When Speech Becomes a Crime

RAPHAEL GOLB

Copyright © 2025 Raphael Golb.

All rights reserved. No part of this book may be used or reproduced by any means, graphic, electronic, or mechanical, including photocopying, recording, taping or by any information storage retrieval system without the written permission of the author except in the case of brief quotations embodied in critical articles and reviews.

Because of the dynamic nature of the Internet, any web addresses or links contained in this book may have changed since publication and may no longer be valid. The views expressed in this work are those of the author and do not necessarily reflect the views of any other person.

Cover design and formatting by Victor Rook

Illustration: drawing by Franz Kafka (ca. 1923)

ISBN: 979-8-218-79189-6

First Amendment Issues

Wherever the truth is injured, defend it.
Ralph Waldo Emerson

Contents

Preface vii

1. A Small Controversy in Lower Manhattan 1
2. Concocting a Case: The DA at Work 18
3. Toward the Criminalizing of Satire in America 51
4. Ideology, Power, and Censorship: The Dead Sea Scrolls Monopoly 68
5. The Deans, the Dons, and a Curator 113
6. Objection? Sustained 138
7. "A Parody over the Line" 159
8. "If They Nab You Again, You're Finished" 201
9. "Like Shooting a Gun": The Logic of Censorship 242

Epilogue 268
Appendix 279
Notes 285
Index 345

PREFACE

My book, *The Qumran Con*, was published in the summer of 2024. Its subjects include the First Amendment, the value of the truth, the history and nature of satire, and the academic scandal surrounding the Dead Sea Scrolls, a topic explored at length in the six chapters comprising the second part of the book.

Since then, the country has endured an upheaval that has gradually morphed into a full-scale assault on First Amendment rights and values—one that might have been unimaginable to most people a decade ago. Is this just an aberration? Or is it the result of a slow process of degradation, one that was somehow blithely discounted or ignored while it was unfolding?

The present book is a new edition of my story, meant for readers especially interested in freedom of speech, in the criminal justice system, and in the social implications of my prosecution. The focus in this book is squarely on the nine-year-long assault on freedom of speech waged by New York prosecutors in the widely publicized "People v. Golb" case. The story of the Dead Sea Scrolls controversy is summarized in a single chapter providing just enough necessary background.

In the prologue to my first book, I wrote about "the value of the truth that my father had fought for, and the lesson his long scholarly struggle had taught me: don't be afraid of authority." Many events that followed the 2024 presidential election in the United States made it clear to me—and others—that the public needs to wake up to dire threats to these values. Towards the beginning of 2025, David Enrich of *The New York Times* published a work whose title succinctly captured developments that had long been in the making: *Murder the Truth*. The book examined how the "wealthy, powerful, and corrupt" had been engaged in a "secret campaign" to shield themselves from criticism, "weaponizing the legal system" to silence dissent and "make people scared to print … the facts."

Enrich rightly understood that truth and freedom of speech are closely intertwined, most pointedly when we speak truth to power. The strength of his book, however, was somewhat marred by its narrow focus on efforts to overturn the standards that have made it extremely difficult, over the past sixty-five years, for public figures to sue journalists for defamation. Enrich's concern with *civil* defamation cases—with lawsuits, and threats of lawsuits—seems to have made him oblivious to the long history of what is commonly known as *criminal* libel. It is certainly chilling to threaten someone with the loss of his or her livelihood (the aim of civil litigation); but it is perhaps worse to throw people into the prison system, potentially for years, because they made a joke deemed to be insulting or said something a jury finds offensive.

Enrich, like many others, appeared to be under the impression that the threat of prosecution had been used to suppress unwanted speech only in centuries past, and only in particularly egregious instances. This latter notion was particularly misguided; it seemed to open the door, once again, to imagining that some forms of expression are worthy of protection while others can appropriately be suppressed or punished with incarceration.

The same idea, as documented in *The Qumran Con* and in the present book, is in fact shared by influential figures who teach in a number of American universities today. These figures present themselves—and are widely acclaimed, especially on the internet—as defenders of the First Amendment. But their vision of the Amendment's meaning is limited by varying degrees of faulty reasoning and historical ignorance. It is also limited by apparent ideological motivations that seem difficult to reconcile with humane principles of justice.

The result, as I indicated in my prologue to *The Qumran Con*, is that "the agitating pamphleteers, the provocateurs of centuries past—including Benjamin Franklin and the other founders of the United States—if they were alive today, could find their free speech rights as easily restricted as we are finding our right to make our own decisions about our bodies and our private lives."

It is not by surveying the easy cases, presented in support of one ideological perspective or another, that one learns the meaning, breadth, and application of the First Amendment; it is by struggling to find a path towards principle in difficult cases, even when doing so creates tension with one's own moral inclinations. This process is similar, in certain respects, to studying the textual strategies that authors have used for centuries to evade censorship. The difficult legal case, just like the narrative designed to elude the censor, must be *interpreted*. That process requires critical thinking; it cannot be accomplished through a "two-minute read," through rote mastery of institutionalized jargon, or through simplistic classroom exchanges of "alternative" viewpoints.

The point is worth emphasizing: the great axioms enshrined in a century of legal interpretation of this crucial portion of the Bill of Rights are not designed to protect, for example, only popularly approved religions or forms of expression; they are, rather, designed to protect ideas that *nobody* likes, to shield the minority from the majority, the weak from the powerful. Like the Bill as a whole, they are a corrective to democracy: that is, they are meant to protect democracy from its own inherent weaknesses. They are a basic part of what *could* prevent democracy from sliding over the line, fragile and variable as it is, into authoritarianism or fascism.

To paraphrase Franklin: We had, and we might still have, a Republic, if we can keep it.

* * *

I again wish to acknowledge the invaluable comments and encouragement received from Arthur Hayes, professor emeritus of Communication and Media Studies at Fordham University, whose principled integrity and insight with respect to my prosecution—an assault, as he sees it, on the First Amendment—are a matter of public knowledge. Professor Hayes's crucial assistance is deeply appreciated. I also again wish to thank the staff of the Elmer Holmes Bobst Library of New York University, who were helpful to me while I was writing the first draft of *The Qumran Con* there during 2014–17. Many other friends and family relations have given me meaningful advice and feedback; they are too numerous to acknowledge.

"*I read in today's NYTimes ... that while your basic approach ... now predominates ... you were excluded* [at the Brown conference] *by people who would not come if you were invited ... That is chilling, a disgrace to the scholarly world.*"—Jacob Neusner, email to Norman Golb (2002)

"*Institutions and museums, international conferences and books may ostracize the scholar who transmits a new message ... A crisis emerges ... Eventually ... the new paradigm gradually gains adherents and replaces the old.*"—Joel Kraemer, essay on Norman Golb (2012)

* * *

"*When you parody and satirize someone on the net, that is your absolute constitutional right... We are surprised that this matter will go to criminal trial.*"—Tzvee Zahavy (2010)

"*Neither good faith nor truth is a defense....*"—Judge Carol Berkman (pretrial order, 2010)

"*He knows how to twist language, stir up controversy. As a result ... the defendant is a menace....*"—John Bandler (Prosecution's summation, Raphael Golb trial)

The defendant's "*criminal intent ... brought you a parody over the line.*"—Judge Carol Berkman (Raphael Golb trial sentencing hearing)

The case's "*implications ... on internet free speech are enormous.*"—former prosecutor Scott Greenfield (2010)

"*This statute, literally understood, criminalizes a vast amount of speech that the First Amendment protects.*" —New York Court of Appeals Chief Judge Jonathan Lippman (dissenting opinion, People v. Golb. 2014)

"*The bad news is that we see, over and over, bizarre exercises of prosecutorial discretion.*"—Santa Clara University law professor

x

Eric Goldman, commenting on People v. Golb appellate decision (2014)

The People v. Golb decision is "*arguably an unconstitutional attack on free speech.*"—Blog of a New York criminal law defense firm (2014)

"*Golb never should have had to face criminal charges … The court … drew a constitutional line with little justification.*"—Fordham University media law professor Arthur Hayes (2017)

1

A Small Controversy in Lower Manhattan

The time is 6:45 a.m. The place is my tiny fifth-floor apartment in a Greenwich Village, New York City, walk-up. I'm deep asleep in the little alcove where I have my futon bed. Suddenly I'm jolted awake by a loud, booming voice shouting, "WHERE IS HE?" Seconds later, I make out a red-faced man in a formal tailored suit, pointing a gun in my face. Behind him, in my living room, I see what appear to be five or six law enforcement agents, some of them wearing jeans, others police uniforms. In the stress of the moment, I don't understand who or what the red-faced man is.

"What's this about?" I manage to stammer, barely conscious.

"*This*," the man replies, "is about the Dead Sea Scrolls. And," he adds (his tone is menacing), "your computer."

The man orders me to put on a pair of underwear, pants, and a T-shirt; to stand up; and to come out from my alcove. Once I'm on my feet, I'm ordered to turn around, and for the first time in my life, I feel the cold metal restraints being tightened around my wrists.

While this is happening, my houseguest from Paris, Annika, tries to come out from my other little room off the kitchen area, and one of the uniformed men, livid with rage, shouts at her to go back in. She must have opened the front door and let them in when they demanded access.

Voices start crackling on walkie-talkies. One of the agents waves some kind of paper at me and says it's a search warrant. I'm allowed to pee in the bathroom—the red-faced man momentarily releases me from the cuffs, keeps the door open, and watches over me. Meanwhile, the others begin to search the apartment, rummaging through my possessions and boxing up my personal items: journals, laptops, financial statements, scraps of paper with names and numbers of my friends scribbled on them, flyers for social events, stubs from old plane tickets, a photo of me taken in France when I was nineteen years old, a paper entitled "Anti-plot in Modern Literature" that I wrote at Oberlin College in 1980, an envelope dating from the late 1980s addressed to me at Harvard (where I was preparing my PhD thesis on the "problems of privacy and trust in modern literature"), and my alumni card from the New York University law school, where I had received my JD degree in 1995.

The search-and-arrest team also takes photographs.[1] One of these focuses on my DVD box set of Larry David's *Curb Your Enthusiasm*. Another shows a shelf containing various books, including *The Moral Decision* by Edmond Cahn, gifted to me when I graduated from law school; *A Confederacy of Dunces* by John Kennedy Toole; and a volume entitled *Who Wrote the Dead Sea Scrolls?* This one is by my father, Hebrew-manuscripts scholar Norman Golb of the University of Chicago, a pioneering figure in scrolls research whose work has earned him the enmity of an entire establishment. *Who Wrote the Dead Sea Scrolls?* is merely photographed, but among the items boxed up and seized by the team there are several scholarly articles by my father, which they locate on another shelf.

As these items are being photographed and confiscated, I am cuffed again and removed from my building—past several astonished neighbors, who are ordered to shut up when they try to ask questions—to an unmarked van.

"How long will this take?" I ask, still not fully grasping the seriousness of my situation.

The red-faced man says it depends on me: if I "speak to the DA," I can "go home a whole lot faster." As the van pulls out, I urgently insist on speaking with the DA.

I'm then driven to the infamous "Tombs" jail complex in Lower Manhattan, where I'm taken upstairs in an elevator and locked in a small barred holding cell where there's a little bench I can sit on. It takes me around fifteen minutes to realize I'm in big trouble. Questioned by the same large red-faced man, I am uncooperative and deny any knowledge of dozens of email addresses on a list that he shows me through the bars—"charlesgadda@gmail.com," "robertdworkin@hotmail.com," "criticalreader@yahoo.com," "larry.schiffman@gmail.com," and so on and so forth. It is too important to preserve my anonymity.

But I do know all those addresses. What should I say to the man? "Sir, Officer, whoever you are, I'd like to inform you that for the past two years, I've been waging an anonymous campaign related to corrupt scholarly practices involving the historic Dead Sea Scrolls, to which you referred in my apartment.[2] On a whole slew of online venues, I've been using pen names to post criticism of an old boys' club of Bible scholars implicated in what I believe to be fraudulent activities involving the scrolls and their exhibition in American museums. I've even resorted to satire! My aim, you see, was to call as much attention as possible to the most embarrassing dirty scrolls laundry. Even worse, I've sent out email parodies. With links to articles I've written about some of the outrageous conduct that strikes me as so rampant in the field.

> The Dead Sea Scrolls were originally thought to have been written at the desert site of Qumran by members of a small radical proto-Christian sect called the Essenes.
> This hypothesis was refuted by my father, Norman Golb, in a series of writings starting in the early 1980s. My father's opposing interpretation of the scrolls as texts produced by *many different Jewish groups*, hidden in the desert during the siege and sacking of Jerusalem by Roman forces in 70 CE, has since come to be supported by major Israeli archaeologists. But the process that led to this development was long, arduous, and characterized by roiling controversy. Defenders of the Essene idea, apparently often motivated by reasons both professional and religious, wielded their power to impose their views in museum exhibits, encyclopedias, and other venues where misinformation can be purveyed.

"In one such instance, intent on calling attention to deeply troubling allegations of plagiarism of my father's ideas made long ago by an Israeli journalist and then stifled here in the United States, I sent out mock Gmail confessions in the name of an academic department chairman. These, sir, were directed toward four student teaching assistants, two deans, the provost, and members of the Jewish studies department at New York University, just blocks away from the apartment you entered earlier this morning. And please take note, sir! That action of mine created a certain amount of controversy at NYU. One faculty member even sent an angry response to the 'confession' itself, oddly enough hinting that *legal action* should be taken to stop whoever was making these accusations. Similar threats were reported to me through friends who heard them being aired at private occasions …"

I prefer to say nothing. One thought echoes over and over in my head as I sit in the cell: someone at NYU must have used his connections to get me arrested.

I am exhausted, having slept for only two hours before the armed raid on my apartment, because I was up very late corresponding with several readers about my most recent anonymous article, "Antisemitism and the Dead Sea Scrolls."[3] The arrest provokes an acute stress reaction on my part.[4] The large policeman tells me again that I have not yet been charged with a crime and that if I agree to "speak with the DA," they will let me go. He then reiterates this suggestion several times. More and more giddy and reckless with fatigue, I decline even to request an attorney, and despite my legal training, imagining that I can clear everything up with the DA and go home—surely he will understand once I talk with him directly—I demand to speak with him at once.

> Throughout the morning, I experience the classic symptoms of acute stress reactions as described in the psychiatric literature. I shoot through a chaos of contradictory mental states. My exhaustion puts me in a fog. At moments, I feel myself receding into a state of distance from what's unfolding around me; at other moments, I'm assailed by an urge to stop the dissociation and to figure out what's happening. I'm aware I'm being illogical, but I feel an overwhelming need to do whatever is necessary to return to the warmth and safety of my bed.

But they keep me waiting, and only an hour later am I taken down a flight of stairs to an interrogation room where, contrary to the advice any competent lawyer would give me, I deny involvement in any online activities dealing with the scrolls—let alone the parody Gmail confessions—and attempt to engage with my interrogator. He is a stiff, starchy man with a marine-style crewcut. He begins the "interview," as he describes it, by introducing himself.[5]

"My name is John Bandler," he says grimly. "I'm an assistant district attorney or a prosecutor. I'm assigned to the investigation of this case. We're here in the DA's Early Case Assessment Bureau, where cases are evaluated. It is 10:46 a.m. on March 5, 2009. You're Raphael Golb. I'm John Bandler. We have senior investigators Patrick McKenna and Terry Williams also present."

"Can I speak?" I interrupt him: a first mistake. He then reads me my Miranda rights and asks me if I'm "willing to answer questions."

"That depends on the questions," I answer. Growing even more reckless, I then launch into an exposition, foolhardy if not self-destructive. "I would like," I begin, "to tell you what I think is going on, and if you say this is a preliminary investigation and you're deciding what to do, I think you should know about certain things."

Nodding at my offer, Bandler first insists on going into an even more detailed explanation of my rights: if there is any form of question whatsoever that I'm uncomfortable answering, I can interrupt the interview at any point I decide I want an attorney. After a lengthy back-and-forth about whether I understand that I'm waiving my legal right to counsel, Bandler again agrees to let me "speak." Increasingly distressed and incapable of fully registering the implicit warning in his words, I now, without any heed for the consequences at all, directly and irrationally lie and claim to have no knowledge of the emails the red-faced man accused me of writing. "A few months ago," I go on to assert—and this much is true— "I heard that at a dinner party, a professor at NYU ... declared to a bunch of people ... that I'm going to have legal problems because I'm 'using false names.' So I think that this person filed a complaint against me, and that this is why I'm here now ... And he has a motive—a big motive—to do anything he can to damage my father."

I proceed to explain to Bandler, who sits listening with an air of casual perplexity, that Norman Golb, in his book on the scrolls, had disproven the ideas promoted by this professor. In fact, he had disproven the claims of an entire gallery of characters (many of them will appear later in this book), and had exposed their actual misconduct—including even rank falsification of evidence. I assert that the purpose of any complaint filed against me would be "to get back at my father. It's very simple ... It's out of maliciousness toward my father."

Bandler is nodding in assent; for several moments, he almost seems well informed about the controversy surrounding the scrolls. But already I get the sense he is dissembling, that he is trying to trick me into saying things he can use against me. My growing awareness of a duplicity in his position, of the fact that he appears to be feigning interest in my situation while his actual intent must be to entrap me into an admission, hardens me in my resolve: I will not cooperate, but I will try to figure out exactly what crime they're saying I committed. I'm beginning to realize that the "interview" is turning into a detailed interrogation about my two-year-long internet campaign. It's becoming clear that my plan—to just tell Bandler a few facts about the scrolls and clear things up—is not what's happening at all. My resistance starts crumbling; my responses become more and more erratic. I alternate between refusing to answer the questions and uncontrollably denying any involvement whatsoever. My denials, all of which are being carefully videotaped to be shown to a judge and a jury, are so absurd even the two "senior investigators" sitting to my right can't keep themselves from laughing.

At one point, I manage to pull myself together and ask my interrogator to clarify why I'm being investigated. "[Is it for] posting things on the internet? Opening an email account ... ? I'd like to know what I'm accused of doing."

Bandler eyes me with a mix of condescension and derisive contempt. "You understand you're not allowed to pretend to be someone else," he says, "and do an act while pretending to be someone else, right?"

The question stuns me. Apparently the man has ignorantly misunderstood what I did. Clearly he is alluding to the Gmails I sent parodying the well-known Dead Sea Scrolls pundit and distinguished department chairman Lawrence Schiffman of New York University—parodies that made him appear to be accusing himself of misconduct. I know there is something deeply wrong with Bandler's statement about "pretending to be someone." But I am so distraught—there is so much coming at me at once—that I cannot grasp exactly what it is. Unprepared to defend myself and still under the delusion that if I avoid admitting any knowledge of the Gmails' contents I can somehow salvage my two years' anonymous stealth campaign, I grasp for at least some kind of a response. "Well, when you say 'someone else,' people post blogs using pen names all the time—does that qualify as pretending to be someone else?"

"Well," Bandler responds, a touch of condescending scorn in his voice, "when there's someone like Dr. Schiffman, and someone pretends to be Dr. Schiffman and does something in his name, you understand you're not allowed to do that, right?"

I freeze on the spot. I've been right all along. He's nailing me on the NYU emails.

From this moment on, an invisible presence looms in the room: the figure of my accuser, "Dr. Schiffman," as Bandler respectfully calls him.

> *"When there's someone like Dr. Schiffman ... you understand you're not allowed to do that, right?"*

That an NYU department chairman, understandably displeased by my Gmail parodies and articles alluding to the old allegations of plagiarism, might retaliate with threats is not particularly surprising. But that he would actually seek to have Norman Golb's son incarcerated is a possibility that has never seriously occurred to me.

Why on earth would he do something that would bring so much attention, both to the plagiarism allegations themselves and to his willingness to retaliate against someone who clearly felt that he had indeed violated scholarly norms and committed academic theft?

Bandler, I suddenly realize, has been *taken in* by Schiffman—by his air of good repute and authority, by his status as a "Dead Sea Scrolls star."[6] It would be ludicrous to imagine that I can somehow get my interrogator to see the NYU Jewish studies chairman the same way I see him: as a prominent example of a scholar who has used his position of power and influence to *actively cause professional harm to others*. And whose research conduct—on more than one occasion subjected to allegations of impropriety—should be investigated by his institution.

I begin to feel like a noose is tightening around my neck. Bandler is sounding increasingly smug. It's as if I'm confronting a dire embodiment of the New Seriousness,[7] one of the dreaded legacies of America's puritanical past. I sense that my journey is only just beginning.

By now I am simply too exhausted to grapple seriously with what Bandler is asserting. It's all a jumble in

> Implicit in the prosecutor's attitude is a puritanical requirement that every form of interaction be straightforward and up-front. By failing to point out to him that "pretending to be" someone else is a basic element of parody, I miss an opportunity to have his ignorance of cultural history recorded on the video of my interrogation that will later be shown to the jury.

my head, but somehow it seems to criminalize any kind of "pretending in someone's name" that conveys an idea about people in positions of authority—that speaks truth to power. Bandler, I suddenly realize, *is* power. I double down on denying any involvement in sending out controversial emails under Schiffman's name.

"Well, yeah," I state, realizing that my whole body is shaking with cold. "I've certainly never done that."

"You understand," Bandler continues, "that some speech is protected under the First Amendment, and that you can go over that line, right … where it could be criminal."

"Well," I say, "tell me what you're talking about."

"Where speech could be criminal?"

"Yes, for example, do you mean pushing someone to commit a murder?"

Bandler vigorously assents, then reverts to his droning lawtalk tone, informing me that if I frighten and torment someone verbally, my speech could be considered harassment. "Or if you engage in a *pattern of conduct* through your speech—that includes emails, electronic communications and stuff—*that* could become harassment of an individual."

"So basically I'm being accused of harassing Dr. Schiffman—is that the idea?"

"Look, you can get the truth out. I work for people who have to decide what to charge you with, if anything. People are going to think your father is behind it—so, if you can own up to whatever you did ..."

I'm now quite aware that he's threatening me. "Show me the harassment ... You say that there are emails ... Could you put [them] on the table? The 'harassment' of Schiffman on the table?"

"You mean literally on the table?"

"Yeah. Can you put it—why don't you want to show it to me?"

"I'll say them to you."

"Sure."

For a second, it seems that I now have at least an opportunity to bring some kind of rationality back into the situation. If he actually recites the emails, I can explain that they must be parodies of Schiffman; I can point out what the "admissions" issued under the name "Larry Schiffman" must have meant; I can enumerate—on video, because everything is being taped—the signs of an academic lampoon in the "confessional" texts.

Bandler ignores my request. Instead, he changes course and cleverly skirts the issue. He is following a technique drawn from the same protocol so effective at producing results in most interrogations. It is important to show who is in control and to keep the accused in a state of uncertainty. This generates fear, which in turn usually leads to a time-saving, and cost-saving, guilty plea. So instead of reciting the "Larry Schiffman" emails and allowing me to impede the criminal-legal process, Bandler pulls out his list and begins a monotonous rendition of all the seventy-odd other email addresses I invented. Addresses from which I sent messages critical of the unbalanced and exclusionary policies set in place by the creators of a Dead Sea Scrolls museum exhibit that had been traveling around the United States.

Bandler clearly has no intention of showing me the emails. So much for my naive plan of having a conversation with him. I'm finally seeing reality, as if I were beginning to come to my senses. I interrupt him and inform him that I won't be answering questions about any addresses he's reading.

"I'm just curious," he says. "If it was you that's trying to influence the Dead Sea Scrolls debate, just admit it and we can move on from there."

Influence the debate! A small wave of nausea passes through me. If I'm not careful, he might also try to get me for disrupting academic life with an act of protest that forced people to pay attention. Then I would *really* be in trouble.

"Did you do that using aliases?" he insists.

My head is still swirling with the almost incomprehensible fact that Bandler has been conducting a criminal investigation of my effort to influence a debate—not only of my "pretending to be" Larry Schiffman but of my entire internet campaign with all its anonymous and pseudonymous blogs and emails about a roiling controversy. "I'd rather not answer the question," I conclude.

"Okay, well, the time is now 12:36 p.m., we're still in Early Case Assessment Bureau, it's still March 5, 2009, we're going to end the interview, the investigators are going to take you back upstairs."

We head to a small elevator, and I am returned to the holding cell. After a short wait, I am joined by someone who, from casual remarks that I hear the "investigators" dropping, appears to be a convicted murderer in transit from another state. It occurs to me that part of their purpose in inserting him into this small confined space with me may have been to unnerve me, and my uncertainty at their motives increases my sense of unease. We sit side by side and say nothing. An hour later, he is removed from the cell and taken away, and I'm provided with a yogurt, a banana, and an apple. Then I'm cuffed and led to a public toilet down the hallway, where the same large red-faced man who earlier awakened me at gunpoint in my apartment stands guard to prevent me from escaping. It is a large facility with many stalls; we are the only two people in there.

As we enter the holding area again, boxes are being carried in and dumped on the floor: objects seized from my apartment. The man has me sit at a table, where he shows me a long handwritten list of crimes labeled under various categories: "aggravated harassment," "identity theft," "criminal impersonation," "forgery," and "unauthorized access to a computer."

"I'll just have to get a lawyer," I say.

The man nods. He then takes me on a long complicated walk through gray narrow corridors, down stairways, then elevators, followed by more corridors. Occasionally we cross paths with guards and cops heading in various directions. Along the way, we enter a huge bustling room, where I am searched and fingerprinted. Here we experience a short delay because there is a problem with a machine that can't read my palm. We try over and over, and eventually the matter-of-fact woman operating the machine seems satisfied with the result. I'm feeling more and more numb, but by now I'm also more awake, cooperating as politely as possible, without resistance or complaining. I try to respond more alertly to orders.

Then, almost without warning, we are met with a huge noise of yelling and banging. We are five stories underground, in the massive holding cells of the Tombs. As soon as we reach this area, I begin having more difficulty breathing on account of the stale air. The red-faced man seems to be satisfied at the job he's done handling my arrest and processing me. He tells me to relax: "Take it easy, and you'll be out in a couple of hours." It's three thirty in the afternoon. There are large cages everywhere, filled with hundreds of people behind bars. The guards walk me down the rows and lock me in with the others. It's a gray space, around fifteen feet by twenty, with metal benches lining the walls, a fouled metal toilet in the rear to the left. The cage is packed with around thirty male prisoners, some of them on the benches, some lying on the floor, some standing. I'm immediately stricken by the basic fact that they are all, without exception, Black and Latino men. "White boy," someone says with a quiet laugh. He makes room for me next to him on one of the benches. I sit down. He's right: I'm the only white person in the room—an obvious result of the racial profiling practiced on a daily basis in New York City.

Almost immediately, the guards bring in another man. He is disheveled, dressed in a ragged overcoat. A commotion breaks out as he lies down on the dirty linoleum floor in the cell's center, because he exudes an unbreathable stench. I see a white insect or larva crawling over his torn coat. The other prisoners in the cage start screaming at the guards: "Get him out of here." Throughout the next fifteen hours, he will stay put on the floor, except for feeding and mop-up time.

It is hot, and the foul odor emanating from the man on the floor hangs everywhere in the cell. There are complaints about the heat and lack of air. At times, the man removes his shoes, revealing ankles and shins covered with oozing white scabs. When he does this, an even more powerful stench suddenly hits everyone in the face. He's got the "stink" on him, he's got "tuberculosis," he's got "lice," my cellmates shout. The guards come and give him a glance and then walk away.

As the hours pass, the guards, shouting orders, move the prisoners out in packs of three, six, eight, and pack others into the cages. The incoming prisoners also shout at the man on the floor. They threaten him, tell him to move away, to put his shoes back on. Some people are lying on the benches where there is room. I find a spot to lie down, with my legs folded and my shoes on the narrow metal bench. But the metal is slippery, and my shoes keep sliding down away from me. This keeps me from falling asleep, because I'm six feet tall, and my main fear is creating any sort of disturbance by touching one of the other prisoners with my shoes.

By now I've figured out that the purpose of this place is to hold people and then move them up to the court for arraignment. Hundreds of arraignments are held each day, and the system keeps the arrestees down here until the judges can hear the cases. Every time they remove a batch of people from the cell, I keep imagining it might be my turn, but someone else is moved instead, until at some point I realize the cage is full of different people from the ones who were here when I arrived. I begin to sense (am I growing paranoid?) that the guards have been instructed *not* to move me out but to keep me in confinement all night long with new arrivals.

I'm also feeling more and more thirsty. I avoid the stinking aluminum toilet and sink at the back of the cell. I try to breathe as little as possible to avoid the ghastly smell. I'm no longer lying down, but sitting hunched over on the metal bench. My mind is rushing everywhere. *This is actually happening. Schiffman and the DA. The policeman said a few hours. Could someone else at NYU have pulled strings with the DA to get me arrested? How long can they keep me in here?*

Something I notice: at least several of my fellow prisoners appear to be decent people. One of them asks me if I know whether he has committed a felony by selling his subway pass for a dollar, which is why he is locked up down here. Later, I realize that some of them are in transit, awaiting trial for serious crimes, like the person I shared the small cage with earlier. But most of them seem to have been arrested for petty offenses like jumping a subway turnstile. Just when I have lain back down and am falling asleep, though, a fight breaks out—two of them seem to be trying to kill each other, and most of the others, apart from the man on the floor, rush away to the bars at the other end of the cage. They shout for them to stop because it could mean trouble for everyone with the guards.

At six thirty in the morning, the guards come and order everyone out from all the cages. We are placed in three lines. We are marched single file down a long corridor. Orders are again shouted at us: we're to stand facing ahead; we're to turn our backs to the wall. The guards warn us that any deviance from these instructions will be met with severe punishment: "One of you does any shit, you all go back!" Then we're taken upstairs to another cell closer to one of the arraignment courtrooms. Here we wait three more hours, lying on the floor and on the benches, which are wooden and even narrower than the metal ones in the cell below. My mind is now utterly burned out. I can't stop it from rehashing bits and pieces of the deranged "interview" with Bandler.

I get released later in the morning. Irena, a friend who is learning the ropes of criminal law, comes and pleads for me in front of one of the judges. He lets me out on my own "recognizance"—no need to pay bail. Slaphappy with fatigue, I exit the courtroom through a crowd of reporters who shout questions and take photographs of me, bulbs flashing. Irena hails a cab that takes me straight to the offices of David Breitbart, one of New York's top criminal defense lawyers, about three miles north to midtown Manhattan as I call my parents from her cell phone—it turns out that they were informed of my arrest by a *New York Times* reporter who called my father at his office while I was in the Tombs.

Irena is convinced Breitbart is the best. She watched him one day in court, eloquently defending Naomi Campbell, when the model was charged with assault after throwing a phone at an employee. Irena has already made an appointment with Breitbart on my behalf. His assistant greets me like a king. They have read the *New York Times* article on my arrest that came out while I was in the Tombs. They ask me to run through the circumstances. Breitbart tells me he will take particular pleasure in "picking apart" Schiffman's plagiarism. He speaks on the phone with my mom, and we agree on the spot to hire him. He tells me everything will work out. I should go home, get some rest, and come back to see him in a few days. When I arrive back at my apartment building in the West Village, I manage to avoid a *New York Post* reporter who is lurking at my front door by ringing a neighbor's apartment, climbing onto the fire escape, and crawling into my place via an unlocked window. The living room looks like it has been trashed by burglars.

The next few hours are a blur. I sleep for a bit. Later in the afternoon, I take a closer look at a press release that Breitbart printed out for me about my arrest, issued by the office of Manhattan DA Robert Morgenthau while I was in the Tombs. "The defendant, RAPHAEL GOLB," the release asserts, "is charged with Identity Theft in the Second Degree … which is punishable by up to 3 to 4 years in prison," as well as with numerous other offenses, "each punishable by up to 1 year in prison."

Dated March 5, 2009, the release explains that the defendant is to be prosecuted "for creating multiple aliases to engage in a campaign of impersonation and harassment relating to the Dead Sea Scrolls and scholars of opposing viewpoints." The author notes that "the investigation is continuing" and invites reporters to contact Maxey Greene, the director of public information at Morgenthau's office.[8]

> The release ominously charges that the defendant "masked his identity" and "engaged in a systematic scheme on the Internet ... in order to influence and affect debate on the Dead Sea Scrolls"—still worse, he "promoted his father's theories" and "criticized the manner in which the Dead Sea Scrolls have been exhibited."

Around five in the evening, I go out for a walk. It feels good to get out in the open after a night in the Tombs, but I'm still dazed by the events of the past thirty hours. Surrounded by the noise and commotion of the NYU neighborhood, I keep going through everything that happened, starting with "WHERE IS HE?" and the gun in my face. I'm as yet unaware that Morgenthau's press release has been picked up by hundreds of news services around the globe. And I have no way of knowing that it is merely the opening salvo in a public relations campaign that will be aggressively waged by employees of the DA on behalf of powerful interests. Even further from my mind is the possibility that all of this is just the beginning of a fight that will end up creating new law, simultaneously expanding and restricting the reach of the First Amendment.

What I do know is that all my actions involved disseminating information that is clearly of public concern: precisely what the First Amendment is supposed to protect. Further, they were all fueled by moral indignation at the misconduct of a group of public figures at the center of a scandal that they themselves had set in motion. Does the DA really want to get involved in a matter that so obviously raises free speech issues?

* * *

A week after my arrest, Tuvia Stern, an affluent prisoner held in the Tombs, whose crime consists in having swindled $1.7 million from Jewish investors, will be allowed to celebrate the engagement of his daughter in a lavish jailhouse party funded in part with taxpayer dollars, his journey to an upstate prison being delayed, also at considerable expense to the city, for the purpose. News of this occasion will eventually leak to the press, causing a certain amount of scandal focused on the special treatment given to certain inmates.[9] Meanwhile, my own personal journey through the system begins to unfold in a way that I, a lawyer with a PhD from Harvard, could never have come up with in my most vivid imaginative moments: I am charged with fifty-two criminal counts involving six different alleged types of felonies and misdemeanors, relating to six different complainants located in California, Oregon, North Carolina, Massachusetts, and New York.

And to what end? After nine years of litigation, only ten of those fifty-two counts will, under a brand-new legal interpretation of existing law, remain standing. And those ten counts will pertain to just five short emails (each of them treated as two separate crimes) sent, in the course of two consecutive days at the beginning of August 2008, in the "name" of a single academic: Lawrence Schiffman of NYU.

Most notably, at one critical juncture around halfway through the process, the New York law that allowed the prosecutors to criminalize my alleged campaign of "harassment"—the prosecution's preferred term for criticism and satire—will be declared unconstitutional on First Amendment grounds. Most of the other charges will also be thrown out, either in view of a complete lack of evidence that I acted with the requisite criminal intent or because the laws invoked simply had no relevance to anything I did.

How did the use of centuries-old methods of verbal provocation to make a point, expose the truth, and thereby produce some measure of justice end up causing so much mayhem in the system? Was it right to divert taxpayer dollars to a concerted effort to jail an individual who, by availing himself of such methods, had perhaps caused some small degree of embarrassment to a university professor? To see how this all came about, we need to take a closer look at the events and circumstances that led to the decision to have me arrested, then charged with crimes, and then aggressively prosecuted for nearly a decade.

2
CONCOCTING A CASE: THE DA AT WORK

By 2004, accusations of scholarly malfeasance had become so commonplace on college campuses that they were popping up as a topic of polite academic inquiry. In *Scandals and Scoundrels*, a book published that year, history professor Ron Robin of NYU lavished praise on the flood of "inflammatory" email complaints bouncing around university offices.[1] According to Robin (who would later be named president of the University of Haifa), these complaints signaled a "powerful public yearning for moral transparency, intellectual integrity, and stable standards in unsettled times." The internet, he insisted, had enabled "a debate where ... information flows in multiple directions with no central authority exercising control." Hoaxes, he added, were "nothing out of the ordinary." They offered "distinct advantages over more conventional forms of criticizing the academy," enabling those who had messages to convey to "penetrate ... the bastions" of their opponents in ways they couldn't with a mere "straightforward critique."[2]

Four years after Robin's defense of such provocative and unconventional "forms of criticizing the academy," several messages emanating from a Gmail account created in the name "Larry Schiffman" were received by Jewish studies department members, graduate students, two deans, the provost, and the student newspaper at NYU. The messages, drafted by me in the evening and afternoon of August 4 and August 5, 2008, were sent from a computer room in the Elmer Holmes Bobst Library, the university's main center for study. The theme of the messages was the fictitious effort of the professor they impersonated—Lawrence Schiffman—to suppress discussion, particularly among students, of his own "minor failing" consisting of plagiarism.

The allegation that the real-life Schiffman had plagiarized the research of his fellow Hebraist Norman Golb was not, of course, invented by me; it was first formulated by journalist Avi Katzman, in an interview with Schiffman published in the Israeli newspaper *Haaretz* on January 29, 1993.³ During the ensuing years, Schiffman never addressed the allegation again, and the matter was never investigated at NYU. Perhaps by virtue of the peculiar silence surrounding this affair, he had been appointed chairman of the university's Jewish studies department.

As chairman, Schiffman wielded considerable authority and influence over students and colleagues. His responsibilities, however, seemed to have extended beyond ordinary scholarly affairs to include such matters as the expansion of NYU's real estate capital. He had, for example, been involved in negotiations for his department to acquire the Center for Jewish History, an independent institution a few blocks from Greenwich Village that hosts the Leo Baeck Institute and the Centro Primo Levi, among other organizations. In the envisioned agreement, "most of the center's archives would be moved to an off-site warehouse … and the public's access to materials curtailed," so that NYU Jewish studies faculty, staff, students, and guests could use the site for their offices, recreational rooms, and related purposes.⁴ (The negotiations eventually failed.)

> In the 1993 interview, Katzman challenged Schiffman: "But also, in different articles you have published, you have not hesitated to adopt portions of Golb's theory without acknowledging as much, and without giving him appropriate credit." Schiffman did not answer Katzman's question directly. Instead, he replied, "This isn't the issue. There's no innovation in Golb's theory … Does he think that he wrote the Bible?"

Schiffman was clearly held in general esteem. He had, for a time, been president of the Association for Jewish Studies, and he was soon to serve as a representative for the Union of Orthodox Jewish Congregations of America to the International Jewish Committee for Interreligious Consultations (IJCIC)—that is, to the organization responsible for representing the Jewish people in negotiations with the Catholic Church.[5] In this latter capacity, he would meet officials at the Vatican, including the Pope, and, according to his own description, exchange pleasantries with them on various occasions.[6] His status as a spokesperson for the Orthodox Jewish community, as well as his ubiquity as a declared Dead Sea Scrolls authority, would give weight to views of his quoted in the press—including views denigrating secular Judaism.[7] At the same time, his public prominence was unmistakably also enhanced by an aptitude in cultivating interfaith relations. The *New York Times* had identified him not only as an expert on early Christianity, but also as a rabbi—a description also found on various websites.[8]

Two years later, Schiffman would testify under oath that he was not a rabbi. But already in 2008, I did not believe he was either a rabbi or an expert on early Christianity, or indeed that his historical and archaeological presentations had any solid scholarly weight. Rather, for the most part, I was convinced they were popularizing apologetics, tending to project the author's own religious faith onto the screen of ancient history and palpably aimed at defending a largely discredited hypothesis of Dead Sea Scroll origins.

All of this formed part of the context for my "Larry Schiffman" Gmail missives of August 4 and August 5, 2008. The messages presented their purported author as defending himself against accusations that he had failed to credit scholar Norman Golb for ideas that he (Schiffman) had appropriated. If he had acted properly, the impersonated professor stated, he would "have been banned from conferences around the world." In the same breath, he justified his "minor failing" as an instance of the "politics of Dead Sea Scroll studies," and sternly instructed the various recipients that they were not to discuss the matter with students or "mention the name of the scholar involved." Declaring that not a word must be said because his "career" was "at stake," he expressed his hope that the recipients would "understand."

A large bold link inserted between the body of the text and the signature line prompted the email recipients to read an article on the NowPublic website (also written by me, under the pen name "Peter Kaufman"), which set forth a case against Schiffman for plagiarizing arguments originally developed by Norman Golb, and for misrepresenting, on numerous occasions, Golb's interpretation of scroll origins.[9] By falsely attributing to Golb the implausible views of another scholar, the NowPublic article alleged, the NYU department chairman had disseminated misleading information that obscured the history of research in this field.

Just a few days after these emails were sent, the deans at NYU received, by regular campus mail, photocopies of various pages authored by Golb in 1980 and passages revealing an unmistakable similarity published a decade later by Schiffman.

Schiffman would later explain to a reporter that "nobody at NYU believed the emails."[10] But this statement was not quite accurate, for a few recipients seem to have been initially duped, back in that summer, by the blunt tone of the messages—so much so that, according to a Bobst Library representative, NYU's security forces, known in the Greenwich Village neighborhood as "Public Safety," were mobilized to counter the perceived threat.[11] When Mark Smith, NYU's Skirball Professor of Bible and Ancient Near Eastern Studies, received his copy of the initial "larry.schiffman@gmail.com" confession, he replied that he did understand and that he was "concerned about any wider impact that this might potentially have."

Cory Peacock, one of Schiffman's teaching assistants, replied at greater length, expressing his view that the author of the linked blog must be someone who was "in the class this spring"; that he didn't "like seeing this go unanswered"; and that "we could tear that piece apart, but it would seem tendentious to do so." Peacock then received the following reply from "Larry Schiffman": "This is definitely ruining my week. I don't know if you can under-

> Smith's teachers included Frank Moore Cross, at the time professor emeritus of Harvard Divinity School, whose fraudulent claims about a document found at Qumran are described in chapter 7 of *The Qumran Con*. Smith would later move from NYU Jewish studies to the Princeton Theological Seminary (not affiliated with Princeton University), where he would serve as professor of Old Testament language and exegesis. "Old Testament" is the Christian term for the Hebrew Bible.

stand how I feel, but it is as if someone had set fire to my beard. The last thing I need now is to be investigated by the dean."[12] Apparently comprehending that he had become the butt of a joke, Peacock fell silent, returned to his studies, and went on to receive his degree in 2012.[13]

"The Allegations of Plagiarism Are False"

There was never any doubt that my NYU emails had been "inappropriate." In fact, sending them had been an overt impropriety, the rather plain purpose of which was to make a point, to speak truth to power, and to provoke discussion of the situation they encapsulated. Regardless of that motivating intent, the emails were even more inappropriate when viewed from within the specific canons applicable to legal practitioners, who at all times are sworn to the very highest moral standards. But did delivering such messages constitute a crime? A good deal hinged on the answer to this question.

At the outset, at least one person thought the answer was yes. And that number would grow.

Soon after the exchange with Peacock, Lawrence Schiffman paid a visit to FBI special agent Catherine Begley, who in the past had once sought out his advice on a case apparently dealing with a forged Hebrew document. Apprised of the situation at NYU, Begley explained to Schiffman that the nature of his complaint did not fall within the "bailiwick" of the bureau, and she sent him to see a special friend of hers at the Manhattan district attorney's office.[14]

As Schiffman would later explain to the *New York Times*, "You know how the FBI says, 'once you're one of ours, you're always one of ours'? It's totally true." According to the same article, Schiffman asked the prosecutors if they couldn't just intimidate me a little: "Send some police in there to scare him and he'll stop." But the prosecutors did not feel that this type of coercive control or manipulation would go far enough; they wanted more, and the more that they wanted entailed Schiffman's cooperation in unleashing the full force of the criminal justice system against me. Their response, according to the *Times*, was to explain that "you have to understand, we don't do that. We investigate a crime, and if we find there's a crime, we prosecute."[15] A response, it should be noted in passing, that was not true, because it left out the *discretion* to prosecute or not to prosecute that is an inherent part of prosecutorial practice. The criminal justice system would simply not be able to cope if charges were filed every time a crime is purportedly committed.

Seven months after the New York University incident, and as a result of Schiffman's contact with the office of the Manhattan DA, assistant district attorney John Bandler prepared a search warrant affidavit aimed at getting a close look at me and my belongings. According to the affidavit, I had committed "identity theft," "criminal impersonation," "forgery," and "harassment" by sending out the fake "confessions."

> Bandler had graduated from the New York Police Academy in 1994; he then served in the National Guard and US Army Reserve before attending Pace Law School and becoming a prosecutor in 2002.

Patrick McKenna, a policeman assigned to the New York County DA's identity theft unit, then signed this affidavit (dated March 2, 2009) and submitted it to New York criminal court judge Carol Berkman, who granted the warrant. In one paragraph of the signed affidavit, McKenna declared under oath, "The allegations of plagiarism are false." This statement itself seemed to imply that the affidavit's author realized the email confessions, to paraphrase the title of a book by a late professor of mine at Harvard, might not "mean" what they "said."[16] Did McKenna recognize that if the allegations were *true*, then the meaning and intent of the emails would be altogether different from the ones attributed to them by the prosecutor?

McKenna was a New York City policeman, and knew little or nothing about plagiarism. His declaration was based on an assertion by Schiffman himself, who had submitted a statement to the police denying the allegations. Neither Bandler nor McKenna acknowledged that Schiffman had long stood accused of plagiarism.

Instead, they engaged in a disingenuous effort to paint the professor as simply an innocent victim of smears. In having a police officer sign such a misleading declaration, the prosecutor had taken the step of endorsing one side in a heated dispute over scholarly ethics that had been playing out over decades.

> Plagiarism allegations are normally examined by academic committees, not prosecutors. But faculty officials at NYU had chosen to ignore Dr. Avi Katzman's allegations, rather than investigate them in accordance with faculty regulations and ordinary academic protocol.

Other statements, also apparently supplied by Schiffman, pointed in the same direction; these included the assertion in the warrant that the scrolls had been the subject of "conspiracy theories." Schiffman's collaboration in drafting the district attorney's description of Dead Sea Scrolls research would later be attested to by his testimony in criminal court, and by the revelation of an email exchange between him and Bandler. He had attached to it a "confidential letter" attacking Norman Golb that he had previously sent to NYU faculty officials.[17] But already during the days after my arrest, the purportedly "knowledgeable" jargon in the warrant suggested that District Attorney Morgenthau had in effect expanded the role generally played by New York City prosecutors by allowing one of his employees to publicly take on the role of private counsel to a professor who had been accused of violating his university's faculty code of conduct.

McKenna's sworn statement does not appear to have troubled Judge Berkman, who would later suggest that even if she had known the statement to be false, she would still have considered the warrant application valid. The granting of the warrant also appears (although no such conclusion can be drawn with certainty) to have taken place without any consideration being given to the possibility that the "Gmail confessions" might constitute a First Amendment–protected parody meant to expose the truth about a public figure's professional malfeasance. That possibility simply seems to have been ignored during the proceedings that led to my "interview" with Bandler and to my night in the Tombs; at least there is no sign to the contrary, for McKenna's affidavit contained no mention of any possibility of the sort. On the morning of March 5, 2009, armed policemen raided my Greenwich Village apartment both to arrest me and to seek out evidence of my ostensibly criminal conduct. While I was incarcerated, Morgenthau, via Maxey Greene, issued his announcement on my illegal "scheme to influence a debate." The press release did not include the—normally required—statement that the accused person is innocent until proven guilty.

Tracking the Trail of Clues to a Criminal Mind

The ransacking of my apartment had turned up incriminating evidence. Personal email correspondence that the DA's investigators found on my laptop showed that by the summer of 2008, I had concluded from reading Schiffman's writings that he had appropriated some of the core elements of my father's theory without attribution—this in the course of trying to develop his own version of the old hypothesis of Dead Sea Scroll origins that my father had refuted. When I read that Schiffman was involved in an important scrolls exhibit to take place at the Jewish Museum in New York in the fall of 2008, I expressed my dismay in an email to my family— one that would later be introduced into evidence as decisive proof of my guilt. I told them that a lecture by Schiffman would "egregiously misinform the public with respect to the fundamental disagreement between scholars concerning the scrolls."[18]

In the same correspondence, I suggested that my father write to the Jewish Museum exhibit curator "pointing out that the speakers are not balanced" and that he would be "willing to give a talk at his own expense to rebut them." I reiterated that the rebuttal could be delivered either by my father "or another proponent of the Jerusalem theory so that the talks are balanced."

Similarly, in an incriminating email to my brother, Dr. Joel Golb, I had mentioned that letters of complaint I planned to address to UCLA faculty were aimed at "embarrassing" two individuals at that institution who had been involved in creating a biased and misleading Dead Sea Scrolls exhibit hosted in 2007 at the San Diego Natural History Museum. As I explained in the email, I planned to cause such embarrassment "by informing people of the truth (which many of them might not know)." A second email, also to my brother, revealed my knowledge (and authorship) of a NowPublic "article exposing the plagiarism of Lawrence Schiffman." A third indicated that my focus was the "institutional" problem: NYU's failure to investigate the allegations of plagiarism raised by *Haaretz* journalist Avi Katzman. My computer also contained an email from a professor of religion at California State University at Chico who coauthored that institution's academic integrity policy, stating that he had "heard about" Katzman's allegations and that there was "no question," in his view, that Schiffman had "crossed the line."[19]

> According to the "Jerusalem theory," the Dead Sea Scrolls are the remains of multiple libraries from the Jerusalem area, hidden in the desert at the time of the siege and sacking of the city by Roman troops during the Great Jewish Revolt of 70 CE. The theory was originally developed by Norman Golb and has since been supported by the research of other scholars. The history of this theory and of its reception is explained in chapter 4.

Incriminating drafts of my various NowPublic articles, including the one "exposing Schiffman's plagiarism," had also been seized in my apartment.[20] The Schiffman article draft in particular displayed my conviction that the department chairman's writings were imbued with "charlatanry" and contained plagiarism, as that term is defined in NYU's faculty code of conduct. The article signaled two facts in particular: (1) that Schiffman had apparently never responded to the detailed account of his actions presented in Norman Golb's 1995 book, *Who Wrote the Dead Sea Scrolls?*, and (2) that for fifteen years New York University, in disregard of its own rigorous standards, had failed to investigate Schiffman's conduct.

All my pseudonymous articles pertaining to the academic "politics" of the Dead Sea Scrolls traveling exhibitions now quickly vanished from the NowPublic site; officials there had received complaints from at least one of the individuals I had criticized, and apparently decided that the most prudent course on their part was to remove my writings, even before I was put on trial. The anonymity that protected and gave impetus to my campaign had been torn away. Those who had planned and promoted the museum exhibits would now be able to use an optimal publicity stunt, a criminal prosecution, to cast doubt on the legitimacy of my call for neutrality and balance in their exhibitions. In the new narrative presented to the public in a range of widely read electronic and printed media, I would be treated as an "exposed Internet troll"; instead of being described as someone who had sought to criticize the actions and policies of an ideologically driven interest group, I would be marked as a blogger who wanted to "promote" (a word favored by the district attorney and first deployed, as we saw earlier, in Maxey Greene's press release) the "unpopular" claims of Norman Golb. The idea taking shape, while not yet explicitly announced, would eventually find formal expression in the outlandish charge that I planned to gain a thousand dollars from my "fraudulent scheme." Not coincidentally, this is the minimum amount of money that needs to have been stolen for a felony scheme-to-defraud conviction in New York State.

The decision to turn me into a financial fraudster had less to do with any form of reality than with the universe of Franz Kafka. The decision, however, was only part of a broader strategy, for at some point the prosecutorial team had reached the conclusion that not only my "Larry Schiffman" emails but as much of my internet campaign as possible must be criminalized, regardless of any First Amendment or other legal issues that might ultimately impede this way of proceeding.

Already in her press release, Maxey Greene had explained that one of my "victims" was an individual known as "Jonathan Seidel," who was "active in the field of Dead Sea Scrolls scholarship." Later, it would turn out this referred to one Rabbi Jonathan Seidel of Oregon—unknown to me and, in this press release, identified as a scrolls scholar apparently for the first time in his life. Other purported victims were Frank Moore Cross (1921–2012), professor emeritus at the Harvard Divinity School, at the time confined to a nursing home; Robert Cargill, at the time a graduate student at UCLA and an employee in the "Digital Humanities" program at that institution; a Duke University stacks maintenance employee named Stephen Goranson; and Jeffrey Gibson, an adjunct professor at Columbia College in Chicago. My alleged crimes consisted in "harassing" Cargill; in harassing, impersonating, forging, and stealing the "identities" of the others; and in perpetrating, through misuse of my NYU alumnus card for "uncivil" purposes, the crime of "unauthorized access" to the computers at the Bobst Library, all as part of a criminal "scheme" to "influence a debate."

For the most part, all these various, highly publicized criminal charges were patently ludicrous, unsupported either by my intent or by the facts, and a direct violation of my constitutional rights—as the courts would in fact be forced to reluctantly recognize during nine years of painstaking litigation, at one point even declaring New York's "aggravated harassment" law unconstitutional on its face in view of basic free speech rights. But no matter how *legally* defective the charges were, they were crucial to the prosecutor's case against me, because they would enable him to tell the story he needed to tell—a story in which he would paint my entire internet campaign as a criminal enterprise with "harassment" at its core. This abuse of the charging process would heighten the likelihood that the jury would be convinced that I acted with a pernicious, criminal motive when I sent out those fake confessions at NYU.

Throw enough mud, some of it is bound to stick. In the course of its effort, the prosecution took dozens of context-free excerpts from email exchanges with my parents and brother, publishing them as "evidence of intent." In doing so, the prosecution also conceded there was no proof of my father's involvement in my supposed crimes. Complainant Robert Cargill of UCLA then reproduced the excerpts on his blog, trumpeting them in red type as demonstrating family collusion.[21] The facts: My campaign evoked various reactions from my parents and brother. My father seemed to find my NowPublic articles interesting, as I had discovered details pertaining to the Dead Sea Scroll museum exhibits that he himself was unaware of; he commented that one of the articles was extremely funny and that the tone of another was lurid. My mom exhorted me to stick it to my detractors when she saw that several individuals were denouncing my use of handles.[22] On the other hand, she warned me not to meddle with Schiffman, whom she termed a "snake." Wishing to avoid being reproached by my father, who was a stickler for scholarly decorum, I informed only my brother that I was planning on contacting UCLA and NYU faculty members about Cargill and Schiffman, respectively. He urged me not to, since, academic culture being what it was, my criticisms of their work and behavior would be labeled harassment. In an email of January 17, 2023, he writes,

> Surprised to be reminded that I warned you. That was bad judgment on my part: I should have approved your trolling an asshole with the truth regarding his Scroll-related academic striving. And I like to think that deep down, famous "maverick" scholar Norman Golb, despite his adhering to academic protocol, would also have thoroughly approved.

The outrageousness of the criminal charges themselves was bad enough. But what really struck me as sinister in the DA's willingness to distort my intent for the sake of winning the case against me was something that went beyond legal cynicism. The prosecutors were pushing a mendacious Dead Sea Scrolls narrative. The actual issues raised in my campaign were dismissed and distorted. The DA, in fact, was acting in harmony with the interests of one particular group involved in the struggle over the scrolls unfolding since 1980. This group would relish the idea of such charges chipping away at the reputation of Norman Golb. He was, after all, the Hebrew manuscripts specialist who had gathered evidence refuting the hypothesis the group had defended and embellished for half a century. And who, in his 1995 book, had also signaled inappropriate financial dealings, plagiarism, and other unethical conduct on their part. In turn, the charges against me would spill over to weaken the work and position of others who largely agreed with Golb's research conclusions, including such distinguished scholars as Yizhar Hirschfeld, Yuval Peleg, and Yitzhak Magen.

Clearly I was facing formidable adversaries. My father, on the other hand, always kept a positive outlook and consistently offered me encouragement. He reminded me that the internet was filled with all kinds of nonsense—and that Schiffman in particular was no angel but had, in his view, behaved disgracefully on various levels, over many years. He indicated that he himself had been on the receiving end of a great deal of electronic garbage for decades. He also told me that several years before, a new University of Chicago dean had been impersonated in a good number of emails by people who evidently felt the appointment was wrong; in view of the institution's strong free speech tradition, it had never occurred to anyone to file a complaint about that incident. With respect to my prosecution, he expressed his belief that people would surely come to their senses. As it became clear that the claims being made about me were going to be used to try to smear him as well, he reiterated that the facts were what mattered. My internet campaign, he mentioned, was more important than I might imagine. He read me sympathetic messages he had received from colleagues. Everybody, he said, knows Schiffman.

> I distinctly remember my father stating, "Everybody knows Schiffman. He's doing this to you because he sees it as an opportunity to try and damage me." He ironically referred to Schiffman's use of criminal charges to fend off, as he saw it, allegations of plagiarism as "a new criterion for academic debate."

* * *

I quickly learn that many national and international news agencies have offices down the hall from the director of public information at the Manhattan district attorney's office. All the director needs to do is communicate with them briefly from time to time, and the proper contours of the narrative, from the DA's perspective, are fixed. As my trial and, later, appeal start to slowly proceed through the court system, more and more reports on my averred crimes appear in the press.[23] That a decision has been made to treat my case in a particular manner rapidly becomes clear: most of the articles closely adhere to the district attorney's characterization of the facts.[24] In most instances they fail to even mention the controversy over the "DSS" exhibitions or the history of charges of plagiarism and other unethical conduct in the scrolls milieu.[25] One notable exception will be a lengthy article in *Tablet* magazine, in which Avi Katzman's serious allegations against Schiffman are cited verbatim, but even after the piece is published, other journalists, including reporters from the *New York Times*, ignore the allegations.[26] Virtually all the news coverage of the case also avoids discussing how my email campaign fits within a context of satire, parody, and similar expressive conduct frequently reported on in the media—including, for example, the phenomenon, well known to academics, of tweets impersonating various university presidents.[27] One early news account, in the *New York Post*, reports that I "hijacked" email accounts of various academics—a term that undercuts the legal difference between hacking into an account and inventing a new one, in another person's name, for satirical purposes.[28]

    Later treatments will either continue not to mention or else simply misrepresent the contents of the criminalized communications involved, together with the claims being made by the district attorney's office. One *New York Times* article, by Jim Dwyer (1957–2020), will state, not inaccurately as far as it goes, that I engaged in "raucous online debates about the origins of the Dead Sea Scrolls," explaining that according to prosecutors, I am guilty of "sock puppetry that spiraled into … identity theft, criminal impersonation and forgery."[29] But, curiously, Dwyer's commonsense observation that "there was no question of anyone making money in this cyber-brawl" is in flat contradiction to the district attorney's accusation that I "hatched a scheme" to "falsify the business records" of New York University and to defraud the Jewish Museum of roughly a thousand dollars. A later article by Dwyer's colleague John Leland, in the *New York Times Magazine*, will rely on Lawrence Schiffman as an "authority" while describing me as a "gadfly," an "irritant," and a "noxious partisan" living in a cluttered apartment.[30] Throughout this piece, Leland's journalistic strategy will be to offer ostensibly neutral but in reality biased reportage, ad hominem in tone. The article, following Dwyer's effort, will serve as a second "human interest" substitute for even halfway serious exploration of censorship, plagiarism, and the other issues forming the backdrop of my prosecution. I will be especially surprised to see this sort of trash appearing in the *Times*, a newspaper that played an important role in breaking the earlier monopoly exercised over the scrolls by the "editorial team" that controlled access to them, mainly through the reporting of (now retired) science journalist John Noble Wilford.

"There was no question of anyone making money in this cyber-brawl."

During the first four years of appellate litigation, my identity theft convictions will be overturned as based on mere "speculation."[31] This, however, will not stop a federal district court judge from declaring that I engaged in an "outlandish scheme of identity theft," in part with the possible *financial aim* of "securing employment" for Norman Golb in the form of a potential lecture at a scrolls exhibition held in Toronto.[32] But the reasoning that supports such a conclusion is not easy to follow. In fact, the evidence seems to include nothing at all suggesting that I have any financial motive in wishing to see the public properly informed, but it does include emails in which I suggest that my father give a *free lecture* at a museum. While converting my insistence on the simple truth into a repugnant profit-making motive would seem to require precisely a form of speculation that reaches far beyond the evidence, it does have the merit of helping to clarify the nature of the persistent distortions that I will spend months upon months, even years, attempting to set right.

In fact, inaccurate and misleading assertions about the case, all of them elevated into purported statements of fact, characterize dozens of items appearing in various media outlets throughout the period discussed in these pages. That many of these items amount to a simple echoing of the Manhattan district attorney's statements to the press does not stop seasoned scholars and legal analysts from relying on them in their own presentations. Seemingly unfamiliar with the opinions of Ron Robin cited at the outset of this chapter, Mark Goodacre, a specialist on the synoptic Gospels at the Duke University religious studies department, dramatically condemns my "unacademic, uncivil and completely unacceptable behavior." And he does more than that: he also declares that I cast a "disgraceful slur" on Lawrence Schiffman—even though it is not clear how he could know this is the case, since he admits in the same breath that he himself is "not an expert on the scrolls," and fails to acknowledge the previous history informing the "slur" in question.[33]

Yet, given the charges I'm facing, Goodacre's priggish remarks are perhaps not as noteworthy as those that four days after my arrest appear in an article by Jonathan Turley of George Washington University, in which my campaign is described as having given rise to "a bizarre case that intersects criminal law and academia."[34] Citing a variety of news items that present the case from the prosecution's perspective, Turley comments that the quarrel over the scrolls "sounds like fighting words." He accurately asserts that I am accused of "impersonating Lawrence Schiffman, a New York University professor." Relying, however, on the offensive reporting of the *New York Daily News*, he quotes a portion of one of my emails both inaccurately and out of context, and says nothing of the possibility that the "impersonation" in question was actually an act of satirical mimicry.[35] Turley will become known above all for his Senate testimony opposing the impeachment of Donald Trump; Aaron Blake of the *Washington Post* will refer to him as "Fox's favorite constitutional lawyer."[36] As it happens, he is also ranked as America's "second most cited law professor."[37] With friends of such caliber, the prosecutors have little need to fear negative public feedback as they proceed with their special efforts.

A "Crime," a "Foul," and a "Cause of Action" …

Several exceptions do seem to emerge from the general journalistic pattern, all in the form of comments posted online. Tzvee Zahavy, a rabbi and former Jewish studies professor, puts out this response to the March 5, 2009, *New York Times* article by John Eligon on my arrest:

> This sad *Times* story must be incorrect. If indeed Schiffman discovered Golb was impersonating him, I am sure that he would have called Golb and his father and demanded that he stop the charade. That's how things are done within a civilized community. The *Times* reports that Schiffman went to the district attorney to have Golb arrested, saying that "he believed that Mr. Golb was impersonating him on the Internet." It's unbelievable to me that if he knew it was Golb, that Schiffman would have gone and had Golb arrested without any prior attempt to let him know he'd been discovered, to reason with him and demand that he stop and repair the damage that he did. Nine out of ten times that approach is effective. This account by the *Times* must be a mistake.

In a later blog entry, Zahavy then follows up with further remarks:

> His inconvenience of defending himself at his university is part of Schiffman's decision to seek public notoriety as an expert on the Dead Sea Scrolls. When you choose to be on TV as a world scholar in the wacky field of the scrolls, that is precisely when it is like you pick up the gun to play the game of Russian Roulette. However, when you parody and satirize someone on the net, that is your absolute constitutional right. It may not be a nice thing to do, but it is no crime, no foul and no cause of legal action. We are surprised that this matter will go to criminal trial. It should be disposed of without hesitation by the judge on an opening motion by the defense.[38]

To be sure, the matter is *not* disposed of by the judge without hesitation. Perhaps realizing that it might seem inappropriate for him to have weighed in on the case, Zahavy removes both of his comments from his blog on the eve of my trial. Following the trial, he will remain silent.

> *"We are surprised that this matter will go to criminal trial."*

On the other hand, Bible scholar Steve Wiggins, an author of books and articles who has taught in several universities, begins his response to an article on the trial in the *New Jersey Star-Ledger* by noting that "anyone who's spent much time with the Dead Sea Scrolls knows the name of Norman Golb." He then comments that "it is still not clear what Raphael Golb has done that is either newsworthy or illegal," and then suggests that the "most disturbing element" in the article "is not that Raphael ... has allegedly committed identity theft" but rather that "a professional journalist describes him, apparently without a hint of irony, as 'a brainiac.'" Wiggins pointedly entitles his blog entry "Crimeless Victim?" In a later entry, he reiterates that "the name of Norman Golb is familiar to just about any Hebrew Bible scholar. His work on the Scrolls is highly regarded." He goes on to hint that he has read, as it were, between the lines of one of the various AP articles by Jennifer Peltz on my prosecution: "In a case whose details rival the minutiae of the Scrolls themselves, the younger Golb is accused of sending emails putatively said to have been sent from his father's rivals confessing plagiarism. To what point, beyond alleged family honor, *one hesitates to speculate*." Wiggins adds that the "Scrolls date from that troubled time period when Christianity was just beginning to emerge from Judaism. Tempers flare at implications masked or insinuated."[39]

Scott Greenfield, a former prosecutor, is equally clear sighted; writing on his *Simple Justice* blog, he calls the prosecution "beyond belief" and warns that its "implications ... on internet free speech are enormous."[40] But perhaps the strongest moral assessment of the case and its implications takes the form of a comment by Greg Supina, a Baptist minister in Alberta, Canada. Commenting in the

Chicago Maroon around a month before my trial, Supina explains that he has just finished reading *Who Wrote the Dead Sea Scrolls?* This reading project, he indicates, has led him to conclude that a "terribly unjust slandering of an innocent man has taken place." He adds that the conduct of those doing this slandering has been "disgraceful," and that "the almost psychopathic cruelty and vanity of the petty and vindictive opponents of [Norman] Golb have been disgusting." Here are a few more excerpts from his statement:

> Although I am not a scholar by any means, I am beginning to see why slick and smooth-talking men—like those who oppose the rather un-slick Golb—seem to be drooling so much over the pain they cause him. After all, I have never seen a devil who likes to be exposed. Golb is obviously right about their complete lack of evidence in support of their views.
>
> I am a Baptist, of the old kind, the kind that supports freedom of conscience … As Calvinists, we believe only God can truly change the opinions of the inner heart. All we can do is preach and do what God gives our hands to do each day to keep basic order and life. So, if we differ in opinion, we debate, whenever our opponent might be willing. If he isn't willing, we wait. But we always keep the door open for an exchange of dialogue, just as Golb has done.
>
> Yet … Golb's opponents have attempted to suppress any fair exchange of scholarly dialogue in their fear of being exposed … And how can they say they didn't do such things? Their injustice is fully documented, even by themselves, even on their own websites over the last year or so!
>
> In the sciences, the use of inductive logic gathers all the facts and eliminates the implausible and untenable first. After that, the possible outputs are weighed and the theory which fits ALL the facts best is chosen—constantly subjecting that theory to review as new input is received.

One does not simply imagine whatever one wants. There are the boundaries of the facts to deal with, for the sake of the truth and for the sake of the lives who depend on that truth.

God help us all if we continue to support more lies of more scientists, allowing them to hurt others directly or indirectly through their lies.

Raphael Golb was wrong to lie, in my opinion. But the far, far greater lies of the others—hurtful, incessant, self-serving, un-repented lies—make R. Golb's lies look [like] fluffy little white clouds for God's good angels to rest upon.

What injustice to the Golb family!!![41]

"I have never seen a devil who likes to be exposed."

Perhaps reflecting a general lack of interest in anything other than the scandal and "flaring tempers" surrounding the scrolls, Supina's statement will go without response. In fact, almost three years will go by before comments indicative of dissent start popping up again. Carl John Hinke—a pacifist and anticensorship activist who was arrested thirty-five times for civil disobedience during the 1960s—will assert that my trial shows how "legal abuse by the misguided excesses of rampant government" can even disrupt the lives of scholars.[42] With still greater concision, Lawrence Kaplan, a professor of Jewish philosophy at McGill University, will refer to me as a "self-appointed, bumbling armor-bearer" and to my prosecution as an "abuse of justice."[43]

"Let Not These Matters Be Published Abroad!"—*Letters of Obscure Men*

Looking back on the affair long after my trial, Arthur Hayes, a media law specialist at Fordham University, will argue that "parody, satire and other forms of outrageous speech have the capacity to reveal truths that provide valuable information and wisdom about the human condition that may yield great benefit to substantial portions of any community."[44] Offering a similar insight on the phenomenon of satirical pranks, Kembrew McLeod, a sociologist at the University of Iowa, will remark that satirists "lie and tell the truth at the same time," and that they "often use falsehoods to reveal deeper truths," or "deceit to expose hypocrisy and inequality."[45]

> *"Pranksters often use falsehoods to reveal deeper truths."*

There is nothing radically new about either of these insights; they serve, rather, as reminders of common understandings. "Satire," according to Michael Bugeja, professor of media ethics at Iowa State University, "remains one of the best vehicles to express an uncomfortable truth."[46] It "is almost always criticism," wrote the critic Martin Seymour-Smith in 1984.[47] Its particular purpose, wrote the scholar of Oriental studies Yosef Y. Rivlin in 1971, is "to show things in their true light."[48] Similar statements can be found in myriads of other sources. Already more than five hundred years ago, Erasmus had explained that Momus, the Greek god of mockery and satire (whose Roman equivalent is named Querella), "is not as popular as the other [gods], because few people freely accept true criticism ... Nowadays," he added, "our Joves shut out Momus ... preferring flattery to ... truth."[49]

During the long period leading up to my trial, it is clear that the New York prosecutors handling the affair are not interested in the truth-manifesting capacity of satirical speech, or in the fine lines separating parody, hoaxes, and other similar forms of critical expression, or the ambiguous zones in which they converge and overlap. Instead, they are intent on portraying my campaign as a "fraudulent scheme" aimed at "promoting" unpopular research and at disseminating "false allegations." As the months go by, I occasionally receive reports of the prosecutor's hardball tactics in negotiations with my lawyer. Rather than dwell too much on the threats periodically conveyed to me, I try to take a broad view, and find it more useful to frame Bandler's posturing in the context of the ample legal precedents that exist for criminalizing "falsehoods that reveal deeper truths." While I've worked my way through a good deal of satire over the years, I've hardly given any serious thought to the genre's legal status. In many instances I have only vague memories of works I read years ago in college. But I'm aware enough to know that those memories fed into my campaign and that I should start gathering material for my defense, so I'm now led to pull down old volumes from my shelves and reread them from a different perspective.

Efforts to suppress "outrageous" satirical writings date back at least to the eve of the Protestant Reformation, when the anonymous authors of the *Letters of Obscure Men* (1515–17) viciously mocked several distinguished academic figures and church authorities who believed the books of the Jews should be burned. The Catholic antisemites pilloried in the *Letters* did terrible harm to the Jews, but their reputations were permanently damaged by the ridicule to which they were subjected.[50] Three of them, including the dean of the Theological Faculty of Cologne, were impersonated in the work, and educated readers around Europe continued to be fooled until a single letter at the end of the second volume directly addressed the satire's pious victims: "To the gallows then with you all … But let not these matters be published abroad, lest all the righteous discern what manner of men ye are."[51] My old paperback

> In 1517, Pope Leo X banned the *Letters of Obscure Men* under pain of excommunication—an action that increased their fame and popularity. The word *obscurantism* was coined in reference to this work.

edition of the bawdy *Letters*—it sits on my shelves next to the *Praise of Folly* by Erasmus—mentions the fooling of educated readers only in passing. I verify at the library that in the original hardback edition, a lengthier introduction by the work's English translator provides much more detail on this episode and includes the remark that "it has been, in every age, the fate of satire to be misunderstood."[52]

It is in fact the inherent instability of satirical expression, its endlessly subversive incapacity to be pinned down as merely a form of humor, its dangerously *serious* deadpan message—so often taken as *true* by the gullible—that has led legal authorities through the centuries to view it with such suspicion and dead seriousness. As George Test puts it in his classic study of the genre, the "understandable willingness to identify the satirist with his or her persona and his or her characters has plagued satire since, in all probability, the original curse itself ... Because of the passionate and partisan nature of their attacks, satirists have long been forced to seek refuge behind anonymity."[53]

Those who sought such refuge included the authors of thousands of licentious epigrams affixed, during many decades of the sixteenth century, to the statue of Pasquino, near Piazza Navona in Rome. When guards were posted at the statue, other monuments were put to the same use. These satirical barbs became known as "pasquinades," regardless of where they appeared. They "victimized" popes, cardinals, princes, and in general hundreds of members of the ruling classes. Their fame spread throughout Europe, and at least until the beginning of the seventeenth century, they continued to manifest themselves at regular intervals—even though they were "prohibited under the heaviest penalties."[54] One of them, ironically referring to the persecution of the Spanish priest Miguel de Molinos (the founder of the Quietist sect, charged with heresy and imprisoned for life in 1685), neatly summarized this situation:

"If we speak, the galleys; if we write, the gallows; if we stay quiet, the Inquisition. Eh! what are we to do, then?"[55]

Not much more than a century after hundreds of Roman pasquinades were first collected into a 647-page printed volume in 1544,[56] the passionate and partisan nature of satire played a key role in one of the great religious controversies of European history. In 1656, special police forces in France engaged in an elaborate effort to identify the author of a series of writings entitled the "Provincial Letters." The author of these vivid and highly believable satirical texts, as eventually became widely recognized after his death, was none other than the philosopher Blaise Pascal, whose friendship with Jansenist theologians had led him to write this "deeply personal, angry response to the use of political power and church censure"[57] to suppress the members of that religious order. Pascal's letters contained portrayals of fictional characters rather than impersonations, but the self-justifications and arguments against the Jansenists that he put in the mouth of a fictitious Jesuit priest were considered so embarrassing to the powerful Jesuits that he was obliged to avoid arrest by using pseudonyms and clandestine presses and by hiding in taverns.[58]

Pascal died in 1662; in 1678, the publication of another anonymous work changed the entire course of literary history. Entitled *La Princesse de Clèves*, the work was remarkable not only because it inaugurated a new genre that would come to be known as the modern novel but because it viciously satirized the courtly social milieu in which, as the eponymous heroine's mother warns her in the opening pages, "appearances are not what they seem." While *La Princesse de Clèves* is not presented in epistolary form, one of its key narrative threads depicts the prurient interest evoked by the discovery of an unsigned letter revealing the secrets of a discreet personal relationship, with the consequent ruin of the letter's recipient despite his desperate denial that he had anything to do with the affair in question (he is referred to only as "you" in the letter).[59] The author of this remarkable work—the Parisian socialite countess commonly known as Madame de La Fayette—denied having written it throughout her life to all but a few close friends.

The same year, 1678, also saw the publication of a key work of English narrative: John Bunyan's *The Pilgrim's Progress*. Bunyan wrote much of his parable in the foul Bedford prison, where he was jailed for twelve years as a punishment for his illegal preaching activities. The book, which has been republished over two hundred times, is laced with satirical invective aimed at "lords" and "great ones," as well as at "professors" who may seem very honorable but "when they are by themselves ... drink iniquity, and swallow down sin like water."[60] Bunyan's characters, with names like "Talkative," "Hypocrisy," and "Mr. Worldly-Wise," personified human vices in a broad, and at bottom somewhat conservative, Christian allegory; the technique of abstract personification (which Bunyan called "similitude") was perhaps partly what enabled the preacher to use his own name to critique the social and religious forces that had kept him in prison for so long. He had also, perhaps, wisely chosen prose, rather than verse, as his medium. In 1599, the archbishop of Canterbury and the bishop of London had jointly issued a decree that appeared to ban verse satire altogether.[61] A modern authority on one of the works burned pursuant to the decree explains that

> Elizabethan satirists ... used generic names (Coscus, Rufus, and so on) to describe people with highly idiosyncratic quirks—obsessions with music, or fencing, or their mistress's corsets. This encouraged readers to identify the names with people they knew, but at the same time ensured that any identification could be denied by the author. This was a highly dangerous game to play, especially when ... the people satirised included corrupt vicars and hypocritical puritans.[62]

While the decree of 1599 had been only sparsely enforced, in view of widespread awareness of the very real risks involved in the act of authorship, *concealed* authorship would become more and more typical during the ensuing centuries. One of the reference works that I consulted, dealing solely with English-language writings, listed "17,000 pseudonyms of more than 10,500 authors." I also came across similar works focused on Jewish authors; the entry entitled "Pseudonyms" in the *Universal Jewish Encyclopedia* (1943) explained that "first in Hebrew and then in Yiddish writings," the use of fake names ultimately rose to such prevalence that the real names of authors are "in many cases no longer known." The article added that "this is particularly the case when the writing was of such satiric or personal nature that the author was afraid to reveal his identity."[63] While I knew practically nothing of the figures who had produced this vast body of literature, their fear had resonance for me. Had they perhaps also cast "disgraceful slurs" and schemed to influence debates?

When satire victimized "great men" of the English "realm" (or kingdom), it risked being treated as a serious crime of libel called *scandalum magnatum*.[64] In some circumstances, it could also be criminalized as "seditious" libel—that is, as inciting rebellion. At the outset of the eighteenth century, Daniel Defoe got himself into trouble with his mockery of political views that he found reprehensible. In 1702, he anonymously published a pamphlet entitled *The Shortest-Way with the Dissenters; Or, Proposals for the Establishment of the Church*, in which he sarcastically argued that Protestants who wished to leave the Church of England should be "crucified." The pamphlet's utterly deadpan imitation of the style used in Tory publications was considered so outrageous that the decision was made to hunt down and imprison its author. He was sent to Newgate Prison for six months and exposed in a pillory for three days; fortunately, however, he ended up being pelted with flowers rather than rotten fruit, because the public supported his views.

Defoe's younger contemporary Jonathan Swift, himself a priest, was somewhat more cautious in his choice of satirical subjects, but he did perhaps more than anyone else to show how effective a weapon satire could be. Angered by a sarcastic reference to the "infallible Church" made by the astrologer John Partridge, Swift perpetrated what turned out to be perhaps the most famous hoax of his time, first "astrologically" predicting, and then falsely announcing, Partridge's death. The hoax was notoriously taken seriously by hundreds of readers, including church authorities. Partridge tried to insist that the announcement of his death was false, but he then became the butt of so many cruel jokes that his reputation was damaged beyond repair. Like many satirists before him, Swift cautiously authored the hoax under a fictitious name (in this instance, "Isaac Bickerstaff"). Throughout his career, likely in fear that his satirical inclinations could ensnare him in legal trouble, he used dozens of pseudonyms, and claimed (despite what he had done to Partridge) that he had always satirized social institutions rather than individuals.[65] His "Modest Proposal" (first published anonymously in 1729) illustrated how unsettling the technique could be by suggesting that poverty and hunger could best be solved by eating children. The work has continued to be misunderstood—and to anger audiences—even in recent decades.[66]

While Swift appears to have been just cautious enough to avoid prosecution, the Italian author Girolamo Gigli (1660–1722) was not so lucky, no doubt because he was more easily carried away by his passions. He was arrested when he poked fun at his contemporaries in the series of fake letters constituting his *Gazzettino* (1713–16), which he "signed" with the name of a well-known Jesuit missionary, and peopled with characters also bearing the real names of known contemporaries, with the result that these satirical writings were commonly mistaken for "true accounts."[67]

> Gigli was spared imprisonment thanks to the intercession of a prominent clergyman with whom he was acquainted.

Despite its inevitable dangers, satire's value as a provocative tool led to its enduring popularity during the Enlightenment period. In France, Montesquieu, in *The Spirit of the Laws*—a work familiar to the authors of the United States Constitution—argued that neither spoken words of an "indiscreet" nature nor written satire should be criminalized: the former, because words are by their very nature "equivocal and ambiguous," their meaning often even depending on how they are pronounced; the latter, because "being generally levelled against men of power and authority," satire "may amuse the general malevolence, please the malcontents … give the people patience to suffer, and make them laugh at their sufferings." This, he suggested, is why satire is not "hindered" in democracies (governed as they are by the people), but is "punished with death" in aristocracies and "prohibited," albeit with lesser punishments, in monarchies.[68]

Regardless, however, of such prohibition, as resentment of royalty began to proliferate, the spread of subversive epistolary satires became unstoppable. Powerful figures, including the likes of

Madame de Pompadour, Madame du Barry, and Louis XV, were subtly ridiculed in scandalous pseudomemoirs and pseudocollections of letters that appeared under their names—written so convincingly that even sophisticated readers took these works seriously. Many of the authors who sought to convey the truth in this manner were tracked down, arrested, and imprisoned.[69]

That fact may help make it clear why, on the new continent, Benjamin Franklin repeatedly availed himself of anonymity to issue dangerously anti-British satires. In September 1773, Philadelphia's *Public Advertiser* printed an "Edict by the King of Prussia" that was actually written by Franklin. This satire induced hundreds of unwitting readers into thinking that the Prussian ruler, in order to retaliate against the British monarchs for their immoral actions, had decided to impose the same sort of cruel restrictions and tariffs on England as England had on its colonies. Franklin followed up with several epistolary hoaxes (some of them falsely signed by Captain Samuel Gerrish and naval fighter John Paul Jones) that continued to both fool readers and harm British reputations long after his death. One of them, distributed all over Europe in 1782, took the form of a forged Boston *Independent Chronicle* "supplement," part of which consisted of a message purportedly intercepted from a British agent that detailed shipments to the British Canadian governor of scalps sliced from the heads of dead American soldiers, farmers, and infants "ripped out of their mothers' bellies."[70]

William Hone, a bookseller (and former law clerk) in London, was only ten when Franklin died in 1790. In 1817, he was prosecuted for authoring "blasphemous and seditious pamphlets" that parodied a number of influential politicians and "savagely attacked the government of the Prince Regent."[71] Hone was thrown into a dungeon, where he prepared his own legal defense over a period of several months. Reduced to abject poverty and ill health as a result of his incarceration, he was nonetheless able to display an immense "erudition on the subject," which "carried him through three trials by his proven plea of past usage."[72]

In spite of severe sickness and exhaustion, Hone spoke on each of the three days for about seven hours, guiding the jury through famous examples of parody that he had gathered from many books. The prosecution "urged that to bring forward any previous parody was the same thing as if a person charged with obscenity should produce obscene volumes in his defense."[73]

Despite the judge admonishing the jury that they were to ignore such testimony, Hone was acquitted on each count. Soon afterward, a public collection was made on his behalf. He was able to get his life back together and to continue writing his satirical works, but he died some twenty-five years later at the age of sixty-two; Charles Dickens was one of those who attended his funeral. Hone's case remains one of the most famous in the annals of English law; no British citizen has ever again been prosecuted for "seditious libel." (Such prosecutions would, however, sporadically take place in the United States, where the Sedition Act of 1918, for example, would criminalize the uttering of "profane, scurrilous, or abusive language about the form of government of the United States." Not until 1964 would the Supreme Court declare such prosecutions unconstitutional in view of the First Amendment.)[74]

While Hone's trial showed that prosecuting an ordinary person for ridicule could rebound against the governing authorities in England, no such result was possible in Italy and in France, where acts of satire were repeatedly criminalized during the nineteenth century. Those imprisoned included the Venetian poet Pietro Buratti, who was imprisoned at least twice for his vicious descriptions of aristocratic figures, and Paul-Louis Courier, an author of many brilliant satires.[75] In 1884, the young author Louis Desprez made the mistake of cowriting, with his friend Henry Fèvre, a novel of rural life filled with coarse satirical passages, including scenes in which the village abbot was portrayed as having an intimate affair with a secular-minded schoolteacher. A few weeks after the novel's publication, the two authors were charged with public indecency. Desprez agreed to assume all responsibility for the book; he was tried, convicted, sentenced to a month in jail, and incarcerated in one of the worst wings of the Sainte-Pélagie prison in Paris, where he soon came down with a bronchial condition that rapidly turned into TB. His ordeal, followed by his death nine months after his release, provoked a wave of outrage in literary circles. From Edmond de Goncourt's journal:

> This child, this writer, at the age of twenty-three, has just died from his imprisonment with thieves and muggers, by the good grace of our republican government—this kid, a literary convict! Such an assassination won't be found even in the annals of the Old Regime.[76]

Meanwhile, some of the moral ambiguities of satire had been illustrated by its continued use in nineteenth-century America. "God defend me from Irony, and from Satire his bosom friend," the confidence man declares in Melville's 1857 ironic satire of an American dream mined by racism, masks, trickery and suspicion.[77] We owe the word *obscurantism* to perennial fascination with the pre-Reformation *Letters of Obscure Men*; but the term *miscegenation* was coined in a seventy-two-page satirical hoax pamphlet, *Miscegenation: The Theory of the Blending of the Races, Applied to the American White Man and Negro*, anonymously published in 1864 by two staff members of the racist *New York World*, a leading organ of the Democratic Party (whose moral platform at the time was roughly equivalent to the one adhered to today by the radical right). The aim of the widely disseminated pamphlet was to mock Lincoln's antislavery agenda and to "rile up" antiabolitionists by extolling the virtues of racial mingling; its suggestion that intermarriage was the true, and worthy, goal of abolition provoked a massive controversy, with its satirical nature often going unnoticed even decades after it was published.[78]

Only a few months earlier, editors throughout the United States had been fooled into reprinting "A Bloody Massacre near Carson," a satire of Mark Twain's in which he went so far as to portray the frontiersman Philip Hopkins as having decapitated his wife and children before slitting his own throat.[79] Twain's actual intent had been to criticize an unethical dividend-cooking scheme going on in San Francisco, and so he decided to portray the mild-mannered Hopkins as having been driven mad by the scheme. Twain made the hoax more convincing by naming a known resident of Carson

City, Abram Curry, as his purported "source." The reading public, it turned out, had little interest in Twain's target—the rigged-dividends scheme—but was eager to soak in the gory details of the purported massacre.[80]

Recalling his "reformatory satire" in 1870, Clemens explained that he had laced it with "telltale absurdities and impossibilities," and that "the idea that anybody could ever take my massacre for a genuine occurrence never once suggested itself to me." The real Hopkins, he insisted, did not have a family at all, but was "well known to every creature in the land as a bachelor."[81] But three years later, Twain told the Monday Evening Club in Hartford, Connecticut, that he knew "from personal experience the proneness of journalists to lie. I once started a peculiar and picturesque fashion of lying myself on the Pacific coast, and it is not dead there to this day."[82] By acknowledging that his satire consisted of a "lie," Twain was merely putting his finger on the subversive, deadpan instability that had always plagued the genre. Like Edgar Allan Poe and many others before him, he had been led to see how difficult it can be to separate satire from hoax.[83]

But the instability itself was far from useless. It served to vividly, indeed almost *experientially*, highlight some of the age-old social lies (the polite manners of the exploiter, the general willingness to ignore abuses whose impact is felt only indirectly, and so on) that we are all expected to tolerate. With the widespread resurgence of satire, pranks, and hoaxes of all sorts in the age of the internet, this "insecurity" factor helped galvanize a vehement public reaction, even against "lies" that speak truth to power. Robert Cargill, one of the key complainants in the criminal indictment against me, would capture the essence of this reaction when he asserted that "in the case of *known* satirists like Stephen Colbert, or *known* parodists like Saturday Night Live, there is an *expectation* of parody or satire," whereas "Raphael Golb was not *claiming* parody, but was actively attempting to *disguise his identity*. ... At no point was there ever an *expectation* or *acknowledgement* of parody or satire."[84]

When I read this statement, I could not help shaking my head in disbelief. Since when in the history and practice of satire in all its forms were authors bound to announce their satirical intent? The words about "disguising identity" struck me as particularly disingenuous. Many American courts had recognized that anonymous and pseudonymous speech are protected by the First Amendment, holding time and again, for example, that "anonymous speech is a great tradition that is woven into the fabric of this nation's history," or that there is a "legitimate and valuable right to participate in online forums anonymously or pseudonymously."[85]

> Courts have insisted on the right to anonymity because "this ability to speak one's mind without the burden of the other party knowing all the facts about one's identity can foster open communication and robust debate."

Certainly aware of this legal reality, John Bandler, the prosecutor, had not gone so far as to suggest that my use of pseudonyms was illegal; but it was clear that he intended—following Cargill's lead—to argue that my effort to conceal my identity showed I was a sneaky, disgraceful liar, and that my accusations of misconduct on the part of the scroll exhibitors lacked credibility. What would his reaction have been had he been alive in 1764, when the anonymous author of an eight-page pamphlet shocked the public with the revelation that Jean-Jacques Rousseau, whose works included a major treatise on education, had brutally abandoned his own children in an orphanage? Rousseau, in his *Confessions*, admitted that the accusation was true; but he attempted to mitigate its impact on his reputation (he was pelted with stones during his exile in Prussia) by arguing that its author was a coward, hiding his identity in an unseemly fashion.[86] Would the pamphlet rightly have been criminalized if it had been issued as a self-mocking "confession" of Rousseau?

Arguments about the moral status of anonymity had been going on for centuries. Good heavens, I thought, is this really where we're heading? Are parodies and satire supposed to be "expected" or "acknowledged"? Are they supposed to be accompanied by trigger warnings, the way certain academics alert students to the potentially troubling content of various literary works, including

Alexander Pope's classic satire (first published anonymously in 1712) *The Rape of the Lock*? Are the people who produce them supposed to openly "claim" to be doing so, and to politely present them as *being* satirical, like John Bunyan with his evangelical similitudes? Are people who send out parodies *really* expected not to "disguise" their identities? Such notions might fit the popular televised formats of Stephen Colbert and *Saturday Night Live*, but they struck me as having little to do with broader historical or even current-day reality.

3

TOWARD THE CRIMINALIZING OF SATIRE IN AMERICA

"I don't know," novelist Howard Jacobson once said, "what kind of trouble this gets somebody into, a disputatious mind."[1] As I sit at computers in a variety of cafés around my neighborhood in the days and weeks following my experience with Bandler and the Tombs, I begin to get a fuller picture of the direction an answer to this question might take.

To be sure, I am able to figure out rather quickly that no one in the United States has ever been arrested for this sort of thing. I dimly recall, for example, reading once about mockery posted in an online forum under variations of the New York Stock Exchange's director's name. A Google search allows me to verify that the stock exchange initially tried to sue for trademark infringement, but that the lawsuit was dropped when the defendant raised the specter of "satire."[2] A stock exchange spokesman explained that "sometimes there are wrongs without remedies."[3] Looking further, I find the same basic position reflected in a November 2004 statement issued by a committee of the American Association of University Professors (AAUP). The statement asserts that "electronic messages are protected [from censorship or legal assault] to an even greater degree than their print-era counterparts," because "proximate, 'in-your-face' risks simply do not exist when the combatants are seated at keyboards an unknown distance apart." (As one sign among many others signaling the academic world's long-standing ambivalence with respect to freedom of debate, this statement will be removed from the AAUP's website in 2013.)[4]

Still, just because something hasn't previously been criminalized doesn't mean it can never be criminalized. There is always a first time. I know that parody and satire are generally considered, as Tzvee Zahavy indicated, an absolute constitutional right. But the full picture is more complicated. True enough, the US Supreme

Court has suggested that social and political satire is protected by the principle of the "free interchange of ideas and the ascertainment of truth."[5] But the court has never specifically held that *personal* or *academic* satire taking the form of false confessions and similar written material is necessarily entitled to such constitutional protection. This lack of a specific, decisive, on-point precedent will in fact play a major role in my prosecution. In pursuing his case, the Manhattan DA will seek to benefit from the Supreme Court's silence on this matter, evading general First Amendment principles and deliberately muddying the waters with outlandish legal arguments. The federal courts will then uphold just enough of the charges to get the matter sent back down to the New York criminal court, partly on the grounds that federal constitutional law simply is not clear enough to compel dismissal of the charges.

While the exact contours of the First Amendment's application to "deceitfully" deadpan email parodies remains unclear, one thing I *am* clear about, as I await developments in my case, is that fakery has long been a basic part of print- and news-driven satirical hoaxes that seek to embarrass powerful people and organizations. The general pattern is that groups who seek to catalyze social change find ways of luring the media to pick up invented news items as if they were real, with the result that such reports are discussed, and sometimes believed, by thousands of readers. An example from before the age of the internet is Leonard Lewin's best-selling *Report from Iron Mountain* (1967), which purported to be a secret government-panel report concluding that a transition to a permanent state of world peace would require drastic measures such as starvation, slavery and increased pollution (compare eating babies in Swift's "Modest Proposal"). Ample press coverage ensued, with the report variously being described as a "satire," "parody," "hoax," or as a genuine document. Lyndon Johnson was said to have ordered the suppression of the "secret report." Lewin's avowal, several years later, that the work had been a "satirical hoax" designed to "provoke discussion," would be ignored—and indeed, with tragic consequences, turned on its head—by right-wing propagandists who would insist on the *Report*'s legitimacy.[6]

As observed at length by Kembrew McLeod, the many satirical hoaxes perpetrated on the internet by the antiglobalist, "culture jamming" duo known as the Yes Men (along with similar groups) are precisely an extension of the print- and news-driven historical tradition of satire and hoaxes.[7] At least two popular documentaries have shown how the Yes Men brilliantly mimic the websites, email addresses, and phone numbers of entities whose alleged corruption they wish to expose. This enables them to entice reporters to fake company presentations, where they proceed to subtly ridicule their victims by making increasingly improbable but utterly deadpan statements that are often taken seriously by those attending these meetings.[8]

> The Yes Men call their imitative techniques "identity correction," as opposed to "identity theft."

While I await developments in my prosecution, I'm already well aware that the elaborate hoaxes of the Yes Men have set a standard for impersonation strategies commonly seen both online and off-line. "Western history," Lani Boyd writes, "is filled with pranks and trickery intent on enlightening audiences by blending fiction with reality ... With an arsenal of parody, satire, interventions, and tactical obfuscation, the Yes Men attack those who they feel abuse their positions of power. They have impersonated public persons and infamous entities, including President George W. Bush, the World Trade Organization, and Dow Chemical. Their mimicry is so convincing, that the audience cannot decipher between satire and the real thing."[9] One of their most widely recognized interventions took place on December 2, 2004, the twentieth anniversary of the Bhopal gas tragedy, when they succeeded in falsely announcing on the BBC that Dow Chemical would take full responsibility for that horrifying industrial disaster. In front of a worldwide audience, the impersonators offered a $12 billion settlement to the victims—an incident that reminded viewers of Dow's failure to acknowledge the role it had played in the more than twenty thousand deaths attributed to the catastrophe.[10]

As the prospect of a trial starts to take shape, I focus on trying to synthesize some of this material, in the hope that it will help point the way toward a defense against Bandler's sweeping harassment charges. Gradually it becomes clear to me that online hoaxes and pranks aimed at challenging power and authority have actually been a feature of internet culture almost since the creation of the World Wide Web. As early as 1994, an "AP news release," perhaps designed to make a point about the marketing of religion, perhaps simply to make fools of media pundits, announced that Microsoft had agreed to acquire the Roman Catholic Church in exchange for "an unspecified number of shares of Microsoft common stock." When Rush Limbaugh read the fake release on his national television program, "the company found itself fielding calls from outraged viewers."[11]

Not all such telling-truth-to-power pranks are internet based. Not long after the Microsoft affair, a highly provocative hoax was perpetrated by NYU physics professor Alan Sokal. Aghast at the vacuity of "postmodernist" academic culture, Sokal contributed an article, which he presented as a serious study on the "hermeneutics of quantum gravity," to the "theory" journal *Social Text*.[12] In fact, Sokal's analysis consisted of deliberate, patent nonsense based on the type of jargon used by typical contributors to the journal. Despite its absurdity, the article, apparently on the basis of Sokal's scholarly reputation, was seen through editorial review to publication. Three weeks later, writing in the May 1996 issue of the magazine *Lingua Franca*, Sokal revealed that the article had been a hoax, a revelation that humiliated the journal's editors and prompted them to accuse Sokal of "fraud."[13] (At the time, *Social Text* had apparently not yet implemented an anonymous "peer review" process. In the wake of Sokal's hoax, other similar articles would eventually also make a mockery of that process as practiced in the academic publishing industry.)[14]

As I gather more and more items, I compile a dossier that I label "satire." With each article that I add to the file, it becomes more and more obvious that a common theme in all such incidents is the anger they provoke, particularly when gullible "recipients" of the prank are fooled, or when there is a fear that some of them might be fooled. A few years after the Microsoft and Sokal affairs, George W. Bush tried to have the satirical GWBush.com blocked, claiming it was "malicious" and stating that "there ought to be limits to freedom." The Federal Election Commission dismissed his complaint without ruling on the issue.[15] Many news articles appearing at the time reflect the confusion and controversy caused by such hoaxes; one article, commenting on a similar website meant to ridicule Al Gore but taken seriously by many internet surfers, blandly notes that "the satire is lost on some visitors."[16]

As I await the first pretrial hearings in my case, I begin to realize that all these controversies fit into the same pattern: they are media events dealing with raging social and political issues. Somehow the satirical nature of the incident that catalyzes the controversy becomes the scapegoat, allowing anger to be focused on the messenger. The media, in turn, thrives on such anger, leading to further magnification of the controversy.

And that—a gross magnification of my "crimes," through the lens of popular anger—is what has happened to me. This understanding helps me rationalize the process. I remind myself that there is sometimes a place even for the "good trouble" of civil disobedience, and that Thoreau himself had only scorn for the "weak tyranny" of public opinion.[17] I shrug off the stress, set myself the goal of seeking justice, and put myself in a Zen mode. I have no difficulty sleeping; I eat regular meals, exercise daily, begin a regime of reading, and spend several hours a week adding one news report or another to my satire dossier. As the file grows bigger, I wonder whether any of the reports stand a solid chance of affecting the trial, once the decision has been made to prosecute me to the full extent of the law. Isn't there any court decision on point that would demonstrate the ludicrous nature of the prosecution's distortions? Eventually I start looking for some direct, current-day legal precedent, but all I can ascertain is that people who file lawsuits complaining that they have been damaged by parody, satire, and the like quickly come to learn that the process can be cumbersome and expensive, with chances limited by the First Amendment rights of impersonators—rights that have tended to be liberally interpreted by civil court judges.

One example that I come across early on has to do with author Ted Rall suing cartoonist Danny Hellman for attributing outrageous statements to Rall in a series of satirical emails that he sent under Rall's name. A judge called the emails an "act of literary impersonation," and the case never went to trial.[18] But Ted Rall was not a well-connected NYU professor featured in televised interviews about a notorious field of religious studies; he had not gone to the FBI or the police but had merely filed a lawsuit; he was not backed by the power of a zealous prosecutor dead set on getting Hellman sent to Rikers Island.

> Lawsuits are filed in *civil* court, a government-run forum in which disputes take place among individuals regarding their responsibilities toward one another. The typical result of a civil lawsuit is money damages. Crimes, on the other hand, are committed against the *state*, which in America is called "the People." The state itself prosecutes crimes, a process that takes place in *criminal* court.

Gradually I come to see that developments, both legal and social, in this field are happening almost every day; but none of them have to do with the criminal law. Along with the continual expansion of hoax "culture," a body of scholarly literature discussing it is also beginning to proliferate. Several years after my trial, Kembrew McLeod will survey many such contributions and come up with a useful definition. Hoaxes, according to him, are "staged provocations designed to persuade." He will observe that "pranks, at their most productive, inspire critical inquiry and thoughtful reflection."[19] Still later, in 2022, Elon Musk's takeover of Twitter will be met by an outpouring of impersonations on that platform, creating what the *New York Times* will describe as "chaos" and "disruption."[20] Internet scholars will quickly recognize the impersonations as "parody and mocking," as a "dissent against Musk's leadership," as a "form of digital protest" belonging to a genre of "rhetorical practices that use irony and detraction to catalyze conversations about power and capitalism."[21] While these types of practices are already common at the time of my arrest, they are not yet as widely studied as they will eventually be.[22] Not one of the legal decisions in the trial and the appellate courts handling the *People v. Golb* affair will mention a single item from the body of literature describing the social value of hoaxes, satire, and the like.

To be sure, despite these difficulties, already from the outset I'm dead sure of my innocence, because there was nothing criminal about my intent at all; rather, I was seeking to spark much-needed awareness and debate. But it's also clear that many "victims" of satire won't share this perspective, regardless of the long history and pervasive presence of the genre. Judging from the constant complaints about "harassment" that I read about in the newspapers, many targets of unwanted parody will naturally derive satisfaction and comfort from a regime of criminalization. Though the First Amendment is theoretically on my side, I'm still fighting an uphill battle, if only because so many individuals subject to mockery are clamoring to satisfy their desire—in itself often understandable, even if subject to criticism—for legal retaliation, whether in the civil or the criminal courts.

Efforts at telling truth to power do have a flip side—for instance, in the "fake news" sent out by an autocrat's bots to subvert elections. Some originally saw the internet as a tool for democracy; its susceptibility to being turned into a vehicle that aids the suppression of freedom has led various commentators to predict the platform's death.[23] The medium can also be used to engage in particularly harmful forms of false speech, such as when X, jilted by Y, posts a fake blog in Y's name featuring nude photographs and highly embarrassing statements purportedly by Y. Fear of the "dark" side of false internet speech will feed into the portrait prosecutor Bandler will set out to paint of me as a trained criminal. I am skilled, he will argue, at "twisting words," a purported talent rendering me a "menace to anyone who crosses [my] path."[24] Capitalizing on the public's outrage at revenge pornography and other similar phenomena, he will casually presuppose a false equivalence as the unquestionable truth and present my criminalized emails not as parodies, not even as malicious parodies, but as "maliciousness" *rather* than parody.[25]

In reality, Bandler's fearmongering will conceal the actual nature of the charge he is pursuing, which in normal legal discourse would be considered a claim of *libel* or defamation.[26] The implicit charge is that I damaged Lawrence Schiffman's reputation by—so it is alleged—falsely accusing him of plagiarism. But there is a problem with this unstated claim. Even setting aside the legal complexities involved in proving it, ever since 1967, libel has been dealt with in New York (as in most American states) as a civil and not a criminal matter.[27]

What Bandler has really set out to do is to find some pretext, some excuse, to make a crime out of something that is no longer a crime. The charge of criminal libel will be *disguised* under that pretext—but it will be hinted at from the start in the disingenuous assertion, issued by prosecutors who know nothing about the Dead Sea Scrolls, to the effect that my campaign consisted of "false accusations." That assertion, in turn, will gradually be transformed into an elaborate prosecutorial strategy relying on a systematic obscuring of the academic scandal forming the context of the criminalized emails.

> In theory, conduct can be criminalized only if lawmakers conclude that it poses a *threat to public safety*. But in the United States, "hard on crime" legislators are continually criminalizing even the most trivial forms of perceived misconduct, leading some commentators to point out that average Americans daily commit a variety of felonies without being aware of it.

At the heart of that scandal is the pointed question put by Avi Katzman to Lawrence Schiffman in 1993, along with the unethical "power politics" of scroll-controversy protagonists using science-museum exhibition halls for propaganda purposes that have nothing to do with science. Katzman's interview with Schiffman in particular is well known to the community of scholars. Norman Golb himself quoted Katzman's exact words in *Who Wrote the Dead Sea Scrolls?*—and he explained that Schiffman's conduct had been "inappropriate."[28] Later, I will testify that my knowledge of the entire episode stemmed originally from reading *Who Wrote* in 1994, because I had done some line editing on the final manuscript before it was sent to the press, while I was still a law student at NYU. Always alert to an opportunity, Bandler will seize on my testimony.

The details regarding Schiffman in *Who Wrote*, he will declare, are simply "irrelevant" and can be ignored. Hinting that I may have coauthored the book, he will suggest that I *myself* could be responsible for Norman Golb's critique of the NYU professor's conduct.[29]

Bandler's insinuations confuse *editing* and *coauthoring* a scholarly book. In fact, even if I *had* coauthored the book, which I did not, it would make no difference; Schiffman's conduct would still have been subject to exactly the same criticism. But Bandler and his team need to suggest that it *does* make a difference. They need to define me as an amateur lacking in expertise, as a "real estate lawyer" who sent poison pen letters lacking all credibility, and as a liar making up foolish claims about satire. In the universe created by the moral outrage brigade, the law itself can also safely be simplified: "You just can't do that," Bandler will assert, no matter what your aim is. So much for the First Amendment.

Over and over again the system charged with evaluating my case—*beyond a reasonable doubt*—will be transformed into a platform for the same type of crass manipulation. This feat will be performed with vital gravitas by trained legal practitioners. What impelled me to take action—my desire to expose the conduct and misdeeds of others—will be lost in the furor over my purported "false accusations." If the reasons *motivating* parody are denied or misrepresented, should the grounds, the pretexts, the excuses offered for criminalizing it be taken seriously?

A Special Method of Random Selection

The long initial wait is over some five months after my arrest; various press photographers, alerted by the weekly criminal-cases calendar, rush at me and flash photos in my face as I enter the court building on the day of the formal unveiling of the indictment or charges against me. Basic notions of what is normally called fairness (or, in constitutional parlance, "due process") are generally thought to control any legal proceeding, even one involving satirical verbal communications. Almost as soon as the brief hearing begins, I am immediately offered some insight into what these notions involve, when the New York court rule regulating judicial assignment of criminal cases is simply disregarded at the prosecutor's request. That rule, which is designed to offer some degree of protection by preventing prosecutors from shopping for judges of their choice, states that "upon commencement of a criminal action ... the action shall be assigned to a judge by the clerk of the court ... *pursuant to a method of random selection.*"[30] Contrary to these instructions, which, after all, are not so difficult to understand, there will be *no* random selection of a judge to preside over my case, despite its obvious classification as a criminal matter. Rather, at the prosecutor's specific request, the case will be sent directly to the same judge, Carol Berkman, whose signature figured on the search warrant of March 2, 2009.

This decision happens so quickly that it seems to catch my attorney, David Breitbart, off guard, leaving him no time to object to the assignment when it is made by a magistrate. Afterward, however, he submits a motion to Berkman, politely asking her to recuse herself and to have the random-selection rule applied. On September 23, 2009, at a hearing held in her own courtroom, Berkman acknowledges that "the rule is not that the case goes to the judge who did the warrant," and further instructs the prosecutor that "for your information, the ... court administration did not believe that the case should follow the judge who did ... the warrants." At the same time, however, she clarifies that she has discussed the matter with the Honorable Michael Obus, the court's administrative judge, who, she indicates, has "directed" her "to keep the case."[31] It then becomes clear that as a defendant, I have no recourse against my case being assigned to the selfsame judge who granted the search warrant—despite the potential conflict of interest this involves—for at least one New York appellate court has held that criminal defendants have no "right" to have the random-selection rule enforced.[32] In essence, this means that application of the rule is a matter of discretionary choice; magistrates, prosecutors, court clerks, and judges can simply handle such affairs as they see fit among themselves. The civil rights community has been so besieged by injustices that it seems not to have thought of adding, so to speak, a more authentic random-selection rule to the long list of reforms it has lobbied for over the years. If a rule of such obvious significance for criminal defendants is not actually enforceable, where exactly does that leave the "rule of law" underpinning our system of justice?

"If You're Going through Hell, Keep Going"—Winston Churchill

Once it becomes clear that my case has been assigned to the judge requested by the prosecution and that we are heading toward a trial, Breitbart warns me that the "danger" we are confronting is serious and that I must, above all, cease any blogging activities and not speak with the press, for any further speech on my part can, and will, be used against me. I then learn that in 1999 the defense lawyers of the Legal Aid Society, invoking Judge Berkman's "systematic rudeness," as they put it, and "mistreatment of ... lawyers and defendants," publicly petitioned against her reappointment to the criminal court, to no avail.[33]

Soon after the assignment of the case to Berkman, I ask Ron Kuby, the well-known ponytail-sporting civil rights attorney, if he would be willing to work together with Breitbart on my defense. Breitbart's repute is largely based on defending high-profile mafia bosses and supermodels. I've decided to stick with him because he is already immersed in the case, because of his vast experience with the system, and also because I like his grim humor and his skeptical approach—his uncanny ability to see things through the eyes of the prosecutor, and the way he uses that perspective as a starting point to solve each problem as it arises. Ever since the weeks following my arrest, though, it has seemed off and on that arguing about the First Amendment and the range of expressive conduct that it protects might not exactly be his forte ("You did all this stuff," he grunts at me during one of my visits to his office, before acknowledging that all the statutes being used against me seemed to have been strangely diverted from their original purpose, which was to combat financial fraud). Criminal defense lawyers generally have little experience with problems like defining the nature of parody, and I fear that Breitbart, who was admitted to the bar in 1969, might also not be thoroughly in touch with today's fast-evolving internet scene.

Kuby, on the other hand, is younger and clearly more experienced with issues involving freedom of speech. When I first visit his office, he tells me that he has never before seen a case where fraud charges and potential hard prison time are based on the idea that the defendant intended to "influence a debate." Clearly concerned about the implications, he readily agrees to join the team. Breitbart is also happy with the arrangement, so we set up meetings and get down to work.

Kuby's first task will be to submit a set of written arguments to the judge arguing that the charges should be thrown out because I could not have known that my emails violated a set of criminal laws designed to suppress financial fraud. He will argue as well that the case should be dismissed on First Amendment grounds, and that most of the complainants are motivated by an ulterior motive to harm Norman Golb. As the brief takes shape, I begin a process of close collaboration with Kuby on the development of our written arguments. Our initial product seems thoroughly convincing. I show it to another lawyer, who spends an hour reading it and agrees we've made a powerful argument that the charges are unconstitutional.

On November 4, 2009, another routine hearing is held in Berkman's court—and then, three months later, things start to take shape, although not quite in a manner any of us had expected. On February 11, 2010, Berkman sides entirely with the district attorney, issuing a three-page order in which she declines to address our First Amendment claim of satire and rules that for me to be appropriately convicted of identity theft (and, she adds, of "related charges"), all the prosecutors have to do is show that I have "assumed the specific identities of actual people ... with the requisite intent to obtain a 'benefit,' as the statute broadly defines that term."[34] Breitbart, having read this little order, informs me that he finds it "deeply troubling," and urges me to consider whether it is worth continuing in the face of such odds. Kuby adds substance to his senior colleague's warning by pointing out that the "benefit" concept can, in theory, simply include a feeling of moral satisfaction at scoring a point in a debate. Berkman's order in fact states point-blank that the prosecution does not need to specify at all what sort of "benefit" I intended to "obtain," just as they would not need to explain what benefit is sought from an act of burglary. The truth or falsity of my allegations of plagiarism is, moreover, irrelevant, because, as she puts it, libel no longer being a crime in New York, "neither good faith nor truth is a defense to any of the crimes charged here."[35]

The parameters of the case are now set. I stand indicted for "aggravated harassment," apparently on the grounds that I engaged in "annoying" speech; and for "unauthorized access to a computer," on the grounds that my use of computers at NYU's Bobst Library to convey certain messages was "uncivil" and, accordingly, forbidden by the library's code of conduct. (Court decisions from around the country have made it clear that the enforcement, whether threatened or real, of a "civility" code by a public university would violate the First Amendment.[36] NYU is a private institution, but it maintains that "free speech" is one of its "bedrock principles."[37] My use of annoying words, as well as my alleged failure to adhere to the Bobst civility requirements, will be skillfully exploited by the prosecutors maintaining that the First Amendment and the values enshrined in it are utterly irrelevant to my case.) Setting aside these two statutes, all the charges—for identity theft, criminal impersonation, and forgery—are premised on my use of the name of another person in authoring electronic communications with the requisite criminal intent defined in the judge's order.

"Neither good faith nor truth is a defense."

A good part of the proceedings will bear on whether I engaged in a "scheme to defraud" by somehow seeking to have Lawrence Schiffman's Jewish Museum lecture canceled. The difficulty confronting my trial lawyers will be enormous. Whenever they try to raise the question of whether I sent out the "Larry Schiffman" emails in a context where serious and valid accusations of plagiarism had been hushed up ever since 1993, they will risk being ruled out of order. Trying to suggest that I intended to engage in a provocative joke, taking the form of a parody or satire, can likewise get them in trouble, because "good faith" is not a defense. On the other hand, the state's task is remarkably simple. All that the prosecutor will need to do, according to Carol Berkman's three-page order, will be to convince the jury that I attributed outlandish statements and admissions to Schiffman with the intent to obtain any "benefit" at all. This will be expanded at trial, to also allow the prosecution to suggest that I intended to cause some kind of "harm"; again, there will be no need to define *what* harm, or to explain to the jury what constitutes a legally cognizable harm. For example, if I sought to *embarrass* someone by exposing his alleged misconduct, would that suffice for my conduct to be criminalized and punished with hard time in prison? The jury will never receive any instruction about this and a similar range of questions.

Any attempt to suggest to the jury that Schiffman is a plagiarist will be extremely perilous for my lawyers, in part because of an understanding that doing so would, at a minimum, reassert my own effort to "harm" him. It would, moreover, cause "annoyance" to him for the sake of promoting the "unpopular" views of Norman Golb. According to the prosecution, my intent is to use the trial as a "bully pulpit." Since neither good faith nor truth is a "defense," my lawyers will also risk crossing the line into impropriety if they suggest that the criminalized emails used parody to poke fun at statements made by Schiffman himself over the years, both in his own writings and in his frequent interviews with the press. The reason for this again seems quite clear: I, not Lawrence Schiffman, am the one on trial. Yet if my attorneys were allowed to introduce such statements and explain their logical nexus with my emails, a jury might find it difficult to conclude beyond a reasonable doubt that the "Schiffman confessions" are really anything more than a rather clumsily perpetrated effort at satire.

After the judge issues her pretrial order opening the door to a virtual infinity of possible criminal "benefits," my legal team attempts to negotiate a plea deal ("a misdemeanor and a walk," as

Breitbart puts it). In light of the "deeply troubling" developments, I am told it would be folly to proceed with Berkman presiding over the trial. The district attorney, however, will only agree to reduce the charges to three misdemeanors, two of them considered "serious crimes" that could be cause for disbarment. I mull it over for a few days. The press has spoken of a "response to the plagiarism allegations" that Schiffman says he was obliged to write at NYU,[38] and I sense that this is a crucial document that I will get my hands on only if I go to trial. On the other hand, I am repeatedly warned that in view of Berkman's rulings in her order, I stand little chance at trial and will only be able to prevail on appeal.

Ultimately, I refuse the deal when I realize that Berkman might still send me to jail (she will later assert to a journalist that this was precisely her intention), and that as part of a mandatory probation period I could be deprived of my right to express myself on the internet for three years. In fact, the deal being offered would predictably hamper my ability to opine about issues involving the Dead Sea Scrolls, religious beliefs, freedom of speech, and other such matters in any context, both online and off. Still worse, I would have to plead guilty to charges brought under statutes that strike me as flatly unconstitutional, in part on their plain surface ("as written") and in part as applied to my particular circumstances.

In line with a national and local judicial system that is, notoriously, grounded on plea bargains,[39] my refusing the deal means, from the prosecution's perspective, that I must now be punished not only for the purported felonies and misdemeanors but also for failing to cooperate with the system.

> If all criminal defendants in America refused to plead guilty, the criminal justice system would collapse.

From the prosecution's perspective, the facts are simple: I "punked" the old boys' club. The entire book of "aggravated harassment," "identity theft," "forgery," "criminal impersonation," and "unauthorized access to a computer" will now be thrown at me. Each of my speech acts will be broken down exhaustively into every variation of conceivable delinquency, all of it combined into a single accusatory chorus.

* * *

In addition to his responsibilities as district attorney, Robert Morgenthau also serves as the chairman of the Museum of Jewish Heritage, an institution of considerable cultural importance located in New York City's Battery Park. One of the museum's major donors is Ira Rennert, a chemical-mining magnate described as America's "biggest private polluter"[40] and funder of the Ingeborg and Ira Rennert World Center for the Dead Sea Scrolls. Some nine months after my arrest, Morgenthau, who is now ninety years old, resigns from his position as district attorney. On October 5, 2009, Ira Rennert donates $34,500 to the election campaign of Morgenthau's chosen successor, Cyrus Vance Jr.[41] On November 3, 2009, Cyrus Vance is elected. Eventually he and his team of assistants will issue the same type of statements as Morgenthau, to the effect that I have violated academic protocol and engaged in an illegal scheme to "promote" Norman Golb's "unpopular" research.

When the case is finally heard by a federal court of appeals eight years later, Morgenthau, at the age of ninety-eight, will still be employed as a lawyer by the Wachtell, Lipton, Rosen & Katz law firm. One of the other lawyers at the same firm is Adam Emmerich, who serves as a fundraiser for Cyrus Vance Jr., Morgenthau's DA successor. Emmerich is also the president of the American Friends of the Israel Antiquities Authority (AFIAA), which advertises the Rennert-funded "World Center" on its website. The AFIAA, which appears to be located at precisely the same address as the Wachtell firm,[42] is chaired by Shelby White, who is the widow of Leon Levy (1925–2003), after whom the Leon Levy Dead Sea Scrolls Digital Library is named. White and her late husband will themselves eventually come under legal scrutiny due to their collecting activities; by 2023, White will have relinquished dozens of looted antiquities "valued at nearly $20 million."[43]

During his unprecedented nine terms as district attorney, Morgenthau has become famous for conducting an astonishing three and a half million criminal prosecutions, many of them important—including his effort to have art stolen by Nazis during the Holocaust restored to its rightful owners—others aimed, for example, at individuals who have displayed controversial signs or spoken through megaphones in public squares without a permit. A member of the wealthy Lehman family, he is married to the Pulitzer Prize–winning journalist Lucinda Franks, a frequent contributor to the *New York Times*. Morgenthau will pass away during the summer of 2019, over a year after the final resolution of my case.

How did such a towering figure, along with certain prominent members of the city's cultural establishment (I will see them in action later, when they testify at my trial), become the public advocate for a professor accused of academic fraud?

It all goes back to the Dead Sea Scrolls—those famous writings mentioned by the police officer who pointed the gun in my face—and that, since their discovery in caves in the Judaean Desert, have become the subject of a roiling scholarly controversy … and a billion-dollar business.

4

IDEOLOGY, POWER, AND CENSORSHIP: THE DEAD SEA SCROLLS MONOPOLY

Sometime during 1947 (the exact date is unknown), on a desert cliff near the western shore of the Dead Sea, two Bedouin shepherd boys ventured into a cave and, quite by accident, made one of the most important archaeological finds of the twentieth century. Hidden deep within the recess were seven parchment scrolls containing texts that had not been read since the first millennium. Over the next nine years, hundreds of such scrolls—some in small fragments, others fully intact, many surrounded by the remains of linen packets or pottery jars—would be unearthed in this and other caves near the ruins of an ancient archaeological site known as Qumran. The findings would consist of a broad array of biblical and nonbiblical Hebrew, Greek, and Aramaic writings, among them a list of treasures written on copper.

These discoveries are of massive importance for our understanding of the origins of Western civilization. A central theme developed by Manhattan prosecutors—and by criminal court judge Carol Berkman—during my trial will be that the "truth" about the Dead Sea Scrolls is "irrelevant." My lawyers will need to show why it *is* relevant, not just to me personally but to everyone working in this field, as well as to anyone interested in the scrolls and the origins of the world that (for better or worse) we live in.

By the mid-1950s, a general belief had taken shape that the thousands of scroll fragments found in the caves were the work of a sect, usually identified as the Essenes. The Jordanian government had assigned Father Roland de Vaux, a Dominican monk, the task of organizing a team of biblical scholars to study the texts. Almost in their entirety, the scrolls were held in the Palestine Archaeological Museum (today known as the Rockefeller Archaeological

Museum) in East Jerusalem. De Vaux appointed a group of team members under his leadership. Not only no Israeli, but no Jewish expert was invited to participate.[1] The reason was clear. Before becoming a priest and moving to Jerusalem, de Vaux had been a member of the far-right, antisemitic Action Française, an organization admired by Mussolini and regarded by many as one of the faces of the European fascist movement.

It was de Vaux and his team who, as the *New York Times*' Edward Rothstein observes, gave the Essene idea a special twist: Qumran housed a "monastic celibate group ... isolated from other Judaic movements," espousing messianic views that "embodied almost proto-Christian sensibilities." Rothstein explains that while this argument was being developed, Jews "were deliberately excluded" from the team, which was "dominated by Roman Catholic priests and scholars."[2] De Vaux rejected "offers by Israelis to help" with his investigations and persisted in "referring to Israel as Palestine." Other team members also had a "scorn of political and religious aspects of Judaism."

This situation was a sign of things to come. The methods developed by the editorial team rapidly diverged from standard, generally accepted research practices; its work ultimately ground to a near halt as it became mired in a scandal involving the monopolization of access to the manuscripts, inappropriate financial arrangements, and antisemitic pronouncements. It is important to bear in mind, however, that during the first several decades of its existence, the team benefited from enormous popularity. Few of the hundreds of researchers who were not allowed to see the texts dared voice any complaints, while de Vaux and several of his colleagues slowly plodded on with their project.

The Essene hypothesis, first based on just seven scrolls, could not convincingly account for the astoundingly large and heterogeneous body of texts that emerged from the caves. Still, its creators and their disciples stood by it. Rather than concede that such diverse texts might have been written by diverse authors—and not by a small, isolated group of claimed monks—they expanded their characterization of Essenism itself.[3] The Essenes were made out to be a large and important group, and Qumran came to be seen as a major center of Hebraic literary production.

The literary critic Edmund Wilson embraced the hypothesis in his popular 1955 book, *The Scrolls from the Dead Sea*, and it rapidly came to enjoy virtually universal acceptance. By the 1980s, encyclopedias, museum catalogs, textbooks, and even scholarly journals and doctoral dissertations were regularly propagating the same idea. Readers of the *Encyclopedia Britannica* learned in those days that the scrolls were "all part of a library belonging to a Jewish religious sect (viz., Essenes) that flourished at Qumran from the mid-second century BC to AD 68." And visitors to an exhibition entitled "Treasures of the Holy Land," which opened at New York's Metropolitan Museum of Art in 1984 and moved the following year to the Los Angeles County Museum of Art, read in the exhibition catalog that Qumran was "the center of the Jewish sect that owned and used the scrolls."[4] Even today, those who see selected scrolls displayed in many exhibitions continue to be told essentially the same story.

What visitors to the exhibits are *not* told is that the Qumran-sectarian idea, however popular, is at odds not only with the large number of scrolls and conflicting doctrines found in the caves, but with almost every shred of evidence that has surfaced during the past seventy years. In fact, the evidence makes demonstrably clear that the Dead Sea Scrolls originated not with an obscure monastic sect but with various groups among Palestinian Jews at large. And if the theory that Essene monks wrote the scrolls is dubious, so are the larger historical beliefs it has inspired. That early Christian doctrines are "related" to Essenism is now a tenet of conventional wisdom. But the actual analysis of the scrolls has failed to reveal any influence of an obscure, isolated Jewish sect on early Christianity.

My father, who had done his PhD work on one of the earliest known scrolls at Johns Hopkins, gradually became suspicious of the traditional hypothesis as he saw more and more manuscript fragments being subjected to bizarre interpretations due to the fixation on Qumran and the Essenes. In a steadily increasing flow of publications, imagined sectarian events had gradually come to be imbued with the status of historical reality, flawed presuppositions had been transformed into essential scholarly dogmas, and ordinary artifacts found at Qumran had taken on special religious significance.

For a historian and manuscripts scholar like my father, it was simply difficult to accept the claim that any single group living in a small desert outpost would have gone about gathering a massive quantity of scrolls containing such varied contents. Many of the scrolls consist of all sorts of works of Jewish literature comprising the apocryphal and apocalyptic writings, including works of these genres previously unknown. It is highly unlikely that that a small sect living in the desert would have been able to guard and preserve such a large corpus of writings.

The hiding of hundreds of extremely diverse literary and religious texts in the caves, and the fact that the vast majority of them were copies of earlier texts, clearly suggested that the scrolls derived from various literary collections or *libraries*. (In ancient times, most libraries were small, private literary collections in people's homes.) This fundamental recognition helped lay the foundation for the new theory of Dead Sea scroll origins first formulated by my father towards 1969. Despite efforts to belittle, misrepresent, and even suppress the emerging research conclusions, ensuing lectures and publications ultimately led to one of the great intellectual controversies of the past half century. Today, my father's theory, in slightly modified form, is defended by major archaeologists in Israel.

Scholars were aware of the emerging picture by 1970, because my father, during that year, had given a talk on the topic in Jerusalem, which journalist and senior editor Malka Rabinowitz had covered in a long *Jerusalem Post* report.[5] Word of my father's views spread quickly, for at the time, well before the arrival of the age of the Internet, the *Post* was a leading international source for news on Israel. Beginning in 1980, my father then published a long series of critiques of the Qumran-sectarian theory.[6] Qumran, he had concluded, was not inhabited by any sect, the scrolls had not been written there, and they were not the product of any single sect to begin with. Rather, they were writings of Palestinian Jews in general and remnants of "library collections" showing a "wide variety of practices, beliefs and opinions." The scrolls, he argued, were hidden at some point by Jews fleeing Jerusalem during the Great Jewish Revolt and the siege and sacking of the city in 70 AD—a horrifying event with massive historical consequences. The precise date of the scrolls' hiding during that time-frame cannot be defined with greater precision, because even during the siege, Jews were able to leave the city through several well-constructed tunnels whose remains have been excavated on various occasions.[7]

According to this view, the scrolls should be interpreted "not by pressing them into the single sectarian bed of Essenism, but by separating them out from one another, through internal analysis, into various spiritual currents which appear to have characterized Palestinian Judaism of the intertestamental period."[8] Several of those spiritual currents, my father suggested, fed into the apocalyptic themes found among the Dead Sea Scrolls. These themes, viewed in their relation to historical events, showed that the mentalities and beliefs of various Palestinian Jewish groups prior to 70 A.D. were "factors which may…help to explain the zeal which led to the Jewish War"—the great revolt that ended with the sacking of Jerusalem and the suicide of refugees at Masada.[9]

Forty years of research had been shattered. Famed classicist Moses Finley wrote that the arguments put forward in the article "seem to me wholly unanswerable, though many with vested interests in the E[ssenes] will certainly not lie down quietly."[10] The remark was prescient: the enthusiasm signaled in various scattered replies would soon be swept aside by "fierce polemics," as the renowned Maimonides scholar Joel Kraemer would put it in his introduction to a volume of essays honoring my father's fiftieth year at the University of Chicago.[11] Noting that my father "was in the vanguard of scholars pressing for release of the Dead Sea Scrolls for study by the scholarly public," Kraemer explained that his "opposition to the Essene hypothesis was received with hostility… Resistance to Professor Golb was particularly keen in Jerusalem, at the Hebrew University, the Shrine of the Book, and Israel Museum."[12] Kraemer added that he himself had become convinced that my father's "doubts were warranted."

In their zeal to present my prosecution as having nothing to do with freedom of speech—or the freedom to speak truth to power—the Manhattan DA's staff would do their best to conceal the import of the struggle that emerged in the wake of my father's devastating critique of the sectarian hypothesis. In the aftermath of the 1948 Arab-Israeli war, virtually all the thousands of text fragments retrieved from the caves near Qumran, as explained by Edward Rothstein, had been "passed among generations of scholars like esoteric possessions," and the sectarian theory became "orthodoxy, made immutable because until the 1990s the texts were largely inaccessible to outsiders."[13] De Vaux ran the monopoly itself almost like a monastery: "The scholarly cult devoted to these scrolls," Rothstein observes, "was as tightly knit, self-regarding and monastic as the cult those scholars imagined produced the scrolls." This situation would continue for decades, because when Israel conquered the West Bank in 1967 and took over management of the Rockefeller Archaeological Museum, it failed to "assert any real authority over the project."

By the late 1980s, complaints had begun to emerge, to the effect that members of the official "editorial team" had been hoarding—or monopolizing—hundreds of unpublished texts and refusing to allow anyone who disagreed with the sectarian theory of scroll origins to study them. In 1991—a year marked, among other events, by the creation of the World Wide Web[14]—a roiling dispute over the hoarding controversy would play out in the press. Further quarrels and recriminations, including a highly consequential lawsuit filed by a member of the scrolls monopoly team, would then follow.

To fully comprehend the significance of this episode and its sequel, we need to bear in mind that the monopolists' narrow, sectarian view of the scrolls was directly imperiled by the growing recognition of the pluralistic character of the discoveries seen as a whole. In the course of criticizing the monopoly, my father had predicted—accurately, as it turned out—that the hundreds of unpublished texts would, once they became available, demonstrate an even broader range of ideas and larger number of scribal hands than seen in the ones already published.

Such predictions clearly posed a serious problem for the editorial team members, for the emerging interpretation of the scrolls could not easily be reconciled with the monopolists' ideological background. In that regard, there had been clear warning signs from the outset, which scholars from around the world chose to remain silent about, apparently for fear of the consequences of speaking out. De Vaux's decision to exclude Jews from his team established a mindset whose consequences have trickled down to this day, and on which, in retrospect, two later episodes would shed considerable light.

In 1971, a scholar who had been a member of the original team, John Allegro, published a book entitled *The Chosen People*. Allegro had been responsible, as it happens, for unraveling and deciphering the important scroll written on copper, and de Vaux had fired him from the team after he had signaled the difficulty involved in reconciling that scroll's contents—listing treasures no desert-dwelling sect could ever have owned—with the Essene hypothesis. Allegro then went on to publish his little book, almost simultaneously resigning from his academic position. Over the decades, this work would become a reference for antisemites—one that is still cited on certain cult websites, like the Vanguard News Network Forum, which praises Allegro as a "theologian who focused on 'macro-theology' and the Essene connection to Christianity," and explains that "the best study ... for the general anti-Semite to read is John Allegro's *The Chosen People* ... which details just how blood-thirsty, organized and generally genocidal the Jews were."[15]

Given Roland de Vaux's own overtly antisemitic personal history, the scandal that came to surround John Strugnell (1930–2007), a disciple of de Vaux who had been appointed head of the editorial team in the 1980s, should perhaps also come as no surprise. The scandal is described in Strugnell's *New York Times* obituary, where we read that

> at a time when the scrolls team was coming under sharp criticism for its exclusive control over access to the documents and its sluggish pace of publication, he [Strugnell] was in Jerusalem and gave an interview to the Tel Aviv

> newspaper *Haaretz*. As quoted by the newspaper, he said of Judaism: "It's a horrible religion. It's Christian heresy, and we deal with our heretics in different ways." Mr. Strugnell later denied accusations of anti-Semitism, noting that he was the first editor to have included Jewish scholars in the project, which had been dominated by Christians … But the damage was irreparable. He was replaced as the scrolls editor and forced to retire from Harvard.[16]

Strugnell (who, incidentally, had never received a PhD) was relieved from his editorial-team responsibilities after making his antisemitic statements in 1990. Already during his tenure, in view of increasing complaints about the team's policies, the monopoly had been expanded to include a few Orthodox Jewish members, and the same expansion continued during the 1990s. This development seems to have been catalyzed in part by complaints of Oxford scholar Géza Vermes (1924–2013; himself a convert to Christianity), who, although a defender of the traditional sectarian theory, observed as early as 1977 that the editorial practices of the official team were "likely to become the academic scandal par excellence of the 20th century."[17] As we will see, Vermes's own decisions pertaining to open research on the manuscripts would not exactly converge with these words.

One of the first Jewish scholars allowed access to the scrolls was Lawrence Schiffman of New York University, who, at many venues, was given the privilege of lecturing on scroll fragments, special copies of which were supplied to him that hundreds of qualified scholars around the world were not allowed to see. At my trial, Schiffman would hotly deny belonging to the official team that had arrogated publication rights over the scrolls to itself.[18] But in 1992 he had been quoted in *New York Newsday* as acknowledging that "important" texts were "made available" to him by the group's members. As he put it, "Any text that I decided I needed, if I worked on the politics long enough, I got."[19] The "politics" of the scrolls appeared to mean, among other things, that after earning special-access favors through persuasive efforts taking one form or another, one would then pass those favors along to other similarly favored colleagues. Schiffman, as a *Washington Square News* staff writer observed at the time, saw fit to allow his own graduate students to "receive" photos of "unpublished fragments of the Dead Sea Scrolls."[20]

The Monopoly Collapses—and an Assault on the First Amendment Begins

After Strugnell's removal in December 1990,[21] Emanuel Tov, a biblical scholar at the Hebrew University—who had already been named codirector with Strugnell despite the latter's vigorous protests—would remain as head of the team in the face of mounting complaints about its modus operandi. Tov's immediate task was to select new team members, so as to accelerate the publication of the previously monopolized fragments. In effect, he was charged with an exercise in academic damage control.[22]

As part of Tov's efforts, during the first few months of 1991, an arrangement was worked out with Géza Vermes: photographs of the unpublished scrolls were to be handed over to the Oxford Centre for Jewish Studies—located in Oxford, England, but not affiliated with Oxford University—under the explicitly stipulated condition that *only individuals approved by the official team could see them*. Vermes himself—a defender of the sectarian view who, it is again worth emphasizing, had acknowledged that the monopoly was an "academic scandal"—would serve as director of the new archive. Upon learning of this arrangement during a trip to England, my father criticized it sharply in a public letter that appeared in the *Times* of London on July 10, 1991.[23] The agreement, he argued, was an offense to a long-standing British tradition of free and open access to ancient documents.

> Pursuant to the arrangement, the photographs were to be sold by the Israel Antiquities Authority in exchange for 250,000 British pounds, to be supplied by a private entity called the Wolfson Foundation.

A few days later, William Moffett, at the time the newly appointed director of the Huntington Library in Claremont,

California, looked at a copy of the *Times* that contained Norman Golb's letter. It just so happened that following his appointment, Moffett had ordered that an inventory be taken of the library's possessions, and as a result learned that the library had a complete set of photographs of the Dead Sea Scrolls. Apparently, in 1980, Elizabeth Hay Bechtel (1904–87), a wealthy philanthropist and founder of the Ancient Biblical Manuscript Center in Claremont, had paid a significant sum of money to have this photographic record of the scrolls deposited with the Huntington for safekeeping in case of a war. Accompanying the arrangement was Roland de Vaux's stipulation that no one be allowed to see the photographs. Moffett, however, having read Golb's letter to the *Times*, now announced that he had decided to ignore this stipulation and to make the photo collection available to scholars at large. According to Sara Hodson, a curator at the Huntington, Moffett knew he faced the risk of being "stopped by a legal injunction," so he decided to fight in "the court of public opinion, where [he] knew he could win." As Moffett put it, the library would drop such a large media bomb "that the [proprietary] wall surrounding the Dead Sea Scrolls would be knocked down permanently."[24]

With this single act of resistance, the team's physical monopoly over the content of the scrolls collapsed. The *New York Times* reported that the editorial team had reacted with anger and suggested that legal action was being contemplated.[25] This specific threat would fail to materialize, but ultimately a member of the monopoly group claimed, in a widely publicized lawsuit, that he held a copyright over his unpublished transcription of a scroll, and indeed over the scroll itself. The *Chicago Tribune* quoted James Gardner, deputy director of the American Historical Association, as stating that the claim had "implications that go far beyond biblical studies." Gardner was further quoted as explaining that historians "already feel threatened, a trend that would accelerate if any one scholar could establish an exclusive claim to a major historical document like one of the Dead Sea Scrolls."[26] Bill Ziobro, secretary-treasurer of the American Philological Association, was likewise quoted as objecting to the new expansion of copyright.[27]

When Israeli courts upheld the rights of the monopoly member, various First Amendment and intellectual property specialists were quick to criticize the decision.[28] The editorial team itself—which is to say in its institutional capacity—never followed through on the reported threat of legal action in retaliation for the Huntington Library's announcement. Instead, Emanuel Tov took steps to hasten the preparation of "definitive" commentaries on the unpublished scrolls by a handpicked group of academics. The earlier institutional effort to prevent scholars around the world from seeing the unpublished texts before their appearance in volumes prepared by the editorial team would from that point on be rechanneled into other forms of containment.

That process would be all the more necessary, because in the meantime, other skeptics had begun openly lending their support to my father. In the early 1990s, the *École biblique* had engaged two professional archaeologists, Robert Donceel and Pauline Donceel-Voute of the University of Louvain, to examine the unpublished notes of Roland de Vaux and various artifacts excavated by him. When the Donceels reported that the notes and artifacts contained no evidence confirming the sectarian theory, they were promptly dismissed; the results of their investigation were published in 1994 without official *École biblique* approval.[29] Around the same time, the Israel Antiquities Authority decided to put together a team, led by the eminent archaeologist Yitzhak Magen, first accompanied by the IAA's founder General Amir Drori (1937-2005), and then, following Drori's retirement in 1997, by Yuval Peleg (1968-2014). The team's purpose would be to conduct renewed excavations at Qumran and to reassess the known evidence.

Beginning in 2002, the team began to publish its findings, together with a nuanced version of the same conclusion that had been reached by my father. The scrolls, the team concluded, were deposited in caves by refugees fleeing the suppressive actions of the Roman forces in the Jerusalem area—possibly the city itself, but also the surrounding towns, villages and hamlets. In their final report, published in 2018, Magen and Peleg point out that the large number of biblical scrolls found in the caves points to multiple synagogues in various communities. The team's emphasis on the entire

Jerusalem region being devastated by the Roman siege is a useful nuance that arguably improves on my father's original theory.[30]

The team, acknowledging its debt to my father in this regard, also concluded that the evidence uncovered was consistent with identification of Qumran as initially a strategic Hasmonaean observation fort.[31] They indicated that after its agricultural and industrial expansion under King Herod, the site took on a pottery-manufacturing component.[32] And they announced, with devastating consequences for the sectarian hypothesis, that their reexamination of all the facts had produced no evidence of Essene or other sectarian habitation at Qumran.

Most importantly, however, the team was in complete agreement with my father's view that there is no evidence the scrolls themselves were either written or copied at Qumran. "We have brought the site down," they wrote, "from the unwarranted height to which it had been raised by various scholars ... and placed it firmly on the somewhat mundane ground of the Second Temple period and the destruction of Jerusalem."[33]

"The facts," Magen and Peleg explained, "do not support" a variety of opinions of the traditionalists, including the claim made by Jodi Magness of Chapel Hill that boiled bones buried at the site (visibly to avoid attracting carrion-seeking animals) somehow had a ritual or sacrificial purpose. This claim, they suggested, was one of various misguided efforts to "explain perfectly straight-forward phenomena in the irrational terms of ritual."[34] The team asserted that the Qumran-Essene hypothesis of scrolls origins was "baseless," and that "there is not even the slightest thread connecting the scrolls to the Qumran site or…Qumran to the Essenes, and any connection created between them is artificial and has no basis in the archaeological study of the site or the content of the scrolls."[35]

Meanwhile, in a lengthy study, Hebrew University archaeologist Yizhar Hirschfeld (1950-2006) had already himself concluded there was no evidence at all that a sect had ever inhabited Qumran, or that the site's inhabitants had anything to do with the authorship of the Dead Sea Scrolls.[36] Additional scholars, such as Jürgen Zangenberg of Leiden University, soon came out seconding the new research conclusions with their own contributions.[37] All of these archaeologists naturally had their own differences of opinion on the exact nature of the site. But they all concurred in expressing views that gave full support to the earlier formulated conclusion of my father: the scrolls were neither written nor copied at Qumran and were brought from Jerusalem to be sequestered in the caves. As Magen and Peleg put it in their final report, the scrolls, including even the so-called sectarian texts found among them, "may represent not only the Essenes, but all sects and streams of opinion present in Judaism at the end of the Second Temple period."[38]

These conclusions were clearly highly damaging to the viability of the old idea that a radical sect lived at Qumran and wrote scrolls there. But the advance of scholarship in this field would be hindered by highly unusual factors. By the early 2000s, the Dead Sea Scrolls, and their interpretation as sectarian writings with a link (however baseless) to early Christianity, had become a form of ideological merchandise. As a consequence of *opposing* the marketed sectarian claims, my father ultimately come to face a reality similar, in certain respects, to the one confronted by the Metropolitan Museum of Art curator Oscar White Muscarella (1931–2022), who in his aptly titled book, *The Lie Became Great* (2000), would describe in minute detail "the corrupt practices of curators and collectors."[39] Muscarella had become the victim of brutal efforts to silence him: he was fired three times by the Metropolitan Museum under false pretexts, but he fought back, hiring a civil rights law firm and ultimately seeing himself reinstated pursuant to court orders. His accusations, dismissed as eccentric rantings at the time they were made, are today recognized as scandalously true and have led to the return of looted artifacts by museums around the world.

While taking place in a smaller archaeological niche, the implications of my father's analysis of Qumranology—the term he had coined to describe the unscientific, speculative approach that had become dominant in scroll studies—were equally devastating. As a result, soon after the Huntington Library episode, the first of a series of damage control mechanisms was set in place in the United States. This, ironically, took the form of Dead Sea Scroll museum exhibits—displays consisting largely of propaganda for the old sectarian idea. Other initiatives would follow, including television "documentaries" produced by Nova, National Geographic, and BBC, strictly adhering to the sectarian hypothesis, and closed "international" conferences where only defenders of the sectarian claim were invited to lecture. Various figures in the field were apparently adept at rigging academic conferences by carefully limiting participation only to colleagues who would agree with their positions.[40]

Adherence to a highly popular dogma, rather than science, lay at the core of institutional efforts to silence my father and his allies. Those efforts also coalesced with a personal element that would have long-lasting consequences. Nahum Sarna was a Bible scholar at Brandeis University who had once been friendly towards my father; he took his distance from him after the publication of his research conclusions on the scrolls. Sarna's students included Lawrence Schiffman and William Schniedewind, who would eventually become department chairs at their respective universities (NYU and UCLA). While studying with Sarna at Brandeis, Schiffman himself developed a friendship with Sarna's elder son, David, who, following my arrest, would ultimately elljjjjknd up posting invective about my hundreds of purported crimes online.[41] Schniedewind, in turn, would serve as thesis adviser to one Robert Cargill, who would post at least thirty blog entries presenting a running narrative of my case as it unfolded from his perspective. In an entry of November 8, 2009, Cargill would write, "*I* knew, as did a host of others…I knew who it was. I tracked everything he did…I contacted Schiffman…and handed what I had collected over to the NY district attorney's office."[42]

Fooling the Public: Theory Distortion

One way of exercising control involves misinforming the public as to the nature of an opposing theory, with the result that it looks less convincing than it actually is. This form of falsification is one of the most flagrant of the many mechanisms that have frequently been employed by participants in intellectual controversies to try and prevent undesired outcomes.[43]

The truth: Norman Golb always consistently emphasized the *plurality* of the collections that were discovered in the caves. In his 1980 article, as well as in *Who Wrote the Dead Sea Scrolls?*, he explicitly distinguished his theory from the "overly specific" proposal of Karl Rengstorf, who, in the early 1960s, had argued that the scrolls were not a sectarian hoard, but *a single library belonging to priests of the Jerusalem Temple* who, he had speculated, used Qumran as an occasional retreat of sorts.

According to Golb, the multiplicity of doctrines found among the scrolls made it clear that Rengstorf's proposal was erroneous, "narrowing down the conception of intellectual and spiritual life prevailing within Jerusalem before the war."[44] The possibility that some *number* of scrolls from the Temple library may have found their way into the sacks of scrolls hidden in the caves was of course acknowledged by my father—but only when specifically addressing Rengstorf's hypothesis. When formulating his own view, he always spoke of various "literary collections" or "libraries," the implication being that these were in the nature of the sort of *private* collections one would expect to have abounded in a major center of culture at the time.

His view was clearly stated from the outset. That, however, has not stopped the Jerusalem-library theory of scroll origins from being repeatedly misrepresented over a forty-year period in publications of some of the most adamant defenders of the Qumran-sectarian hypothesis—several of whom would testify against me at my trial.

Not only my interest in my father's work and its impact but my own educational background had made me more than just a little bit sensitive to the nuances here. If I had learned anything during my studies, it was that scholarship required careful and accurate description of sources and opposing views. Then I came to realize that the scholarship of Lawrence Schiffman of NYU involved publishing misleading descriptions of my father's theory.[45]

To the best of my knowledge, this problem first emerged in an article printed in 1990, in which Schiffman offered this remark: "I should perhaps comment briefly on the hypothesis recently put forward by Professor Norman Golb of the University of Chicago. According to him the Qumran scrolls are the library of the Jerusalem Temple, brought from Jerusalem and hidden at Qumran during the First Jewish Revolt against Rome."[46] To put forward a false claim of the sort in a popular magazine article oriented toward Bible fans was bad enough. But Schiffman repeated his misrepresentation in his 1994 book, where he informed readers that "the hypothesis that the scrolls are the library of the Jerusalem Temple is put forward by Golb."[47]

Similar misrepresentations would then reemerge in the writings of other defenders of the sectarian theory.[48] The publication of the work entitled the *Encyclopedia of the Dead Sea Scrolls* (2000), was paramount in this context. This self-defined "reference" work—edited, again, by Lawrence Schiffman, along with James VanderKam—amounted, in fact, to a sustained polemic from which any writing opposing the sectarian hypothesis had been excluded. Not that the key opposing view went altogether *unmentioned*. The task of addressing Norman Golb's theory of scroll origins, in a few short lines of the two-volume encyclopedia, was allotted to Dr. Charlotte Hempel, at the time a young research fellow who had received her doctoral degree at King's College in London in 1995. In her article on the "Qumran Community," Hempel asserted that according to Golb, "the texts belonged to the library of the Jerusalem Temple (as suggested by Rengstorf in the 1950s) as well as to individual wealthy citizens and were hidden near the Dead Sea just before the fall of Jerusalem to the Romans in 70 CE."[49]

With the misleading statement "as suggested by Rengstorf," Hempel had obscured the basic thrust of the Jerusalem-libraries theory. While more subtle than Schiffman's earlier misrepresentation, her distorted summary lent credence to that effort; in fact, precisely because of its subtlety, her own effort was arguably worse. Readers of the "encyclopedia" had no way of knowing that in Golb's view, the scrolls revealed a *wide range of social, religious, and legal complexities* contained within intertestamental Judaism.[50]

Hershel Shanks, the editor of *Biblical Archaeology Review*, obtained a review copy of the encyclopedia—and felt compelled to object.[51] "Shouldn't Norman Golb," he asked, "have been given an opportunity to make his case?" The Chicago scholar, Shanks noted, "has published a large body of work relating to the scrolls, including a major book ... Well, my perverse mind would like to hear what Golb has to say."

Shanks, of course, was right to protest. The Schiffman-VanderKam effort stood in direct, if tacit, defiance of the norms of neutrality in scholarly disputes to which encyclopedia editors are generally expected to adhere. Encyclopedic reference works are normally not tools for ideological warfare; what they aim for is scientific neutrality. According to a policy statement published by the editors of the *Stanford Encyclopedia of Philosophy*, encyclopedias should "offer a broad perspective ... rather than advocate a point of view," and "not be idiosyncratic or polemical ... but rather strive for balance by presenting the important arguments that have been put forward on both sides of an issue."[52] But for the defenders of the sectarian hypothesis of scroll origins, neutrality was anathema; editorial policies needed to be set in place, and acted on, to *prevent* as many people as possible from understanding "both sides of the issue."[53]

The emerging picture will sound familiar to experts on public opinion manipulation.[54] In his famous book *The Structure of Scientific Revolutions*, Thomas Kuhn signals a tendency by the defenders of traditional scientific models to "resort to the techniques of mass persuasion, often including force." Kuhn suggests that as a result, textbooks are "systematically misleading," because their function is to "disguise not only the role but the very existence of the revolutions that produced them."[55] However precisely or imprecisely Kuhn's interpretive model fits the facts of scientific revolutions in general, it fits the battle over the scrolls with considerable accuracy.

Inevitable Facts: the Multiple-Judaisms Neurosis

Already during the 1980s, a different set of strategies had also emerged. It was, in fact, during this period that champions of the sectarian hypothesis began to emphasize *special modifications* introduced into the old paradigm. Ultimately, this tendency developed into the remarkable claim that the purported sect had gathered a massive collection of scrolls, most of which were not writings of the sect at all.[56]

How did this claim become part of the sectarian defense strategy? In his 1995 book, Norman Golb wrote of an effort "to evade the import" of his own interpretation of scroll origins "both by studious denial of its originality and the simultaneous dismantling of its components into disparate sections that were then presented without attribution or as original ideas of the presenters."[57] In the same book, Golb quoted Avi Katzman's *Haaretz* exchange with Lawrence Schiffman, adding that the NYU scholar, while misrepresenting the nature of the Jerusalem-libraries theory, had also adopted as his own "several of its most essential elements."[58]

In 1989, while I was a graduate student at Harvard, Thomas Mallon's *Stolen Words* had appeared. An excellent historical treatment of plagiarism, the book included a lengthy chapter devoted to the case of Jayme Sokolow, who had lost his teaching position when it was revealed that his NYU dissertation had been riddled with unacknowledged "curious parallels" to the work of another historian.[59] Dwelling on Sokolow's denials of his plagiarisms and on the "bluff and bluster in [his] character," Mallon signaled the tendency among academics to "shut up, to keep the dirty secret from spreading through the extended professional family, and perhaps above all, to keep from getting sued."[60]

Mallon's discussion was stored in a niche in my memory, and came back to me years later, when I started to think more closely about the academic debacle surrounding the scrolls—and about the role Lawrence Schiffman had apparently played in it.

Schiffman had prepared his doctoral dissertation at Brandeis University, where his thesis adviser was the late Nahum Sarna, one of the Bible teachers who had reacted, apparently with some indignation, to my father's critique of the traditional theory.[61] Schiffman had completed his doctoral work in 1974. At the time, like Sarna and many others, he appears to have simply assumed that the scrolls were the product of a "sect." Fifteen years later, however, he began to insist that the claimed "sect of Qumran" had not only written some of the scrolls, but had gathered writings of "widely varying Judaisms" of the Second Temple period.[62] Schiffman's suggestion that a single group of *sectarians* had gathered hundreds of manuscripts containing so many doctrines would be described by Philip Davies (1945–2018) of the University of Sheffield as leading to "little but methodological chaos," which he contrasted to the "valuable method" that he found in Norman Golb's approach to scroll origins.[63]

There was, arguably, a reason for the chaos, one that Davies left unsaid, but that seemed implicit in his juxtaposition of the two scholars.[64] Schiffman, in making his "widely varying Judaisms" claim, had failed to appropriately address the actual *history of research* on this topic. Perhaps his work might have seemed more cogent, if Schiffman, in developing his idea, had discussed the valuable method and previous multiple-Judaism conclusions of his Chicago colleague. But there was no such discussion—a failure that clashed with my own understanding of everything involved in university research, across its many disciplines.[65]

This understanding was informed by various seminars, for example, that I had taken at Harvard taught by the literary historian Dante Della Terza (1924–2021), who felt it so important that we engage with past scholarship that he would sometimes end up spending the whole hour addressing that theme. Later it would occur to me that Norman Golb's entire approach, constructing his own theory step by step through careful critical analysis of earlier views, was in line with what Della Terza had tried to teach me, and the opposite of the approach taken by authors like Schiffman.[66]

Judging from his published writings, Schiffman began developing his own conception only after Norman Golb's first articles on the scrolls' origin and nature appeared. In email correspondence with Richard Goerwitz dated May 29, 1990, Schiffman displayed his familiarity with the basic claim made in these articles, writing that "Golb is correct that the collection represents a wide variety of Jewish groups."[67]

In his published works, however, Schiffman failed to inform his readers that Norman Golb had developed precisely this idea; rather, he presented it as his own. As a result, uninformed readers had no way of reflecting on the developments that had led Schiffman, in the late 1980s, to begin arguing that the scrolls have "an enormous amount to tell us about the widely varying Judaisms of the Hasmonaean and Herodian periods."[68]

In stunning contrast to Schiffman's failure to acknowledge the relationship between his own proposals and Norman Golb's contribution, the well-known scholar of Judaism and rabbinical texts Jacob Neusner (1932–2016) would put things like this in a letter to my father:

> Time and again I come back to your pioneering insistence ... Your *akshanut* [= "brave perseverance"] placed the whole scholarly world in your debt ... Again, I come back to your pioneering insistence that [what] we have is ... not a system, not a community represented by those writings. When you first wrote along those lines, I was puzzled and surprised, since I ... assumed that the prevailing consensus—Essene or whatever—was so. But I parked it in my mind for future reference. Now I have found that ... the only way to approach it is within your perspective.[69]

Schiffman had not merely failed to acknowledge that general "pioneering" perspective. As I looked deeper into the material I had gathered, it struck me that starting in the late 1980s, the NYU professor's writings had adopted *several* specific ideas and arguments previously developed by Norman Golb without even once citing him as a source. Realizing that this could be a serious matter, I gathered some of Schiffman's statements, set them side by side with earlier ones by Golb, and saved them with a number of relevant news clippings in a folder that I labeled "Schiffman."[70] (See Appendix, pages 279-84.)

Like anyone else, Schiffman had every right to argue the case for variety in the scrolls. But he had advanced—to be sure, in his own special way—arguments that appeared to be derived from ones previously put forward by another scholar, without signaling that previous scholarly history. Looking for guidance in the *New York University Faculty Handbook,* I read that "every member of the University ... is expected to conform to the highest standards of honesty and integrity. Activities such as plagiarism, misrepresentation, and falsification of data are expressly prohibited ... Plagiarism is the appropriation of another's ideas, processes, results, or words without giving appropriate credit."[71]

Reviewing the section on plagiarism in the American Historical Association's *Standards on Professional Conduct,* I further read that "all who participate in the community of inquiry, as amateurs or as professionals ... have an obligation to oppose deception ... Every institution that employs historians ... is expected to investigate charges of plagiarism promptly and impartially."[72] In fact, not only did New York University's faculty code of conduct forbid plagiarism in the severest terms, but it encouraged its anonymous denunciation: "An initial report of suspected research misconduct should be brought ... either anonymously or in person."[73]

In *Stolen Words,* Thomas Mallon observes that when an author is accused of plagiarism, "apologists" will invariably come to his defense.[74] Two former NYU deans would later testify under oath that they decided not to investigate the allegations against Schiffman because he had a "reputation for honesty" and because the details were "very technical."[75] To which it must be replied that when good people choose to remain silent, their inaction may give rise to an appearance of institutional impropriety.

Why does the truth about any of this matter? The American Historical Association's *Statement on Standards of Professional Conduct* declares that historians

> should practice their craft with integrity ... They should acknowledge their debts to the work of other scholars. They should respect and welcome divergent points of view even as they argue and subject those views to critical scrutiny. They should remember that our collective enterprise depends on mutual trust ... No matter what the context, the best professional practice for avoiding a charge of

plagiarism is always to be explicit, thorough, and generous in acknowledging one's intellectual debts.[76]

Another way of putting this is to say that university teachers are expected to err on the side of caution when it comes to attribution of ideas first expressed by others.[77] Authors must properly footnote others' arguments and ideas—regardless of whether they are citing them verbatim or merely paraphrasing them—because they need to "place their own ideas in context, locating their work in the larger intellectual conversation about their topic."[78]

When I attended the Oriental Institute ceremony in honor of my father's eighty-fifth birthday, Joel Kraemer told me that he, too, when he had read Schiffman's book (with its significant title *Reclaiming the Dead Sea Scrolls*), had "the same reaction" I did; he then realized, he said, that "these people were going to do everything they could to avoid giving credit to Norman for what he's done."

Every institution that employs historians *is expected to investigate charges of plagiarism promptly and impartially*. And yet, in his 2005 book *Historians in Trouble*, Jon Wiener argued that plagiarism charges usually only lead to serious consequences when those making the allegations are backed by powerful interest groups.[79] Seen in that light, my concerns were bound to be simply ignored, because to the extent power was involved in this situation, it was squarely weighted in favor of all the defenders of the sectarian dogma. Not only did I lack the backing of any interest group; I was directly opposed to one.

In law school, one learns the basic principle that authors must be given due credit and recognition for their ideas and creations. That principle rests on the underlying utilitarian premise that such credit and recognition help spur the great debates that enable the progress of knowledge. In Jewish legal thought, there is a different rationale. By deceiving the public, the plagiarist develops a "false self" and a fake persona; he engages in a form of *impersonation*.[80] A point precisely echoed in my parodies of a puffed-up NYU professor announcing that he would not have been invited to lecture in conferences around the world had he given due credit to Norman Golb. That point, however, was not one to the liking of Manhattan's cutting-edge prosecutors. While insisting that the case had nothing to do with the First Amendment, the prosecutors were in fact intent on stigmatizing and suppressing the message of my parodies.

The Censorship Regime, as Enforced by the "New Essene Sect."

In the absence of the objective controls that exist in fields like medicine and physics, the sectarian ideology's promoters were also free to give full rein to other suppressive strategies. This process would unfold with the assistance of a remarkable new tool: the internet.[81] That medium of communication, often described as having a revolutionary social impact, could be used for "subversive" ends—that is, to speak truth to power. But it could just as easily be used for propaganda and related purposes.

The defenders of the old ideas were quick to spot the value of the new medium, especially as younger, social media–savvy students were indoctrinated into their ranks. Toward the summer of 2006, anyone interested in quickly gaining information about the Dead Sea Scrolls could run a few Google searches. What he or she would encounter resulted from the internet's use as a publicity tool by defenders of the sect-based approach to scroll origins. Often enough, their efforts took the form of "news" items based on press releases apparently written by themselves, and then disseminated through a network of Bible blogs. Sometimes exactly the same, slightly sensationalist, propaganda pieces would appear, with minor differences, under the bylines of several different reporters working for competing agencies. A basic feature of such articles is their careful, studied silence regarding any research developments or evidence contradicting the sectarian theory. This silence, in fact, would represent a consistent dimension of Dead Sea Scrolls "politics" extending from 1980 until at least 2024, a dimension contrasting with the investigative reporting of a few major journalists, including Avi Katzman and Pulitzer laureate John Noble Wilford.

There was nothing really too surprising about the sectarian propaganda effort. After the publication of Norman Golb's *Who*

Wrote the Dead Sea Scrolls? in 1995, and of further works with similar conclusions by several major Israeli archaeologists during the decade that followed, there was a sense in which the outstanding issue in this field was no longer what the evidence showed. Rather, the issue was *who could be more publicly persuasive*—and what methods of persuasion would be employed to achieve the desired goal.

The ensuing struggle played out, for the most part, against the social ethos of contemporary academic life, especially as it is experienced in many American institutions of higher education. This has been described with acuity—and without exaggeration—by Russell Jacoby in his book *The Last Intellectuals*.[82] Academic culture is largely built on establishing "connections with reputable institutions or people," rather than on the quality of one's work. Participants in this culture "desire to be surrounded by individuals marked by charm, a conforming personality and skills in interaction."[83] In a climate of "vague general fear," all are expected to behave with "discretion." Disciplines are "armed against critical inquiry." They shun dissenters. They "turn inward ... towards more receptive colleagues." Rather than risk losing their jobs, members of the community focus their talents on "hyper-specialization," on demonstrating their mastery of the "jargon" that they share with their colleagues in each of their respective fields. Disciplines of study become "organized enterprises," where the focus is on applying for grants rather than investigating the truth.

All these special imperatives had long been important in scroll studies. By the mid-1990s, the key requirement for belonging to the inner sanctum of the Qumran-sectarian ideological group seemed to be less a matter of devoting oneself to critical scholarship than of agreeing to participate in suppressing dissent. The defenders of the sectarian hypothesis were declining to debate or even, for the most part, to cite their critics—a practice that would continue for decades.[84] They were also turning increasingly to personal arguments of a rhetorical nature, suggesting, for example, that their opponents were isolated eccentrics who were harassing the true scholarly world with mere "polemics."[85]

Much of this process took place in full public view, leaving a record difficult to reconcile with ordinary notions of academic collegiality. This type of phenomenon, of course, was not new; it had been observed as far back as the nineteenth and early twentieth centuries by such figures as Thorstein Veblen and Henry Adams among many others. Veblen had signaled the "reluctant tolerance" and "attitude of deprecation" with which new ideas were generally greeted in universities; Adams had observed the "conspiracy of silence" that "inevitably meets ... all thought which demands new thought-machinery."[86]

In their turn, students entering the field of scrolls scholarship would be left to puzzle over the hostility, so well documented that it could hardly escape their attention. One doctoral candidate would note, in the course of her own rather devastating critique of Qumran-sectarian claims, that the "most famous" rejection of the traditional paradigm was Norman Golb's, and she would observe that the "strength of the critical questions" Golb and others had posed was "invaluable to the progress of Qumran scholarship." She would then, however, add that the "radical" nature of the skeptics' rejection of the old paradigm had led to "negative reactions."[87]

I had an opportunity to see this process at work firsthand, soon after I began my doctoral studies in comparative literature at Harvard. I no longer recall the exact date of the lecture on the scrolls that was announced all over campus, but it must have been the spring of 1987 or sometime during the 1988–89 academic year. The lecture was to be given by Magen Broshi, the curator of the Shrine of the Book museum in Israel, under the auspices of the Department of Near Eastern Languages and Civilizations.

Thinking this would be a good opportunity to have an exchange about some of the questions involved in the debate over scroll origins, and assuming that various people in the audience might be asking such questions, I made some copies of one of Norman Golb's articles and went to the lecture—which turned out to be rank Qumran-Essene propaganda. When it was over, questions were solicited from the audience, and I duly raised my hand and proceeded to ask why Broshi had not addressed any of the objections to his claims that had been raised during recent years.

In response, Broshi squinted at me, apparently recognizing me, and observed, "I think I see where this is coming from. Is this Norman Golb?" Taken aback by the direct, ad hominem vulgarity of his words as well as the anger in his voice, I could think of nothing to say but yes; I was, after all, referring to published critiques that had been written by Norman Golb. Then came the direct, categorical answer from the podium, announced with sharp venom in the tone: "I am not going to talk about Norman Golb."

I immediately began to ask the short follow-up question that this statement seemed to invite—namely, "Why don't you want to talk about Norman Golb?"—but the professor who had introduced Broshi rapidly intervened, sternly waving his finger at me and asking if anyone else had any questions. The other audience members seemed uninformed and rather befuddled by what had happened, and one graduate student in the department approached me afterward and asked me what it was all about, as his professors had never informed him of the existence of any opposition to the Essene theory. I gave him one of the copies of the article I had brought along. When he had read it, he eventually spoke with me again. He seemed more disturbed by Norman Golb's critique than by Broshi's behavior; I came away with the uneasy impression that in the course of his education he had learned to comply with a particular set of rules established by the Qumran ideologues.[88]

By this time, Qumranology had hardened into precisely the kind of connection-based cultural apparatus described by Jacoby and other critics of academia. In his preface to the final *Back to Qumran* report, Yitzhak Magen would describe doing research in this climate as remarkably "difficult and unpleasant."[89]

As Magen put it, the sectarians had themselves formed a "new Essene sect" or a "guild," whose research was pervaded by "antiscientific" attitudes. The members of the guild padded their résumés with coded, jargon-filled articles, published in journals edited by themselves and their associates. If an opposing voice emerged, the Qumran-sectarian gatekeepers took measures to suppress it. Magen's description was frighteningly clear: Anyone who deviated from the "general opinion" was "ostracized." Dissenting views were excluded from "the journal of the 'Qumran researchers sect.'"

Still worse, any sign of defiance was met with a "chorus of insults and slander."[90]

These famously included the description by M. Broshi (whose lecture I had attended at Harvard) of Norman Golb as a "revolting ... opinionated trouble-maker" who had "filled the world with his filth," and of whom "we will be free ... when he dies."[91] Yitzhak Magen did not need to mention this incident: everyone in the field remembered it and would immediately know which "insults and slander" he had in mind.

The *New Humanist*'s Daniel O'Hara would describe Golb's book *Who Wrote the Dead Sea Scrolls?* as "a fascinating case-study of how an *idée fixe*, for which there is no real historical justification, has for over 40 years dominated an elite coterie of scholars controlling the scrolls, who have not only sought to restrict access to those who are prepared to toe their party-line, but have abused and rubbished those 'heretics' who have attempted to place a different interpretation on them." The elite scrolls coterie openly reviled the University of Chicago heretic, and anyone who dared to take his side had good reason to be afraid of professional repercussions. As Joel Kraemer would wryly observe in his biographical essay on Golb, "Those who believe in academic freedom may be disappointed to learn that Norman Golb was not invited to the sixty-years celebration of the Dead Sea Scrolls at the Hebrew University."

During the years following its publication, *Who Wrote the Dead Sea Scrolls?* would be repeatedly vandalized from the shelves of the Albright Institute library in Jerusalem; to this day, it apparently remains unavailable to students and scholars using that facility.[92] About the same time, a subtle pattern of vilification began in internet chat rooms, with Stephen Goranson, a stacks maintenance assistant at the Duke University Libraries and one of the most doctrinaire defenders of the Essene theory, suggesting that Norman Golb withdraw his work from publication. The scholar Niels Peter Lemche even seems to have believed that some of Goranson's remarks had an antisemitic tenor.[93] Moderators warned that the conversation must remain civil.

In 2002, Pulitzer laureate John Noble Wilford, writing in the *New York Times*, offered another look at ongoing efforts to silence Norman Golb. Discussing the scrolls conference held that year at Brown University, he pointed out that certain academics had agreed to attend only under the condition that certain *others* would not be invited.[94] Jacob Neusner, himself a former professor at Brown, understood exactly what was being referred too and wrote to Golb, in an email of December 24, 2002,

> I read in today's NYTimes … that while your basic approach to Qumran now predominates, you were not invited to participate in the … conference. The report said you were excluded by people who would not come if you were invited … That is chilling, a disgrace to the scholarly world. [Y]ou raised the fundamental questions and defined the shape of scholarship for generations to come … The people who excluded you are nourished by your ideas, whether they want to be or not, whether they acknowledge it or not.[95]

In emphatically asserting that Golb had "defined the shape of scholarship for generations to come," Neusner stated a fact known to scholars around the world—but that none of them could openly admit. Clearly, the traditionalists could not prevent a growing public recognition of the polarization between two fundamentally opposing theories of scroll origins.[96] In response, publications, conferences, and media campaigns organized by the monopolists and their heirs would continue to systematically present the sectarian hypothesis as a fact, often suppressing any mention, let alone discussion, of the evidence supporting the contrary view.

Some news items hinted at a public relations struggle; an article in *Israel Insider* explained that on August 16, 2004, archaeologists "financed by Christian fundamentalist organizations" gave a press conference to reassert, in the face of research to the contrary, that Qumran was a monastery inhabited by a sect or "community."[97] In the preface to *Back to Qumran,* Yitzhak Magen would report that during this period "there were requests to excavate from various people with strange theories ... all accompanied by endless pressure and supported by lawyers." Their aim, according to Magen, was "to promote personal agendas and baseless theories. One ... dig ... was carried out by a very senior archaeologist using heavy machinery, causing the destruction of antiquities until the dig was stopped by us."[98]

Despite the personal agendas and their destructive results, and with no reference to the reassessment of Qumran by the Magen-Peleg team, the sectarian idea would prevail on the website of the Israel Nature and Parks Authority. The unnamed author of this page—presumably a governmental employee—would point-blank describe Qumran as the home of "members of the Essene sect, the writers of the Dead Sea Scrolls," and would further misguide readers with the statement that the scrolls "have fired our imagination with the information they provide on the lifestyle of the ancient residents of Qumran."[99]

The emerging picture pointed to religiously oriented efforts to shore up a largely discredited theory—efforts including the fabrication of a "consensus" and the spreading of sensationalist claims in the media along with propaganda supporting the theory and masking the strong evidence against it.[100] Clearly, part of what was at stake was money. The rise of evangelical tourism would bring in more than half a billion dollars a year to Israel's economy.[101] According to the Israel Ministry of Foreign Affairs, over two million Christians visited Israel in 2013, some 420,000 of them Protestant; and 60 percent of all Christian "pilgrims" to Israel visit Qumran.[102] Three years later, a large increase in tourism to Israel would result from a publicity campaign targeting "Evangelical, Catholic and Jewish audiences in New York, LA, Atlanta and Florida, with a particularly high budget for online promotion."[103]

In the midst of this process, came the announcement, on the website of the American Friends of the Israel Antiquities Authority, of plans to build a massive new complex in Jerusalem for housing and studying the scrolls.[104] Unsurprisingly, the presentation treated the sect scenario as a fact. The envisioned complex was to be part of a "national campus for the archaeology of Israel" on Museum Hill, across from the Knesset. It was funded by and named after New York business tycoon Ira Rennert, the "biggest private polluter in America," and his wife, Ingeborg, director of the Lincoln Center for the Performing Arts.[105]

As mentioned at the end of chapter 3, soon after my indictment and around a year before my trial, Rennert himself would donate $34,500 to the election campaign of Cyrus Vance Jr., Robert Morgenthau's chosen successor as district attorney, who would see my prosecution through to its end while seeking reduced sex offender status for Jeffrey Epstein, dropping charges against accused rapist Dominique Strauss-Kahn, and allowing Harvey Weinstein to go uncharged until the arrival of the #MeToo movement ultimately persuaded him to take a firmer stand.

The Traveling Exhibition: Gaslighting the Public?

Soon after Yizhar Hirschfeld, Yitzhak Magen, and Yuval Peleg announced their research conclusions, various American science museums became the venue for a traveling Dead Sea Scrolls museum exhibit. The idea of scroll origins favored by the original monopoly team and its heirs was now marketed across the country as a widely accepted fact. "News" items written by defenders of that idea were released to the press by museum PR departments (sometimes working in tandem with publicity firms) and, toward the summer of 2006, began to find a natural path for further exposure through evangelical blogs. Viewing these internet pages, anyone aware of the actual situation could not help but realize that in its staging, the scrolls exhibit amounted to something like a public, evangelized American farce, one meriting popular debate and discussion.

Soon, the exhibitors would begin to realize that the internet itself was being used to challenge the claims they were making, to document their perceived abuses, and to embarrass them along with other defenders of the sectarian claims. In short, my campaign of criticism and satire dealing with the exhibits was having an impact. Although I was, at the time, an anonymous figure, I was well informed about the scrolls controversy, about the exhibitors' academic network, and about their effort to defend a particular ideology, and I had set about divulging the actual facts to readers.

Testimony at my trial would later confirm that discussions were held in museum offices, and that certain steps were taken to contain any possible damage that might ensue. With such discussions in the background, the exhibits, always featuring one-sided displays favoring the assumptions of the scrolls "editorial team," would continue unabated in a process extending well over a decade—and even into the indefinite future. The frequency of the exhibits would lead to condemnation from two scientists at the Federal Institute for Materials Research and Testing in Berlin, Germany. According to them, the manuscript fragments were "not receiving proper care from the Israeli cultural institutions responsible for their well-being," for "frequent travel, exhibitions and the associated handling induce collagen deterioration ... covered up by the absence of a proper monitoring program."[106]

Judging from available figures (and unfortunately figures are not easily available), the various scroll exhibits of the 2003–18 period would be lucrative ventures not only for the Israel Antiquities Authority—which rents out fragments of the manuscripts for a sizable "conservation" fee of $250,000—but also for the institutions involved.[107] At a ticket price of some twenty to thirty dollars per adult, the exhibits would bring in around $80 million, donated by the misinformed public over a ten-year period.

What struck me most, as I increasingly followed the developing story of the exhibits online during the 2006–7 period, was that the institutions hosting the exhibits could not plead ignorance. In a series of articles, my father had documented poor scholarship and misleading claims made in the exhibits, along with conduct of the exhibitors (including their receipt of money from interested parties) that he condemned as unethical.[108] If the exhibits, according to criticism by a specialist at the University of Chicago's Oriental Institute, consisted largely of false and unsupported claims designed to mislead visitors, then wouldn't one normally expect the directors of the prestigious exhibiting museums to investigate these claims?

Clearly that *would* be the normal expectation, if American science museums followed the rules laid out in the code of ethics promulgated by the London-based Museums Association.[109] According to that code, the duties incumbent on museum governors and employees include

- "enable … others to keep up to date with developments in their field";
- "make the museum a forum in which ideas can be discussed and tested";
- "cultivate a variety of perspectives";
- "indicate clearly the part played by opinion or conjecture in interpretation"; and
- "reflect differing views striking a balance over time."

A London ethics code, however, has as much influence as a dead letter in American exhibiting institutions. The "Code of Ethics for Museums" promulgated by the American Alliance of Museums is drafted in a genteel-enough way to avoid generating too many disputes about such matters: it states merely that museums are to ensure that "programs respect pluralistic values, traditions and concerns."[110] Blithely ignoring this latter requirement, the American science museums hosting the scroll exhibits would engage in a concerted effort to hide the polarized nature of scrolls scholarship from the public. The exhibits were nothing short of an assault on the truth, and the unsuspecting public was the victim. Disputed, and in many instances disproved, claims were being marketed as accurate in order to normalize what a major archaeological team had described as a baseless theory.

Over and beyond the question of scientific accuracy, there were other irksome issues. The exhibits were created largely by Christian scholars, some of them affiliated with evangelical institutions such as the University of the Holy Land and Trinity Western, others tied, in one way or another, to the scrolls monopoly group.[111] A few Orthodox Jewish scholars were also involved, but the more secular-minded Jewish scholars who fundamentally opposed the sectarian theory were being excluded point-blank from participating in the lecture series accompanying virtually all the exhibits.

Science and education were the stated missions of most institutions where the scrolls were being exhibited. In the surrounding cultural context, the scroll exhibits stood out like a sore. To make matters worse, reviews of the exhibits generally lacked any critical dimension. As a result, the deception involved in the displays was taking place without public knowledge, so that thousands of visitors were literally buying into a biased point of view masquerading as fact. With the scroll exhibits, the sectarian ideology had become a spectacle, and as such, it would thrill the public like fashion, coronations, action films, or any of the myriad other "events" that blend into a run-on, repetitive narrative that Americans absorb from one day to the next throughout their lives.

San Diego: "A Lively Debate over the Dead Sea Scrolls"

In the summer of 2007, the defenders of the sectarian cause worked to set an example for all future exhibitors of the scrolls, marketing a $6 million exhibit at the Natural History Museum in San Diego—and rigorously controlling precisely what type of ideas were presented in it.

An article in the *San Diego Union-Tribune* summed up the facts: "The exhibition's journey to San Diego began with a lunch and a phone call."[112] David Noel Freedman had invited his "former student" Risa Levitt Kohn (later to become chair of the religious studies department and director of the Jewish studies program at San Diego State University) to meet Weston Fields, executive director of the Dead Sea Scrolls Foundation, which "raises funds ... through exhibitions." Levitt Kohn had suggested the Natural History Museum "as a possible venue." Another item specified that Fields had "visited Freedman at UCSD while Levitt Kohn was completing her doctoral studies."[113]

Soon thereafter, the Natural History Museum agreed to host the exhibit, with Levitt Kohn as its curator. While the museum was gathering $6 million from various philanthropists (including Irwin Jacobs, the founder of Qualcomm), she began to put together the exhibit and its accompanying lecture series, from which the various contrarian researchers were excluded. In January, she would try to respond to criticism of the upcoming exhibit on the San Diego Jewish World website, pointing out that "of the museums hosting the scrolls, SDNHM is the only museum that has its own curator for the exhibition. As a Dead Sea Scrolls scholar and professor of religious studies ... I am fortunate to have been selected for that position."

Interviewed by the *Voice of San Diego* several months later (June 2, 2007), Levitt Kohn would offer a different formulation, admitting that she was "far from an expert" and "didn't really study Dead Sea Scrolls much, other than in kind of a tangential way."[114] (Meanwhile, as the exhibit opened, the Israel Ministry of Tourism would invite "publishers of 10 American Christian newspapers to tour Israel," with Qumran high on the agenda.)[115]

A few weeks later, Levitt Kohn would again attempt to justify the exhibitors' approach. On June 26, 2007, the *Los Angeles Times* reported on the opening of the exhibit, in an article by Mike Boehm entitled *"A* Lively Debate over the Dead Sea Scrolls." After some general description of the exhibit, Boehm quoted my father's critique: "Instead of guiding viewers toward an understanding of the controversy over the origin and significance of the scrolls, it manifestly undertakes to manipulate the layman's comprehension of them." He then quoted Levitt Kohn's reply: "You don't want to confuse people with so many competing theories, so they walk away, saying, 'Well, nobody really knows anything!'"[116]

Reading Boehm's article, I was struck by how concisely Levitt Kohn had managed to define a basic ideological perspective. The last thing in the world that the "official" editorial team—that is, the monopoly group and its heirs—would want was for ordinary members of the public to realize that there was more than one interpretation of the facts. According to Levitt Kohn's statement, if the conflicting interpretations at the core of the scrolls controversy were actually presented in a museum exhibit, people might become *confused*—a state of mind, apparently, that could have serious consequences. Some individuals might even start asking unpleasant questions.

During the ensuing months, Levitt Kohn's performance as curator of the San Diego exhibit continued to be feted in the local press. Soon after the exhibit opened, Delle Willett, the Natural History Museum's marketing director, moved to control any potential damage, explaining to the press that "a guy named Norm Golb just loves to follow these Dead Sea Scrolls around the country and talk about how we've got it all wrong."[117] In an interview published on June 2, 2007, Levitt Kohn clarified the exhibit's agenda, stating, "The truth is, I wouldn't classify these as Jewish texts ... Because I would say Judaism, the way we tend to think about it, even early Judaism, is not yet fully crystallized in this period."[118] Unfortunately, the "truth" voiced here by Levitt Kohn tripped over the abundant historical evidence supporting a "Jewish" interpretation of the scrolls—facts that would be concealed from the public in the exhibit.

One important dimension of the museum's strategy was to remain silent in the face of criticism: Norman Golb's discussion, on the Oriental Institute website, of gross factual errors and misinformation in Levitt Kohn's exhibit catalog went unanswered.[119] The exhibitors appeared to have concluded that for some time, the "dissident" view would continue to subsist in its own parallel universe, but that just as long as they shielded themselves with merely a *modicum* of distortion and obfuscation, their own interpretation would surely prevail.

The strategy had a flaw. By now, motivated by an increasing sense of outrage at the exhibitors' strategy, I had learned how to post articles on NowPublic—and, apparently by virtue of some business arrangement between NowPublic and Google, almost as soon as each of these articles appeared online, a link to it would automatically shoot to the top of the first page of a search for the words "San Diego Dead Sea Scrolls."[120] Any potential visitor to the exhibit who did a Google search, even just for schedules or for the museum's address, risked encountering one or more of my articles, replete with background documentation and a dose of measured indignation at the exhibitors' misconduct—indignation that would later play into the New York prosecutors' claim that I was motivated by personal "resentment." Contrary to that claim, my campaign was not merely some sort of a strange personal vendetta against scholars who happened to "disagree" with Norman Golb. My goal was to call out a systematic effort to cheat the public of the truth.

In one of several critiques of the San Diego exhibit that I published under the pen name "Charles Gadda"—an Americanized version of Carlo Emilio Gadda (1893–1973), an Italian novelist whose principal themes were irrationality and digression—I wrote that the display gave "rise to an appearance of impropriety." The exhibit, I continued, was "tainted by intellectual antisemitism and with an obscurantist, seemingly irrational fear of debate." Seen from *this* perspective, I suggested, the exhibit was the resurrection, in a somewhat different form, of the same monopoly that had collapsed in the midst of scandal during the early 1990s.

Not surprisingly, my article evoked furious comments from someone who seemed to be closely involved in the exhibit and who, using the pseudonym "B. Ralph," accused Charles Gadda of using a pseudonym, of being a "bigot," and of declaring "guilt by association."[121] The comments contributed to drawing more attention to the article and to keeping it at the top of the Google search results.

My efforts (this goes almost without saying) could have only a small impact when compared with the sensationalist media campaign emanating from the museum's marketing department—a campaign that in effect marketed not only the exhibit but the sect-centered hypothesis to as large a local and national audience as possible.[122] Furthermore, an elaborate Bible blog network *organically publicized* the exhibit, a phenomenon with religious overtones that vastly broadened the impact of the sectarian propaganda campaign.[123]

In the midst of all the lectures, blogs, and press releases, a particularly potent tool for boosting the sectarian claims was a "virtual reality" film that the San Diego exhibitors promoted. The role given to this computer-generated work quickly became the focus of my own quarrel with the techniques the museum's staff members were using to convey disinformation. The film, produced at UCLA, consisted of a 3D reconstruction of what Qumran may have looked like, together with an explanatory script that docents read aloud to visitors gathered in the museum's auditorium. The film was entitled *Virtual Qumran.*

To guarantee the film's realization, the museum and the Righteous Persons Foundation—that is, Steven Spielberg's Holocaust foundation—joined forces to allot $100,000 to Robert Cargill, at the time a graduate student at UCLA. Cargill, it turned out, was writing a doctoral dissertation on the topic of "the Qumran digital model." His thesis adviser was William Schniedewind, who together with Cargill formed the "team" responsible for the film's production. Schniedewind, presented as the "project's principle investigator," was the chairman of the Department of Near Eastern Languages and Cultures at UCLA.[124] As for Cargill, he had previously attended the Church of Christ–affiliated Pepperdine University,[125] where he had received both a master of divinity degree and a master of science in Christian ministry. The late journalist Tom Tugend, writing in the *Jewish Journal* shortly before the San Diego exhibit opened, summarized Cargill's Pepperdine background by stating that he had majored in "biblical studies." Schniedewind and Cargill, according to the same article, were both "practicing Christians with a deep appreciation and knowledge of Judaism and Israel."[126]

Within the sleek, popularizing package of its special virtual reality format, *Virtual Qumran* seemed designed to slickly convey the idea of desert-dwelling monks practicing a pure, proto-Christian form of Judaism at Qumran—even though that idea had recently been rejected by the "Back to Qumran" archaeological team in Israel. The film, in effect, set out to convince viewers that even though Qumran was originally a fortress, this did not conflict with the theory that a pacifist, purity-loving "community" lived there while gathering and writing the Dead Sea Scrolls. Claims made about the film in the press gave the distinct impression that its key purpose was to serve as one of various propaganda tools for the San Diego exhibit.[127]

As I signaled in several internet articles at the time,[128] the claim touted in the film, far from being original, was in fact virtually identical to an idea previously proposed in 1994 by Israeli archaeologist

Yitzhak Magen—who later, after further reflection, had rejected the idea.[129] The producers of the film, however, failed to divulge the history of previous scholarship bearing on this central claim.

This led to one plain result. The team's "findings," as they were called in a UCLA press release, came across not as a hypothetical development related to an idea previously proposed, and then dropped, by a leading Israeli archaeologist. Rather, they came across as an original conception. Their apparent willingness to create this impression opened a question of credibility, especially because Cargill's dissertation, in which the same claim was reiterated, turned out to be plagued by other weaknesses that would be signaled in a review by Eibert Tigchelaar of the Catholic University of Leuven.[130] According to Tigchelaar, the dissertation was characterized by a dubious "reliability of the adduced arguments," a lack of "thoroughness," and an absence of "concrete evidence" to support the hypothesis advanced.

What came next shed further light on the San Diego exhibit and the nature of Cargill's involvement in it. Cargill, in fact, would send a series of emails to the University of Chicago, demanding that Norman Golb's critique of the *Virtual Qumran* effort be taken down from the university's website. By virtue, Cargill indicated, of having affixed a "proprietary clause" to the cover page of his film script, he had a special ownership privilege that prevented Norman Golb from quoting anything from the script in his critique.

In response to Robert Cargill's demands, on June 3, 2009, Russell Herron, associate general counsel of the University of Chicago, would write a formal letter explaining that "we have carefully considered the matter and are quite comfortable that Professor Golb's article does not violate any copyright or other legal right you may claim in your script.... Nothing in the nature of your work or in the purportedly restrictive legends it contains compels a different conclusion." Herron ended his letter by stating, "We understand that you may not like Professor Golb's criticism of your work. We encourage you to respond to Professor Golb openly and on the merits, rather than attempting to silence academic commentary and criticism through legal posturing."

Herron's words about the "silencing of academic commentary" stood completely at odds with the principles and practices of the parochial scrolls scholarship universe. I understood from Cargill's emails to the University of Chicago, as well as from remarks that he would offer later to justify what he had done, that something was felt to be wrong with Norman Golb's ability to publish his academic criticisms of a Dead Sea Scrolls museum exhibit without submitting to the control of the proper authorities. Authorities who were self-anointed experts representing a sect-like, and well-funded, group defending a highly particular ideology.[131]

Ultimately, all this would lead to a remarkable, and seemingly rather inexplicable, development—one that involved not museum exhibits or doctoral dissertations but a televised admission by Cargill himself. During the summer of 2010, some three years after the San Diego exhibit—and, ironically, while I was preparing for my criminal trial—he would appear on a National Geographic program, where he would announce that he had been on a spiritual journey through the world of Dead Sea Scrolls research, and that he now was able to conclude that the scrolls "were written by Jews—not just one specific group, but by lots of Jews." The program's narrator, André Sogliuzzo, would explain that "there is one event that ties the fate of all these groups, with all their scrolls, together—the Great Jewish Revolt."

Much to my surprise, Cargill went on to vividly describe how Jews fled from Jerusalem during the sacking of the city in 70 CE: "They grabbed their valuable possessions, they grabbed their Bibles, they grabbed their scrolls, and they ran, and they hid those scrolls in caves all throughout the Judaean Desert ... I went from thinking," Cargill continued, "that the scrolls were written by one single group, to understanding that the scrolls were perhaps written by a vast array of different Jewish groups. It really does allow me to understand the scrolls as documents that speak directly to me." What had caused this change?

It was, of course, possible that something had been edited out of the film, but judging from its viewable contents, Cargill had not mentioned Norman Golb's name during his National Geographic appearance.[132] His statements in the film, though, were quite different from those he had made in his doctoral dissertation.

Cargill's apparent shift would ultimately be followed by another development—one that was remarkable not in itself but in the use to which it would be put in the *New York Times*. During his Pepperdine and UCLA years, Cargill had to all appearances been a believing Christian. At Pepperdine he had served not only as an adjunct religion teacher but as a "faith counselor."[133] According to the résumé he posted online, he had also worked in a variety of capacities at a company called "Christianity.com."[134] While less directly apropos, it is also worth noting that he had tutored a world-renowned movie star on biblical topics. One celebrity news website reported that "Hollywood beauty Nicole Kidman is returning to her Catholic roots by taking a detailed course about the Bible's Old Testament. The 37-year-old Australian actress has employed *acclaimed Professor of Religion* Dr. Robert Cargill, of America's Pepperdine University, to teach her about theology and its connections to Middle Eastern Politics."[135] Coverage of the sort seemed to indicate that Cargill, far from being a mere student, was a public figure of considerable consequence, known for his theological expertise.

Then, around six years later, in a lengthy *New York Times Magazine* article focused on my misdeeds, Cargill would be described not as a "practicing Christian" (as Ted Tugend had put it) but as an "agnostic." This description, made without biographical nuance, helped guide readers toward believing that I had been libelous and inflammatory in suggesting, in 2007, that Christian fundamentalism had been playing a role in the ongoing scroll exhibits, and that those exhibits were tainted by intellectual antisemitism.[136]

By the summer of 2008, following the success of the San Diego display, the exhibit had moved on to the North Carolina Museum of Natural Sciences in Raleigh. Unlike the privately owned natural history museum in San Diego, this was a state-run institution. But here, too, Risa Levitt Kohn was involved. In Raleigh as in San Diego, the evidence brought to light by various secular-minded researchers who had rejected the sectarian theory was downplayed and concealed. Those researchers themselves were physically excluded from participating in the lecture series accompanying the exhibit. My blogs, on the other hand, seem to have had some impact on a local reporter, who acknowledged in a review that "the exhibition, while paying lip service to the controversy ... gives the secular interpretation short shrift."[137]

More and more people were flooding into scroll marketing displays across the country, while in New York, taking occasional breaks from my own reading projects at Bobst Library, I continued to avail myself of the library's open-access computers to write pseudonymous articles that questioned the efforts of Levitt Kohn and her associates. These pieces included, to quote playwright and drama professor Margaret Rose, an assortment of satirical "arrows drawn from the quiver of caustic criticism," and were aimed at exposing, ridiculing, and attracting attention to "what is chimerical and false."[138]

Soon, I was challenging the museums in an increasing number of blogs, comments on news sites, and an array of other communications (all of them always either pseudonymous or anonymous) focusing on the exclusionary policies behind the exhibitions. In many of these items, I linked readers to scholarly reviews by Norman Golb of the exhibits—reviews that the Oriental Institute had been publishing on its website for years but that the scroll exhibitors had been ignoring.[139]

Traveling curator Levitt Kohn's statement regarding the necessity of protecting the public from "confusion," provided fodder for an argument that I included in various postings: God forbid people should become uncertain about something, lest they have unpredictable and possibly dangerous reactions upon leaving the exhibit![140] Unwilling or unable to justify their efforts to avoid public confusion on scientific grounds, the exhibitors found themselves increasingly taunted in various online forums in postings that I signed with a variety of handles and pseudonyms.[141] One scholar, commenting on one of the articles, thanked me for my "good work in the public interest."[142]

No doubt the exhibitors felt a mounting threat to their reputations and to those of their associates.[143] When an upcoming

Canadian exhibit was announced (again with a curatorial role for Levitt Cohn), Toronto's *National Post* referred to the Jerusalem-libraries theory and questioning its exclusion from the exhibits. It is worth emphasizing that during this period, from San Diego to Toronto and beyond, I did not hesitate to send variously signed pseudonymous emails to the museums hosting the Dead Sea Scroll exhibits, as well as to academic associates of the group involved in creating and propagandizing the exhibits. In fact, I felt morally obliged to do so. In these emails I pointed to a pattern of institutional mayhem in respect to the treatment allotted to the scrolls.[144]

At the same time, I dogged the exhibitors with equally pseudonymous online articles focusing on their association with the ideological efforts of the "official" scrolls editorial team or monopoly. Why these pseudonymous complaints of mine would never be the subject of specific criminal charges is a bit of a mystery. Interviewed by the *National Post* in 2009, Levitt Kohn would express the view that my criticism of her work *should* have been criminalized, a statement that reminded me of the efforts of police officials in seventeenth- and eighteenth-century France, England, and elsewhere to track down satirists who had caused public confusion by mocking Jesuit authorities or other influential parties.[145]

The Jewish Museum Exhibit: An Outbreak of Confusion

Then, toward the end of July 2008, the Jewish Museum in New York made a major announcement: this prestigious institution would soon be displaying an exhibit of the Dead Sea Scrolls, in which the public would be informed of two clashing ideas regarding the origins of the texts. According to published reports at the time, the exhibit would introduce the public to the "two basic theories" of scroll origins. In a striking exception to the general exhibition policy that had emerged in the United States, the announcement described the sect-centered theory as merely one among several possibilities "still being debated by historians and archaeologists."

The museum's press release forthrightly informed the public

that in an exhibition gallery, "visitors will learn that *scholars still do not agree* about the origins and meaning of the scrolls decades after their discovery." It asserted that "many years" might pass "before scholars can come to a consensus on who wrote and used the Dead Sea Scrolls, where they lived, and how this impacts on our interpretation of their meaning for our lives today."[146]

In a separate press release, the museum explained that the scrolls "have opened up a complex world of Jewish diversity and inquiry from which Christianity eventually emerged," and that of the "two basic theories" of scroll origins, one "proposes that the scrolls were a random collection of texts reflecting the beliefs of many Jewish groups of the period," that "there is no connection between the scrolls and the settlement at Qumran," and that "during the Jewish revolt against Rome beginning in 68 CE, refugees ... hid their precious texts in the Dead Sea caves."[147] The release further stated that "in assembling the exhibition ... Susan Braunstein, Curator of Archaeology and Judaica ... selected texts that illustrate the diversity and transformations in Judaism during the Second Temple Period."

These statements fed into my campaign. They bluntly contradicted the agenda of the North Carolina exhibit that was taking place precisely at that time. I quickly raised this issue on various websites; posting under the alias "Timothy Fishbane," I asked how the presentation of a *single* doctrine in Raleigh could be reconciled with the approach taken in New York.[148] Stephen Goranson of the Duke University Libraries then came to the defense of the Raleigh exhibit; in the course of the exchanges that followed, he pointed out that I was using pseudonyms, a fact, he suggested, that invalidated my arguments.

Toward the same time, Goranson posted a series of comments defending the Essene hypothesis on the Ancient Near East (ANE) online forum. This chat room had initially been run out of the Oriental Institute library, and had then been opened up again by Jeffrey Gibson, an adjunct professor at Columbia College in Chicago. Oddly enough, the name Jeffrey Gibson was known to me because of humorous online accusations made by a British blogger to the effect that many online comments on the scrolls (including ones by

Goranson) were actually posted by Gibson using a variety of pseudonyms.[149]

It was thus no surprise that when I attempted to engage with Goranson's ANE arguments, Gibson blocked me from doing so under the pretext that I was using ... a pseudonym.[150] I then messaged various participants in the forum directly, with emails lauding Gibson for his rigorous control over his forum, and Goranson for his courage in standing up to what I referred to as the "filth from Chicago." I sent these emails using the pseudonym "Jonathan Seidel." I also used this handle to contact several museum officials (including in Toronto) to ask them if they planned, in light of the Jewish Museum's dramatic announcement, to continue with the biased policy of presenting the public with only one side of the scrolls controversy.

My use of the words "filth from Chicago" (language that directly mimicked Magen Broshi of the Shrine of the Book)[151] elicited a furious reply from a participant in Israel who insisted that even if, as he wrongly assumed, I disagreed with Norman Golb, the University of Chicago historian was a serious scholar who had never done anything to deserve such an outrageous insult. Several other replies to the "Seidel" emails expressed no such dismay.

Meanwhile, the Raleigh museum failed to respond to any of my online comments, or to acknowledge in any way to visitors that they were viewing a biased presentation. Viewed against that silence, the exhibit about to take place in New York appeared especially significant. The Jewish Museum's announced change of policy—to present *both* sides of the story, rather than just one—was a radical departure. But my sense of satisfaction about this unexpected shift was short lived. The museum soon issued a follow-up press release, making it clear that the *lectures* accompanying the exhibit would consist only of the usual presentations delivered by two defenders of the sectarian idea. The first was Lawrence Schiffman of NYU, and the second was Sidnie White Crawford, another defender of the sectarian idea, who, I surmised (as it turned out, accurately), had been "recommended" to the museum by Schiffman.

I phoned Daniel Friedenberg (1923–2011), a close friend of my parents (who at the time were in Jerusalem) and a retired curator at the museum. Filling him in on the two press releases, I asked him if he had any insight into how the lectures accompanying the museum's exhibit had been converted into a propaganda exercise. He expressed dismay at the museum's lecture choices but thought there was nothing to do about it given the local politics of the situation—and Schiffman's influence in New York Jewish circles.

As the prosecutors in New York prepared their case in consultation with Lawrence Schiffman, it rapidly became clear that none of the ethical difficulties inherent in continuing support for a "baseless" hypothesis would be officially acknowledged. This strategy would fully coincide with the position staked out by defenders of the sectarian view who even today—forty years after many of that view's weaknesses were first exposed—continue to carefully evade the manifestly valid points raised by critics rather than openly address them. The task the adherents of the Qumran-sectarian belief set themselves when confronted by ever-increasing amounts of criticism was not to grapple rationally with the new ideas but to defeat the opposition with any means at their disposal.

5
THE DEANS, THE DONS, AND A CURATOR

After my indictment, I'm forced to wait for a year. The district attorney seems clearly motivated to follow the case through to the end, despite all the other ones coming up in the news. If they think of a good-enough reason, the police could even come bursting into my apartment again any day. But the DA's team is actually using the time to prepare all their witnesses, and then, on Monday, September 13, 2010—around eighteen months after my arrest—my trial begins. Now I will get used to the *New York Post* photographer following me around, to the mostly empty courtroom, to the prosecutor's obvious difficulty reconciling the facts with the law, and to my own constant struggle to try to make sense of a situation that, on a variety of levels, seems inherently deranged and incomprehensible.

If I have to single out one impression that will remain with me from the entire trial, it is Judge Carol Berkman's frequent interruptions of my lawyers as they attempt to cross-examine various witnesses. Interruptions accompanied by a variety of puzzling expressions, which at one point will lead one of my attorneys to ask, "Have I disaffected you, Your Honor? You're making faces again."[1] It would be cynical and misleading for me to suggest that any sort of personal bias against me or my lawyers motivates these interruptions; my aim here, to the extent I cite the honorable judge's statements, will be to examine the relation between her vision of the law, as it manifests itself during the trial, and the issues the jury will ultimately be instructed both to examine and, more significantly, not to examine.

That judicial vision, the clarity of which cannot be disputed, has already been concisely asserted in Berkman's ruling, some seven months before the trial, that "neither good faith nor truth is a defense to any of the crimes charged," a decision rendering the "truth" about the Dead Sea Scrolls controversy simply "not relevant to any issue actually presented in this case."[2] As a result of this ruling, the jury will be prevented from weighing the actual evidence pertaining to what speaking truth to power confronts and challenges, including for example:

- the suppression of plagiarism allegations at New York University;
- the documented misrepresentation of Norman Golb's research conclusions, and the suppression of empirical evidence supporting those conclusions in museum exhibits;
- the blackballing and exclusion of Norman Golb from normal venues for debate, a phenomenon Jacob Neusner described as a "disgrace to the scholarly world."

If, as Berkman ruled, the "truth is not a defense," then clearly discussion of all such matters becomes simply irrelevant and can be suppressed at trial. No wonder, I keep thinking as I sit in my assigned chair, this particular criminal court figure was the DA's judge of choice, both to sign the necessary arrest warrant and to preside over the trial.

My own feelings as a defendant sitting in that chair, however, are not affected only by an awareness of the limitations imposed on my ability to defend myself in the pretrial "neither good faith nor truth" ruling. I have also read various media items about Berkman, which include one explaining that the Legal Aid Society, invoking her alleged "systematic ... mistreatment of ... lawyers and defendants," publicly petitioned, in 1999, against her reappointment to the criminal court.[3] Additional articles have led me to understand that Berkman, a graduate of Harvard University Law School, is known for her oversight of many controversial criminal cases. In one of them, she sentenced poet-musician Gil Scott-Heron, who suffered from an addiction problem, to one to three years in prison for possession of crack cocaine. In another, she sentenced a man suffering from Asperger's syndrome to five years in prison; his obsession with the city transit system (and with stealing buses and trains) rendered him a "threat to society."[4]

Even during the months and years following my trial, I will continue to take note of news items on Berkman's judicial career. Her cases will come to include one that is declared a "gross miscarriage of justice" by an appellate court, after she sentences a pregnant governmental informant to three years in prison despite an agreement of leniency with prosecutors. Reporting on this case, the *New York Post* will call Berkman a "tough-as-nails" judge, noting that, according to the five appellate judges who throw out the sentence, she "exhibited hostility, even disdain," toward the woman and, "more importantly, a total disregard for her safety and welfare relating to her role as a drug informant for the District Attorney's Office." Berkman, the *Post* article states, "refused prosecutors' request to close and seal the courtroom ... even after being told the woman's life would be in danger if she didn't."[5]

Those events will take place in 2012. But already by the time of my own trial, I have read enough to offer me some sense—no doubt distorted by the filtering of reality through prurient media reports—of what I might expect to experience as I try to avoid jail. A 2002 *Harper's* essay by Jeff Tietz described Berkman as listening to court proceedings "with her chin on her upturned palms and her incredulous mouth open," rolling "her eyes with unusual vigor and range, her head following ... until it almost touched her shoulder."[6] I cannot help but notice a similar range of expressive behavior. The above-cited *Post* article includes a photo that, when I see it, will vividly remind me of my own experience. But I would again like to emphasize that it would be unfair, in my view, to leap to a conclusion about any sort of personal animus toward me or other defendants from such photos. What they certainly do achieve is capture the intensity of the judge's concentration as she

> The appellate judges will note that Berkman "routinely mocked the woman." Among Berkman's statements: "I don't think she is worthy of sympathy ... She's pregnant again with, what is it, five or six other children that she has, none of whom she is the mother to ... I have no idea what she has been doing the last couple of years, other than getting pregnant."

focuses on the difficult task of applying the law to the situation and facts as they emerge and unfold before her during the trial.

In retrospect, far more significant than the aura surrounding the judge's persona in the media or its effect on me is the bewildering nature of the testimony itself that will unfold over a two-week period, reflecting the complexities associated with a roiling academic dispute over an abstruse intellectual topic. It is in fact not clear that the actual implications of the various assertions made by one witness after another as I sit in my special chair—constantly suppressing an urge to protest—could possibly be fully evident to any of the court personnel and other individuals participating in the implementation of justice. This includes even my two lawyers, who are apparently so used to hearing outrageous claims that they have grown almost immune to them, and whose attention is focused on trying to get me off the charges.

My lead attorney, the accomplished David Breitbart, has secured not-guilty verdicts for an entire series of murder defendants by picking apart the testimony of the unreliable witnesses who testified against them. He is now balding, in his early seventies, with a dead-serious face and bushy eyebrows. No longer the firebrand he once was, he still projects a tough image. According to news stories, he carries a gun on him. He is as gruff as a prison guard, despite his elegant suits; yet he has a soft side and a sense of humane sarcasm that occasionally announces itself, as when he audibly comments on one of the incriminating "Larry Schiffman" emails introduced into evidence by the prosecution, "Ooh, that's a good one!"

Breitbart is assisted by Ron Kuby, who, under the arrangement we've agreed on, will cross-examine a few of the many witnesses, but whose main job will be to keep a lookout for rulings along the way that can be appealed, and for issues involving "social media" and the internet, an area he is potentially more familiar with than Breitbart on account of his relative youth.

Kuby, in fact, has a "radical" image, which his dark-gray pinstripe suits seem unsuccessfully designed to counteract (they are solid, imposing, perhaps a bit too flashy, not as elegant as Breitbart's). He was once a partner of the famed left-wing lawyer

William Kunstler and in this capacity was mentioned by "the Dude" (played by Jeff Bridges) in *The Big Lebowski*, a Coen brothers' film ("I want a fucking lawyer, man. I want Bill Kunstler man ... or Ronald Kuby"). His radio show is a big hit, and some of his past clients have been so controversial that he feels obliged to explain to Berkman, before the jury selection begins, that he has a tendency to evoke either positive or very negative feelings among jurors, depending on their backgrounds.

* * *

During jury selection, John Bandler, the prosecutor who interrogated me before sending me to the Tombs, eliminates anyone who reveals any knowledge of the Dead Sea Scrolls controversy. This includes the retired college professor who asserts that he knows all about scrolls "politics," the corporate saleswoman who has spent a lot of time in Israel and has a "personal belief" about the scrolls and "how they should be published and where they belong," and the head of a credit union who has "always been really, really annoyed over the years" that the scrolls have "been kept secreted and somebody had control over them."[7] Breitbart, in his big booming voice—it will serve as a counterpart to Schiffman's—that helped make him a famous courtroom lawyer, asks the potential juror, "If you find that some of the witnesses for the government in this case were members of that monopoly, would you take that into consideration?" Berkman immediately interrupts: "I'm sorry, sir, you are assuming a fact not in evidence. There is no evidence, actually as to the truth of that conclusion."[8] She later "excuses" the potential juror for "hidden biases."

Performing artists and a musician are also eliminated. When Breitbart asks another potential juror who states her profession as "actress-comedian" if she is familiar with the concepts of parody and satire, Berkman immediately tells him that his time is up. This is no doubt so, but I'm left feeling that a few seconds more for a yes-or-no answer might not have done too much harm to the schedule.[9] Both attorneys become wary of even mentioning parody, an issue that Kuby feels has been implicitly ruled out under the "good faith is not a defense" prong of the pretrial ruling.

From the outset, there is a sensation of latent hostility in the air, something waiting to be set on fire. One potential juror explains that she is embarrassed because she "already dislikes" me.[10] Another asserts that if any IP addresses lead back to me, she will definitely vote to convict me. During a break, a juror in the hallway is overheard saying that he doesn't understand why my shirt was untucked. When the selection process resumes, a ceramic artist explains, "I just already feel like I'm being prejudiced and this is crazy, I know, and I want to do my civic duty but I feel I'm already forming opinions and nothing has even been said so I'm just being honest." She adds, "I just get a funny-ish sense of kind of an angry attitude" from Breitbart. "I just find it confrontational, it makes me nervous. I would want my attorney to have a different kind of attitude, to speak with respect to jurors. I don't know why I feel this way but I feel very uncomfortable."[11] Breitbart (who holds a college degree in psychology) then begins to question all the remaining potential jurors: "Does anyone else feel some disrespect by counsel to any of the jurors that were being questioned?" One answers, "I think some of your questions are kind of annoying," and another adds, "I'll be frank, I've seen you for about two minutes and you're already getting on my nerves. I mean how else do you want it?"[12]

At various points, the judge makes her own preliminary feelings about the case clear to the jurors. She explains to them that it doesn't involve a "private matter," because "we're supposed to allow people, I guess peace and quiet." The "charge," she declares, "is identity theft, not quite where somebody gets your credit card number or access to your bank account, but it's in that category."[13] Later, she modifies this formula slightly and asserts that financial crime is "a very different kind of thing" from what's "going on here as identity theft."[14]

But it turns out several of the potential jurors have been victims precisely of identity theft in the way that term is normally understood. One of them is a documentary filmmaker whose award-winning work includes a film on prison conditions. When Berkman asks him if he feels he can be a fair juror despite the theft of his credit card, he answers, "There's been a lot of talk about identity theft here but it doesn't come out very clear."[15] Berkman then makes an effort to clarify what it is all about: "Well, it's not identity theft in the financial sense which many people unfortunately are victimized [sic]. So does that change your answer at all?"

After a slight pause in the silent room, he replies, "No." He is rapidly eliminated from the pool. Meanwhile, Bandler seeks to clarify things further and explains that I have been charged with "impersonating some people and harassing some people."[16] His stance throughout the trial will be to casually presuppose, as if it were a fact that everyone understands, that "you can't use other people's names," regardless of whether any kind of tangible harm is intended.

The panel is chosen. My fate is to be decided by seven women and five men (apart from Berkman and Bandler). The women, listed by their professions, are as follows:

- a branch manager at a bank
- an employee in HIV/AIDS "surveillance" for the health department
- a marketing director at Macy's
- the director of a Model UN high school program (the court transcript inaccurately states "modeling program")
- an events marketer for Ralph Lauren
- an employee in "client services for an investment management firm"
- an account supervisor in a pharmaceutical advertising firm

And the men are as follows:

- an insurance representative
- a residential real estate broker
- a former retail manager (currently unemployed)
- a budget director at the Children's Aid Society
- an assistant administrator at Queens College

There are also four alternate jurors, whose job will be to replace any of the actual jurors who might need to be dismissed for any reason once the trial begins. They are a woman (at the time unemployed) who has worked in an office dealing with women's health and HIV prevention, and three men: an advertising specialist whose job is to "determine where advertisers should place their ads," an independently wealthy former investment banker, and a retiree who once worked at the UN and taught electrical engineering at Columbia University.

By virtue of separate enunciations made by the judge and the prosecutor, at this point, the carefully chosen panel understands that there is a "different" kind of identity theft, in which the harm caused is not financial but rather any selection (or combination of selections) from an amorphous infinity of undefined "benefits," "gains," or "advantages." So far, there has been no divergence from the general principles made clear in Berkman's pretrial order, where she explained that just as one does not have to prove what harm someone intends to cause inside a home that he burglarizes, in my case, there is no need to show what harm or benefit I intended to cause or gain by my "theft" of names.[17] Enough knowledge, at this point, has already been inculcated to give jurors the impression that sending a series of pseudonymous emails designed to provoke controversy and debate is itself without doubt a crime that offends the "peace and quiet" of its victims. It is against the background of this impression that the jury will watch the trial take place.

In addressing the jurors, Berkman has not mentioned that the case they are going to decide might be the first of its kind in an American criminal court. It would not, of course, be reasonable to expect her to mention that fact. Nor should she be expected to mention (even though this was pointed out to her in my pretrial motion to dismiss the charges) that a California State Senate committee, in a report on legislation aimed at criminalizing electronic impersonations, warned that the proposed statute would raise "First Amendment" concerns. The California committee decided that the statute should "not include an element that the defendant intended to obtain a *benefit*," because "arguably, an impersonation that caused no harm but that created some sort of benefit or sense of satisfaction to the impersonator does not involve criminal conduct."[18] Again, she should not be expected to mention that the Texas legislature eschewed using the term "benefit" in a similar statute enacted six months before the trial; or that, like the California lawmakers, the ones in Texas included a provision requiring that the defendant intended readers of the communication to "reasonably believe" that it was authored by the impersonated individual. There is also no need for Berkman to point out that dozens upon dozens of groups and individuals, from the Yes Men, to many a Democratic or Republican propagandist, to all sorts of recalcitrant subjects whose names are unknown—for such activities are almost always engaged in anonymously, to protect their authors from retaliation—have impersonated people on the internet and elsewhere for purposes of social criticism or to make a "political" point. The jurors will not be aware that I have been singled out for prosecution; it is implied almost as a given that texts such as my "Larry Schiffman" emails are to be considered a crime as long as there was some intended "benefit," and that my actions, if verified, must therefore be construed as criminal.

"And So the Defendant's Illegal Scheme Was Hatched …"

The following morning, his appearance marked by a casual hint of swagger, assistant district attorney John Bandler enters the hushed chamber, shuffles his papers, and begins his opening statement. This is, he explains, a "simple case" of impersonation, harassment, and identity theft—technical details that he spices up with assertions that go to the heart of the matter. While "pretending to be someone else," I made "false accusations" and "false complaints."[19] From the trial's start, this line of attack raises the specter of criminal libel inscribed, as it were, within the "pretending to be someone else" identity theft charges. Bandler adds that my emails generated an "inquiry and a reaction" at New York University based on "false premises."[20] His discourse is tailored to appeal to the jury's emotions and to their sense of belonging to the New York social system, a strategy he will make use of throughout the trial.

After all, "neither good faith nor truth" is a defense. The implied theme is that the academic "victims" of my misdeeds enjoy a prestige they have a right to maintain unsullied. The presumed crimes almost speak for themselves—the jurors would not want emails going out in *their* names.

A touch of anti-intellectualism is unmistakably part of the mix: my belief in the merits of controversy and debate is treated as a rank criminal motive. This idea was in fact already discernible in the terms employed in the district attorney's press release issued on the day of my arrest, and it will continue to inform the prosecution's presentation of the case long after the trial is over, from one appellate court to another. An array of disinformation regarding the scrolls controversy, some of it apparently based on communications with Schiffman, will help undermine my credibility and endow my defense with an air of irrelevant whining: any criticism of the prosecution's strategy must be motivated by childish spite for "perceived adversaries."

One theme consistently raised will be that the Jerusalem-libraries theory of scroll origins is unpopular, or unaccepted by the majority. Any effort to respond to such innuendos will make it look like I simply lack the required remorse. If I suggest that the prosecution is actually engaged in the same assault on freedom of debate as the Qumranologists, this must mean I have no regard for academic propriety. Indeed, my speech had no academic value: I "twisted language," "stirred up controversy," moved to "derail careers," "targeted" my victims, "schemed," "plotted," "promoted" the unpopular theory, "maligned" museum exhibits, "tricked" people into investigating plagiarism, and used words like "demolish," or "it's time to finish him off now [viz., in the discussion forum]," or "they will realize they have a devoted adversary who is out to get them" in my casual, private correspondence—words that in their full hyperbolic thrust reveal a manifestly criminal intent directed at the particular victims involved.[21] And on top of that, I tried to conceal evidence of my crimes—what else is a pseudonym, if not an attempt to cover one's tracks?

Standing—with solemn dignity—in front of the jury on the first day of the trial, Bandler, sporting a gray business suit that perfectly accords with his stylish crew cut, asserts that I made a "false allegation" of plagiarism that "smeared" Schiffman, a "lead [*sic*] scholar," and that I engaged in a scheme to "influence the Jewish Museum" because of a "disagreement" that was "mostly of [my] own mind."[22] He expresses contempt for the controversy that I purportedly fabricated, and reduces my online discussions of scientific standards, due credit, and open debate to a personal whim. He explains that "the defendant does not like the fact that many in the academic world do not agree with his father or they don't acknowledge his father's theory properly, or perhaps he feels they misstate his father's theory or they don't give his father the credit his father deserves for developing that theory." Misguided anger over a little "disagreement" among scholars—personal resentment based on an inflated view of my father's scholarly importance—was, the prosecutor explains, my "motive" for "hatching" an illegal "scheme."

    David Breitbart then rises to his feet and gives a short statement, asking the jury for patience and suggesting that I'm best seen as a "whistleblower."[23] He seems surprised, when he sits back down, that the judge even let him say that much in my defense. But it is not clear how the jury will react to the approach taken. Synonyms for the word "whistleblower" include "snitch," "traitor," "fink," and "informer." In an article entitled "Why We Love to Hate Whistleblowers," clinical social worker Diane Barth explains that people who report wrongdoing often find themselves "attacked and vilified" because they "make us aware of a reality … that we don't want to know about." Assaulting whistleblowers' legitimacy, she adds, makes us feel "like we are protecting our own credibility." Especially when accusations focus on a group we deeply love or respect (examples include colleges and religious organizations), we prefer to "blame the person who is accusing" the group in question; "rather than try to find out the truth, we attack the person who is trying to help us see that truth."[24]

    And this is why the First Amendment matters: its fundamental purpose is to protect those who put themselves on the line.[25] A jury, along with the government, may seek to punish such people; the First Amendment is designed to invalidate that entire process. In some contexts, such as when vital state secrets are revealed, certain laws override this basic principle. This much I had learned in law school. But nothing, until now, had led me to imagine that the embarrassing practices of an academic clique could have the special legal status of privileged governmental information.

"I Have Written 139 Scholarly Articles"

Following the opening statements, there is a tension in the courtroom—for the first witness, Lawrence Schiffman, is apparently waiting somewhere in the building to give his testimony (several remarks exchanged between Bandler and Berkman make it clear that the prosecution has had to make special arrangements to accommodate the department chairman's busy schedule). When he finally makes his entrance and is led to the stand, a hush falls on the gathered public, which includes a group of uniformed female students (navy skirts down to the calves, gray button-down shirts) apparently bused in from a Brooklyn yeshiva. Pallid and thin, with a pointed gray beard, Schiffman strikes me as looking ten years older than his age, and I wonder if his health has declined. But with his black Garment District suit and his stern demeanor, he quickly establishes a professorial and highly charismatic presence: the courtroom becomes a classroom, even an auditorium, where he can assert his overwhelming prestige. Bandler's immediate goal is precisely to exploit the social and cultural status of his witness: he begins by establishing Schiffman's expertise through a series of questions about his career—and about the Dead Sea Scrolls.

Soon, photographs of dozens of blogs and emails begin to pop up on a giant screen to the side of the jury, and Bandler moves back into the crucial theme of his opening statement by eliciting statements about my "false accusations."[26] This line of questioning—which will be repeated with several other witnesses as well—serves as a mechanism for introducing all the criminalized blogs and emails into evidence, with Schiffman briefly summarizing the contents of each item, always making it clear that he is an innocent victim. "Again he calls me a rabbi," he observes, glancing at one of the items, "which I am not." (Schiffman has apparently forgotten that multiple sources, including the *New York Times*, had described him precisely as a rabbi before I wrote the item in question, with no hint of a correction ever appearing in any of those sources.) When asked by Bandler if there is any "truth" to Avi Katzman's allegations, he answers, "Yes," but then immediately adds, "I do not see that he charged me with impropriety."[27] Asked whether he has any "knowledge that it was the defendant that did this to you," Schiffman answers, "No, absolutely not." Asked to verify that he is not "directly accusing the defendant," he again answers, "No."[28]

> Schiffman's suit would seem to have been purchased in the same Manhattan Garment District shop where my father once took me during my law school years. Upon recognizing my father, the owner of the shop had informed us that a certain scholar who "did not see eye to eye" with my father, as he indicated with humor, was one of his regular clients. He had then mentioned Schiffman by name, leaving us both slightly bemused.

After a lunch break, Breitbart begins his cross-examination. He speaks with the gruff, combative tone that had contributed to making him famous—a strategy in itself not without risk, for the jury could take it as a sign of disrespect and might not like seeing a professor addressed in such a manner (especially one who has been falsely accused of being a rabbi). Schiffman seems a bit out of his element for a few minutes, and then he begins to hem and haw, modifying his earlier testimony with special explanations and revealing an extraordinary skill at equivocating about certain facts. When he is asked to explain his correspondence with Bandler in which he provided him with my address in Greenwich Village, he answers that the information was provided to him by Robert Cargill—but that he "doubted it could be true because I didn't know that anybody would do such a thing to me and I had not had any negative or other type personal experiences with Professor Golb."[29] (Throughout his testimony, Schiffman and I will avoid any eye contact.)

Breitbart quickly has to confront an even more serious problem. According to the judge, anything having to do with the Dead Sea Scrolls controversy is merely irrelevant "background." Bandler has been allowed to elicit whatever claims he wishes to make about this "background," but when Breitbart tries to challenge and controvert what has been elicited, Berkman rapidly makes it clear that inappropriately detailed cross-examination will not be permitted.[30] Her pretrial ruling that "neither good faith nor truth is a defense" seems to apply only to me (as its very terms indicate) and to my efforts to have certain issues fleshed out during the proceedings. As a result, Bandler's recurrent allusions to my "smears" and "false accusations" become a fundamental part of the record, to which no real response is permitted. At one point, Berkman informs Breitbart in what strikes me (no doubt unjustly) as a very angry tone that Schiffman is "not on trial for plagiarism."[31] Documents pointing to the textual basis of the plagiarism charges will not be admitted into evidence.

And yet it is blatantly obvious, as I follow what's unfolding in front of me, that not only Schiffman himself but the other complainants as well are intent on convincing the jury that I harassed them by disseminating false and defamatory accusations about them.[32] Could Berkman possibly be unaware, after Bandler's brilliantly prepared duet performance with Schiffman, that the prosecution's aim is to communicate this belief to the jury? And assuming she *is* aware of Bandler's plan, won't she give Breitbart the full opportunity to litigate this point and to attempt to prove, to the best of his ability, that my accusations were in fact true?

That no such reciprocity is in the offing becomes increasingly clear as the cross-examination proceeds. As soon as Breitbart starts to ask Schiffman about delicate matters, he is warned to stop. Time and again the witness dances around the questions that do get asked and that often end up sounding like nothing more than stabs in the dark. Schiffman vehemently emphasizes, for example, that he received "only a very small group of texts" from the monopoly, a statement that potentially raises a host of questions. Did these texts include the famous *Acts of Torah* on which Schiffman largely based his career? How many years did he and a few others sit on these texts without publishing them? Precisely how many other scholars around the world were allowed to see them at all during that period? Doesn't the statement ("only a very *small group* of texts") perhaps conflict with other statements Schiffman has made in the past about being able to obtain "any" material

> On her own volition, even without any prompting from the prosecutor, Berkman, at least eight times, blocks Breitbart from asking Schiffman about plagiarism and the nature of his association with members of the Dead Sea Scrolls monopoly group.

he needed? None of these questions get asked: Breitbart is already walking a fine line every time he even hints at the issues that Berkman has declared irrelevant because "neither good faith nor truth is a defense."[33]

Nor, it seems, is there any point even attempting to raise any questions about Schiffman's self-touted use of academic "politics." Or about his assertion in his book that "scholars agree" the scrolls were written by a sect at Qumran. Or about any knowledge he might have of satire. A slight feeling of nausea overcomes me as Schiffman dances around one question after another, occasionally treating Breitbart like an ignorant pupil. When we run out of time, Berkman explains that there will be a break the next day, to accommodate the court's schedule as well as Schiffman's.

On Thursday morning, Breitbart doggedly resumes his cross-examination, and eventually he does succeed—almost by virtue of ignoring Berkman's repeated remonstrations—in pressing Schiffman about the 1993 article by Avi Katzman. But Schiffman, clearly agitated by the questions, manages to gain the upper hand again with a powerful display of indignation. At a culminating moment, flushed with rage, he pounds his fist on the lectern. "I have never plagiarized Norman Golb!" he shouts. And not only that; he also asserts that he has never previously *been accused* of plagiarism.[34] Schiffman's performance clearly resonates with the jury—his anger serves as a decisive rebuke to the disrespectful tone and bearing of the lawyer asking him all these questions. Under further cross-examination, the professor delivers this translation of Katzman's

Hebrew-language statement: "But you also in various articles that you published did not hesitate to adopt pieces of the theory of Golb, without admitting it or acknowledging it, and without giving him appropriate credit." But he then haughtily glosses the statement as merely "an accusation of too few footnotes to a guy," adding that "Norman Golb is footnoted in everything I've written. I have written seven books on the scrolls. I have written 139 scholarly articles. No one has ever accused me of plagiarism."[35] The distinguished department chairman backs up his "too few footnotes" interpretation of Katzman by emphasizing that "nobody reads" the New York University faculty code of conduct. And he indicates that falsely attributing the Temple-library theory to Norman Golb was merely a little "mistake."[36]

All in all, it is a powerful huff-and-puff performance, one that projects an overwhelming sense of righteous indignation at being asked foolish, uninformed questions by an ignorant man. I myself am particularly stricken by the shocking signs of an apparent disdain for intellectual culture that continually come to the surface. They give me the same strange feeling I had when the San Diego curator pontificated about not wishing to confuse people with so many different theories, or about how the scrolls were not really Jewish texts. I remind myself, as the dignified, elegantly dressed professor is excused from the witness stand, that I'm confronting a gang of Philistines; and of the suggestion, in one of Cicero's works, that the historian has two complementary duties: never to say anything false and never to refrain from saying anything true.

"Nobody reads it."

No sooner is Schiffman ushered out of the courtroom than former NYU dean Catharine Stimpson firmly walks to the podium to testify on behalf of her colleague. Stimpson is a sharp, wiry lady with short gray hair and a dignified, commanding presence: she is in full control of her wits at seventy-four years of age. She has honed her skills as an eloquent public speaker for decades. In

1991—just when controversy was raging about the Dead Sea Scrolls monopoly—she argued in a televised debate that there was no real threat to academic freedom in the United States. As she put it, "The American campus has seen a few bad things," but "is there a Galileo in a cell? Show me the prison."[37] Whether any issue of academic freedom is implicated by Lawrence Schiffman's role in the "politics" of the Dead Sea Scrolls is a question that does not seem to have occurred to her during her years of service as a dean at NYU. She testifies that being a dean was "a wonderful job," and that her responsibilities included "making sure the students are taught by the best possible professors, making sure they learn things that are true and on the cutting edge of thought," and making sure "that all policies and procedures are taken care of."

A professor of law and literature known for her acceptance of "postmodern theory about the death of the author and the overwhelming power of discourse,"[38] Stimpson concedes that she knew there was something "wrong" when she read the "Larry Schiffman" Gmail she received, because it clearly had not been written by Schiffman. She explains that the "details" of the plagiarism allegations "were very technical," that Schiffman "made it clear" to her that he was innocent, and that she did not seek any outside opinion on the matter; but she acknowledges that the words used by Avi Katzman in his interview with Schiffman constituted an accusation of plagiarism. She gives me a dirty look as she exits the courtroom, her arrogant posture conveying all her disdain.

Nine years later, I will recall Stimpson's testimony when I come across her name toward the top of a list of fifty-two people in academia—mainly teachers of literary theory (twelve of them teaching at NYU)—who have signed a "confidential" letter in defense of a colleague accused of sexual harassment.[39] The colleague is Avital Ronell, a member (and former chairperson) of NYU's German department who, in a heavily publicized case, has been charged with drastically inappropriate and abusive conduct toward a much younger male graduate student. The defense offered in the confidential letter is along the lines of "We all think highly of our esteemed colleague Avital Ronell, who after all has an international reputation, a reputation now under malicious attack." After an internal investigation, Ronell will be found guilty by the university and punished with a year's leave from her teaching duties.

Eventually, it becomes clear that the letter was composed by probably the most well-known theorist on the list, Judith Butler, whom University of Chicago philosopher Martha Nussbaum has, as it happens, christened the "professor of parody."[40] Alongside the letter, several of its signatories make public statements suggesting that Ronell's behavior should be regarded as a kind of "campy," parodic, postmodern acting out that cannot be understood by those uninitiated into postmodern theory and practice:[41] an explanation unmistakably harmonizing with Ronell's own view of her teaching method as a "pedagogy of ... syntactical disturbance," with her stated desire to "make a point of scandalizing students," and so forth.[42]

When I read about this developing academic scandal in the *New York Times*, the *Chronicle of Higher Education*, and elsewhere, I cannot help but be struck by an apparent contradiction in Dean Stimpson's quite clear positions regarding my prosecution and the accusations leveled at Ronell. On the one hand, there is the explicit support offered by Stimpson to Ronell, a colleague who has manifestly abused her power and whose conduct is belittled and explained away as mere parody that has been taken far too seriously. On the other hand, there is the at least implicit support offered by Stimpson to prosecutors engaged in criminalizing very *real* parodies dealing with the conduct of Lawrence Schiffman, another of her colleagues.

But then it becomes clear to me that the apparent inconsistency is in fact none whatsoever, and that Stimpson's ostensibly differing responses in a sense encapsulate the key motivations that led to my prosecution. Simply stated, the thread tying the responses together is a fundamental interest (apparently transcending any concern with either truth or ethics) in maintaining institutional power—and in protecting the collegial networks to which Stimpson is professionally attached. The networks at stake, of course, include the internal administrative power structure of NYU. That university has, after all, given Schiffman its full backing as one of its own, and has done so quite likely in collaboration with district attorney Cyrus Vance Jr. and his staff.

> Dean Stimpson represents the power structure that protects its own. She is also an intellectually alert professional who would likely never read a fake, pompously "confessional" letter as anything *but* parody.

One Thousand Dollars; a Puzzled Philosopher

As the day gets longer, it becomes increasingly clear that the judge's rulings are preventing us from adequately cross-examining the witnesses. The situation she has put us in also forces us to hold back, out of fear that the answer to one or another question might make matters worse. This caution seems to be allowing the witnesses to demonstrate their dignity, superiority, and highly specialized expertise, thereby garnering sympathy and adding to the general climate of disdain for those who dare to cast doubt on anything being said by the distinguished, confident, knowledgeable members of the academy who have come to offer their important testimony. I decide to assign a bit more of the questioning to Kuby, wondering whether the infusion of his own particular style into the proceedings might shake things up a bit.

Meanwhile, in the midst of the gradual poisoning of the trial atmosphere with the incessant focus on my "false accusations," there is a small change of pace when the judge informs the prosecution that she is having difficulty understanding the object of the "scheme to defraud" in which I engaged.[43] Apparently, after explaining to the jury at the outset that this case involves "the other kind" of identity theft, she has given some further thought to the matter and come to the realization that under New York law, a "scheme to defraud" requires that the defendant defraud one or more people of the minimal sum of $1,000.

Since my attorneys raised the issue at length in legal memorandums submitted a year earlier, Bandler himself is already aware of this difficulty. In order to fit the criminalization of the fake "Larry Schiffman confession" into known legal precedent, he offers a "financial fraud" argument. While Bandler did not present the argument to the grand jury that approved the indictment, he now runs it by the judge and obtains her approval as well—despite her own acknowledged difficulty in understanding it.[44] This is the argument that in sending emails to NYU faculty members, I must have intended to induce the Jewish Museum to cancel a lecture that Schiffman was scheduled to give there, and to get Norman Golb invited instead. Since Schiffman was paid $650 to give his talk, and since one could assume that travel and hotel expenses were to be involved for Golb, by somehow adding these things up, Bandler argues that I actually intended to defraud Schiffman and the Jewish Museum of at least $1,000.

If this was my intent, then why, in email correspondence with my family, did I suggest that my father counter Schiffman's lecture by giving one of his own "free of charge"? I never suggested that anyone's lecture should be canceled; what I did argue was that scholars opposed to the sectarian theory should *also* be invited. Yet the jury, during Schiffman's testimony, has been introduced to a pseudonymous blog of mine from September 25, 2008, in which I announced Schiffman's upcoming lecture and asked whether the Jewish Museum was aware of allegations that the scheduled lecturer was a plagiarist. On the other hand, there is no message in which I state, for example, "I have attributed a fake confession to the professor; let us hope this convinces the Jewish Museum to drop his lecture." From the evidence revealed in the chain of emails flashing unreadably across the giant screen, I might simply have hoped that Schiffman's lecture would itself help draw further attention to his role in the ongoing saga of the Dead Sea Scrolls controversy.

No worries. A lack of direct evidence is never an *absolute* bar to determining that an intent to injure, defraud, or otherwise engage in subversive or criminal activity existed in a defendant's mind at the time of a crime. On a practical level, the prosecution can deal with these little problems by simply not drawing too much attention to the pertinent passages in my blogs and emails. The complicated ethical issues raised in this material have in any case already been declared irrelevant, a fact obviating much of the risk that the jurors might focus on it during their rapid deliberation.

Potentially more damaging to Bandler's "thousand dollars" premise is the testimony of Susan Braunstein, curator of the Jewish Museum scrolls exhibit, who takes the stand after Stimpson. In response to Bandler's question, she testifies that she has met me before, but when he asks her to point me out in the room, she suddenly seems to poke fun at him—and in fact at the entire trial—by waving her finger at me with an absurd, theatrical exaggeration. At the moment of her gesture, Braunstein and I rapidly exchange a grin of recognition, and I directly sense her conveying one simple message: she knows damn well I don't belong in this place. There is no way the curator's comic finger-pointing could go unnoticed by Ron Kuby, who is sitting right next to me. As soon as Bandler is done eliciting a number of facts from her about Schiffman's lecture at the museum—apparently part of his strategic effort to highlight the status, dignity, and victimhood of my chief accuser—Kuby steps up to do the cross-examining, and I quickly realize that he is treating her as a friendly witness.

Braunstein's self-assurance now quickly makes itself felt and conveys a strong impression that she is to be trusted to tell things straight. Well dressed, with meticulously coifed dark brown hair, she seems alert, as if ready to pounce on something—almost as if she has been planning and hoping for this moment—and she promptly explains that complaints about upcoming lectures are frequently received from the public; that I never contacted her about Schiffman or any other matter during the course of the exhibit; that I never even met her until the exhibit was over, several months after Schiffman gave his talk; and that when I did meet her, at a lecture that *she* gave, we simply discussed the content of the exhibit in an utterly polite manner.[45] She also testifies (although all such information would appear to be "irrelevant" pursuant to Berkman's pretrial ruling) that there are indeed "two basic theories" of scroll origins, the sectarian theory and that of Norman Golb, Yitzhak Magen, and others of the opposing school—and that the Jewish Museum scrolls exhibit, for the first time in history, broke with the standard approach by making this fact known to the exhibit's visitors rather than suppressing it.[46]

These statements strike me, sitting in the grim, gray, and slightly stale atmosphere of the courtroom, as immensely helpful to my case—and, in the broader context of the scrolls, as nothing short of sensational—but their impact quickly seems to be drowned out by additional exchanges that are more difficult to follow. In response to a number of questions, for example, Braunstein explains at some length that Daniel Friedenberg, an elderly art collector and curator emeritus at the museum who was a friend of my family, *had lunch* with her before the exhibit opened, and that, although Friedenberg never suggested that the museum should drop Schiffman from its roster, he actually urged her to invite Professor Golb to participate in the museum's lecture series—even offering to fund the lecture and the travel expenses involved himself.[47] (Friedenberg, who was harassed by members of Bandler's team after my arrest and refused to cooperate with them, would pass away while my case was being litigated in the appellate courts.) She also testifies that before inviting Schiffman to lecture, she was herself aware he had been accused of plagiarism by Norman Golb in his 1995 book, *Who Wrote the Dead Sea Scrolls?*[48]

Kuby holds back from asking about the politics at the museum that may have led to this situation, or whether Braunstein has any regrets about the ethical conundrums they might raise. When he wraps up his questions, he seems to feel that he has made progress by establishing quite simply that nothing I did was designed to have any effect on Schiffman's lecture. But the jury, by now, seems to have grown numb to the details. Will Braunstein's testimony be remembered at all? And if so, will it be taken seriously, or will it ultimately merely contribute to a muddled impression that a linkage has been established—*beyond any reasonable doubt*—between my "Gmail confessions" and a criminal intent to get Schiffman's lecture canceled?

The next day, Friday—we are now four days into the trial—a second NYU dean, philosopher Richard Foley, takes the stand on Lawrence Schiffman's behalf. Solemn yet with a polite demeanor, as if he is trying to appear as relaxed as possible, the distinguished professor is a few years younger than Catharine Stimpson. He has a full head of hair and a few days' growth of beard. He wears one of the best suits I will see during the trial, but he seems to squirm a tiny bit behind his elegant, professional veneer. He asserts that Schiffman has a "reputation for honesty."[49] Breitbart, during cross-examination, then starts to ask him about the plagiarism allegations, but as soon as this topic is raised, Foley actually helps to prevent any unwanted discussion of such matters, for he claims that he cannot remember the events he's being asked about—or what was involved in the plagiarism allegations. Yet he does remember discussing the matter with Schiffman.

Because of Foley's advancing age and many academic responsibilities, his claim of selective memory loss seems almost credible. At the same time, he is perhaps unaware that, under the view of the case set forth in the judge's pretrial ruling, the truth as to whether or not Schiffman committed plagiarism is simply an irrelevant detour in the trial proceedings. Nevertheless, Breitbart somehow manages to elicit some answers—especially when I write down two questions that I want him to ask the witness and slip them to him on a piece of paper. In response to these questions, Foley ends up admitting not only that the words Avi Katzman used in his article do constitute an accusation of plagiarism but that it would "not be appropriate" for a professor to falsely deny, in a written statement submitted to NYU officials, that he had ever been subjected to such an accusation.[50]

Foley appears genuinely disquieted, almost a bit broken, when, after "refreshing" his memory by reading the relevant paragraph in NYU's faculty code of conduct, he makes this admission. For all his reluctance to recall the exact events that occurred two years before his testimony, he must realize that a somewhat unflattering picture of what happened after I posted the NowPublic article on Schiffman ("Did NYU Department Chairman Pilfer from Chicago Historian's Work?") and sent the email "confessions" is now beginning to emerge.

> *"No, that would not be appropriate."*

It turns out, in fact, that the article, along with the "Larry Schiffman confessions," did produce an effect, but not the one I had anticipated. The two faculty deans, Foley and Stimpson, possibly pursuant to instructions from the provost, chatted with Schiffman a few times on the phone. Following these conversations, they decided not to pursue the matter, both because of Schiffman's "reputation for honesty" and because the source of the allegations lacked "credibility" by virtue of his use of impersonation as a technique for dissemination of the emails.[51] Despite this decision, toward the end of August 2008, Schiffman drafted an eleven-page "response to Internet accusations," which is to say to the allegations of uncredited use of Norman Golb's research originally leveled by Avi Katzman, backed up by Golb himself in his 1995 book, and then reasserted in my own NowPublic article and email "confessions."

After filing his criminal complaint, Schiffman then delivered the document to John Bandler, in response to an inquiry from Bandler as to whether he had answered the "plagiarism allegations." Following my arrest, Schiffman would declare to the press that he had been obliged to write a "response" to those "allegations," so I knew there was some sort of text in which he had sought to justify his scholarship. I was eager to see that text; but Bandler would hold on to it for two years and then hand it over to my lawyers, buried in a mass of other "evidence," a few days before the trial. At the time, New York law (unlike that in most American states) allowed prosecutors to withhold whatever they had until the eve of trial, the rationale being that early release of evidence would give gangsters an opportunity, for example, to threaten or eliminate a witness once they knew what they were confronting. In my case, it must have been understood that a favorable result might become more difficult to obtain should Schiffman's response fall into my father's hands and become the subject of open academic debate.

Indeed, once I have access to the response, I promptly forward it to my father.

Possibly unaware of the rule requiring that evidence eventually be handed over, Schiffman, when he sent the document to Bandler back in 2008, may have been under the impression that the matter would remain confidential. Looking extremely worried on the witness stand, Richard Foley denies that Schiffman was required to prepare any written response at all to the plagiarism allegations. In fact, Foley denies remembering that he ever *saw* the response. But the "confidential letter," having been introduced as evidence at a criminal trial, is now part of the historical record. Bandler will effectively use it to argue that I made "false accusations," and in the end, the jury will have no reason to ponder the puzzling statements with which Schiffman's effort is laced, an examination of such details having been excluded as irrelevant by the judge.

As Foley leaves the courtroom, I'm dimly aware that Schiffman's confidential letter might have other consequences after the trial is over. But it's not over yet. In fact, it's just getting started.

> Schiffman's "response," at the top of its first page, features a special warning that it is "confidential" and not to be shown to anyone other than the parties to whom it is "addressed." But the text will become a public document when introduced at my trial.

6
OBJECTION? SUSTAINED

The day is Monday, September 20, 2010, and Bandler is looking particularly solemn. In the morning, several forensic analysts testify about the technicalities of computer logging systems and how they confirmed that I was the one who sent the criminal parodies. When they are done, Patrick McKenna, the arresting officer who signed the search warrant affidavit, takes the stand. He is tall, with a blue suit and shirt, a beet-red face, and short gray hair that barely covers his otherwise bald head. He has a calm, cautious aura about him, and he looks older and somehow weaker than he did when he stood over my bed pointing his gun at me and explaining that "this is about the Dead Sea Scrolls." It quickly becomes clear that the point of the testimony is to introduce my videotaped interrogation into evidence and have the jury watch it. I sit aghast as the tape begins to play, but after ten minutes or so have gone by, Breitbart leans over with an intrigued expression on his faces and says, "You know, this really isn't that bad." Kuby vigorously nods his assent. Do they think that some of the reality of Schiffman's role and actions might be starting to seep through to the jury? When the tape is over, we break for lunch.

When we get back, McKenna resumes his spot at the podium, and Breitbart starts asking him about how he got assigned to investigate me and what steps he took once he was on the job. Waving a document that was prepared by McKenna himself while he was investigating me, Breitbart asks him if he did "any or all" of the things written down on it. "Yes," McKenna answers, and then Breitbart, his voice becoming just a bit louder, asks, "What did you do, sir?" At this point, Bandler calls out, "Objection," and Berkman immediately rules: "Sustained." Momentarily taken aback, Breitbart asks the judge, "I may not ask him what he did?" She promptly answers, "I don't see any relevance."

Persevering despite this initial setback, Breitbart tries to ask some questions of a more specific nature about the manner in which the "investigation" was conducted, but when Berkman finds these questions objectionable, she starts interrupting him, leading him to state, "I object to the way Your Honor is treating counsel by not allowing me to ask a question and jumping in … to take away any impact." After several additional interruptions from Berkman, Bandler visibly gets the hang of what's going on and starts to lob one objection after another. At one point, this exchange occurs:

Bandler: I still don't see the relevance of all of this, Your Honor.
Breitbart: I'll be happy to explain it to you, Your Honor.
Berkman: Okay.
Breitbart: This was a targeted investigation where Raphael Golb was named by Professor Schiffman and the only one they focused on, off a set of allegations, was Raphael Golb.
Berkman: That was not the question you asked, sir.
Breitbart: Well, that's what I'm trying to prove, but I'm having a little trouble because of the things that are going on.
Berkman: Whatever that means.
Breitbart: You don't want me to explain that one, Judge.

The attempt to conduct a cross-examination then resumes. Despite being repeatedly hindered by objections from the prosecutor and interruptions from the judge, Breitbart gradually gets around to the main topic his questions have been building up to: the search warrant affidavit signed by McKenna and approved by Berkman on the eve of my arrest.

Breitbart: There are many facts in this affidavit about the Dead Sea Scrolls, is that correct, sir?
McKenna: That's correct.
Breitbart: Do you know anything about the Dead Sea Scrolls?
Bandler: Objection.
Berkman: I presume that's because the affidavit is on information and belief, Mr. Bandler. [Is that] the basis of your objection?
Bandler: Does he know anything about the Dead Sea Scrolls?

Berkman: I don't know what the question means either, that is true. [To McKenna:] You're not personally a Dead Sea Scrolls scholar, I take it?

McKenna: I am not, Your Honor, no.

Breitbart: May I have the last question read back?

Berkman: I don't see any purpose of that.

Breitbart: Of the reading back or of the question?

Berkman: Of the reading back.

Breitbart [to McKenna]: I didn't ask you whether or not you are a Dead Sea Scrolls scholar; I asked you whether you knew anything at all about the Dead Sea Scrolls. Do you, sir?

McKenna: Yes.

Breitbart: What do you know about the Dead Sea Scrolls?

Bandler: Objection.

Berkman: Sustained.

Breitbart: Doesn't this affidavit … purport to indicate that you know a great deal about the Dead Sea Scrolls?

Bandler: Objection, misstating it.

Berkman: Sustained.

Breitbart: Did you not swear to the authorizing judge that you knew a great deal about the Dead Sea Scrolls?

Bandler: Objection, it misstates it.

Berkman: Sustained.

Breitbart: Would it be fair to say that you know nothing about the Dead Sea Scrolls?

Bandler: Objection, asked and answered.

Berkman: Sustained.

Breitbart: There came a time that you said here under oath that you read this affidavit and you know that it's true, is that right?

McKenna: Yes.

Breitbart: Do you know if it's true?

After further objections, Breitbart resumes:

Breitbart: Is that the affidavit that you signed and swore to—I think it was on March 2nd or 3rd of 2009?

McKenna: Yes, it looks like, yes.

Breitbart: What were you swearing to?
Bandler: Objection.
Berkman: Sustained.
Breitbart: Were you swearing to the truth of that affidavit that you knew was going to be submitted to a judge?
McKenna: Yes.
Breitbart: Did you swear to that in front of a judge of this court?
McKenna: Yes.
Breitbart: Now, when you were swearing to the truth of that affidavit, was it the truth? Don't look at him. [Bandler is the person McKenna is looking at, apparently hoping for assistance.]
McKenna: No, I'm looking at him to look at this.
Breitbart: Please look at it, take your time, look at it carefully.
McKenna: Can I ask you what would you like to know about what is the truth?
Breitbart: Well, first of all, you in that affidavit swear that Lawrence Schiffman is not a plagiarist; is that correct?
Bandler: Objection.
Berkman: Sustained.

Apparently Berkman now decides that this has gone far enough, for she suddenly intervenes and takes over the questioning herself:

Berkman: Sir, there is a whole bunch of stuff in that affidavit about the Dead Sea Scrolls, right?

> Berkman in effect prevents Breitbart from eliciting any "objectionable" testimony from McKenna. Yet this is Breitbart's best moment in the trial. For a moment, his own silencing by the judge almost appears to mimic the suppression of the "dissenting" theory of scroll origins by the DSS monopolists and exhibitors.

McKenna: Yes.
Berkman: And did you swear to the truth of that information about the Dead Sea Scrolls?
McKenna: Yes, I did.
Berkman: But you really are not a Dead Sea Scrolls expert?
McKenna: That is correct.
Berkman: Can we move on, please?

Either ignoring or, perhaps, freely interpreting the judge's instruction, Breitbart somewhat brazenly continues on with the same perilous theme, asking the witness "what information" he had that allowed him to "swear to the truth with regard to the Dead Sea Scrolls" when he signed the affidavit. McKenna explains that he did his scrolls research on "some Google pages." When Breitbart tries to elicit more precise information, further objections erupt.

Breitbart then attempts to ask some questions about what sort of financial-crimes evidence (a category referred to in the search warrant affidavit) McKenna was looking for at my apartment—an "objection" from Bandler, "sustained" by Berkman—but eventually circles back to the value of the internet as a forum of knowledge, asking whether McKenna indicated in the affidavit that "Raphael Golb modified a Wikipedia page." To which McKenna answers, "Yes, I did." Breitbart then asks him, "When you swore to that, did you know that anybody at any time has the authority to modify a Wikipedia page?" Apparently caught off guard by this proposition, the police officer answers, "I did not"—words that may serve to shed some light on the mindset of those who were charged with mounting a case against me. Breitbart then again focuses in on Schiffman, which leads to this exchange:

Breitbart: During the course of your investigation, did you read any of the blogs or writings … which Mr. Golb is alleged to have created?
McKenna: I don't recall yes or no.
Breitbart: You don't recall if you read anything?
McKenna: I don't recall.
Breitbart: Did there come a time when you read something that indicated that Dr. Schiffman was a plagiarist?
McKenna: No.
Breitbart: Do you know what a plagiarist is?
McKenna: Yes.
Breitbart: What is a plagiarist?
Bandler: Objection.
McKenna: A plagiarist—

Berkman: Sustained. Don't answer the question.

Breitbart: Well, did there come a time where you were asked to swear through an affidavit that Dr. Schiffman—that the allegations against him of plagiarism are false?

Bandler: Objection.

Berkman: Sustained.

Breitbart: Did you do any reading with regard to Dr. Schiffman and what he wrote?

Bandler: Objection.

Berkman: Sustained.

Breitbart: Do you know anything about Dr. Schiffman's work?

Bandler: Objection.

Berkman: Sustained.

Breitbart: Do you know who Norman Golb is?

Bandler: Objection.

Berkman: Sustained.

Breitbart: Did you read and compare the work of Norman Golb to what Schiffman had done ten years later?

Bandler: Objection.

Berkman: Sustained.

Breitbart: Did there come a time when you learned that Dr. Schiffman actually did plagiarize Norman Golb?

Bandler: Objection.

Berkman: Sustained.

Breitbart: Did you read any of the blogs containing this allegation?

Bandler: Objection.

Berkman: Sustained.

Breitbart: Did you indicate under oath when you swore to this that there are examples of plagiarism?

Bandler: Objection.

Berkman: Sustained.

Breitbart: Is this with regard to form or substance, Your Honor? I want to get it right so that I can get an answer.

Berkman: Substance.

Breitbart: Substance?

Berkman: Yes, sir.

Breitbart: So you don't think it's appropriate to ask these questions?
Berkman: That's why I sustained the objection, because I think there is a substantive issue.
Breitbart [to McKenna]: Did you read any of the material that you swore was correct in the affidavit?
Bandler: Objection.
Berkman: Sustained.
Breitbart: Well, how did you swear to this affidavit as being correct if you didn't read anything in it?
Bandler: Objection.
Berkman: Sustained.
Breitbart: Did you read anything about which you swore?
Bandler: Objection.
Berkman: Sustained.
Breitbart: Do you know what parody is?
Bandler: Objection.
Berkman: Sustained.
Breitbart: After reading anything, sir, either in the investigation or in the affidavit in support of the warrant, did you determine that Larry Schiffman didn't write what he was accused of writing?
Bandler: Objection.
Berkman: Sustained.
Breitbart: Did you read anything that made you laugh?
Bandler: Objection.
Berkman: Sustained.
Breitbart: Did Larry Schiffman, is Larry Schiffman reputed to have confessed to his own plagiarism?
Bandler: Objection.
Berkman: Sustained.

And so on.[1] Abraham Heschel once remarked that asking questions, rather than imagining one has the answers, is what brings man closer to God. When Breitbart is done asking the officer an entire series of questions that are not supposed to be asked, occasionally expressing his own wry sense of humor in the process, he calmly returns to the defendant's table, where I'm sitting with

Kuby. There seems to be a feeling in the courtroom that something important just happened.

"What is a plagiarist?"

Berkman then excuses the jurors. As soon as they file out, she explains, the severity of her tone rising almost to a harsh pitch, that McKenna's apparent perjury in signing the affidavit would not have prevented her from granting the warrant. Later, during Breitbart's summation at the end of the trial, Berkman will interrupt him again to assert, this time with the jurors present and respectfully listening to her, that there is no proof that the officer was *aware* that the affidavit might contain an untruthful statement. And indeed, how could there be such proof, given that Breitbart was blocked, nearly in toto, from eliciting answers to any of the questions that he had prepared for McKenna? In short, Berkman will use her power as trial judge to uphold the validity, and the integrity, of the search warrant that she herself signed around a year and a half before the trial: a possible reminder, for civil rights lawyers, of the type of consequences that can ensue from the neglect of the unenforceable Rule 200.11(c), requiring the "random" selection of judges in criminal trials.

Aged sixty-nine at the time of my trial, Patrick McKenna will continue serving the DA for several years; he will pass away in a Bronx hospital in November 2014, around halfway through the seven years it will take to litigate my appeal.[2]

"Please Explain to the Jury …"

The following day, Tuesday, it all gets swept away. Things now get bogged down in endlessly tedious testimony from government investigators who explain how they put all my blogs, emails, and IP addresses together. Giant charts are projected onto a screen.

Wednesday is a break, but we are back again on Thursday morning, and the tedium continues.

Then, in the afternoon, other criminal complainants start testifying. They have arrived from all over the country and are being hosted in a hotel at New York taxpayers' expense. For the charges, as the jurors will learn, are by no means limited to the harassment and impersonation of Lawrence Schiffman. I have, specifically, also been charged with twenty-one additional counts pertaining to my alleged harassment and/or impersonation of five different individuals: Stephen Goranson of Duke University, Frank Moore Cross of Harvard, Jeffrey Gibson of Chicago, Robert Cargill (fresh from his National Geographic appearance), and Jonathan Seidel, a rabbi in Oregon. Therefore, testimony must be elicited that will allow the jury to understand the full breadth of my criminal scheme to "influence a debate."

First in this line of witnesses is Rabbi Seidel—slightly naive-looking, with a graying beard and a mellow, even mildly cheery demeanor offering no clue that he is testifying in a criminal court.[3] Modulating his voice between a formal and a somewhat conversational tone, as if he were speaking from a pulpit, Seidel explains that a "rabbi is someone who listens with two ears and speaks with one mouth, which means you should listen more than you should speak." He adds that his duties include "teaching, helping people, pastoral visits, education, community organizing." The Dead Sea Scrolls are "not [his] main field," and he admits that he is "not a scrolls scholar," although he "mentioned" the scrolls in his doctoral dissertation. He asserts that he was "shocked to see" that messages regarding the scrolls controversy had been sent from a Gmail address called "Seidel dot Jonathan," although he "suspects" that "about a hundred" individuals share this name in the United States. (These messages, the prosecution has earlier explained, were illegal attempts "to stir up controversy and also draw another victim into a dispute.")[4] Seidel also has his "own Gmail address." He recalls having had a chance encounter with Norman Golb in 1988, apparently in a university lounge in Cambridge, England, and having "talked about his book on Rouen, on the Jews of France for an hour or two and maybe two seconds on the Dead Sea Scrolls."[5]

Next comes Stephen Goranson, the Duke University Libraries stacks maintenance employee who repeatedly attacked Norman Golb on the internet over a period of at least several years. I am accused of criminally harassing Goranson by sending annoying complaints to his superiors concerning his use of Duke library computers for that purpose. Furthermore, I am accused of criminally impersonating him by opening a Gmail account in his name from which no messages were ever sent.[6] (I will later testify that I used this account to store the email addresses of various academics, and named it after Goranson as a personal joke, as he had condemned my use of pseudonyms during the 2008 online controversy over the Raleigh, North Carolina, scrolls exhibit.)

Bearded, haggard, gaunt, Goranson has a fixed look in his eyes that seems to express a slight feeling of horror and indignation, and that doesn't quite fit with his quaint, highly educated accent and general aura of advanced expertise. With his giant beard and chiseled features, he almost brings to mind the character of an eccentric professor in a gothic novel. He defends his online conduct and explains that he has his computer (presumably at the library, although this is never clarified) set to inform him whenever Norman Golb is mentioned on the internet. As he answers the questions, he seems to be taking care to make his testimony as precise as possible. Here are a few extracts from the exchange:

Breitbart: Would you describe your email and blogging activity as being scholarly?
Goranson: Certainly some of it is.
Breitbart: And have you had disagreements online?
Goranson: Yes.
Breitbart: And as a result of those disagreements, have you been thrown off many websites?
Goranson: I'm off one website, one list now ...
Breitbart: And why were you removed from that?
Goranson: The person, the list owner, thought I made an ad hominem attack ...
Breitbart: Is that the only time you were removed from the list?

Goranson: There have been temporary suspensions on some other lists …

Breitbart: How many times have you been banned or suspended on the internet for things that you have written?

Goranson: I don't know.

Breitbart: Many?

Goranson: Four, five maybe, along with other people …

Breitbart: Weren't you removed three times from the Orion list before they gave up?

Goranson: It's possible. I don't remember the number …

Breitbart: Were you known for attacking Norman Golb on the internet, sir?

Goranson: I can speculate to some say that.

Breitbart: How many times did you read that you were accused of attacking Norman Golb?

Goranson: I don't know the number …

Breitbart: Under a thousand?

Goranson: Probably under a hundred.[7]

Eventually, Berkman intervenes: "I don't know where we are going with this, Mr. Breitbart … we are done with the subject."[8] Breitbart conducts the rest of his questioning as cautiously as possible, so as not to provoke further interruptions from the judge; he is careful, for example, not to inquire as to whether the pallid librarian has any ties with doctrinaire Qumranologist Eric Meyers of the Duke religion department. Instead, the point he seems to be getting at is that Goranson enjoys griping about the Dead Sea Scrolls—and, in fact, strangely, that his online attacks are a normal manifestation of intellectual culture. The only problem is that in the poisoned atmosphere of this particular trial, any such effort can backfire; sympathy can be garnered for another distinguished, bearded employee of an academic institution, and Bandler can

> Trying not to inflame the situation, Breitbart is careful not to question Goranson about the episode in which a Danish scholar suggested that a comment of Goranson's about Professor Golb struck him as antisemitic.

succeed in establishing a lust for revenge (in this instance, against Goranson) as a further motive for my "scheme of deceit and fraud." The day is drawing to a close; we are dismissed from the darkening, mostly empty courtroom.

"I Don't Recall"

And then comes a culminating moment in the trial. It is the morning of Friday, September 24, 2010. A hush falls on the courtroom as Robert Cargill, exuding a firm command of the important task he is facing, takes the stand. Slightly plump, he wears a fashionable beige suit and a short, neatly trimmed graying beard and mustache that compensate for the large premature bald patch at the back of his head. He squints intelligently from the podium. There is a faint aura of pique about him; he exudes self-satisfaction, eagerness to tell his story, and the charisma of an archaeological media star.[9]

> Cargill's work experience includes lecturing academics on "talking to the media as a biblical scholar."

The witness's well-rehearsed communication skills are on full display as he expertly answers the questions. His main task is to explain how he compiled the information that the prosecutors used to establish my identity as the author of all the criminalized texts.[10] He testifies that he was the victim of annoying criticism authored by my pseudonymous characters. He denounces my campaign as an "abuse of anonymity."[11] He asserts that he suffered emotionally when confronted by members of UCLA's Near Eastern languages department with emails complaining about his failure to respond to published criticism of the film he had created that was being shown at the scrolls exhibit in San Diego. He remembers that according to the emails, certain statements in the film were "mendacious."[12] Cargill also decries the fact that, in our pretrial motion to dismiss, we suggested that a passage in his doctoral thesis was marred by intellectual antisemitism—a detail that still appears to stir up a wave of indignation in him. (Cargill's protestations will not resolve the question whether his failure to call the Great Jewish Revolt by its name—referring to it merely as "a political uprising" when describing Norman Golb's theory in his dissertation—is in fact symptomatic of a form of antisemitism prevalent in certain academic circles today. Years later, Elon Musk will threaten to sue the ADL for signaling the constant, vicious flood of antisemitic commentary on the Twitter platform; Jennifer Safstrom, director of a First Amendment program at Vanderbilt University, will assert that "whether or not someone is antisemitic is fundamentally a matter of opinion, which is protected expression.")[13]

But Cargill's most dramatic testimony takes place when, during cross-examination, Kuby asks him a number of questions about the special "exclusive" that he submitted for publication to *Archaeology* magazine several months after getting my blogs removed from NowPublic. The article was never published—but Cargill forwarded it to John Bandler, who handed it to my lawyers on the eve of trial. Since *Archaeology* declined to publish this article, it has a status similar to that of Schiffman's "confidential letter": it becomes a public document when it is introduced as evidence at the trial. Unlike with the "confidential letter," however, we have no inkling Cargill's "exclusive" exists at all until a few days before the trial.

When we do learn of this article draft and examine its contents (a process we have to perform very hastily given the DA's policy of holding everything back until the last minute), we find a good deal of material in it that seems to shed a certain amount of light on the circumstances that led to my arrest. Cargill begins by eloquently describing his pleasure at seeing early news coverage of the *Virtual Qumran* film. "These news stories," he explains, "were special: they were all highlighting my work. In picture after picture, there was my research, there was my theory, and there was my name."[14] It was, he adds, "the proudest moment of my young academic career." Then, however, he began to "notice the comments" appearing online about his work, and to "read lengthy, highly detailed critiques of my research, and specifically of my [*sic*] conclusion that Qumran had been established as a Hasmonean fortress, which was abandoned and later reoccupied by a small Jewish community responsible for the Dead Sea Scrolls."

"Some of the comments," he goes on, "accused me of plagiarism, called my research misleading or better yet, 'mendacious,' and … included links that pointed back to … articles … by none other than Dr. Norman Golb, the 81-year-old Ludwig Rosenberger Professor of Jewish History and Civilization … who had written them without the 'hindrance' of peer review, and had slapped them up on the Oriental Institute website."[15] In response to such "highly detailed" critiques, Cargill explains that he and Risa Levitt Kohn "established a few ground rules … including never responding to the comments, and never mentioning Golb's name … we even agreed never to write his name down."

These claims raise two questions that will not be broached during the trial in view of the restrictions imposed by the judge: (1) whether the idea of "never mentioning Golb's name" was not in fact a much older policy of the scroll exhibitors and (2) whether this sort of policy was not precisely what my campaign was designed to expose. In the "exclusive," Cargill himself hints at one purported justification for that policy, by categorically asserting that Norman Golb's research "had been around for over a decade, and had been debated and dismissed by scholars"—a misleading claim evoking Lawrence Schiffman's declaration that "scholars agree" the scrolls were written by a sect living at Qumran. Then, in the crucial passage that Kuby wants to ask him about, Cargill summarizes his own feelings:

> Fringe theories die hard, especially when the scholars proposing them are still alive to defend them … Given Norman Golb's defiant statement that he and his son are "together and united," and Raphael Golb's recent plea of "not guilty" on grounds of "free speech," it appears that Norman Golb is going to do what he has always done: fight his litigious, losing battle until the bitter end. Unfortunately, the words of Shrine of the Book curator Magen Broshi still appear to echo true today: "When will

we be free of [Golb]? When he dies." (brackets added by Cargill)

Magen Broshi's statement about Norman Golb's death had been formulated in a moment of impulsive anger during an interview by the Israeli newspaper *Haaretz*; afterward, Broshi claimed that he had been inaccurately quoted. In resuscitating the statement in his "exclusive," Cargill sought to distribute it to *Archaeology*'s large popular audience. Joined with Cargill's introductory remark ("unfortunately, the words ... still appear to echo true today"), the statement would seem to offer a good occasion to discuss the socialization of postdoctoral Qumranologists into a particular academic environment. Or, if the judge declares such topics irrelevant, the statement might at least offer an occasion to shed some light on the witness's ulterior motives. Kuby seems to have something of the sort in mind as he gets into his cross-examination, as can be seen in this exchange between him and Cargill:

Kuby: And this was an exclusive to *Archaeology* magazine?
Cargill: I've never published in *Archaeology* magazine.
Kuby: I'm sorry? Dr. Cargill, just take a look at the document marked page one, scan it silently to yourself if you please, and after you've satisfied yourself and you know what it is—
Cargill: (The witness complied.)
Kuby: What do you recognize that to be, sir?
Cargill: This is a document that I wrote for consideration of publication for *Archaeology* magazine.
Kuby: So you sent it to *Archaeology* magazine for publication; is that correct?
Cargill: I was working with an editor there.
Kuby: And did they publish it?
Cargill: No, sir.
Kuby: And with respect to this article, you've delivered variations of this article in the form of a lecture; is that correct?
Cargill: I have not delivered variations. I've delivered one redacted variation of that article ...
Kuby: And this article, you wrote this article, right?

Cargill: Yes.

Kuby: Did you end the article by saying, "Unfortunately the words of Shrine of the Book curator Magen Broshi still appear to echo true today"—quote—"When will be we free of [Golb]? When he dies." Close quote. You wrote that?

Cargill: I'm sorry?

Kuby: You wrote that?

Cargill: Magen Broshi wrote that.[16]

Kuby: Well, we'll hold that for now. Magen Broshi—you identified him in this article as the Shrine of the Book curator, correct?

Cargill: I believe so.

Kuby: And what is the Shrine of the Book?

Cargill: The Shrine of the Book is a building that contains many of the Dead Sea Scrolls. It's a part of the Israel Museum in Jerusalem.

Kuby: And you were aware, were you not, that in an interview with the newspaper *Haaretz*, Magen Broshi said, "When will we be free of Golb? When he dies."

Cargill: I read that quote in Dr. Golb's book. That's when I learned of that quote.

Kuby: And you saw fit to quote it in your paper, correct?

Cargill: No, I did not. I saw fit to include it in the original draft of the paper, which was later redacted from the paper. No one ever publicly saw that.

Kuby: Pardon me?

Cargill: No one ever publicly saw that.

Kuby: I'm not asking you that question. You wrote those words, correct?

Cargill: I quoted Dr. Broshi in the early draft of a document that I wrote.[17]

Kuby: And when you say you included it in your paper—that is, the portion where you said, simply to quote, "Unfortunately Broshi's words are still true"—you mean by that it's unfortunate that you wouldn't be rid of Norman Golb sooner than his death?

Cargill: No, sir, that's not what I meant.

Kuby: Do you know how old Norman Golb is?

Cargill: I do not.

Kuby: Do you have any idea?

Cargill: I would have to speculate.
Kuby: Any notion of how long you have to wait to be free of him?
Bandler: Objection.
Berkman: Sustained.
Kuby: You also wrote, did you not, that Norman Golb will, quote, "fight his litigious losing battle until the bitter end?"
Cargill: I'm sorry, are you quoting from a draft of a manuscript I wrote?
Kuby: I am asking you if you wrote the following words—
Cargill: I don't recall. I mean, we would have to see if it's in a draft of a manuscript that was never published.
Kuby: Did you ever deliver those words to the Society of Biblical Literature on November 23rd [2009]?
Cargill: I don't recall.
Kuby: You don't recall. Is this the kind of thing you would remember if you had done it?
Cargill: No.[18]

Up to a certain point, Kuby is allowed to proceed with this line of inquiry, but he runs into difficulty when he tries to question Cargill about the letter he received from the University of Chicago counsel describing his insistent complaints to the Oriental Institute as "threats of nuisance litigation" and encouraging him to "answer criticism of his work on the merits."[19] As soon as Berkman realizes that this topic has arisen, she rapidly intervenes and blocks any testimony about the matter, explaining that the University of Chicago's assertion of Norman Golb's right to engage in scholarly criticism is a mere *expression of opinion regarding Illinois law that is not relevant* to the case.[20] (By "Illinois" law, Berkman will later acknowledge that she meant the federal law of copyright, fair use, and related issues.)

Kuby then turns to questioning Cargill about his own use of numerous online pseudonyms. Cargill denies having used the name "B. Ralph," then his tone changes; perhaps worn down a bit, he seems almost on the verge of stumbling, but then pulls himself together, vehemently points at me, and calls out that his own intent in using pseudonyms was to "let him [i.e., Raphael Golb] know that I knew who he was!"[21]

All this, just a few weeks after Cargill's appearance on National Geographic, in which—without mentioning Norman Golb's name, and with the earnest support of Stephen Pfann—he described his personal spiritual journey toward the view that the scrolls were written by Jews fleeing Jerusalem during the Great Revolt against the Romans. Kuby doesn't even try to raise this issue, knowing, perhaps, that it would be considered "irrelevant" and that it could even do me more harm than good: it might allow Cargill to present himself as a disinterested party in the scrolls controversy, bearing not even the slightest ill will against my father and motivated only by a firm desire for justice.

Following his testimony, Cargill will receive a state-funded assistant professorship in both the classics and religion departments at the University of Iowa. After publishing an article in 2011 in which he will again argue for a link between the "sectarians" of Qumran and the scrolls, he will apparently abandon his Qumranological focus and turn to writing about biblical topics having nothing to do with the scrolls.[22] In 2017, he will be appointed by Hershel Shanks to take his place as the editor of *Biblical Archaeology Review*.[23] Cargill's University of Iowa web page will list him as a member of various organizations, including SBL and ASOR, as well as the American Humanist Association and the American Civil Liberties Union.[24] In 2019, he will be promoted to an associate professorship at Iowa.

* * *

As soon as Cargill leaves, Bandler wraps up the bulk of his case by calling Sidnie White Crawford from the University of Nebraska—the disciple of Frank Moore Cross who lectured along with Schiffman at the Jewish Museum. She is a formidable witness, precisely because, with her nonflashy clothing, her voluminous Janis Joplin hairstyle, and her general attitude of good will and cooperation, she seems to be a completely ordinary person—one who has volunteered to come halfway across the country to help with the legal matter at hand. She speaks in a straightforward tone, with a tinge of sadness, as if to make it clear that she is simply here to do her civic duty, which consists in testifying that Cross, presented by Bandler as one of my "victims," has been in a nursing home for several years. Cross is unable to pursue any charges against me on his own, or to defend himself against any accusations of misconduct, but Crawford is here, at Bandler's request, to fill in for Cross if need be.

Crawford further indicates that several Gmails, sent to the members of the Duke University religion department and signed "Frank Cross," are not in the retired Harvard professor's "style." These messages, the prosecution has explained, contain language "attacking another scholar."[25] This is true, for they criticize the selection of Bart Ehrman of Chapel Hill to lecture in support of the Essene hypothesis at the Raleigh, North Carolina, scrolls exhibit despite his admission, in private email correspondence, that he was not himself an "expert" on the scrolls.[26]

> Ehrman is a New Testament scholar who started out as a fundamentalist Christian but later became an agnostic. He regards the "business" of university professors as being to "generate doubt" and "get people to think."

A fast-witted observer might be able to see the "Frank Cross" email flashing across the screen. And what is the criminal content of this message? "It looks like Bart has gone and put his foot in his mouth again. Are we going to have to take on the Jewish Museum? I'm seeing this crop up everywhere on the web." Two links to my pseudonymous blogs criticizing Ehrman are included in the message along with these rather childish remarks—the total effect being to suggest, in a decidedly nonprofessorial manner, that a scholar of Frank Moore Cross's prestige is alarmed about online attacks on the Raleigh exhibit and unhappy with the Jewish Museum's decision to inform the public about the "two basic theories" of scroll origins.[27]

While this email is projected for the jury on the viewing screen, Berkman is staring at the screen of a desktop computer that is placed in front of her at the bench. For some days already it has dawned on me that she must be reading all the blogs and emails on her computer. The direct relaying of the evidence to her desktop seems to make it more comfortable for her to follow the proceedings, without having to twist her neck to see the screen to her left. Her direct proximity to the evidence also contributes to her ability to control the proceedings, an ability crucial to her role as judge. Occasionally, as she peers at her screen, it seems that she is chuckling, almost as if she were finding something humorous, or perhaps improbable, in whatever she is reading.

As Crawford finishes testifying and is ushered out of the courtroom, one thing that neither Berkman nor I myself can have any inkling of is the precise direction the Nebraska scholar's efforts will take several years later. In 2012, Crawford will inform her readers that my father's theory of scroll origins has been "convincingly refuted," referring them to a few scattered pages in which his theory was by no means refuted at all.[28] Then, in 2016, she will join the ranks of the various Qumranologists seeking to buttress their own arguments by inaccurately describing my father's research conclusions in their published writings. In an article entitled "The Qumran Collection as a Scribal Library," she will inform her readers that according to Norman Golb, the Dead Sea Scrolls belonged to "refugees, who brought them from Jerusalem, *perhaps from the Temple*, prior to the siege of Jerusalem in the First Jewish revolt in order to safeguard them from destruction."[29] (Naturally she rejects this view.) Ironically, this inaccurate description will be put forward in an article considering the Qumran "collection" in view of the known facts about ancient *libraries*, including the difference between *private* and *public* libraries.

Contrary to the implication of Crawford's statements here and elsewhere, my father never argued that the scrolls are a "collection" of writings that may have come from the Temple. What he did argue was that the scrolls are the partial remains of *multiple Jerusalem collections or libraries*. Why, then, in an article dealing with libraries, will Crawford miss the opportunity to discuss the *private* character of many of the theorized collections, in contrast, for example, to the synagogues where, as the Magen-Peleg report signals, a large portion of the biblical scrolls likely originated? *That*—a mixture of private libraries and synagogues—is surely the view against which Crawford's own conception of the scrolls as a single unified collection put together by sectarians needs to be measured. Crawford's effort, when I'm eventually led to read her article, will strike me as losing both clarity and credibility on account of her failure to forthrightly address the opposing theory.[30]

7
"A PARODY OVER THE LINE"

Once Bandler has finished presenting his elaborate case laying out my criminal scheme, Berkman asks my attorneys if they wish to call any witnesses in my defense. After hesitating for a moment and verifying the answer with me, they announce that I myself have decided to testify. There is really no choice: our difficulty asking the witnesses even basic pertinent questions has cornered me into in a position where I am required to justify my criminalized speech.

It is the morning of Monday, September 27. Feeling cold and fatigued after a sleepless night, but staying as calm as possible, I climb to the stand. Breitbart starts with some simple questions about my background, education, and lifestyle, but as soon as we get to the heart of the matter, it quickly becomes apparent that Berkman's control over the trial will now manifest itself directly in my regard: whenever I reach the points that seem most important to me, I am simply blocked from testifying. I will be forbidden from testifying about my knowledge of the various instances in which people have used all sorts of crude parodies to tell truth to power. The pile of material about the scrolls controversy, plagiarism, and the like that I have brought from home will be systematically excluded and ignored. I will be prevented from pointing to Judge Richard Posner's observation in his *Little Book of Plagiarism* that "some types of plagiarism merit ostracism, ridicule, and cancellation of contracts."[1]

The duties enumerated in the code of ethics of the Museums Association are a mere detail mentioned along the way; neither my copy of the code nor any of the other documentation I have brought along will be admitted into evidence. Of pivotal importance for the trial's outcome, I will not be allowed to rebut Schiffman's eleven-page, confidential "response to Internet accusations." Since the record lacks any corrective input from me, this decision will apparently prompt the jury to infer that the department chairman, in that "response," is the one who successfully rebutted the allegations of misconduct that I had leveled against him.

Bandler launches his cross-examination with a dramatic recitation of the entire list of my online pseudonyms: I am to answer, one by one, whether I used each of them in the course of my campaign. Breitbart protests against this "charade," as he calls it. Berkman overrules his objection.[2] During the ensuing exchanges of questions and answers, Berkman guides me to answer questions from Bandler in one or another particular manner that she considers appropriate. When Kuby protests that no such limitation has been imposed on the prosecution's witnesses, she comments, "The record speaks for itself."[3]

> At one point, Bandler sneeringly asks me whether I think I am "smarter" than the jurors—clearly suggesting that I feel superior to them by dint of my academic training and implicitly marking me out as their enemy.

Capitalizing on the poisonous atmosphere that has gradually infected the entire trial, Bandler inflames the situation with as many loaded questions as possible. He displays crass contempt for the serious ethical issues involved in the museum controversy and insists on reducing my "Larry Schiffman" emails to a crude expression of vile motives. The prosecutor's skill at implementing this strategy can be seen in the following exchange:

Bandler: You became *fixated* on the Jewish Museum exhibit, didn't you.
Me: Fixated? I wouldn't use that term. The Jewish Museum opened an exhibit, and I found—
Bandler: How about *obsessed*, would you use that word?
Me: Obsessed, no. I wouldn't use that word either.
Bandler: Very interested?
Me: Sure, I was very interested in it because it was a new type of exhibit, yes.
Bandler: It was very important to you, right?
Me: Not only to me but to many people.

Bandler: And it was important to your *family* also?
Me: Of course.
Bandler: And you *hate* Dr. Schiffman, right?
Me [shocked by the question, I recall a Holocaust survivor's explanation of why she refuses to hate Nazis, and start to explain]: You know, you can only "hate" somebody who is superior to you—
Bandler: Objection. You hate Dr. Schiffman, right?
Me: I wouldn't use that word.
Bandler: You dislike him?
Me [weary, recovering a bit from the shock]: Dislike him, sure, but—
Bandler: You *resent*—
Breitbart: Let him finish his answer, Judge, please. He interrupted him in the middle again.
Berkman: I'm sorry. The question is do you dislike Dr. Schiffman, you may answer the question.
Me [stumbling over my thoughts, confused by Berkman's seeming to side with me for a moment]: That's not the way I would think of it but, yes, you could say I dislike him, as I dislike all plagiarists—
Bandler: And you *resented* that he was speaking at the Jewish Museum, right?
Me: I resented that he was speaking at *all* of the museum exhibits from which my father was systematically *excluded*.
Bandler: Objection. You resented that he was speaking at the Jewish Museum, right?
Me: I resented that he was speaking at *all* of the museums.
Berkman: That would include the Jewish Museum, correct?
Me [in a weary tone]: That would *include* the Jewish Museum, of course.

> One basic definition of the word *resentment* is "indignant displeasure at something unfair." That is the sense I was seeking to attribute to the term, but it quickly became apparent that Bandler wanted to cast my answer in a whole different light.

Berkman [instructing me]: So your answer to that question would be yes.
Me [again in a weary tone]: Sure.

Bandler: And you wanted your father to speak at the Jewish Museum, right?
Me: I wanted my father, *also*, to speak at the Jewish Museum, yes.
Bandler [echoing Berkman]: So the answer to the question is yes.

By now, my thoughts are jumbled up into a dim, exhausted awareness that my thoughts and words are being manipulated, that the point I'm trying to make about the natural resentment that everyone should share in face of an unfair situation is being twisted, and that this can all result in me being sent to jail. This is the point where sarcasm injects itself into my testimony; I begin to dutifully echo—or indeed to *mimic*—whatever I'm asked to say:

Me: "Yes."
Bandler: And you knew your entire family wanted your father to speak at the Jewish Museum, right?
Me: My entire family wanted my father to be able to speak at *all* of the museum exhibits, yes.
Bandler: So the answer to the question is a yes.
Me: "Yes."
Bandler: Your Honor, if it can be answered with a yes or no, could you please instruct the witness to do so.
Berkman: Yes ... Answer his questions.
Breitbart: Judge, most respectfully, I believe he did answer his question. The question didn't call for a single-word response, and if it *could* be answered, it should be answered appropriately.
Berkman: He wanted to add *all* of the museums, so that would *include* the Jewish Museum as I just asked ... Mr. Bandler has the right to ask the questions that he wants to ask.
Bandler: You *knew* your whole family wanted your father to speak *at the Jewish Museum*, right?
Breitbart: Asked and answered!
Berkman [instructing me]: You may answer the question.
Me: "Yes."
Bandler: So you hatched this plan on your own to impersonate Dr. Schiffman, didn't you.

Me [finally getting a grip and making an effort]: I object to the word *impersonate*, and I object to the word *so*.
Bandler: I object to the defendant objecting.
Me: The answer is no. There is no *so*. You're implying something in the question; therefore, the answer has to be no.[4]

Bandler's "objection" to my "objection" seems to indicate that even he can, at bottom, participate in the humor, when he feels that it is in his interest to do so. But his aim is hardly humorous; it is to cast a pall of obscurity over the concept of *healthy* resentment and to generate collective, irrational anger and poison in place of it. The process, in fact, is already the punishment, and at this moment, the retribution for "putting words into Schiffman's mouth" is the extraction of misleading statements from my own mouth as mandatory affirmative responses to the prosecutor's questions. I am both gagged, as it were, and forced to say things at the same time.

Grounding himself on the framework of Berkman's pretrial and courtroom edicts, Bandler wields his sharply honed verbal skills to full effect and succeeds in rendering one essential detail entirely irrelevant to the proceedings. This is the fact that, according to the documentation entered into evidence by the prosecution itself, I sought *neutrality* and suggested a *free-of-charge rebuttal* lecture by Norman Golb.[5] By obfuscating this fact under a cloud of rhetoric, Bandler also obscures its context: the demand for neutrality at the Jewish Museum was one step of a campaign that challenged the conduct of a group of scholars involved in *silencing opposition to their favored theory*. These scholars had created a series of museum exhibits aimed at concealing the current state of research on the Dead Sea Scrolls from the public. They had rigged an accompanying series of one-sided lectures all over the United States.

The mandatory, misleading "admission"—I was motivated by "resentment" of a lecture—will feed straight into Bandler's rhetoric during his closing argument. You see the defendant's scheme? You see his deceitful conduct? You see how he even tried to deny he was resentful? As the *New York Times* will quickly report, a vein swells in my neck.[6] The deft prosecutor then moves in for the kill:

Bandler: You testified that you didn't intend to impersonate Dr. Frank Cross, right?
Me: I intended to *parody* him; that was a kind of parody, just like the other stuff.
Bandler: Objection.
Berkman: *Parody* assumes a conclusion, Mr. Golb. So the question is whether you intended to *impersonate* Frank Moore Cross.[7]

With this concise logic, Berkman both denies me the opportunity to clarify what I testified to and explains what the question "is." But Bandler's question was not "whether I intended" to impersonate Frank Moore Cross; it was whether that had been the nature of my *testimony* regarding my intent. Berkman, not I, appears to have assumed, and, through her choices and restrictions, to have focused the inquiry, through the funnel of a certain way of seeing things. In this instance, she has done the focusing in a manner that directly blocks me from clarifying my own reality—and from invoking my First Amendment rights.

It goes almost without saying that Schiffman and Cargill, for example, were subjected to no such restriction; they were allowed to answer questions from Breitbart and Kuby any way they liked at all, even with offensive remarks. Before my trial, I never knew that special restrictions applied to the testimony of criminal defendants; I had imagined that they were treated just like any other witnesses. I had also imagined that prosecutors were forbidden from asking them questions designed to inflame the minds of a jury. Apparently I was wrong on both counts.

*　*　*

The next morning, when I take the stand again and Breitbart tries to revisit some of the issues that have been distorted by Bandler, Berkman again prevents me from testifying about various things. Her voice seems to become especially irate when Breitbart asks me about the academic misconduct of Schiffman and the other complainants.

When he asks me whether I know of any academic figures who have written that the appropriate response to plagiarism is *ridicule*, I answer "yes" just as Bandler calls out "objection." She sustains the objection and instructs the jury to ignore my answer. Did the question assume an impermissible conclusion? Or was it inappropriate because I, not my accusers, am on trial? When Breitbart tries to elicit testimony from me about Bandler's conduct on the morning of my arrest—in particular, about his mendacious assertion, that morning, that I had not been charged with a crime—Berkman immediately silences him. The jury is thus denied the opportunity to reflect on the honesty of the prosecutors, or the circumstances of my taped interrogation and the illogical, stress-induced conduct on my part that it memorialized.[8]

> Interrupting Breitbart repeatedly, Berkman makes it clear that my motivations have only a peripheral bearing on whether I committed a crime. "The relevance of whether or not these people perpetrated an academic fraud," she says, "is off to the side, and not in the center."

"Have You No Sense of Decency, Sir?"—Joseph Welch

Bandler's job is not just to make me look like a bad person: he has to prove, beyond a reasonable doubt, that I committed a crime. Not long after my arrest, Martin Garbus, the renowned dean of First Amendment lawyers, had told me that, call it what they like, this was a criminal *libel* case: Bandler's actual intent was to convince the jury that I had set out to damage the *reputations* of the complainants by disseminating defamatory statements about them. This, Garbus indicated, was not a proper topic for a criminal trial, because, as Carol Berkman herself had acknowledged, ever since 1965, libel had no longer been a crime in New York. So what the prosecutor was really trying to do was get the jury to find me guilty, under the false pretexts of "harassment" and the like, for something (my alleged libel) that was not even a crime at all.[9]

The course of the trial ends up confirming Garbus's early assessment. The transcript refers at least 170 times to my allegations, made in the course of my campaign, that various members of the Dead Sea Scrolls network had engaged in questionable or inappropriate conduct. The real charge Bandler has set out to prove is that these allegations of mine, contrary to all the evidence I had gathered, were defamatory. He has elicited sworn testimony from several of the parties in question, to the effect that my "accusations" (or "complaints," or "attacks") were "false," or "not true," or that they had "no credibility." I had decided to "craft" my claims. They were a "smear," or a "stain." They were "not substantiated." They were "wrong." They were "personal" and "crossed a big line." They were "negative," "very serious," and "terrible." Even when discussing my campaign in an ostensibly more neutral manner, Bandler has adopted a sarcastic, sneering tone of voice each time he refers to my contentions, implying that everyone knows, of course, that such allegations *must* be defamatory: a verbal technique that doesn't even show up in the transcript at all.[10] When my attorneys, on the other hand, have tried to introduce the evidence that my allegations were *true*, or even just to fully probe the credibility of the witnesses, they have been repeatedly blocked by objections and rulings of the judge.

The hypnotic effect is cumulative; one could just as well be in China, Russia, or anywhere else in the world where such trials take place. When my testimony is over, we break for lunch; in the afternoon, Breitbart sums up our case with an eloquent plea for my innocence. But I sense that the jurors aren't too interested in what he has to say. Bandler's vicious assault on my character has caught their imagination. When Breitbart is done, Berkman gives Bandler a day off to prepare his closing summation—a leniency reflecting, perhaps, not only the court's schedule, but the high consideration in which the office and special responsibilities of prosecutors are held in our country.

The day is Thursday, September 30, 2010. Bandler rises from his seat. He begins his peroration by explaining that the plagiarism accusations are "untruthful"; that Schiffman is "reputable and respectable" and would not have "plagiarized someone with a different theory"; that I have an "obsession" with "wanting [my] father's theory to get more credit"; that Avi Katzman's statements are "irrelevant"; that I am an "angry and bitter" person who "knows how to twist language, stir up controversy"; and that what I can do with this knowledge is "much more devious and disturbing than what a less educated person can do."[11] I do my best to maintain a proper appearance of composure in my chair, but I cannot help feeling my jaw drop as I hear these accusations from an officer of the law who maintains that the First Amendment is irrelevant to the prosecution he is charged with conducting. And I feel it dropping a bit more when I hear him explain that my attaching of a "smear" to Schiffman's "name" was timed to "influence the museum, get Schiffman booted, get Dr. Golb added and it's not just an honorarium, it's travel, lodging, meals, and everything else that comes with this."[12]

> "He knows how to twist language, stir up controversy. As a result, what he can do is ... devious and disturbing."

Here Bandler does have a problem: there is no actual material evidence that I authored the "Larry Schiffman confessions" with the specific intent to get Jewish Museum personnel to cancel the professor's lecture. So he uses a different sort of argument. By the sum total of my emails and blogs, he suggests, I "created developments" that *must have been* designed to get the lecture canceled.[13] The jury members, the argument suggests, need only speculate a bit about my calculations as to how readers of my communications would react. From these speculations they might conclude that I expected word to reach the Jewish Museum that Schiffman had "admitted" to being a plagiarist. And they might further conclude that I expected this would lead the exhibitors to inflict a grievous injury on Schiffman by canceling his lecture.

As Bandler puts it, "Thus the defendant's elaborate scheme of deception was hatched."[14] Throughout the trial, the prosecution has sought to justify its effort to criminalize my campaign under New York's fraud laws by emphasizing my "deceitfulness"; my motivations have been repeatedly trashed, while Schiffman's huff-and-puff displays of indignation have been given the status of authentic declarations. As I watch the prosecutor's own displays, I am reminded of something I once heard about the art of persuasion, in the courtroom as in politics. Orators—whether virtuous defenders of truth and freedom or populist demagogues—are always at their best when *imitating* anger, never when actually angry. What passion itself cannot produce is rapidly gained by a *facsimile* of passion.

Bandler's skill at radiating a sense of indignation will, above all, offer him an effective way to deal with the satire issue during his summation. This is an important issue because it potentially poses a serious impediment to winning the case. God forbid that the jury should come away thinking that I had engaged in a merely "pious" fraud, with no criminal intent at all, or, even worse, in what critical theorist Bernard Harcourt would call an act of "resistance" or of "principled disobedience."[15] The strength of the material evidence would be significantly weakened if even one of the jurors— perhaps the solemn-looking director of the Model UN program who seemed to smile at me encouragingly when I mentioned the use of over seventy pseudonyms by the Portuguese poet Fernando Pessoa—should conclude that the "Gmail confessions" were satirical in nature and that no one was meant to seriously believe that Schiffman, the department chairman at a major university, had authored them.[16]

In fact, it is generally understood that even the most offensive parodies are shielded from governmental suppression by the First Amendment. That is potentially a very serious problem indeed— and so Bandler, pursuing his effort to incarcerate me for my crimes, goes a step further: he sets out to suggest that my intent in sending the emails could *not* have been satirical. Under Bandler's guidance, the jury is now asked to play its role in enacting a *trial by intent*. A wrongful motive is attributed to me, which, because of the deadpan nature of the evidence, cannot be disproved. As I sit listening to the prosecutor's rhetoric, it suddenly dawns on me that the presumption of innocence has been reversed: I will be presumed guilty because I was unable to produce blatant, compelling proof that I did *not* have the intent attributed to me. I'm aware that this kind of reversal has characterized, through the centuries, certain American legal cases, such as the charges brought against Communist sympathizers by Senator Joseph McCarthy,[17] but it's not exactly what I was expecting in a courtroom in New York in the year 2010.

Hinting to the jury that they can presume my guilt, rather than my innocence, is in fact a highly effective prosecutorial method. Given the circumstances, Bandler's accusations can be confirmed on the simple basis of *not being entirely implausible*. Efforts to cast doubt on them can even be recast as additional criminal acts aimed at impugning the good names of Schiffman, Cargill, and the others. It is crucial that the people assigned with doing the assessing—the jury and, to some extent, the judge—not be persuaded by suggestions that another, *non*criminal intent was actually at play.

> The McCarthy trials have been described as venues where a defendant is understood to pose a "threat so grave that—the prosecutor may hint without exactly saying it—it is all right, just this once, to pronounce the guilty verdict we know is true even if the evidence doesn't quite prove it."

Not only does Bandler skillfully avoid such a development, but he actually creates a situation in which the jury itself, by virtue of my very presence in the courtroom, feels victimized by a diffuse sense of dereliction. After all, if I thought my emails were so funny, why isn't anybody laughing now? Bandler's voice booms across the floor; he denies, he attacks, and he nails me, the cybercriminal, to the wall: "This was not for parody, this was for maliciousness!" There is "no way," the skilled prosecutor adds, "to sugarcoat this: the defendant is a menace to anyone who gets in his way."[18]

For a moment, I feel myself suppressing an urge to laugh. In Bandler's vision, somehow it seems that the world has been turned upside down and the victims have become abusers. The gravity of the danger I pose, he demonstrates, is shown by my use of *fictitious personae* to inquire of several dozen faculty members at UCLA whether it was okay to award a PhD to a young, sympathetic doctoral candidate in their department—merely because he had apparently participated in implementing an exhibition policy of not writing down the name of a particular professor. And who could *not* be swayed by Bandler's logic, when he suggests that by sending such messages, I perpetrated a devious *falsehood* about my actual identity and sought, yet again, to *deceive* the recipients of my messages! (Incidentally, this is exactly what Fernando Pessoa did; only long after his death was it discovered that many of the various personae he created, and under whose names he published numerous articles in journals all over the world, did not actually exist.) Bandler's self-possessed bearing, gained both from years serving as a platoon leader in the army reserve and from his natural sense of indignation, lends his declamations about my criminal "scheme" strength of conviction.

Emphasizing the lack of appropriate, comic impetus in the criminalized communications, Bandler also demonstrates that I committed a second felony running alongside the various misdemeanor charges: I engaged in a fraudulent scheme to falsify New York University's business records, so as "to generate an inquiry and a reaction based upon false premises."

This charge, of course, rests on another not-entirely-implausible premise that no one could possibly disprove: I engaged in a double-sided criminal calculation. First, I am presumed to have calculated that people would *actually believe*, with no further investigation, that Lawrence Schiffman was *confessing to plagiarism*, and that he was enjoining them to read—but to withhold from students—a linked article accusing him of that academic misdeed, in a message emanating from a freshly minted "Larry Schiffman" Gmail address. Second, I am presumed to have calculated that university officials would make false entries to their important business records on the basis of just that belief. Despite the seemingly speculative nature of this accusation, as well, the proof here again is in the pudding: my character is putatively deceitful. How could the jury not convict me of this crime as well?

Perhaps the most intriguing of all the charges that Bandler alludes to during his peroration concern "Jonathan Seidel," the handle I claimed to have invented by combining the last name of the award-winning poet Frederick Seidel with a typical "Jewish"-sounding first name.[19] As with most of the aliases I used (Joshua Reznick, Simon Adler, Jesse Friedman, Albert White, Peter Kaufman, Sam Edelstein ...), it turns out that many people actually have this name. Prosecutors, legislators, and others who are indignant about this form of anonymity may wish to take a look in the white pages. There they will also find many reiterations of the name Richard Saunders—an alias widely understood to have been used by Benjamin Franklin (even though this founding father of the United States never admitted he *was* Richard Saunders).

My "Seidel" emails made no claim to be written by a rabbi, or to come from Oregon. Seidel himself has apparently never published anything about the Dead Sea Scrolls. I have testified that I never heard of a Rabbi Jonathan Seidel in Oregon, not from Norman Golb and not from anyone else. Yet Bandler easily demonstrates that the weighty impact of the evidence—divinity classes with Schiffman, Oberlin College, a chance encounter in England with Norman Golb in 1986—is enough to convict me of several additional counts of forgery and criminal impersonation, on the grounds that I assumed the rabbi's name (beyond reasonable doubt!) with the "intent to obtain a benefit or injure another." The notion that the conflicting messages sent under this name (some of them criticizing museum exhibits, others attacking the "filth from Chicago") expressed a variety of ideas and might therefore be protected speech under the First Amendment was of course not even broached.

Ultimately, as Bandler pulls all the incriminating facts together, one crime stands out more than any of the others: I am charged with harassment, on the grounds that I intended to "annoy" the victims of my email complaints, precisely in violation of the statute's interdiction of communications sent with the intent to "annoy." This charge in effect criminalizes my entire campaign, for my annoying messages had a sort of giant harassment ripple effect: as my criminal scheme unfolded, the *recipients* of the emails became my weapons, spreading annoying speech through museum offices and academic departments all the way from New York to Los Angeles.

Few fraudulent schemes, however, are ever prepared with the requisite mental agility; few crimes are perfect. Seeing things from the prosecution's perspective, my impersonation of Schiffman was actually a disastrous blunder on my part, in which I revealed the true nature of my vast, carefully planned illegal enterprise: a modern illustration, as it were, of Raskolnikov's observation in Dostoevsky's *Crime and Punishment* that even the most quick-witted felons cannot help making mistakes, because they suffer from a "failure of will and reason ... a phenomenal, childish thoughtlessness, just at the moment when reason and prudence are most necessary."[20]

It is all very well put together, and it capitalizes on the fact that the jurors' very first impressions of the trial include the judge informing them, during the selection process, that what the case is about is everyone's right to "peace and quiet." What she failed to mention was that no professor, no matter how privileged and distinguished he may be, has the right to remain undisturbed by criticism, ridicule—even in its most biting forms—or the irritating necessity of defending themselves when facing accusations of misconduct. Bandler's "harassment" argument breaks with that basic fact, as well as with the principles, established in many cases around the country, that speech cannot be criminalized merely because it is annoying, that harassment must not be confused with allegations of libel, and that emails can constitute harassment only if they are sent directly to their victims.

But such technicalities are of little consequence. It is, after all, always legitimate to argue that the law should be changed. And what matters most at this point is convincing the jurors and securing the conviction, not complying with abstract principles and legal precedents that can be endlessly debated by judges and professors.

"People Generally See What They Look For"—Judge Taylor in *To Kill a Mockingbird*

After the prosecutor's summation, it is Berkman's turn. Before she reads her instructions to the jury members, she explains that she is "neutral."[21] After going on for some time about the jury's duties, she catches me and my defense team by surprise and suddenly mentions parody and satire. She then makes clear her own "assumptions" (the word she used in silencing me when I sought to clarify that my intent had been to engage in parody), by giving definitions of these terms that highlight their role as light comedic techniques, while skirting their more provocative, socially controversial range of meanings. She defines *parody* as "the close imitation of the style of an author or a work for *comic* effect or in ridicule," and *satire* as "a *form of humor* where a writer tries to make the reader have a negative opinion of another by *laughing* at that person or making that person seem ridiculous or foolish, and the like."[22]

These definitions appear to have been chosen to the exclusion of others that are quite different; for example, the definition in the authoritative Merriam-Webster dictionary. The ninth edition of that work defines *satire* as "a literary work holding up human vices and follies to ridicule or scorn," or "trenchant wit, irony, or sarcasm used to expose or discredit vice or folly." Various definitions of *parody* include "humorous *or satirical* mimicry"; "a false, derisive, or impudent imitation of something"; and "imitating another work or style with intention to ridicule."[23] The late Simon Dentith defined it as "any cultural practice which provides a *relatively polemical allusive imitation* of another cultural production or practice."[24]

Having provided her own chosen definitions, Berkman instructs the jury that the First Amendment is not an excuse for breaking the law. "Words," she explains, "can be the tools by which crimes are committed, as, for very obvious example, when a robber says, 'Your money or your life,' the First Amendment doesn't protect that."[25] (I wonder, as I listen, what would happen to someone who unwisely utters the words "Your money or your life" in satirical contexts including blogs, emails, or rap songs.)[26]

Berkman concludes this portion of her instructions by explaining to the jurors that "the questions for you are not the legal issues of freedom of speech ... but rather whether the elements of a charged crime have been proved beyond a reasonable doubt."[27] She goes on to indicate that if they decide that I "assumed the name of another with the intent to gain a benefit," they are to find me guilty of identity theft. She underscores, again, that the word "benefit" means "any gain or advantage," and she firmly declines to impose any specific definition of what type of "gain" or "advantage" is meant, despite my lawyers' repeated requests that she do so. As for "injury," she declines to define the word at all.[28] She instructs the jury that I committed a crime if I acted with "the intent to deceive ... as to the source of the speech," or to "trick" the recipients of my emails,[29] but she does not explain how long the false impression must have been intended to last. It thus appears that even if the emails were mere clickbait designed to send recipients to my NowPublic articles, as long as the "trick" was intended to last for a moment, I committed the crime. On the other hand, whether my educated audience was intended to *reasonably* believe that a department chairman had sent out instructions that an investigation into his own ostensibly admitted plagiarism be squelched is an issue not mentioned during the jury instructions.[30]

> After instructing the jurors not to examine the "legal issues of freedom of speech," Berkman explains to them that Tina Fey will still be able to continue imitating Sarah Palin if they find me guilty.

It is difficult, in fact, to reconcile Berkman's instructions with the simple reality of parody. That reality will be plainly reasserted, almost twelve years to the day after my trial, in an amicus brief submitted, on behalf of an individual wrongly arrested for ridiculing the police in Ohio, to the United States Supreme Court by the *Onion*. The authors of the brief will assert that "parody functions by *tricking* people into thinking that it is real." They will add that "because parody *mimics* 'the real thing,' it has the unique capacity to *critique* the real thing"; that "a *reasonable* reader does not need a disclaimer to know that parody is parody"; and that "it should be obvious that parodists cannot be prosecuted for telling a joke *with a straight face.*"³¹ The words I have placed in italics capture in a nutshell some of the key factors excluded from the analysis of my case pursuant to the vigorous legal vision laid down by Berkman in her instructions to the jury.

In effect, Berkman's definitions of the law are so clear sighted, and so exclusive of the actual polemical nature of satirical "cultural practice" both in its historical usages and in its current-day manifestations, that it is almost impossible to see how the jurors could fail to conclude that I committed a crime of deceit and provocation, or how they could fail to find me guilty. And it is not particularly surprising when, on the same day as Bandler's summation and the judge's instructions, after a mere five hours of deliberation over a case that involves hundreds of pages of detailed documents—virtually none of which they request to see, for they have no need to see them—the jurors do in fact find me guilty of nearly all the numerous charges leveled against me. Uninformed stragglers attending the trial might wonder whether the verdict results not only from Bandler's rhetoric and Berkman's guidance but also perhaps from sheer fatigue on the part of the jurors—and this not only brought on by the rapid flashing of incomprehensible emails across the screen but also from being forced to sit through so much testimony about all sorts of recriminations whose truth or falsity has been declared irrelevant.

The verdict reached is in fact the only logical result of the processes involved: I am guilty because I sent the emails. I am guilty because Norman Golb's theory is allegedly unpopular, because the witnesses have angrily pointed their fingers at me, because the prosecution has denounced my ability to "twist words" and "stir up controversy." The single crime of which I am *not* convicted involves Jeffrey B. Gibson, the Chicago-area lecturer in humanities who is the author of various works on Jesus and Christian prayers and the owner of the ANE-2 website. Perhaps I am spared because I testified that I actually found Gibson, who "confessed" to a slightly checkered past and revealed a certain sense of humor on the witness stand, to be a tolerably sympathetic character with whom I could probably settle my differences over a cup of coffee.³²

Whatever the explanation, since I must have intended to "gain a benefit" by assuming so many different names, my combined provocations, regardless of the jury's particular feelings about Gibson, reveal dangerous criminal propensities that clearly need to be corrected through incarceration.

"A Parody over the Line"

News of the verdict spreads quickly. On October 1, 2010, Jonathan Turley of George Washington University informs his thousands of readers that I have "been convicted of 30 counts of identity theft and impersonating a law professor [*sic*]."[33] "Golb," he continues, "insists that setting up accounts in Schiffman's name and those of other academic critics was merely a parody ... Golb now faces as much as four years in prison." When a friend points me toward Turley's article, I find his choice of words disconcerting. Anyone, in the United States, is free to "set up accounts" in any name he likes on Gmail and similar platforms; we have not established the verified-identity regimes of China and other similar countries. The issue at trial had nothing to do with setting up accounts; it had to do with the content of the *messages* sent from those accounts—content quoted inaccurately by Turley in his article, on the basis of the *New York Daily News* item he had read some eighteen months previously. Moreover, one would not normally expect a principled defender of "free speech values" to take such a flippant attitude toward what Turley calls "merely a parody." Is he suggesting that certain forms of expression are less worthy of protection than others? Turley's article provides no clarification of this matter. Ironically, years later, Turley will publish a lengthy law review essay lamenting the "decline of free speech in the United States." In it he will have much to say about the so-called "cancel culture" and the wrongful (according to him) banning of right-wing figures from social media platforms; but the terms "satire," "parody" and "criminal libel" will not appear in his essay.[34]

Several weeks slide by. Then the sentencing hearing takes place. It is the morning of November 18, 2010. I have gone without sleep the night before, due in part to the impending confrontation with Bandler at court but also heightened by my reading of additional reports about my trial—these ones posted online by David Sarna, the elder son of the late professor Nahum Sarna of Brandeis. Among other noteworthy statements in David's articles are the accusation that "greed" led to my downfall and the assertion that "knee-jerk liberals ... down played [*sic*] the conviction and misreported that it was 'only' 30 counts rather than 482 on which [Golb] was actually found guilty by an impartial jury of his peers." David's articles also mention that he has been present at my trial, and remind readers that according to Kuby, I could in theory be sentenced to thirty years in prison. None of which contributes to a restful night's sleep on the eve of the sentencing hearing. His vehement remarks about the "free speech" lawyers (his quotation marks) who have taken up my cause keep popping up in my head, along with his insistence that "greed ... is not just money" and that "the pursuit of status and power," which he suggests is the key to understanding my campaign, can itself "be criminal."[35] I am aware, of course, that David Sarna was a classmate of his father's student Lawrence Schiffman at Brandeis; the two had even collaborated on a computer-aided "critical edition" of certain rabbinical writings in 1970, before either of them received his bachelor's degree.[36] This fact only contributes to the faint sense of nausea that I once again have as I drag myself down to the court.

A large crowd has packed itself into all the available seats on this particular morning, and listens in silence while John Bandler vigorously argues that the appropriate punishment for my crimes is three years of incarceration in a New York State prison. Berkman—visibly asserting her control over this final stage of the trial—again brushes aside the "constitutional" arguments that had been raised during the trial. *Giving an impression*, she explains, has nothing to do with expressing ideas. "Your criminal intent," she admonishes me, "brought you a parody over the line," a statement whose full, concrete import may seem almost incomprehensible, but which somehow makes perfect sense in the context in which it's uttered.

> *"Your criminal intent brought you a parody over the line."*

"Accordingly," she continues, "there needs to be a clear message as to the consequences of continuing in such behavior."[37] The crowd grows even more silent as these words echo through the room. Perhaps it is only the idea that the sentencing hearing itself will somehow help clarify the nature of the trial as a whole that allows me to stay reasonably alert and focus on what she is saying regardless of my fatigue.

Rejecting the Department of Probation's recommendation of no jail time, Berkman pronounces the sentence: six months at the Rikers Island penitentiary and five years' probation, during which time my so-called free speech rights are to be limited by a variety of restrictions. Enforcing the forgery statute's terms that criminalize "deceitful" speech in a rigidly literal manner, she forbids me from engaging in online discussions using *any pseudonym*, whether invented or historical, other than the word "Anonymous."[38] It goes without saying that neither Schiffman nor any other complainant is present; nor will any of them ever raise, at any subsequent opportunity, the slightest objection to the sentence imposed.

Only after announcing the sentence does Berkman suddenly realize that I haven't been given an opportunity to speak. Alerted to this inadvertent lapse by court staff, she asks me if I would like to say something. This puts me in a bit of a dilemma: Can I be sure she won't increase my punishment if I speak out? I nonetheless make a short statement, in which I point out that the term "impersonation" is often used as a synonym for "mimicry" of someone for satirical purposes, and signal the existence of the Yes Men and similar groups, none of whom have ever, at least in America, been hunted down by the police and incarcerated for "tricking" their audiences.

Despite my obduracy, Berkman leaves her sentence intact—but she declines to grant me a stay; I am to be immediately incarcerated at Rikers Island. She explains that only this punishment will teach me not to "imitate someone in that manner."[39] I am handcuffed and taken into a little cage behind the door. There they remove the cuffs, search my bag and shoes, and prepare to send me on a journey through the New York correctional system.

"It Was the Daytime, but It Felt Dark"—Former Detainee in the Film *Rikers: An American Jail*

After a while, they take me down a hallway and elevator into another area where some new guards fingerprint me and search my bag again. They do this in a rather casual, matter-of-fact manner and seem a bit puzzled at my sentence of six months at Rikers for a bunch of emails making fun of a professor. After a short period, they take me to another cell, where I begin to wait. There is only one other person in there with me, a Latino kid with long hair; he stands at the bars and keeps moaning to be let out, and eventually they take him away.

After sitting for a while and trying to read a few pages from a paperback copy of the *Confessions* of St. Augustine, which I have brought with me in my bag, I get up and walk back and forth in the cell, trying to relieve my legs and back from the pressure of sitting on the narrow bench. Several hours go by before they come again and take me down to the Tombs.

Here again my bag is searched. The guards down here are more meticulous. They let me keep the book, but they throw out my toothbrush. They place me in a cell with another Rikers-bound inmate, a big fellow with dreadlocks named Joe, who is on the phone when they bring me in—the free phone one can use to make calls, but only within the city. I mind my own business, urinate in the filthy metal contraption that serves as a toilet—the first of many such receptacles I will see during the next thirty-eight hours—and pace around in the cold. When Joe is off the phone, I ask him if he thinks I can call 411 on it. We quickly confirm this is impossible. Then we start talking.

Joe can see I'm scared about going to Rikers. He says it will be okay, asks me what I did, and gives me some advice: everyone will want to take me under their wing, some for the wrong reasons. He would do it himself, but he is only going to be there for a day or two at most since he has already served seven days and is going to be released maybe even this same night. (Joe has already served most of his ten-day sentence for heroin dealing in the Tombs because, like most inmates in New York, he is unable to afford bail.) But he will get me started. There are good people, but there are some I had better avoid. Never give your PIN to anyone. Just be there reading your book in your corner and you'll be okay. He suggests I will want to ask for protective custody in a cell of my own, something I have already decided on long ago. Joe has obviously been to Rikers many times.

Since in my haste to prepare for sentencing I forgot to copy down Kuby's number, and can't remember it, Joe calls his friend back and asks him if he can look it up. We call again a few minutes later, and he reads it to us. Joe gives me a slip of paper he has in his pocket and a bottle opener, and I scratch the number onto the slip (no pens are allowed in the Tombs). This way I am able to call Kuby's office and speak with his secretary, who gives me his cell number. He doesn't answer, and when I call his office back some time later, the secretary has also been unable to reach him. Apparently he is still in the chambers of the appeals court judge he was planning to apply to with my request for bail.

Maybe, I think, Kuby is rushing down to the Tombs in the subway to try to get there before I'm shipped out to Rikers. Maybe bail has been refused after all. By now it's four o'clock and Kuby still isn't picking up. Joe says I can keep the piece of paper, so I use it as a bookmark for the *Confessions*.

Then Joe and I are removed from the cell. My talk with Kuby's assistant is my last communication with the outside world until the next day. I will not see another phone at all until the morning, and hours will pass between seeing one and being able to use one. Thursday at four, Joe and I are handcuffed together and taken to the boarding area adjacent to the armored Rikers bus. There, in another, more sinister cell, we are soon joined by a flock of other inmates. There is a seething, imploded energy here. Most of them have been brought in on drug busts. Joe stands at the bars, clenching them in his hands, and I do the same on account of the cuffs. Then we sit. He notices that my cuff is too tight and explains to me that I should rest my wrist on his leg so it doesn't swell up. He is entirely matter of fact about it.

I keep hoping Kuby will burst in shouting for my release, or that someone will quietly come and get me, but it quickly becomes apparent that I am actually being hauled off to Rikers Island. Joe and I are led to the bus and find a seat in the back (I can barely fit given his size, and have to struggle not to fall from the seat). Two inmates who have been separated from each other shout back and forth excitedly about the drug raid in which they were caught. The trip is rough, as there is no suspension and potholes abound. I see Chinatown passing, and then we are on highways. An hour later, we are all waiting, still sitting in the bus, in a courtyard in the prison complex.

We may have been waiting on the bus for an hour; my sense of time is beginning to get muddled. During the night, as I try to come to grips with what's happening, it occurs to me that the disorientation involved here is intentional, part of a process of intimidation designed to encourage passivity in hardened inmates.

When we finally get off the bus, Joe and I have our handcuffs removed. We are brought through a door into a space with cages and told to stand behind a red line drawn on the floor some three or four yards from the door. A red-faced man standing by the door shouts at me: "How many crimes you been charged with?" "One," I say. "One?" he yells back, looking at a list of my offenses on a paper in front of him. "There are a lot of counts," I say. He looks at the list again, and then he shouts, with a voice louder than any I've ever heard in my life, "Fuck that! You do this shit in here, I'll take you out in the courtyard and shoot you! You hear? I'll take you outside and shoot you!" At first, I think he must be joking and gently laugh at him.

The man does not take kindly to this friendly gesture on my part. He becomes frantic and screams, "I'll *shoot* you. And get that smile off your fucking face, idiot!" He orders me to place my bag on the counter and sends me into a large cell on the left. Here there is no phone. I'm in the company of only two people: Joe and a thin man who lies exhausted on a bench.

Soon the red-faced man has me come out to fetch my bag, which he has searched. I tell him I'm requesting protective custody, and he shouts furiously, "There's none of that shit here! You'll be treated just like anybody else!" When I tell Joe I've asked for protective custody, he wryly comments, "Wrong man to ask." Joe tells me to ask the medical personnel when I see them. By now I have figured out that we're going to be kept in these cages for some period of time and then taken somewhere else for a medical checkup before going "upstairs."

The thin man on the bench seems to know Joe, and tells us that earlier he was on the floor and a cockroach got into his ear and had to be removed in the infirmary. The thin man asks about my case, and when I tell him, he says, "Fuck that shit—they give you *six months* for sending out a bunch of BS emails. I did something *really* bad, and I got *ten days* for it."

Joe and I are soon moved into another cell across from the red line, with many more inmates. We spend most of the time sitting on the dirty wooden benches or standing; as the night wears on, I stand more and more to try to keep the pressure off my back, shifting my weight from one foot to another as the pain begins to set in.

After hours of waiting, we are moved to another, particularly filthy cell. Here it gets even more crowded as the number of inmates keeps increasing. At some point Joe switches places and takes a spot that has opened up next to me on one of the hard wooden benches. We don't need to say anything. I appreciate it. More hours of surreal waiting go by. Toward midnight, a man comes into the cell and approaches me. He says, "You're Golb?" I nod. "I need to speak with you," he explains, emphasizing the word "speak" in a meaningful and polite manner. "Okay," I say, "should I bring my bag?" "No," he says in a firm, polite manner. "Later in the morning."

Then he leaves. I ask who he is, and someone says he's the "captain." Later, I find out his name is Smith. Captain Smith. But I never see him again. At least a dozen times I remind one guard or another that the "captain" wants to speak with me, but the meaning of this mystery will never be clarified.

Perhaps toward midnight, we're provided with a meal (or "chow") of rice, beans, and chicken and a cup of Kool-Aid. Then the process moves to another stage. Once we have all been numbed from fatigue and waiting, and indeed from a sense of imminent danger induced by the red-faced man screaming at one or another new arrival on the other side of the bars, around two in the morning, my name is called. I will never see Joe again.

I'm taken into a room where I'm forced to strip. One of the guards shouts, "Squat down." I squat. Then they make me put on a green jumpsuit. They give me receipts for my clothes, my bag, and the eighty-eight dollars in cash I have on me, and I'm told to keep all these receipts in my socks, which I'm allowed to continue wearing along with my underwear and shoes. It's cold in the jumpsuit without a T-shirt underneath. If I ever return to Rikers, I will be sure to take along extra pairs of underwear and several T-shirts. These are the only items one is allowed to bring into jail, but apparently they tolerate a book and a watch too.

I'm allowed to defecate in a toilet off the hallway that is open and visible to anyone passing along, and provided with a plastic cup for a urine sample. It's another one of those dirty metal toilets. The waiting now shifts from the cages to the medical checkup room. Here I sit again on a bench along the wall, with seven or eight other inmates. A few of them seem curious about the *Confessions*, which I still have with me.

One of them, Marcus, spent a full year in a Florida state penitentiary. He tells me that St. Augustine, Florida, is the oldest town in the United States. He took a class on theology in college. The *Confessions*, he says, show how you can find faith, which is there in you if you just open yourself to it. With Marcus I also meet Danny, a rock drummer who proudly shows us the tattoo on his shoulder that he shares with other members of his band. Danny has been sentenced to ten days in jail on a DUI charge. He is the only other inmate I meet who has never been in jail before. He is also one of the three or four white inmates I will see at Rikers. Marcus and Danny both listen to details of my case with their jaws dropped.

At three in the morning, my blood is drawn and a TB test administered. I'm seen by a male nurse and a female medical assistant who ask me a series of questions about my health. I tell both of them I'm seeking protective custody. The medical assistant says it's a decision to be taken by the department of corrections, not by medical personnel. The nurse tells me the head intake woman will make the decision. When I ask the head intake woman, she says I was supposed to ask the judge and it's too late. At one point, some guard comes in and tells her Captain Smith wants to speak with me. She nods at him. That's the last I ever hear of Captain Smith wanting to speak with me.

Then I'm sent back to one of the cages in my jumpsuit. Eventually we are taken down a long hall to another cage, where we are fed little boxes of Rice Krispies and milk. After two more hours of waiting, we are lined up and provided with a plastic drinking cup. I wonder whether we shouldn't be provided with a toothbrush and toothpaste too. Later I will learn that those items should have been inside the plastic cup, and since none were provided to me, I will simply have to go without brushing my teeth, at least for the time being. When I ask how long it will be before I can get a toothbrush, I'm told it can take up to a week. During my forty hours of incarceration, I will never be able to brush my teeth.

Most of the inmates are given blankets, but there are none left for me or for Marcus, who, like me, is one of the last in line. The others are also given an ID card and a PIN that gives you access to the phone and to the "commissary," where you can purchase ramen soup, granola bars, a plastic radio with headphones, and other things that might help you make it through six months. Somehow I never get the ID card or PIN, but when we get to the end of the line, I'm sent "upstairs" with everyone else. It's a quiet operation with a few orders barked here or there. It's six in the morning when we make it out of the cages.

"Upstairs" is a vast area that resembles a darkened homeless shelter, with what seems around two hundred cots distributed in rows and a glass booth near the entrance where a guard sits looking out over the prostrate inmates. We are told to pick any cot we want. Since I have no blanket, they give me a few extra sheets. We are forbidden from removing our jumpsuits, although I would keep mine on even if we were allowed to remove them.

I lie shivering on a cot near the aisle in my floppy green suit, wondering if I've been granted bail and when I will be allowed to brush my teeth. I am exhausted, but the images in my head and snoring around the room keep me from falling asleep. By eight o'clock, daylight has filtered into the room through large barred windows and reveals red and orange stains here and there on the sheets they have given me. Most of the inmates are still lying on the cots, but someone shouts out "commissary," and a number of them line up to go to the commissary. I get up, too, and try to figure out what I have to do next.

A female guard at a window in a central booth watches over the entire room. I hesitantly move toward the window, but at that point, an inmate who notices me quickly approaches and explains that he is on suicide-watch duty.[40] It is his job to make sure that none of the new arrivals are psychotic and that they all get what they need. He explains that I can get two free calls on the phone with my PIN. I tell him I never got a PIN. He says I will get one soon. He shows me the list of goods sold in the commissary and explains that I will be able to go there, too, once my account (now worth eighty-eight dollars) is activated. Most importantly, he gives me a blanket. I lie back down under the rough gray warmth and fall asleep for around an hour.

When I awake, the inmate in the cot next to mine is getting up. He is a white man with hair cropped close to his skull, looking clearly a hardened convict. He says, "You're scared, uh? Never been to jail before? It's okay, I'll protect you." He lies reading a copy of the Bible. I show him the *Confessions*. Another inmate approaches and tells him that Bible reading is a form of hypocrisy. "Because you say, if I read this, I'm not gonna do what I do on the street anymore. But then you go back out there and do it again. So it's better just not to do it instead of thinking you can read some Bible and stop. That's just an excuse."

The white man defends Bible reading. Maybe you can find something in that book that makes you a better person. A bit later, he confesses to me that he can barely understand a lot of what they're talking about in the Bible.

Another hour or so goes by. Toward nine o'clock, I and all the other new arrivals (but not Joe, who has been either released or imprisoned somewhere else) are taken down a stairwell to a large gym-sized space in which we are shown a film entitled *Orientation*, which most of them have already seen many times.

Among other details presumably required by administrative regulations, the narrator of this film explains that we have the right to make a phone call to our lawyer during the intake process—the process, that is, that I went through during the night, during which time no phone was available at all.

The film also emphasizes that we must never accept anything from another inmate, and that if we felt threatened in any way, we should speak to our "counselor." After the film, several representatives of charitable organizations give speeches, urging the inmates to take vocational training during their incarceration. We can get drug counseling. We can learn cooking skills that will allow us to seek employment in New York City restaurants. Then we are taken back up to the homeless-shelter zone.

> Unmentioned in the film is the fact that Rikers Island was named after the family of Richard Riker (1773–1842), the first Manhattan DA, who was responsible for enforcing the Fugitive Slave Act in the city. Riker belonged to the "Kidnapping Club," a conspiracy that involved randomly grabbing Black New Yorkers off the streets, declaring them to be fugitive slaves, and sending them to slavery.

After another hour on the cot, I approach the female guard at the window and explain that I have no PIN and no toothbrush. The guard says she will look into it, then calls me back as I move away from the window. "You don't take nothing from any prisoner here," she says. I quietly assert that I will never take anything from anyone, and then she reiterates: "If anyone offers you anything, you don't take it, got it?" During the day, I repeatedly ask for a toothbrush. Eventually she explains to me that since the toothbrushes are "downstairs," and we are "upstairs," I will have to do without one.

Around eleven o'clock, another guard shouts out that it's "chow" time. A wave of excitation sweeps through the cots. Inmates sit up, putter with their stuff, go toward the line-up area, and mill around. Gradually a general groaning makes itself felt. Time is going by again, and nothing is happening. We are taken downstairs for chow nearly two hours later. This is when I fully realize how the guards at Rikers use time as a form of cruelty, to disorient the inmates and awaken them to their lack of control over any aspect of their own destinies. This is like teasing a dog with a bone, except the teasing takes place over hours and hours of time.

When we are taken downstairs, we are made to wait in double file along a red line, facing the wall, then forward, then the wall again, then forward again with the guards shouting at us, before going into the giant eating space. The food is vile—no rice and beans anymore, but mushy pasta with some form of ground beef. This could probably keep a person alive, but I have difficulty stomaching it. Each of us sits in a spot we are sent to by the guards, in the order we came in. There is no sitting with any group of lunch partners like in the movies. Then they take us back upstairs to the cots again.

I'm cold, and for the second time, I begin hastily walking around the room between the cots. At one point, a friendly-looking inmate who is sitting back on his cot chatting with two others calls out to me, "Hey, do you want a T-shirt?" He seems to have a pile of T-shirts, and I immediately think he is passing them out, so I say, "Sure, thanks." He hands me the shirt, and I take it in my hands, but then I realize he's pulling them out from under his pillow. I say, "Is this your own personal T-shirt?" "Yeah," he answers. "I'm sorry," I say. "You need this T-shirt—I can't take it from you." He seems disappointed. "I'm just trying to help you out," he says. "You look cold." A grin flashes on his face, and he adds, "But that's okay. I'm gonna freeze you out!"

This is the one real moment of doubt I have about my interaction with another inmate at Rikers. Did I just offend someone by refusing a friendly gift, or did I wisely follow the guard's instructions and avoid accepting an object for which I would eventually be required to give something else in return, something I might not have? I tell my hardened Bible-reading convict-neighbor about it, and he immediately replies, "He's just trying to help you out, man. It's just a T-shirt. Cautious, huh."

I do some more walking, and during one of my rounds, I spot Russ, the suicide-watch guy, sitting on someone else's cot. He calls me over and asks me if I've gotten my PIN yet. I say no, and this time something moves him to help me. "Well, you're gonna make your call now," he says. "I'm gonna let you make your call on my PIN." He takes me to the phone. I fish the piece of paper Joe gave me out of the book, and manage to read the scratched-in number in the dim light. Russ dials the number and gives me the line. Immediately I'm connected with Ron Kuby's associate. "So they denied the bail?" I say. "No, they granted the bail!" she begins, and finally I learn that I will be going home.

She explains that my parents have cabled the money and she is about to fetch it at the bank and come up to Rikers. She doesn't know, however, how long it will take for the prison bureaucracy to become aware that they have to release me. Some of the other inmates quickly tell me that it can take the entire weekend to get me out of there. This sobers me up a bit, and I lie back down under the blanket.

It seems like I have just fallen asleep, when someone prods my leg. I open my eyes. A guard is standing there looking down at me. "Pack your stuff," he says. "You're leaving." It's three o'clock on Friday afternoon. I have nothing to "pack," but leap up. Marcus is sleeping under his sheets; I lay my blanket over him, as he asked me for it in case I left, and turn to follow the guard. He has vanished.

My exit from the system will be handled with almost as much efficiency as my entry into it. Several inmates notice my relief and warn me that it can still take days for them to actually get me out of there. One man who seems old and wise comes and sits on my cot with me. "This is what they do to you," he says. "They mess with your head. You'll be in here until the morning." He asks me many details about my case and the Dead Sea Scrolls. "That shit is fucked," he says. "You just got carried away with a bunch of BS on the internet, but I did something wrong; and you got six months for that shit."

I don't ask him for details about what he did, but he says that if he had just stayed on the F train and gone home, nothing would have happened. One thing I notice over and over again at Rikers is the necessity everyone feels to talk about their cases, often in veiled terms. I ask the old man what he will do when he gets out of there. "I'm going to stay home," he says, "and raise my daughter. I'm going to watch her grow up."

Another hour goes by. Danny comes over and shares some insights with me into the results of racial profiling on display in this giant chamber. He tells me about his rock band. He asks me if I can give him my copy of the *Confessions* when I leave. I write my number in the back of it so he can return it when he gets out, but I never hear from him again. Marcus is awake by now, and I borrow my blanket back from him as the time goes by. Then chow is announced again, and again we wait. At six o'clock, we are lined up and taken back downstairs; before we leave, I make sure Marcus has the blanket again. In the corridor downstairs, as we stand facing the wall and then straight forward, a woman shouts from somewhere, "There's a discharge down here: Golb!"

I wave a quick goodbye to the line of inmates and head off with the woman, who hands me over to a male guard. He takes me back to the cages where I spent the first night. Along the way, he stops by the room where I was initially made to squat and change into the jumpsuit, but he can't spot the yellow bag with my clothes. So when we get to the cages, I'm still wearing the jumpsuit. "You know about this discharge here?" he says to the red-faced man at the door. "No, there's no discharge," the man shouts back. "We got nothing on him." Then he shouts at me, "You been sentenced. You got no discharge." I explain that the sentence has been stayed by the appellate court and that my attorney posted bail that afternoon. "You got no discharge," he screams. "I'll shoot you!" Then he points to the cage in the corner and shouts, "Go in there."

The time is a quarter after six. Hours pass in the cage. Around a dozen of us are waiting to be discharged while the red-faced man screams abuse at new arrivals. The wait is hard not only because they apparently don't know I've been discharged and could send me back upstairs at any moment but because I no longer have anything to read. I regret having left the book with Danny. Around nine o'clock, we are all fingerprinted again.

Then the nature of the problem begins to clarify itself. Friday nights, we are told, the "box" area with the yellow bags is closed. Some of us have our clothes in that box. I show my receipt to one of the guards, and he takes out a fat wallet from his pocket and lifts it in front of my face. Not sure what this means, I back away. He seems extremely satisfied at this reaction. Eventually, they take me and a few other discharges back to the jumpsuit room and force us to select some old clothes from a huge plastic bag they have there. "It's your choice," they say. "If you wanna go home, you have to wear these clothes."

All I can come up with is a pair of old, sick-looking sweatpants, a gray T-shirt, and a black zip-up sweater, all of it way too big for my 120-pound figure—which is probably thinner now after thirty-six hours in this hellhole. In the rags from the plastic bag, I look like a homeless person. Since no account had been opened for me and my money is unavailable, I'm going to have to go home in the subway wearing this uniform. I will then have to return to Rikers on Monday to retrieve my regular clothes, including my gray scarf and my suede jacket.

When they bring me back to the cage, a wave of snickering mirth goes through the other discharges. "You take that stuff off and throw it out before you cross the door into your apartment," one of them says. Another hour goes by, and then around eleven o'clock, a guard looks in at me.

"Where do you live?" he says.

"In the Village," I answer.

"You know you can go down to the Tombs to get your money next week," he says.

"But I have to come back here for my clothes," I say.

"Let me finish!" he shouts. "I'm going to get your clothes for you!"

This is quite a relief, but then the waiting begins again. The ones who have their own clothes on are frustrated, because the delay seems to be due to those of us without clothes. But they recognize that we need our clothes, and bear it patiently. Toward midnight, I and three other discharges are again taken to the jumpsuit room; this time we are given our clothes. When I reappear in the cage, faces light up. "That's different," someone says. He approvingly touches the suede on my jacket.

I am released from Rikers at one o'clock Saturday morning, ten hours after the guard prodded my leg and told me I was leaving. (Twelve years later almost to the day, news will trickle out of a class action settlement requiring New York City to pay $3,500 "for every instance between October 2014 to October 2022 that a detainee was not released within three hours after bail was paid, as mandated by law."[41] Given the number of victims of the city's illegal conduct, payments are expected reach a total of $300 million. Since illegal confinements before the dates specified are not covered, the agreement will have no bearing on me.)

After waiting another hour for a bus to Queens Plaza, I take the F train home, call my parents, and brush my teeth. Then I fall asleep.

Late in the morning, I go to see Ron Kuby to fetch my cell phone (which I left with him at the sentencing) and to find out what happened. While I was on my way to Rikers, Kuby headed to see Judge Rosalyn Richter of the First Appellate Division, New York's intermediate appellate court. She issued an order staying the sentence. John Bandler objected to this decision on grounds of my moral turpitude and criminal propensities. He demanded that bail, if granted, be set in the amount of $500,000. Richter set it at $25,000. She asserted that the case was one of "first impression," since the issues involved had never arisen before. This assertion, of course, already contradicted Berkman, who had explained to the jury that the case was simply an ordinary, run-of-the-mill instance of the "other" kind of identity theft.

The next day, I sleep again for a long time. When I awake, I put some of my stuff together and start waiting for the appeal.

* * *

Even, however, before the first steps could be taken in the impending fight for my rights, another significant consequence of the criminalization of my Dead Sea Scrolls campaign was to become clear. As we saw earlier, Bandler had been able to withhold Schiffman's "response to Internet accusations" from my legal team until the eve of trial, and then had used the "confidential" document against me, while I was blocked from testifying in response to its contents. The special New York legal rule that allowed Bandler to keep me from seeing this item would be changed ten years after my trial: as of January 1, 2020, prosecutors would be obliged to hand over all their evidence to defendants early on. And in view of what happened with the letter several weeks after my trip to Rikers, it seems fair to ask whether, if the new rule had been in effect at the time of my arrest, my trial would have taken place at all.[42] (Notably, Robert Morgenthau, during his extraordinarily long tenure as DA, had strenuously objected to this and various other urgently needed criminal justice reforms that were eventually enacted by the New York State legislature long after his retirement.)

In the text of his secret communication to NYU administrators—now, as a result of my trial, a public document—Schiffman complained that he had been "portrayed" as admitting to plagiarism and informed his colleagues that the anonymous internet accusations concerning the scrolls were a "sordid attempt to encourage acceptance of [Norman] Golb's theories."[43] The text also contained various paradoxical claims along with a number of familiar assertions: Golb, according to Schiffman, was an "aggressive" man; and there was nothing new about certain fundamental ideas introduced into scrolls scholarship by Golb during the 1980s—a claim made despite the fact that Schiffman himself, in the 1990s, had presented these ideas as a "revolutionary" scholarly contribution of his own. According to the testimony of NYU dean Foley, Schiffman was at no point required to submit this remarkable document to university officials but did so of his own volition.

Once the document did become public as a result of my trial, my father would publish a detailed response to Schiffman's "confidential letter" on the University of Chicago's Oriental Institute website. The response, dated November 30, 2010, pointed to a range of misleading statements in the letter Schiffman had addressed to his NYU faculty superiors, starting with the NYU Jewish studies professor's misleading denial that Avi Katzman had ever accused him of plagiarism. Next, Schiffman's claim that he had himself "called attention to the wide nature of the Qumran library … considerably before Golb wrote any of his works" was not borne out by the text of Schiffman's 1975 doctoral dissertation, to which the NYU professor expressly referred in his "confidential letter."

Schiffman, Golb continued, had coupled these claims with the false and defamatory assertion that he, Golb, had used "threats" and "lawsuits" to "advance ... his point of view." And, he indicated, Schiffman had gone to the length of *fabricating a source* to support another one of his claims—that Golb had "argued at times that the scrolls constituted mainly the library of the Jerusalem Temple."[44]

> In his "confidential letter," Schiffman claimed that Avi Katzman's 1993 *Haaretz* article contained "absolutely no accusation of plagiarism." Schiffman also asserted that on the second page of a "presentation," Norman Golb had argued that the scrolls came from the Jerusalem Temple—an argument Golb had never made and a "presentation" he had never presented. The existence of such a document appeared to have been fabricated by Schiffman.

Toward the end of his response, my father focused on three additional statements in the "confidential letter": that Schiffman was a member of the "organizing committee of the conference commemorating the sixtieth anniversary of the Dead Sea Scrolls, held at the Shrine of the Book of the Israel Museum in July, 2008"; that the committee had "decided not to involve Golb in the program"; and that "some others with dissident theories were invited, but declined to attend." Although in his letter Schiffman had not defined what he meant by a "dissident" in Dead Sea Scrolls scholarship, my father observed that "by the standards of Qumranological belief set ... in the 1950s, most scholars of the subject today are dissidents, with many nuanced theories crowding the Internet." He then addressed Schiffman's role in rigging conferences on the scrolls:

> What S. apparently means by his statement is that any scholar who professes [certain beliefs] is entitled to be anointed a non-dissident and to attend meetings where he and his colleagues lecture to one another. The position of S. and his fellow believers is thus that those scholars who do not accept these ideas of the traditional Qumranologists may or may not be allowed to lecture at meetings on the scrolls, depending on the good grace of the traditionalists ... Schiffman ... in effect suggests that there is nothing inappropriate about keeping lectures and debates on the scrolls under the control of a particular group of scholars who oppose the ideas of certain other scholars. This bizarre view of academic debate ... is obviously contrary to the free and open pursuit of scholarship.[45]

It is unclear how much actual discussion of Golb's response took place within the academic community, at NYU or elsewhere; this remains the case today, even a year after the republication of both texts as appendices in *The Qumran Con* (see pages 381–413 of that work). A comment posted online by Lawrence Kaplan, a scholar of Jewish law and philosophy at McGill University, describes Golb's response as an "expert demolition job ... on Prof. Schiffman's 'Confidential Letter.'"[46] At least one longer comment was addressed directly to my father, by his colleague Joel Kraemer of the Committee on Social Thought, in an email of December 9, 2010:

> Dear Norman,
>
> I read your response to Schiffman the day we had the very pleasant lunch, for which again thanks. You had no choice

but to reply, as unpleasant as it is to indulge in polemics. Although Raph's impersonating him, if that is what happened, was not a good idea, one can understand Raph's reaction to someone who was, in his view, taking positions from your publications. By reacting the way he did, Schiffman pushed the issue of his plagiarism to the forefront of the discussion. He obviously felt the need to inform his university's officers that he was innocent of that.

If I am not mistaken, you made public your dissent from the regnant position in 1980. This, if I am correct, was at least ten years after you began to think in new directions. You took me in the academic year 1969–70, when you were at Tel Aviv U. and I was in Jerusalem, to the Qumran site. There, you raised the question of the main room being a "Scriptorium" and the function of the edifice that once stood there. You obviously gave much thought to your new paradigm before going public.

Schiffman's explanations why you are not invited to certain conferences are, of course, absurd. There were clearly attempts at censorship. Again, I understand perfectly Raph's reaction.

I hope all goes well with him. In a perfect world, fellow scholars would have embraced your findings, as did archaeologists and some others, and you would have been spared *'agmat nefesh* ["grief of the soul"]. You can rest assured that in the future, when the history of the discovery of the Qumran documents and their interpretation are discussed, the truth will win out and you will be thoroughly vindicated.[47]

When my father shared Kraemer's words with me, I had the impression that the great Maimonides scholar, whose learning and sense of humor I had once had the opportunity to appreciate during a memorable dinner-table conversation at my parents' home, had consciously written a document for the historical record.

> *"There were clearly attempts at censorship ... The truth will win out."*

A little over a month later, on January 12, 2011, a press release issued by the president of Yeshiva University indicated that Schiffman was leaving his chair at NYU—with no previous announcement and in the middle of the academic year—and had been appointed to a midlevel administrative position at Yeshiva. The release referred to Schiffman's "reputation as a scholar" and to his "collegial sensibilities," which made him the "ideal person" to "lead the effort to 're-imagine' undergraduate education" at the university to which he had suddenly moved.[48] (In 2009 and 2011, Yeshiva University secured "over $230 million in public funding" by falsely claiming that it was a secular educational institution. Years later, the university would insist that its status as a *religious* institution entitled it to ignore New York State's equal protection laws. Three state senators would demand an explanation. "We will not abide," they stated in a letter, "the use of state funds to support discriminatory behavior that excludes LGBTQ students from their right to an equal education.")[49]

Schiffman would spend three years at Yeshiva, and then, in 2013, he would return to NYU, to serve as the Judge Abraham Lieberman Professor of Jewish Studies. The late Abraham Lieberman, in addition to his role as a municipal judge in Weehawken, New Jersey, was a former president of the Jewish Culture Foundation of NYU and a founder of Yeshiva University. The NYU Jewish studies chair endowed by Lieberman had been vacated by its previous occupant, who had moved to California; as a result, Schiffman would once again be offered a position of power and influence over students at an institution whose faculty code strictly forbids not only the use of another author's ideas without appropriate credit but any form of "misrepresentation." Schiffman, despite having testified under oath that nobody reads the code, was apparently aware of this rule: in his radio interview with Eve Harow a decade after my arrest, he would declare that his job was "to tell the truth."⁵⁰ Perhaps Harow knew nothing of my case, or felt it would be indiscreet to ask any questions about it, for it would go unmentioned during the interview.

One person who of course knew a *lot* about the case was Robert Cargill. From his particular perspective, he had been tracking its course month after month, year after year, in many sensationalistic blog entries featuring titles like "DR. GOLB FOUND GUILTY!"⁵¹ On January 12, 2011—the same day as the Yeshiva University press release about Schiffman's move from NYU—Cargill was still at it; on that day, he posted a "quote of the day" about Dead Sea Scrolls scholarship from his own trial testimony.⁵² In response, Christian Brady, a scholar of rabbinic literature at the University of Kentucky, posted an item of his own, entitled "I Worry for My Friend Dr. Robert Cargill." The item was ostensibly focused on the fact that "for quite some time now," Cargill had been properly capitalizing words like "I," or the opening of sentences, in his blogs. When Cargill replied by acknowledging that he had decided to use capitalization because "people keep telling me more people would read my work if i [*sic*] used actual punctuation," Brady came back with a remark that perhaps meant to convey his point in a more direct way: "I do now take you far more seriously. That and the fact that you can put people in jail."⁵³

* * *

Meanwhile, the ongoing Dead Sea Scrolls museum-exhibit saga had seen a new development, one that initially seemed to hold great promise. During the months before my trial, in an exhibit at the Science Museum of Minnesota, two curators with opposing views—my father's student Michael Wise and Lawrence Schiffman's student Alex Jassen—had guided viewers toward an understanding of the debate over scroll origins and the nature of Qumran.⁵⁴

Unfortunately, this departure from widespread exhibition policy, like that of the Jewish Museum which had sparked my "Larry Schiffman" emails and led to my arrest and prosecution, would remain the rare exception proving the rule. At the Milwaukee Public

Museum exhibit, also showing in 2010, and at ensuing follow-ups in other American cities, the agenda would again be set by members of the "international team" responsible for the earlier efforts at San Diego and elsewhere.[55] Accordingly, all these exhibits would be centered around the idea of the scrolls as the product or library of a desert sect. One of the first signs of the lengths the team would go to in popularizing their propaganda came in October 2011, when a massive display featuring the scrolls opened in the Discovery Times Square exhibition space (New York), with Risa Levitt Kohn of San Diego State University listed as curator and Lawrence Schiffman of New York University as "consultant."[56] Promoting the exhibit in an interview with Fox News, Schiffman declared, "We've got here a house that you can look into and get a sense of what was there. How people live. How people bathed. How they cooked. We've got some weapons. We've got all kinds of things from that real life that you read about, especially in the books like Samuel and Kings."[57]

Discerning visitors did not seem especially impressed. Complaining of a "vaguely unsatisfying" show and a "failure of nerves" on the part of the exhibitors, Michael Satlow of Brown University suggested that perhaps the exhibitors had been unable to "acquire enough objects to mount a respectable exhibition on the Dead Sea Scrolls themselves, so they acquired other tangentially related objects to fill out the show and then didn't quite know what to do with them all."[58] Writing in the *Jewish Forward*, Jenna Weissman Joselit of George Washington University described the "discomfort" she had experienced in face of the "uneasy mix of the authentic and the ersatz that characterized the 'Dead Sea Scrolls' exhibit."[59] And Tzvee Zahavy went so far as to assert that the exhibit left uninformed visitors "ignorant of the basics of the culture and history of the ancient materials," and that "based on this exhibit ... [a] newcomer to the scrolls could not put together a coherent narrative of the contents or the context of the objects."[60]

None of the commentators spelled out the circumstances leading to the exhibit's problematic presentation, which included distorted claims about the origins of Christianity and the "Holy Land." With that crucial context kept in the dark, few observers could spot the signs of an abuse of both power and financial influence to suppress evidence conflicting with the view the exhibitors were defending: a purpose that conflicted with the principles of freedom of information and the public's right to know.

Glaring conceptual contradictions nevertheless emerged in the exhibition. The Discovery Times Square exhibitors at one point observed that "there is too much variety in the scrolls, and they are too numerous to have been written by a single, small community. Scholars have begun to question the Essene connection to Qumran and Qumran's connection to the scrolls."[61] To be sure, the questioning had "begun" thirty years earlier, and there was no mention of the evidence, itself logically intertwined with such "questioning," that the scrolls originated in various libraries in Jerusalem. Instead, visitors were referred to a "tantalizing mystery" and were offered the observations that "the authors of the Dead Sea Scrolls were intimately familiar with Jerusalem" and—in an apparent variation of an argument central to the Jerusalem-libraries theory—that the "scrolls provide a porthole [*sic*] to an era when a variety of Jewish groups attempted to live their lives in accordance with the writings of their sacred past."

Despite these concessions to reality, the heavily visited Times Square exhibition, like nearly all the others that had preceded it, was filled with inaccurate and erroneous statements of all sorts. Of these, one was the claim, entirely unsubstantiated by any historical evidence, that Christianity and Judaism had simultaneously emerged from a commonly shared "Israelite" background. This claim directly clashed with the heavily documented historical fact of Christianity's emergence from the background of intertestamental Judaism. Similarly, visitors were informed that "Israel became the Holy Land" during early Christian

> The Times Square exhibit falsely informed visitors that the Dead Sea Scrolls were written "when Judaism and Christianity were just taking form." The exhibit presented the Christianization of Palestine (which was very short lived, a fact unmentioned in the exhibit) as a natural process, without mentioning the violent persecutions of Jews that accompanied it.

times, when in fact the term is already found in the Hebrew Bible. There is no evidence it was used by most early Christians (for whom only sites associated with Jesus were "holy"), though it later came to be shared by Jews, Christians, and Muslims during the medieval period.

With these and other similar claims, the exhibitors responsible for the 2011 Discovery Times Square scrolls exhibition apparently sought to prevent public confusion from taking root in New York City.[62] From there, the scrolls show headed to similar venues in other cities; visitors in Philadelphia included President Obama and other members of America's political and cultural elite. While the entertainment value of the scrolls was being fully realized, I was slowly heading into seven years of appellate litigation.

8
"If They Nab You Again, You're Finished"

"You committed fraud. If they nab you again, you're finished." The female probation officer assigned to my case is a hardened bureaucrat. Once a month, I am required to show up, put my hand in a palm-print machine, take a drug test, report on whether I have had any "police contact," and provide information on any work or activities I'm involved in that could allow me to commit another crime. Strictly speaking, I am not actually supposed to be on probation, because the sentence was stayed and probation was part of the sentence. But as we know by now, such rules don't matter, and steps need to be taken to make sure I don't "imitate" anyone again in an inappropriate "manner."

Reacting immediately to the conviction, Manhattan DA Cyrus Vance Jr.—who, we recall, had received, a year before, a $34,500 campaign contribution from Ira Rennert, the founder of the Ingeborg and Ira Rennert World Center for the Dead Sea Scrolls—issues, on September 29, 2010, a new statement to the press. Stealing money, he declares, isn't the only type of identity fraud, and "using fictitious identities to impersonate victims is not what open academic debate seeks to foster."[1] Writing on the Simple Justice website, former prosecutor Scott Greenfield comments as follows:

> Say what? Cy, good buddy, those two statements don't go together. You aren't the arbiter of academic debate, and there's no crime of unfostering. Identity fraud requires that something be stolen, that someone be harmed. When we do away with harm, and substitute empty rhetoric in its place, all the really funny jokesters are just as guilty. And there are a lot of really funny (though some are brutal as well) people on the Internet.[2]

201

Cyrus Vance ignores these remarks. He cannot be expected to cry from the rooftops that he colluded with liars, charlatans, and alleged plagiarists. A year later, he will argue for dismissal of the rape charges he himself had filed against the director of the International Monetary Fund, Dominique Strauss-Kahn. Toward the same time, Vance's office will also make a special request for Jeffrey Epstein's sexual predator status to be lowered; later, the same office will decline to prosecute Harvey Weinstein after an actress goes to the police with rape allegations.[3] Both the Epstein and the Weinstein decisions will eventually be reversed in the face of a public outcry, but Vance will never admit that the contrasting decisions were simply based on political opportunism.

> *"You aren't the arbiter of academic debate."*

A number of important principles are set forth on the DA's website, where we read, for example, that his office is "always mindful of the prosecutor's duty to advance the cause of justice. Thus, where it appears that the defendant has been unfairly prejudiced by some error in the proceedings leading to his conviction, the Appeals Bureau forthrightly acknowledges the defect and advocates a remedy that will effectively redress it without unduly harming the public."[4] Such moral scruples are understandable when dealing with rape charges against figures like Strauss-Kahn, Epstein, and Weinstein; but it appears there is no need to apply them when a violation of the rules regulating polite academic discussion is at stake.

"Fear Corrupts ... Perhaps the Fear of a Loss of Power"—John Steinbeck

Thinking back on my trial during the weeks following my release on bail, I was confounded by the amount of charges filed and convictions secured—and, above all, by the ludicrous disparity between the verdict and the complete lack of harm, understood even in the prosecution's sense, caused by my actions. During the trial, the two deans from New York University had testified that the "Larry Schiffman" emails struck them as "weird"; that they did not take them seriously; and that, apart from a few conversations on the phone with Schiffman, they refrained from investigating the plagiarism allegations because the source was not "credible."[5] Schiffman himself had testified and informed the press that he suffered no financial harm and that nobody believed he had committed plagiarism.[6] Since so much was made of so little, clearly there had to be some kind of special explanation for the prosecution's reasoning, motivations, and methods.

For a start, even beyond the personal and ideological agendas at stake in the Dead Sea Scrolls controversy, a lot depended on the case's outcome. Clearly, the district attorney saw it as being in his interest both to preserve and to expand the capacity of prosecutors to prevent, as much as possible, the internet from being used to threaten the public repute or indeed the careers of well-connected, influential, and powerful players in various institutional spheres. In this respect, the concrete institutional reality of NYU seemed especially important. The university's role, for example, in real estate development and expansion was well known, and its chairs, as in all other large and important private educational institutions, were funded by a range of business moguls—including, in NYU's case, by New York businessman Ira Rennert. It did not occur to me that Rennert might be guilty of conspiracy, and I am not making any such allegation now. But his funding of the World Center for the Dead Sea Scrolls, seen in tandem with his near-simultaneous, substantial contribution to Cyrus Vance Jr.'s campaign and his long-standing generosity toward NYU, itself seemed, at the very least, to raise an appearance of impropriety on Vance's part.

In light of Vance's declaration of his personal opinion about "what free and open academic debate seeks to foster," the efforts to suppress opposition to the Qumran-sectarian ideology, at NYU as elsewhere, seemed to merit special attention. During the early decades of scrolls research, a relatively small group of scholars monopolized access to a corpus of ancient texts possessing massive historical importance and imposed on them an interpretation to all appearances in harmony with predetermined religious-ideological tenets. By the time of my trial, especially in light of the significant sums generated both by the popular museum exhibits and by evangelical tourism, that situation had changed. Qumranology, through its major representatives and popularizers, had emerged as a well-funded academic and pseudoacademic structure, one that was even interlinked with New York City political, legal, and business spheres. The impact of these spheres on both historical scholarship and biblical archaeology could well be considered the outcome of a smoothly run form of contemporary multi-institutional networking, and it was quite the opposite of what "free and open academic debate" should be "fostering."

The *tool* taken up by the district attorney to protect what he apparently considered to be his own self-interest was the criminalization of both "annoying" speech and—under arguably bogus pretexts—speech regarded as defamatory. To achieve its purpose, the prosecution had carefully refrained from addressing any evidence that risked pointing to my innocence. This technique was effectively used to conceal several direct statements reflecting the intent that I claimed I *did* have—statements I and my attorneys would only get around to focusing on, within the mounds of "evidence" dumped on us a few days before the trial began, many months after my conviction. There was that email of August 4, 2008, in which I stated that I had written "an article exposing Lawrence Schiffman's plagiarism."[7] During the same period, I had expressed my opinion that a "skewed pair of lectures" scheduled to take place at the Jewish Museum would "egregiously misinform the public." Similarly, several months previously, I had explained to my brother that the "idea" of my letters of complaint to UCLA faculty members was to "embarrass" two academics "by informing people of the truth (which many of them might not know)."

These statements, never mentioned by Bandler, were sometimes contained in portions of lengthy email threads. The prosecutors had culled and patched together scraps of casual banter from these threads to convince the jury that I intended to "harm" various academics who were simply exercising, as it were, their right to pursue their careers. While highlighting such banter, the prosecutors had deliberately skirted the passages that signaled my intent to expose misconduct and to inform people of the truth.

By avoiding such blatant, direct evidence of my intent, the prosecution—whose "duty," we must recall, is to seek "justice"—had been able to subject me to what some might regard as a campaign of vilification. Already carried out through the narrative the DA's "public information" office had presented to the press, the process would later again be reflected in the "facts" cited in the decisions of the appellate courts. In the prosecution's briefs, my use of expressions like "demolish" (as in "demolish an argument" or "demolish an opponent") would be repeatedly cited to suggest that there was something criminal about my mentality. My academic opponents would be described as "perceived adversaries" or as "fiercely despised." My criticism of their actions would be labeled as an effort to "target them in order to derail their careers." My defense of opposing views would be regarded as "promoting" a theory—a hint, particularly when combined with the claim that I sought to gain a thousand dollars, that the prosecution wished to depict academic culture as simply one kind of commercial enterprise.[8]

I was, according to Bandler and his colleague Vincent Rivellese, who would take over in the appellate stages of the litigation, "perturbed" by what they clearly regarded as the perfectly ordinary decision to exclude Norman Golb from museum lecture series; when I suggested that a lecture be delivered free of charge as a public service, I was "scheming," "plotting," and "brainstorming." My demand that Avi Katzman's allegations of plagiarism be investigated in accordance with academic regulations, and my effort to call attention to that demand with mock confessions, was a "trick" designed to entice NYU into investigating them. By criticizing a museum exhibit, I had "maligned" it. And by referring to Voltaire as an example of a figure who used pseudonyms, anonymity, and satire in the context of religious controversies, I had "compared" myself to the French Enlightenment philosopher, as the prosecution would assert in a phrase borrowed from an article by *New York Times* crime beat reporter John Eligon.[9]

From a legal standpoint, the fundamental objection to this entire façade was not only the use of character assassination to sway the jury and judges against me but the prosecution's effort to give a vast, sweeping reach to the various statutes invoked—most of which were part of the "fraud" chapter of the New York penal code. It was in fact only through such expansion that my campaign could be criminalized at all. To be sure, in the context of prosecutions brought under various federal statutes, the United States Supreme Court had held the kind of sweeping interpretations of fraud invoked by the Manhattan prosecutors to be "void for vagueness"— that is, too amorphous for a defendant to have known that he was committing a crime; the scope of such statutes must, the court had held, be limited to bribes and kickbacks or to some other illicit form of monetary gain.[10] My attorneys had submitted lengthy arguments to Berkman pointing out these decisions, urging that the case be dismissed on First and Fourteenth Amendment grounds. She had responded by explaining that there was no need for her to address their arguments; after all, I was free to raise them at the appellate level and to continue pleading my philosophical differences with the prosecution, even long after her mandatory retirement from the bench at the age of seventy.

* * *

The first appeal brief in my case is due in March 2011. During the weeks leading up to the filing, I have a difference of opinion with my attorney, Ronald Kuby. In discussions and emails, I remind him that I have, in my view, been subjected to a prosecution for criminal libel under bogus legal pretenses. Accordingly, the focus of the appeal should, I insist, be the trial judge's ruling that "neither good faith nor truth is a defense," her conduct toward me and my attorneys throughout the trial, and her unfairness in favoring the prosecutor, who was allowed to repeatedly denounce my "false" accusations, against me, the defendant, who was not allowed to introduce any evidence of the *truth* of those accusations. The trial was in fact gutted of the truth: arguably an obvious violation of my right to defend myself against the charges.

Kuby declines to go along with this tactic. The issue, he insists, is "defaulted" because an adequate objection was never made during the trial.[11] Ultimately, a sort of compromise is reached, whereby the matter gets mentioned along the way but never as a separate point of appeal. By the time we get to federal court six years later, the issue will suddenly seem more "relevant," but the district court judge will rule that I have defaulted on the claim by not raising it adequately in the state *appellate* courts: precisely what Kuby refused to do because of the lack of an adequate objection on point at trial.[12] In the very last stages of the appeal, I will for the most part be reduced to arguing the single issue—one so abstract as to be almost devoid of human interest—that Kuby has wished to press all along: the charges, even as retroactively reinterpreted by the state appellate courts, are impermissibly "vague" and "overbroad."

Before we reach that point, however, years go by. As often seen in American criminal cases where the accused declines to make a deal, the process is the punishment. First I am disbarred for felony convictions, resulting in my loss of my means of livelihood; then I have to wait. After the initial appeal is filed, seventeen months pass without a response from Cyrus Vance's prosecutorial team. When the response finally comes, it demonstrates the strength, at the appellate level, of the same tactic used throughout the trial:

- vigorously assault my character (and that of my eighty-year-old mother based on her private email remarks about Schiffman's moral stature)
- show that I am dishonest because I use pseudonyms
- lace the presentation with dozens of innuendos, hints, and suggestions to the effect that my father's views are unpopular and I was upset because he wasn't getting the "homage" I imagined he deserved
- confront the judges with an intricate—at times even oxymoronic—mesh of jargon and half-baked arguments leaving the impression that there must, after all, have been *some* basis for the charges[13]

Even after I get the felonies vacated, readmission to the bar will be far from guaranteed. Who would willingly appear in front of an ethics panel and demonstrate the appropriate degree of contrition required in such circumstances, when he feels he has been railroaded and wrongfully convicted? The number of disbarred lawyers who are ever allowed to practice law again is extremely small (around 10 percent), a fact the prosecutors were well aware of when they filed the fallacious felony charges. The prosecution's easily discernible aim is to strip me of professional standing, and of income, as punishment for my resistance.

"This Is the Rough-and-Tumble of the Internet?"

Meanwhile, I had continued collecting information on internet impersonation as a popular form of polemical discourse; my lawyers submitted the list I compiled to the various appellate courts.[14] The list would go unmentioned in the judicial opinions, but the court clerks assigned the task of examining my appeal must have been aghast at the material they had the opportunity to read when clicking on all the links—proof to them, perhaps, of the deplorable inaction of governmental and law enforcement agencies. To the minds of the clerks, what was at work on the internet must have appeared a plague of steadily worsening fakery. What I had compiled was a jumble of satire and hoaxes telling truth to power, all of them stewing in the same electronic kettle as the most noxious, societally harmful fake news from Russia and innumerable alt-right websites like American Renaissance and the Daily Stormer.[15]

The list included websites opened and messages tweeted out (and emailed!) in the names of dozens upon dozens of public figures—in London, a site had even been opened by music professor Howard Fredrics, my fellow Oberlin alumnus, in the name of Sir Peter Scott, the former chancellor of Kingston University, the feature of the site being its detailed exposure of that institution's acquiescence in blatantly antisemitic campus activity.[16] In the US, campus trolls had repeatedly opened Twitter accounts in the names of university presidents. A report on this phenomenon explained that "fake presidential Twitter accounts have cropped up at Columbia University, Wesleyan University, Georgetown University, Brown University, the University of Texas at Austin, and Vassar College."[17] The report indicated that university officials had occasionally submitted requests to Twitter to remove some of the accounts. Another news item on the same topic informed readers that Michael L. Wesch, a professor of cultural anthropology at Kansas State University, found the "spoofs ... revealing" and liked "how 'authentic' they seem."[18]

Clearly, from the perspective endorsed by Cyrus Vance Jr., authentic-sounding fake tweets in the name of university presidents were "not what open academic debate seeks to foster." Was the criminalization of such activities in New York meant to extend to their entire range and to reach, for example, groups like the Yes Men who impersonate people, companies, and organizations so convincingly that they fool audiences of many thousands? Or was it meant to be limited to infractions that cause annoyance in a refined, networked milieu of institutionally normalized "academic debate"? Quoted in *Inside Higher Education* shortly after my arrest, Lawrence Schiffman, adept at public relations and having dealt with allegations of plagiarism by filing a police complaint, seemed to have left the issue open in his own expression of a victim's innocent befuddlement: "This is the rough-and-tumble of the Internet?"[19] In light of his response to my "confessions," the implication seemed to be that at least this academic form of rough-and-tumble merited police suppression, whether or not it in fact consisted in an *idea or message being conveyed*.

The question, however, remained whether such suppression was meant to be limited to fake communications disseminated in the "name" of faculty members at institutions like NYU. David Mazella, a specialist in satire at the University of Houston, had observed an "entire constellation of fake blogs" impersonating prominent national figures such as Steve Jobs and John McCain. "One of the keys to this kind of online writing," Mazella wrote, "is the strategic mystery surrounding its sources: the satire always works better, I think, when there is genuine uncertainty regarding its origins and therefore its purposes."[20] But if there was uncertainty as to the purposes of a text, then the path lay open toward criminalization by zealous prosecutors. For who was to say that the authors of these strategically mysterious, fake blogs did not intend to cause some "harm" or to obtain a "benefit," as required by the statutes? As Rebecca Greenfield of the Atlantic Wire had pointed out, the "line" between parody and nonparody "blurs quickly";[21] but in the shadow of the precedent that would ultimately be set by *People v. Golb*, future parodists who might be tempted to engage in acts of online impersonation would be well advised to make their innocently comedic intent entirely clear—gutting satire of its subversive heartbeat.

The danger was arguably extremely real, because, as Viktor Mayer-Schönberger, a professor of "internet governance" at the Oxford Internet Institute, had declared, we were living in a "Foucauldian postmodern world where we can't tell the truth from fakery."[22] For philosopher Slavoj Žižek, the "misrepresentations" spawned by the internet were even "part of our own identities"; the internet was nothing less than a "space of false disidentification."[23] Such statements may have presaged the election of Donald Trump; but they also pointed to a convergence between reaction to the "fake news" phenomenon and a palpable, growing fear circulating within the social and professional world occupied by North America's educated elite.

On its surface, this was a fear of internet "trolls" (often amalgamated with "bullies"), fake social media accounts, and other forms of false and devious electronic communication. But false internet speech was also perceived as dangerously undermining the authority of trained expertise—which was, of course, acknowledged to be infected by charlatanry, abuse, and corruption, but was nevertheless seen to be necessary for the functioning of any advanced society. Still worse, electronic fakery was perceived as contributing to the fragmentation (or "disidentification") of our most primary social bonds, soon to be replaced by masses of alienated "social media" users operating in a system defined by uncertainty, confusion, and distrust. That perception was exacerbated by a reality of different social strata living in entirely separated cognitive frameworks shaped by both cable news and the internet.

Such was the tumultuous backdrop to my legal efforts to defend my flouting of the institutional suppression of a historical-religious debate about Western foundations in which my father had played a key role—and my calling attention, with pseudonymous blogs, mockery, and satirical email impersonation, to allegations of malfeasance by prominent members of the network involved in that suppression. This backdrop, itself only clear in the light of societal changes catalyzed by the advent of global instantaneous electronic communication, would undoubtedly play a decisive role in the outcome of these legal efforts.

*　*　*

Waiting month after month—and soon year after year—for the machinery of justice to move, I had plenty of time to follow the growing controversy over the use of electronic means to expose public scandals. During the same period, the judges assigned to my appeal were likely reading the *New York Times*, watching the cable debates, and becoming just as well aware as everyone else of all the internet tumult. They could not help but be aware of the controversies surrounding Edward Snowden, Julian Assange, and Chelsea Manning.[24] News stories, at the time, also provided ample details on MIT prodigy Aaron Swartz's downloading of 4.8 million files from the Massachusetts Institute of Technology's JSTOR ("Journal Storage") repository of published academic articles, for the sake of open access to these articles by everyone, not just those with institutional privileges or money—and on his ensuing arrest by federal authorities and his subsequent tragic suicide.[25] Other stories similarly provided details on the saga of Barrett Brown, an American journalist and satirist who reported about leaked and hacked "military-industrial complex" data, and who was sentenced to sixty-three months in prison on what some claimed, in sharp antithesis to the presiding trial judge's position, to be grossly trumped-up charges.[26] And beyond such highly publicized individuals, controversies, and incidents, the judges were also probably aware of such cases as the impersonation of President Hamid Karzai of Afghanistan, an impersonation not carried out on the net but that, as the

McClatchy Washington Bureau put it, "bounces from cell phone to cell phone." An aid to the Afghan president commented that "freedom of speech should have its limits ... I don't think cursing one's wife—or insulting someone's personality—should have a place in freedom of speech."[27]

In 2014, an anonymous group pretending to be Koch Industries would post deadpan satirical "press releases" that completely fooled reporters. A federal judge would throw the case out, and the *New York Times* would comment that "on the Internet, parody and mockery have never been easier to pull off."[28] Also in 2014, a tweet sent out under the name of Peoria mayor Jim Ardis would portray him "as a foul-mouthed politician with a penchant for liquor, drugs and prostitutes";[29] its author would be arrested, his home searched, but no charges would be filed and he would eventually collect $125,000 in damages from the city.

Considering that my own experience and research might be of use in an academic context, in the midst of the appeals process, I applied for a fellowship to the Berkman Center for Internet and Society at Harvard.[30] My application set forth a research project, the topic being the "Limits of Satire." I proposed "to develop a philosophy of satirical discourse that allows us to elucidate some of its more troubling online manifestations—including anonymous satire—in the broader context of a socio-political theory that accounts for divergent normative attitudes." Noting that the phenomenon of satire was "imbued with the psychology of scandal: the speaking of *that which must not be said*," I suggested that "online interaction, frequently characterized ... by uncertain identities, potentially provides opportunities for a far more potent brand of satire and controversy than the televised, politically correct, and more ritualized formats that we have grown accustomed to viewing in the self-declared parodies of *Saturday Night Live* and similar productions."

Satire's "moral role," I continued, "and its demonstrable relation to a crisis involving identity and scandal, necessitates a *moral taxonomy* of satire. The semiotic uncertainties associated with the genre, resulting from its use of irony, hyperbole, understatement, innuendo, caricature, reductio ad absurdum, and personification; the varying attitudes it confronts; and the unease and feelings of anger and embarrassment that it necessarily evokes, lead to efforts to define its boundaries, to categorize admissible and transgressive satirical forms." Therefore, I argued, it was "important to compile data and create a catalogue of satirical forms."[31]

Focusing on the reaction of the prosecutors and of the judge in *People v. Golb* (and noting that Judge Carol Berkman was herself an alumna of Harvard University), I pointed out that the criminalization of certain emails in that case "appears to be founded on the presumptions that Internet satire must be *comical* or 'just for fun'; that it must be *clear*, or overtly declare itself to be satirical; and that it must be directed towards an audience that has an *expectation* of satire, as when surfers log onto 'satire.com.'" After making a few comments on "the moral and legal ambiguities of online satire,"[32] I expressed my desire to examine these issues "throughout the proposed project ... in the atmosphere of combined rigor and freedom of inquiry fostered by the Berkman Center for Internet and Society."

An office assistant at the Berkman Center rapidly sent me a short rejection letter. Were the internet specialists employed at the center troubled by the coincidence of their institution's name with that of the judge who presided at my trial, fellow Harvard alumna Carol Berkman? Did they feel that my project lacked merit? Did they feel it would be inappropriate to host an applicant facing jail time as a fellow? The answer was apparently one of those little things that must "never be written down."

"Only the Suppressed Word Is Dangerous"—Ludwig Börne

"Whoever Would Overthrow the Liberty of a Nation Must Begin by Subduing the Freeness of Speech"—Benjamin Franklin

"Everyone Has the Right to Freedom of ... Expression; This Right Includes Freedom to ... Impart Information and Ideas

through Any Media"—UN Universal Declaration of Human Rights

From the outset, the various courts handling the *People v. Golb* appeal would need to address the constitutionality of several laws restricting speech based on its content. I had been charged under a wide variety of criminal statutes, each extended beyond its original intended scope to apply to accusatory, provocative, and in part satirical speech. Twenty-one of my convictions would ultimately be vacated for lack of evidence, inapplicability of the statutes invoked, and on First Amendment grounds. New York's "aggravated harassment" statute, employed by the prosecutor to criminalize a variety of my communications on the grounds that they were "annoying"—and to inflame, poison, and prejudice the trial atmosphere, transforming it into a full-scale assault on academic criticism—would be declared unconstitutional by the New York Court of Appeals, on the grounds that the state had no right to criminalize "annoying" speech.

Despite the ruling on the "aggravated harassment" statute, one theme stood out in the litigation: the reluctance of each of the reviewing courts to apply the Supreme Court's freedom-of-speech precedents to my case. At every step of the way, it was as if the Constitution was a mere technicality, a nuisance whose application could be avoided unless there was really no other choice. This tendency was especially visible each time our First Amendment argument was given short shrift. Whenever I saw this happening, my question was "If the judges feel that our constitutional argument is flawed, why don't they directly address the matter and explain why they've reached that conclusion?"

Like anyone who had studied law, I knew that the founders had added the Bill of Rights to the United States Constitution because they recognized that it was not sufficient to enact a constitution that granted powers to the three branches of government; such powers could be *abused*, and to prevent that from happening, they needed to be "restricted by a declaration of rights."[33]

Foremost among those rights was freedom of the press—a doctrine that was later expanded to include freedom of "speech." The

Supreme Court once asserted, in a case decided more than seventy years ago, that First Amendment liberties have a privileged status; "any attempt to restrict those liberties must be justified by clear public interest, threatened not doubtfully or remotely, but by clear and present danger."[34] And in some of its loftiest declarations, the Supreme Court had explained that this liberty was based on the "grand principle of the free and open exchange of ideas," a principle famously expressed by John Stuart Mill, who, in *On Liberty*, argued that the proper way of confronting speech that we dislike is not to suppress it but to engage in *more speech*—that is, in criticism, rebuttal, and refutation.

Like anyone with a legal education, I was well acquainted with this "grand principle." I knew that forms of "hate" speech that could easily be criminalized in many other countries—such as shouting Nazi slogans in street marches or screaming abuse at the parents of a gay man at his funeral—could *not* be criminalized in America. No matter how offensive the idea expressed might be to public mores, the United States Constitution invokes a higher value and imposes tolerance.[35] And, since acts as well as words can be used to convey ideas, the notion of "speech" had progressively been expanded to include not only verbal utterances but expressive conduct such as desecration of a flag, nude demonstrations on the streets of Manhattan, cross burning, and pornography.[36] The court had specifically explained that "First Amendment protections are not confined to the exposition of ideas."[37]

> Speech about political life had often been described as the "core" or "essence" of the First Amendment, but speech uttered in other frameworks, such as art and religion, had likewise been declared entitled to First Amendment protection.

Furthermore, I knew that in a 1966 case, *Ashton v. Kentucky*, the court had held that a legal decision criminalizing libel was unconstitutional. The court emphasized that libel presents no public danger because it doesn't "breach the peace" (contrary to what the old common-law judges assumed centuries ago in England when duels were fought over insults), and that a "function of free speech

... is to invite dispute." They added that "speech is often provocative and challenging" and "may strike at prejudices and preconceptions and have profound unsettling effects as it presses for acceptance of an idea."[38]

And again, in a famous 1988 case entitled *Hustler v. Falwell*, the court held that satire, no matter how damaging to a reputation—and there is no easier way to damage a reputation than to engage in satire—is a form of speech protected by the "great principles of the free exchange of ideas."[39]

I also knew, of course, that certain forms of speech *were* illegal and that speech used to commit crimes was unprotected. For example, child pornography was arguably a form of "expression," but it was also a crime with serious consequences. Similarly, if you lie under oath, you are using words, but if the matter you lie about is important or "material" enough, you may be guilty of the crime of perjury. But there was no real problem here, because there was no real contradiction between the existence of "speech" crimes and the

> In *Garrison v. Louisiana* (1964), the court held that truth must be allowed as a defense in any criminal, just as in any civil, trial for libel—and recognized along the way that there is no longer any compelling state interest in criminalizing libel at all.

grand principles of the First Amendment. Their reconciliation, as laid out in a century of Supreme Court jurisprudence, lay in what was known as the "compelling state interest" doctrine. According to this doctrine, nine specifically defined, exceptional categories of speech were "traditionally" recognized as not benefiting from constitutional protection.[40] *All speech falling outside these nine categories was protected*, unless the state had a "compelling interest" in suppressing it. Notably *absent* from the nine categories of unprotected speech were "harassing," "harmful," "annoying," or "embarrassing" speech; impersonation of an academic department chairman; and any combination of these categories.

The specific nature of the protections accorded to speech falling outside the nine categories had been fleshed out over the decades. Reasonable regulations of speech on the basis of time and place were allowed: it was fair to oblige protestors to remain at a certain distance (say, one hundred yards, or the other side of the street) from a funeral or an abortion clinic. But where a law impinged on speech on the basis of its content, it was considered *presumptively unconstitutional*, the government bore the burden of demonstrating its constitutionality, and the correct standard of analysis was called "strict scrutiny."[41] This referred to a method of inquiry that enabled a court to determine whether the state had a compelling interest in criminalizing any given form of speech, and whether it had done so in an objectively reasonable, "narrowly tailored" manner (as in the one-hundred-yard restriction). In the First Amendment context, a regulation was considered narrowly tailored if it used the "least restrictive means" of achieving the government interest.[42]

In sum, it was clear that an individual's right to engage in speech (or expression), no matter how unpopular, provocative, or unpleasant that speech may be, could be curtailed only if the state first passed the stringent test required to meet its burden to prove that it has a compelling interest to do so.[43] In my case, however, the State of New York would not accept that burden. Instead, the prosecutors offered justifying slogans such as "You can't use speech to commit crimes," "The defendant is to be punished not for his speech but for deceiving others," "The legislature intended to reach the use of another's name to damage a reputation," and so on: seemingly anything to avoid considering whether the statutes invoked by the prosecution restricted speech or expressive conduct based on its content, and whether the state had a compelling interest to do so, according to the specific, widely recognized criteria established by the Supreme Court over many decades.

Every time I heard those evasive declarations of the prosecutors, I couldn't help but wonder, How on earth is this possible in a legal framework? If the First Amendment forbids the criminalization of speech that doesn't enter into one of the unprotected categories, how can anything of the sort take place, right here in New York City? Eventually I came to realize that the rationale used in my case was one that prosecutors and criminal courts had developed over the years to make an end run around the compelling state interest test when they wished to suppress a form of speech that they disliked. Through eight years of litigation, an array of prosecutors maintained that the criminalization of my campaign had nothing to do with its content, because the "subject matter" of the communications was irrelevant. The various prosecutors and courts would claim that I was not to be punished for my *speech* at all; my wrong consisted in engaging in *deceitful conduct* with the intent to cause some vaguely defined harm to others. Since I was to be punished for illicit *conduct* rather than speech, there was no need to address any implications the Supreme Court's "free speech" decisions might have with respect to the prosecution's strategy at the Dead Sea Scrolls trial.[44]

This distinction between words and actions had been appealed to by the prosecution, and had been fully supported by Judge Berkman, at various moments during the trial. It was the key to persuading the jurors that my entire defense strategy, to the extent it had anything to do with freedom of speech or expression, was simply irrelevant to the actual fraud laws of New York. Just as the truth about the scrolls controversy, plagiarism, and other such matters was irrelevant to my intent to gain "any" benefit or advantage. The same rationale would then be passed along from one appellate court hearing to the next.

The issue, the prosecutors urged, was not "speech" but fraud—and at the same time, they urged the appellate courts to expand the definition of fraud beyond its previously recognized boundaries. Antifraud laws are aimed at conduct that causes some kind of substantial (generally financial) damage. But the prosecutors argued, for example, that "there is no First Amendment right to engage in deceptive conduct aimed at duping victims into acting in reliance on the deception." That formula stretched the law and ignored the Supreme Court's directives, because it left out the *material harm* that must be caused by such reliance.[45] Disregarding such stringent requirements, the prosecution would engage in diatribes—analogizing, in one instance, my emails with sexual assault: after all, they suggested, no defendant could commit *that* crime and then get away with arguing that he was merely "expressing" himself. Unlike speech acts that stir up academic controversy, sexual assault is a form of physical violence, and so the analogy had no legal merit; but it did have the merit of pleading to *sentiment*. In fact, it neatly illustrated an observation made by the sixteenth-century French essayist (and magistrate) Michel de Montaigne: litigants commonly believe that to obtain an appropriate outcome in a legal case, they need to make the judges *angry*.[46] Apparently motivated by a similar perspective, the prosecution would repeatedly indulge in forms of special pleading that seemed designed to provoke the reaction of an indignant schoolteacher.

> In his essay entitled "On Wrath," Montaigne suggested that any judge who condemned a criminal defendant out of anger should be punished by death.

At trial, Bandler had used a quite different technique to get people angry at me: he repeatedly elicited testimony regarding the allegedly "false" and hurtful accusatory contents of the emails I had sent. Amalgamating the plainly unconstitutional harassment charges that criminalized "annoying" speech with all the other ones, he had, at a key moment of his summation, exhorted the jury to *examine the emails* during deliberation. I had made a "terrible allegation," I had issued a "false confession and accusations," and the complainants were "very upset" at the allegation; my "attacks" were "personal," they "crossed a big line," I made "accusations," or "accused" others of misconduct, or was an "accuser," and so on and so forth. "So look at exhibit ten," the skilled prosecutor had declared. "These binders down here at the bottom ... that are [sic] emails from the Larry dot Schiffman ... Look at all the evidence. Look at the totality of what he did. Look at why he did it because he hated him and resented him."[47]

These types of harangues had echoed throughout the trial, merging into a single repetitive indictment of the content of my emails as well as of my character, the key claim being that, in my criminalized messages, I inappropriately "attacked," "accused," and "upset" the distinguished complainants.

Having used the content of the communications as the basis for criminalizing me, the prosecution would then casually turn around and claim that the content of the communications was irrelevant.

Even after years of litigation, New York prosecutors—continually acting on behalf of a well-known and well-connected NYU department chairman and public figure—would bluntly assert that "it is not the content of the emails that got Golb into trouble." I was, they would insist, to be punished for my "conduct," not my speech. To be sure, the conduct consisted in conveying messages and had been initiated, evidenced, and carried out by means of written language, but these, they would argue, were only negligible details, minor quirks of the case, with no First Amendment consequences. But the fact that I had disseminated certain ideas was hardly *incidental* to my alleged crimes. I was to be jailed not merely because I chose to convey my messages under the names of individuals from whom I was distinct. It was hard to believe that if I had merely sent out a commonplace "Happy Holidays" in Schiffman's name I would have been arrested, prosecuted, and incarcerated in the Rikers Island penitentiary.

In response to the prosecution's bombast, Ron Kuby signaled that there was no way around this basic point: my emails had been criminalized under laws that distinguished "favored speech from disfavored speech on the basis of the ideas or views expressed," precisely the kind of content-based distinction long held unconstitutional.[48] As the Supreme Court's rulings had made clear, if one must examine the content of a particular instance of speech to determine whether it falls in a permissible or impermissible category, the restriction involved is content based.[49] It hardly seemed possible to reconcile the claim that I was to be punished for my "conduct" rather than my "speech" with the rulings of the Supreme Court in this regard.

Efforts to treat words as if they were acts have a potential impact on every American's life. In 2021, Florida enacted a statute that prohibited professional and academic training programs incompatible with the "anti-woke" value system promoted by the state's governor Ron DeSantis. When the law was challenged in court, the state argued that it was aimed only against the "conduct" of the trainers, not "speech." Rebuking the state for its vicious assault on a type of speech it didn't like, the Eleventh Circuit Court of Appeals declared the law unconstitutional.[50]

Here is another example of an American appellate court decision based on the same fundamental principle: In 2015, the North Carolina high court overturned a lower-court decision that had upheld the constitutionality of the state's cyberbullying statute. The statute had made it illegal to "post or encourage others to post on the Internet private, personal, or sexual information pertaining to a minor." The lower court had tried using the same kind of argument repeatedly invoked in my case: the statute, it held, "is not directed at prohibiting the communication of thoughts or ideas via the Internet. It prohibits the intentional and specific *conduct* of intimidating or tormenting a minor."

> The Eleventh Circuit admonished Florida that "labeling certain verbal or written communications 'speech' and others 'conduct' is unprincipled and susceptible to manipulation."

The North Carolina appellate judges would have none of it. That a speech-restricting law is content based, the court indicated, can be seen "in the plain text of the statute, or the animating impulse behind it, or the lack of any plausible explanation besides distaste for the subject matter or message." The court held that the cyberbullying statute had to be subjected to the strictest level of First Amendment scrutiny because it "criminalizes some messages but not others, and makes it impossible to determine whether the accused has committed the crime without examining the content of his communications." And the statute couldn't make it past that scrutiny, because it created "a criminal prohibition of alarming breadth."[51]

Judged by these basic rules, the solution in my case was clear. After all, everyone involved in prosecuting my case had spent considerable time "examining the content" of my emails to determine if they were comedic enough, or so deadpan as to be merely deceitful—if they were "criminal" rather than parodic impersonations. It bears repeating: if I had sent out an email stating "I am Lawrence Schiffman and I ate an apple this morning," I would likely not have been arrested. Apparently, however, it was far more important to protect the reputation of Lawrence Schiffman than bullied minors in North Carolina.

And, perhaps, the fact that *reputation* was involved is precisely what made litigating my appeal so difficult. In the context of pervasive anger at me—for I was publicly defined by the DA precisely as an "internet bully"—most of those one would normally expect to care the most about such matters had apparently reached a decision, even if only a tacit one, that making a fuss about the "technical" requirement of testing for content-based speech was unnecessary.

The DA's position was also strengthened by widespread indifference, in the age of cut and paste, to the very real evil of plagiarism, and by general ignorance regarding the museum-exhibition scandal that was the focus of my internet campaign. Some observers were puzzled by what struck them as an inexplicable lack of concern for the implications of my case. As Scott Greenfield would put it, that there hadn't been "huge interest" in my trial and appeal was "a mystery," and everyone now had to "live with the consequences."[52] PEN America, the American Civil Liberties Union, and other popular civil rights organizations, evidently aware of a need for caution, would refrain from issuing any statement about the speech-chilling developments presented by the trial.[53] The case was apparently not an "easy win," and the freedom to impersonate Lawrence Schiffman and portray him as justifying inappropriate conduct not a popular cause. Only the National Association of Criminal Defense Lawyers would protest, in an amicus brief signed by noted New York lawyer Marc Fernich, against the broad interpretation of "harm" advanced by my prosecutors.

I was soon to learn the lengths to which the courts themselves would go to avoid engaging in any substantial

> An amicus brief is an argument submitted to a court by a party (often an organization representing a class of potentially affected individuals) that is not involved in the litigation but that has an interest in the outcome of a case. Marc Fernich would go on to be named the 2014 Criminal Lawyer of the Year by the Institute of Jewish Humanities.

discussion, in their published decisions, of the content-based issues raised by the case. These included not only the nature of mimicry and the "strict scrutiny" test but the allegations made by Israeli academic and journalist Avi Katzman, which I had reiterated in my campaign. Instead of discussing any of this, the appellate judges would offer narratives of wrongdoing that seemed to be cobbled together from context-free email excerpts in a manner creating the impression that the case was centered on an "ordinary" crime having nothing to do with speech. But this did not annul the fact that the plain language of the New York State laws invoked as the basis for the prosecution's accusations—the identity theft, harassment, criminal impersonation, and forgery statutes—intruded into the realm of, and inhibited, speech that was constitutionally protected. Criticism, parody, and satire regularly sting, burn, insult, annoy, and embarrass; these forms of speech always diminish or "damage" reputations.

Many law books and Supreme Court decisions spell out that the state's desire to prevent harm of all sorts cannot trump the First Amendment. If the statutes invoked are substantially overbroad and vague, they are unconstitutional. But the scrolls trial, along with the seven following years of appellate litigation, would show just how fragile the foundations are that nominally oblige courts to adhere to this unique aspect of American constitutional law.

* * *

Things slowly began to move. On January 29, 2013—nearly two years after the filing of the first appeal—a panel of Manhattan's First Appellate Division rendered an initial decision that was slightly over two pages in length. The panel left all the impersonation convictions intact, on the ground that I "was not prosecuted for the content of any of the emails."[54] This struck me as a most perplexing conclusion in view of the panel's preceding analysis:

> Defendant's principal defense was that these emails were only intended to be satiric hoaxes or pranks. However, as it has been observed in the context of trademark law, "a

parody must convey two simultaneous—and contradictory—messages: that it is the original, but also that it is not the original and is instead a parody" ... Here, the evidence clearly established that defendant never intended any kind of parody. Instead, he only intended to convey the first message to the readers of the emails, that is, that the purported authors were the actual authors.[55]

How could the panel assert that the emails were not "satiric" without examining their contents and explaining, for example, how the jury could conclude, beyond a reasonable doubt, that the words "If I had given credit to this man, I would have been *banned from conferences around the world*" did not convey the message to recipients that they were reading an academic parody? To what "evidence" was the panel referring if not to the content of the emails?

I also knew full well that what was involved in a trademark case was not whether someone should be sent to jail for a crime but whether he would be allowed to *continue using another person's mark*. The burden of *proof* for such a decision was much lighter than the "reasonable doubt" standard applicable to criminal cases. And the decision itself was always based precisely on the *contents* of the material in connection with which the allegedly infringing mark was used.

Notably, many courts had held that the use of another's trademark as clickbait in a URL address was *protected by the First Amendment*, if the contents of the *website* accompanying the URL were aimed at *criticizing* or *ridiculing* the owner of the mark, rather than at selling a *competing commercial product*. By analogy with *those* cases, it seemed that my "criminal impersonation" convictions should have been immediately overturned! And not upheld on the grounds that the contents of my messages were somehow irrelevant. Would the panel have upheld my convictions if I had "created the impression" that Schiffman had eaten a good piece of pie that morning?

Still worse, the panel passed over the harassment convictions in complete silence, allowing them to stand even though the same appellate division had previously cast doubt in other cases on the constitutionality of New York's aggravated harassment statute. Had the panel simply failed to notice that this same dubious statute had played a central role in my trial?

The panel also offered no comment on the felony identity theft conviction based on my alleged intent to "falsify NYU's business records." It did, however, in an extremely focused manner, vacate one conviction: the felony charge based on my intent to gain a thousand dollars by getting Schiffman's lecture canceled. The panel, foregoing any discussion of the DA's actual chain of speculative reasoning, dismissed this single charge on the grounds that "the People's assertions in this regard rest on speculation."[56]

Inherent in the panel's ruling on this count was its recognition that the DA had brought a bogus charge on the basis of a contrived legal pretext. New York's felony identity theft statute says that the crime occurs if one assumes a name with the *intent to defraud*—that is, to deceitfully obtain someone's money or some other illicit material benefit. The DA's "speculative" argumentation represented an effort to casually comply with the language of the statute, while in effect treating a particular use of someone else's name that the DA disapproved of as itself a form of theft.

> "Identity theft" is a misnomer. This crime does not involve stealing someone's "identity"; it involves the use of an identity with the intent to steal something else.

Since the First Appellate Division, however, did nothing to make this clear, it left entirely open the possibility that the same tactics would be used again with different results in future prosecutions. This possibility would become all the more clear during the ensuing years of litigation. Each of the appellate courts involved in my case, for example, would give remarkably short shrift to (and in most instances would not even address at all) the decision of the United States Supreme Court in *United States v. Alvarez*, a decision specifying that fraud, in the legal sense, must involve deceit, reliance on deceit, and a "material benefit" derived from it. The *Alvarez* court struck down a statute called the Stolen Valor Act, which criminalized false claims to having won military medals. That statute was not an identity theft law, but the decision's logic, based on the premise that even false speech is entitled to protection unless it is used to obtain some kind of tangible benefit or cause some kind of tangible harm, would also seem to apply to the use of a name or identity on the internet. Citing George Orwell to make its point, the court wrote that

> our constitutional tradition stands against the idea that we need Oceania's Ministry of Truth ... Were [we] to hold that the interest in truthful discourse alone is sufficient to sustain a ban on speech ... [we] would give government a broad censorial power unprecedented ... in our constitutional tradition. The mere potential for the exercise of that power casts a chill, a chill the First Amendment cannot permit if free speech, thought, and discourse are to remain a foundation of our freedom.[57]

"Those Innocent Academics Involved in Dead Sea Scroll Research ..."—Simon Tanner, Director of the Digitization Pilot of the Dead Sea Scrolls

The next leg of the appellate litigation, in New York State's highest court, would last over a year—and any public awareness of the case would have altogether subsided were it not for a small incident that arose soon after the First Appellate Division rendered its January 29, 2013, decision. It turned out that Clifford A. Rieders of Williamsport, Pennsylvania, was a lawyer representing Lawrence Schiffman; and acting in this capacity, he had sent an email to conservative First Amendment specialist Eugene Volokh of UCLA, demanding "complete removal" of "blog material" regarding my case, the "removal of any other mention or reference to Dr. Schiffman by Mr. Golb or anyone responding to him," and a "certification as to all efforts made to expunge the material."[58]

Schiffman also had his attorney send this request to at least one other legal website, the *Simple Justice* blog of former prosecutor

Scott Greenfield. Rather than complying with the demand, Volokh and Greenfield both posted Rieders's letters on their websites, together with manifestly irritated commentary about the "threats" received. Volokh, for example, asserted that

> I generally do not publish letters sent to me, but unfounded demands such as this are an exception. This is especially so because demonstrating the unsoundness of the lawyer's argument requires showing the entirety of the letter—both the particular language that the letter included ("criminal postings," the demand for "complete removal of the blog material," the demand for "removal of any other mention or reference to Dr. Schiffman by Mr. Golb or anyone responding to him," and so on) and what the letter didn't include (any specific explanation for why the material would indeed be legally actionable).

Greenfield, on *Simple Justice*, responded with, among other things, a succinct "asshole" and "bite me," commenting, "Eugene is much nicer than I am."

On Volokh's popular legal website, commentators promptly mocked the fact that Schiffman's lawyer joined the word "Esquire" to his name, and poked fun at his firm, which includes colleagues Thomas Waffenschmidt and others, and is oddly located in Williamsport, Pennsylvania: a town whose sister city is the settlement of Maale Adumim in the Israeli-occupied West Bank. In an additional swipe at the lawyer and possibly at Schiffman as well, Scott Greenfield referred to Rieders as "busily trying to sanitize the internet of arguments that might ... not-so-much favor Schiffman."[59]

Rieders appeared not to always work in his client's best interests. For example, he distributed incorrect information about Schiffman's academic position, referring to the Judaica scholar as "Vice Provost of Yeshiva University," while on his own popular website, Schiffman had described himself more accurately as a "Vice Provost for Undergraduate Education." Notably, such inaccuracies were not limited to correspondence sent to owners of legal websites by Clifford Rieders. Erroneous information, in this case that Schiffman was a rabbi (a falsehood, as we have seen, also presented as fact in the *New York Times*), was conveyed in a news service run by students at Yeshiva. The error was then taken up by internet mockery, with one anonymous blogger citing the dicta in Proverbs 27:2: "Let another praise you, and not your own mouth; a stranger, and not your own lips" and "Like clouds and wind without rain is a man who boasts of a gift he does not give."[60]

Perhaps in reaction to the exposure of Schiffman's demands for suppression of commentary on my case, various members of the academic community, particularly ones affiliated with digital humanities programs, now began to approvingly cite my arrest and prosecution in writings critical of anonymous online speech. Simon Tanner, director of the Digitization Pilot of the Dead Sea Scrolls, would go so far as to suggest on the *Guardian* website that "the case ... shows the real invasive power and perfidy of sock puppets." Without mentioning my legal appeal, Tanner would assert that I "got six months in jail," and argue that my blogging and email campaign "severely disrupted ... academic discourse ... while those innocent academics involved in Dead Sea Scroll research were libeled, defamed and smeared."[61]

Tanner's editorial seemed to signal that a new criterion for debate about scholarly ethics and museum exhibits had been established in the wake of my prosecution. According to this criterion, the use of internet anonymity, even for the sake of bypassing channels controlled by one or another academic network to present ideas discomfiting to that network, was not only inappropriate but inherently delegitimized the arguments and theories presented in this manner.

But not everyone agreed with Tanner's perspective. For instance, among various responses posted beneath his article, a Norwegian commentator suggested that the "use of 'sock puppets' to advance Norman Golb's theories seems to me not only justified but, with the ongoing trial process, to have succeeded way beyond Raphael Golb's dreams." The importance of Norman Golb's theories, he argued, was "of a very high degree and, being denied proper academic channels, the increased awareness of his work due to his son's actions is certainly to be welcomed."

"Isn't That a Little Overbroad?"

Schiffman's letters demanding the "expunging" of any mention of his name from the Volokh website had barely been forgotten when things moved ahead: on March 25, 2014, three and a half years after the Dead Sea Scrolls trial, the New York Court of Appeals in Albany held oral arguments on the case. The hearing again followed months of delays occasioned by the district attorney's diligence in making me and my aging parents wait as long as possible. It also followed the filing of the amicus brief on my behalf by the National Association of Criminal Defense Lawyers.

Rejecting the distinction between "speech" and "conduct" emphasized by both the trial court and the First Appellate Division, the NACDL brief asserted that "if Schiffman and others like him feel aggrieved by online speech with academic value, they have adequate remedies in tort"—that is, in civil rather than criminal courts. The brief called my prosecution "unprecedented"; asserted that it was wrong to "jail the actor for causing a bruised ego or, at worst, diminished credibility as a scholar"; and culminated with the suggestion that if the conviction stood, "virtually anyone who impersonates others on the Web for wholly innocuous reasons" could be unjustly prosecuted.[62]

During the long-awaited oral hearing in Albany, an interesting exchange took place between the prosecutor and several of the court of appeals judges.[63]

"Is this aggravated harassment, or just annoying behavior?" the court's chief judge, Jonathan Lippman, inquired.

"It's both, that's for sure," assistant district attorney Vincent Rivellese declared.

"Isn't that a little overbroad?" Lippman asked.

"No," Rivellese answered.

Judge Robert Smith then queried whether he could be prosecuted for harassment if he asked a question that he knew was going to be annoying. Rivellese maintained that he could, if the question was in writing.

His voice rising nearly to a shout, Smith shot back, "Really? Really? If I email somebody an annoying question, I get a year?"

Toward the close of the hearing, Kuby reminded the court of the thousands of other examples of online parody untroubled by any prosecution, whereupon Lippman put a small question that had been lurking in the background of the trial and appellate proceedings for many months: "But why did they choose to prosecute this?"

Kuby explained the nature of Schiffman's connection with the FBI; Lippman politely thanked him, and the hearing was over.

News of the Albany exchange seems to have percolated through legal circles, even reaching some of the civil rights organizations that had cautiously steered clear of becoming involved in the affair. On April 3, a week or so after the hearing, Christopher Dunn, the associate legal director of the New York Civil Liberties Union, chose to publish the first of two articles that he would write about the prosecution—each of them replete with misinformation about the Dead Sea Scrolls controversy and the purpose of my internet campaign. In this first contribution, Dunn puzzlingly eschewed any discussion of the "aggravated harassment" issue, and suggested that whether my NYU emails could be "considered" parodies was a "difficult issue." That issue, he asserted, "turns in large part on whether a reasonable person would have realized the emails were not actually from the professor."[64]

Dunn, a defender of civil liberties, had himself served as an adjunct professor at NYU. One might have expected him to explain to his readers how a *reasonable person* at that institution could possibly have believed that Schiffman had actually sent him a Gmail confessing to misconduct and instructing him to remain silent about the matter. Schiffman had naturally responded to perplexed inquiries from a few gullible readers by explaining that he had not sent the "Larry Schiffman" messages, and no one had any reason to disbelieve him. The prosecution had offered no testimony pertaining to a "reasonable" belief, and Carol Berkman had declined to instruct the jury that such was the standard, despite our explicit request that she do so.

As indicated, Dunn grounded his discussion by parroting Bandler's misleading narrative of the case's background. Notably, however, he failed to inform his readers that "neither good faith nor truth" was allowed as a "defense" at my trial. That is, he failed to inform them that the prosecution had accused me of making "false accusations" throughout the trial—and that I had not been allowed to introduce any of the evidence demonstrating the *truth* of my accusations. Apparently Dunn hadn't noticed this issue in our briefs, or perhaps such matters simply didn't fall within the scope of the New York Civil Liberties Union's legal concerns.

Five weeks later, Albany issued a complex decision authored by Judge Sheila Abdus-Salaam.[65] One law professor informed me that upon reading the judge's summary of the "facts" of the case after locating the court's decision in the Westlaw database, he believed that he must have made a mistake and pulled up the prosecution's brief; he returned to the legal database to find the court's actual opinion, then realized that this is indeed what he had been reading.[66] The decision itself initially seemed to do precisely what many legal experts would expect from a state high court in such a case. It announced (albeit with odd brevity) that my remaining "identity theft" felony conviction—the one predicated on the puzzling claim that I intended to "falsify the business records" of New York University—was vacated for lack of evidence. The conviction for "unauthorized access to a computer" was also vacated, on the grounds that I had quite simply been "authorized" to use the computers at NYU's Bobst Library by virtue of the fact that I possessed an alumnus library card. Abdus-Salaam had no comment on the possible First Amendment implications of the prosecution's claim that my alleged violation of the Bobst "civility" code rendered my access to the library's computers illegal. In this regard, however, and far more momentously, she declared New York's speech-restricting "aggravated harassment" statute (Penal Law § 240.30) unconstitutional, and accordingly vacated my various convictions under this statute—convictions required even just because of the "annoying" nature of my criminalized communications, to Judge Smith's incredulity.

The "aggravated harassment" ruling would have an immediate and, for the state, catastrophic impact on approximately 7,600 pending cases.[67] It would also resonate in the media, with various news items reporting that the "right to annoy" had been upheld.[68]

Christopher Dunn of the New York Civil Liberties Union (and erstwhile adjunct professor at NYU) now found it opportune to weigh in with the second of his two misleading articles. Whereas in the first article, written two months earlier, he had barely even mentioned the harassment charges, in the new one he focused specifically on Albany's stunning ruling—by which he seemed almost confounded, conceding that it was "hard to understand how a statute criminalizing annoying speech could have remained on the books for 50 years in New York and particularly upsetting that thousands of people have been arrested for annoying or alarming speech."[69]

In finally declaring, after half a century, such an unusual law unconstitutional, Abdus-Salaam had taken a great step forward for civil liberties. However, in announcing this portion of the court's decision, she failed to consider whether, during the trial, the "harassment" charges had the effect of "wreaking prejudicial havoc and deflecting attention from the real issues," as Scott Greenfield put it in his online discussion of the decision.[70] And from this point on, the decision took an entirely different turn: most of the criminal impersonation and forgery misdemeanor convictions were allowed to stand, on the grounds that I sought to "harm the reputations" of the complainants—and not, according to Abdus-Salaam, merely to cause "momentary embarrassment or discomfort," which would *not* be a crime.[71] In "narrowing" the statute to create this special "harm to reputation" standard, Abdus-Salaam offered no comment on the "speech with academic value" argument of Marc Fernich's amicus brief, or on my own argument that the trial was a disguised criminal libel prosecution. She did, however, find it useful to embellish her decision by quoting, in a footnote inserted right where she referred to "people ... with a career in academia," the famous words spoken by Iago in Shakespeare's *Othello* (act 3, scene 3):

> Good name in man and woman, dear my lord,
> Is the immediate jewel of their souls.
> Who steals my purse steals trash. 'Tis something, nothing:
> 'Twas mine, 'tis his, and has been slave to thousands.
> But he that filches from me my good name

Robs me of that which not enriches him
And makes me poor indeed.

When I saw the ghost of Iago rising out of the pages of the honorable judge's opinion, protesting against anyone who should "filch" his good name, my jaw dropped. For there is, of course, no more sinister character in all of literature than Iago; of him, the Shakespeare scholar Andrew Bradley once wrote that "evil has nowhere else been portrayed with such mastery."[72] At first I could not fathom why Iago would emerge precisely in a context where I was portrayed as having wronged an individual with a "career in academia." But then it occurred to me that Abdus-Salaam's citation of words spoken by one of the most perverse villains in all of literature was perhaps meant to emphasize, no doubt with a touch of humor, that even the very worst elements of the academic community were entitled to their reputations, and that no effort to besmirch the good name of *any professor* through an act of email impersonation would be tolerated under the applicable fraud laws of the State of New York.

Iago's words did serve to clarify why "good names" are guarded so closely: reputation is not a mere "shadow," as Abraham Lincoln once told his confidant Noah Brooks, of the "real thing" that consists in a person's "character";[73] nor is it an "idle and most false imposition" that can be "got without merit," as Iago himself asserts in act 2, scene 3, of the same Shakespeare play; rather, reputation is the cherished "jewel" of a "soul." But nowhere in her decision did Abdus-Salaam refer to the particular categories of *harm* to reputation that courts might, perhaps, be able to constitutionally criminalize. In the famous *Ashton* case decided by the Supreme Court in 1966, the Kentucky Court of Appeals had, precisely, narrowed a criminal libel charge to cover only *false and malicious* defamation.[74] The Supreme Court hinted that Ashton's trial *might* have been constitutional if the trial court rather than the court of appeals had understood the law so narrowly. In *People v. Golb*, the New York Court of Appeals' narrowing of the statute is much *wider* than false and malicious harm to reputation. Under the rubric of "damage to reputation," the court in effect criminalized any intent to expose actual academic misconduct through an email prank. And the court applied this sweeping standard, even though "neither good faith nor truth" had been allowed as a "defense" at my trial.

Not only did the decision ignore the required distinction between truthful and malicious harm to reputation; it also ignored the fact that the *jury had not been instructed* about Abdus-Salaam's subtle distinction between "damage to reputations" and "momentary embarrassment or discomfort." Rather, the jury had simply been told to find me guilty if I intended to cause "any harm" or gain "any benefit." Abdus-Salaam herself found that standard too broad. And in her effort to fix the problem, she imposed the "harm to reputation" standard retroactively, under the apparent premise that the jury, if properly instructed, *would* have found that I intended to harm reputations. That might very well be an accurate premise in view of Judge Berkman's restrictions based on her "neither good faith nor truth" ruling. But would it still be accurate if Berkman had instructed the jury, for example, that they were to assume that my underlying accusations of misconduct were entirely true?

> Abdus-Salaam did not explain where exactly the line is to be drawn between exposing malfeasance and damaging a reputation. The old specter of criminal libel, removed from the books in New York in 1966, again loomed large.

The chief judge, Jonathan Lippman, dissented from the decision on First Amendment grounds, arguing that the statutes invoked were "unconstitutionally broad, and substantially so," and that "criminal libel has long since been abandoned, not least of all because of its tendency in practice to penalize and chill speech that the constitution protects." Lippman appeared to be even more perplexed than I had been by the looming presence, as it were, of a villain in Abdus-Salaam's opinion. Noting that Shakespeare had engaged in an act of *irony* when he put the "he that filches from me my good name" speech in the mouth of Iago, Lippman objected outright to the implications of the majority's use of the famous quote.

"It is difficult to imagine," he wrote, "that an ill-intended, pseudonymously uttered comment about Iago or his modern equivalent would be actionable civilly, much less criminally." There was perhaps no need to clarify who the "modern equivalent" of Iago was; surely, in a case with so many implications for freedom of speech, the words were not meant to allude to a particular person with a career in academia. Rather, the evident concern was that *any* individual with sufficient power and influence, no matter his moral integrity or lack thereof, might seek to have his "good name" vindicated through the assistance of a willing prosecutor in similar circumstances. According to Lippman, "The use of the criminal impersonation and forgery statutes now approved amounts to an atavism at odds with the First Amendment and the free and uninhibited exchange of ideas it is meant to foster."[75] He concluded that "if [Golb] has caused reputational injury, that is redressable, if at all, as a civil tort, not as a crime."

> Chief Judge Lippman warned that "in an age in which pseudonymous communication has become ubiquitous, particularly on the internet," the court's decision gave "prosecutors power they should not have to determine what speech should and should not be penalized."

The court of appeals' majority decision seems to have caught professional legal commentators somewhat off guard. In the second of his two aforementioned articles, Christopher Dunn, of the New York Civil Liberties Union, focused merely on the aggravated harassment ruling and said nothing about the "harm to reputation" standard created by the court or its First Amendment implications. Jonathan Turley of George Washington University, having twice reported on the case following my arrest and trial on the basis of items he had read in the press, now had nothing to say, and he would ignore all future developments in the case as well. It fell to conservative UCLA law professor Eugene Volokh to support the court's decision, regardless of the unusual email interaction he had had with Schiffman's lawyer. Apparently, Volokh was so enthralled by Abdus-Salaam's reasoning that he saw no need to address Lippman's dissenting opinion in his blog entry on the matter.[76] For all Volokh's readers knew, that opinion didn't even exist, let alone merit reasoned discussion—such lack of engagement being a basic silencing technique practiced by ideologically motivated academics.[77]

In actual fact, despite his reputation as a staunch defender of the First Amendment, Volokh had been arguing for years that the reach of that section of the Bill of Rights *can*, in various debatable circumstances, be restricted.[78] He would go on to suggest that libel itself can be criminalized consistent with the Constitution. In making this suggestion, he would neglect the reasoning of international human rights organizations, special rapporteurs of the UN, and jurists working for various other bodies, all of whom have concluded that there is no justification for punishing defamatory speech with jail, and that states should decriminalize libel and substitute it with civil lawsuits wherever possible to avoid chilling freedom of speech.[79] Is this broad consensus irrelevant to our understanding of the First Amendment?

Former prosecutor Scott Greenfield disagreed with Volokh. Warning of the decision's consequences for the First Amendment, he sought to address the key issue directly. The problem with the case, he wrote, is that

> parody is in the eyes of the beholder, and a crime is in the eyes of the perpetrator. Lawrence Schiffman ... found nothing funny about the emails. So what? The targets of parody rarely do. Parody doesn't have to be amusing, though it often is. Parody is "created to mock, comment on or trivialize" something. It exists to harm a reputation.
>
> The Court implicitly holds that what Golb did was not parody, because neither the judges, the prosecutor nor ... Schiffman thought it was funny. So good parody gets a hearty guffaw, and bad parody gets a conviction? Or more to the point, parody that escapes the technological limits of the judges on the New York Court of Appeals, who failed to appreciate what any slightly astute digital native would

> have immediately realized—that the emails Golb sent could not be real—is a crime.
>
> What makes this particularly troubling [is] that [if] Schiffman's reputation ... within the academic community ... was well-founded, there would have been nothing Golb could do to harm it, and nothing Golb could do that would make Schiffman do more than chuckle. Instead, it caused Schiffman to seek Golb's prosecution.
>
> This act by Schiffman is more damning to his reputation than anything Raphael Golb could have done. So regardless of the sentence imposed on remand for the ... remaining misdemeanors, it looks like Golb wins the battle of Schiffman's reputation.[80]

Such perceptions, however, appeared to have had little impact on Robert Cargill, the key trial witness presented by the prosecution as one of my harassment "victims." While expressing a degree of disappointment that the court had "determined" that he *wasn't* a victim, he indicated that he was "satisfied" that I had been "found guilty on multiple counts," which he called a "correct decision."[81] Just as with Eugene Volokh's blog entry, missing from Cargill's was any mention, let alone discussion, of Judge Lippman's dissenting opinion. Cargill, however, took this polemical approach a step further than Volokh, by failing to directly acknowledge that the statute that had led to his participation in the trial had been declared *unconstitutional*. Contrary to Cargill's suggestion, the court did not merely find that I had "not criminally harassed" him or any of my other purported victims; it ruled, rather, that the prosecution, in *charging me with harassment under an unconstitutional statute*, had violated my First Amendment *rights*. It is that direct encroachment on my rights that allowed Cargill to be presented to the jury as a *victim* to begin with; but this went unmentioned in Cargill's report on Albany's decision. In further blog entries later that year as well as the following year, the Iowa religion professor would continue to proclaim that I was "still a criminal" and "headed to prison," and that my impending "incarceration represents only a modicum of closure," because he, Robert Cargill, was "a victim in this criminal case."[82] By the time my appeal was heard by the federal courts, Cargill, like Jonathan Turley and Eugene Volokh as well, had ceased blogging about the matter. Illustrating, however, the special new directions of research and debate in today's scholarly world, Cargill would devote a portion of his popularizing book entitled *The Cities That Built the Bible* to the same preoccupations.[83]

Following the publication of Judge Abdus-Salaam's opinion, New York legislators rapidly amended the state's aggravated harassment statute to clarify that it did not apply to unwanted or embarrassing criticism of an academic nature, but only to communications that conveyed a "threat to cause physical harm ... or unlawful harm to ... property."[84] During the following months, case after case that had been brought under the unconstitutional statute were dismissed—a result Morgenthau, Vance, and Bandler certainly had not contemplated when they set out to criminalize my annoying emails—but the invalidation of the law would, to the best of my knowledge, never be made retroactive to the thousands of New Yorkers previously convicted of this purported crime. Meanwhile, commentators gradually became aware of the court's creation of a special distinction between intended reputational damage and embarrassment—a distinction the court based on the fact that people "with a career in academia ... value their reputations at least as much as their property"—and many of them were puzzled. Media law specialist Arthur Hayes of Fordham University suggested that Abdus-Salaam's "career in academia" argument is an

> unconvincing ... sidestepping of First Amendment ... precedents. In effect, the court carved out in cursory fashion an exemption from the First Amendment for speech with academic value—or scholarly debates. But why stop with scholars? Don't, say, authors, priests and Buddhist monks, ethicists and artists, political and ideological purists value their reputations as much as their property, oftentimes more

so? They do, of course, but the court did not consider them. It drew a constitutional line with little justification. Moreover, if ... reputations ... were injured, civil actions—libel lawsuits—were the constitutionally appropriate recourse.[85]

With respect to what Hayes called the "constitutional line with little justification" drawn by Abdus-Salaam, the lawyers of one criminal defense firm wrote on their website in a comment on the case, "How do you know when you've crossed that line? And where in the statutory language ... is that line in the first place?"[86] The authors suggested that Abdus-Salaam's decision was "arguably an unconstitutional attack on free speech."

> *"Don't ... authors, priests and Buddhist monks, ethicists and artists, political and ideological purists value their reputations as much as their property, oftentimes more so?"*

Eric Goldman, a professor of internet law at Santa Clara University School of Law, would express similar doubts. The "implications" of the case, he wrote, were "troubling given the ubiquity of 'pretend' behavior online... The bad news," he added, "is that we see, over and over, bizarre exercises of prosecutorial discretion." His co-commentator, attorney Venkat Balasubramani, would be even more blunt in his assessment: "Wow," he remarked, "Golb's creativity in his email campaigns is matched by New York State's creativity in fashioning criminal restrictions on speech!" He went on to define the danger posed by the ruling with precision:

> I suppose you could cast this as a case about reputational harm but ... the status of criminal defamation statutes is uncertain at best. I don't think the Supreme Court has expressly repudiated criminal defamation, but it has certainly implied that criminal defamation ... laws are not kosher

and many states in response have moved away from these laws. Another problem with the court's construction of the statute is that it relies on line-drawing between "temporary embarrassment or discomfiture" on one end and "real harm" on the other. I would think this imbues the statute with a grant of prosecutorial discretion that courts have rejected as being contrary to the First Amendment.[87]

Lingering misgivings about the decision's underlying legal rationale would also become evident when Timothy Wu of Columbia University, an authority on topics such as "who controls the Net," posted portions of the opinion on a Harvard University platform. Wu included Abdus-Salaam's statement of the facts along with her analysis concluding that the aggravated harassment statute was unconstitutional; but he omitted virtually everything else she had written. He did, however, include the gist of Lippman's dissent, as well as the puzzling quote of Iago's ironical speech from *Othello* and Lippman's comment on Iago's "modern equivalent."[88] Wu's omissions seemed to suggest that he was troubled by the implications of Abdus-Salaam's opinion. Ralph Waldo Emerson, had he lived in our day and age, might have been equally troubled. He wrote of the "unfounded pretensions and the false reputation of certain men of standing," and taught us that a man who chooses "rest, commodity, and reputation ... shuts the door of truth."[89]

The court's ultimate disposition of the case was also puzzling. Several major Supreme Court cases require that a new trial be granted when the scope of an unconstitutionally broad statute is narrowed on appeal.[90] Abdus-Salaam, however, said nothing of these precedents and remanded the case for *resentencing*. This move was a tacit admission, perhaps, that there was something not entirely right about the initial sentencing hearing, at which Judge Berkman had allowed me to make a statement only *after* she declared her sentence, in violation of normal protocol at sentencing hearings. But it also opened the door to three more years of appellate litigation that would eventually reach the Second Circuit Court of Appeals—the highest federal court in New York. I would doggedly argue that my First Amendment rights had been violated by the criminalization of my speech, and my due process rights by the refusal to grant me a new trial; and the prosecution would, equally doggedly, argue that my "conduct" and not my speech was the gravamen of my crimes, and that I was not entitled to a new trial because the statute, even as applied at the trial, was perfectly compliant with constitutional principles.

> I was tried on the basis of Carol Berkman's idea that I was guilty of identity theft and related charges if I intended to cause "any harm" or to gain "any benefit" whatsoever. This standard was held overbroad and narrowed by Abdus-Salaam to financial and "reputational" harm alone. Since the other convictions were vacated, this meant that each and every one of Berkman's rulings on which the trial had been based were wrong to begin with.

What was unknown to me at the time was that three weeks before Abdus-Salaam's decision was published, her brother, who had terminal lung cancer, had committed suicide. Three years later, on April 12, 2017, Judge Abdus-Salaam herself would be found dead in the Hudson River. A commentator in the *National Law Journal* would observe that this "suspected suicide shines a light on a silent struggle," noting that "while bar associations across the country have devoted money and resources to help attorneys battle mental health and addiction issues, not nearly as many resources have been focused on judges." The author added that "many jurists are extremely reluctant to discuss those problems."[91]

The media coverage of Abdus-Salaam's suicide dwelled at length on her perceived liberalism, on conflicting rumors regarding her domestic life and religious affiliation, and on the details surrounding her death. Her decision in my case went unmentioned.

9
"LIKE SHOOTING A GUN": THE LOGIC OF CENSORSHIP

Since Carol Berkman had by now been obliged to retire from the bench, the resentencing took place before a different judge, former prosecutor Laura Ward. Without any explanation of why she believed jail was the appropriate punishment, Ward resentenced me to two months' incarceration at Rikers Island: a proportionate reduction, as it were, commensurate with the number of convictions that had been vacated. (Ward is the daughter of the late federal judge Robert Ward, who presided over the famous Alex Haley plagiarism trial. She is active in New York cultural life, and sits on the board of advisers of a theater and film company whose mission is "to find a contemporary vocabulary to tell stories on stage," in view of the fact that "art stimulates new ways of thinking and new ways of seeing."[1]) Ward set a surrender date for a week later, a delay that again allowed me to seek a stay from higher courts, and then to remain at large for an additional four years while my appeal slowly moved forward in the federal appeals system—with the result that, after seeing me appear before her countless times at routine continuance hearings, she would eventually be faced once more with the issue of whether to send me to Rikers Island, almost ten years after I'd perpetrated my crimes.

With the decision of the New York Court of Appeals, at least some clarity had been brought to the proceedings—within which new layers of confusing technicalities would rapidly emerge. The case appeared to resuscitate criminal libel, taken off the books in New York in 1966 following the Supreme Court's *Ashton* decision. Was it appropriate for a state where libel was no longer a crime to criminalize an act of "deceptive" mockery judged to have been carried out with the alleged intent to damage a reputation?

How to reconcile criminal libel with human rights has long been an issue debated around the world. In England, defamation was decriminalized in 2009, and both the European and African Courts of Human Rights, as well as the United Nations Human Rights Commission, have held that jail is never an appropriate sentence for harm to reputation.[2] That is why prosecutions for libel in France, for example, normally end with payment of a small symbolic fine. Most American states decriminalized libel during the 1960s, following the aspersion cast on the old system by the Supreme Court in *Ashton*; many state high courts have also held criminal libel laws unconstitutional; but they have remained on the book in various states, where the past decade has seen a resurgence in prosecutions.[3] The prison sentences for violation of such laws in America are long and arduous.[4] Since New York decriminalized libel half a century ago, Ron Kuby now finally decided to put two questions to the federal district court: (1) Did the New York Court of Appeals legitimately reintroduce virtually the exact same crime of libel, as it were through the back door, by interpreting the term "harm" in the criminal impersonation statute to include "harm to reputation"? And if it did so legitimately, then (2) can libel rightly be criminalized *at all* consistent with the principle that criminal laws must not be unconstitutionally "vague" and "overbroad"?

The question whether libel can appropriately be criminalized had never been explicitly answered by the Supreme Court, but it had been much debated in human rights circles. Those who believe that libel *cannot* be criminalized argue in essence that damage to a reputation can be deserved and that whether this is the case is something reasonable people can always disagree about. In criminal trials, the burden of proof is "beyond a reasonable doubt." The consequences of this principle when dealing with issues like character and reputation seem clear enough, and courts have recognized them in the past. For example, an Indiana school policy permitting discipline based on the principal's conclusion that the students had brought "discredit or dishonor" on the school and themselves was held unconstitutional, for the "notion of good character inherent in each term," as the court put it,

> introduces a nebulous degree of value judgment. Issues of character and values involve such a broad spectrum of

reasonable interpretation (but also strongly-held disagreement) as to be insufficiently conclusive for a disciplinary standard. In other words, the meaning of the terms may be readily understood by persons of ordinary intelligence, but ready agreement about all the conduct and circumstances they apply to cannot reasonably be expected.[5]

When, as Carol Berkman stipulated, "neither good faith nor truth is a defense to any of the crimes charged," and when the prosecution is allowed to repeatedly argue that the criminal defendant made "false accusations" but the defendant is blocked from introducing any evidence that his accusations were true, can the burden of proving guilt beyond a reasonable doubt be met, as required for criminal verdicts?

One objection to criminalizing libel is that doing so discourages free expression, intimidating authors, for example, who are not willing to risk jail to accuse a public figure of corrupt behavior.[6]

> Approximately 170 times, the prosecution was allowed to suggest that my accusations of misconduct were a "smear," a "stain," "wrong," and otherwise worthy of contempt. When my attorneys attempted to probe the credibility and ulterior motives of the witnesses, objections were raised and sustained.

Commenting on the "online impersonation" laws enacted in several states, Matt Zimmerman, an attorney for the Electronic Frontier Foundation, argued that they give too much "discretion to law enforcement to go after First Amendment activity ... The resulting consequence ... is that people will feel chilled and intimidated and hence decide to not engage in perfectly legitimate forms of social protest because they're worried that not only might they be sued, but they could actually go to jail."[7]

Seen in the context of the uninhibited internet confrontations defined as a positive social phenomenon by Ron Robin (see chapter 2, page 18), the intimidating potential of the Dead Sea Scrolls trial—a case redefining the parameters of irony and anonymity, two frequent and perennially controversial elements of such confrontations—seemed evident. As the Supreme Court observed long ago, "It is not merely the sporadic abuse of power by the censor, but the pervasive threat inherent in its very existence that constitutes the danger to freedom of discussion."[8] When a law creates such a threat, the court explained, and lends itself to "discriminatory enforcement by local prosecuting officials, against particular groups deemed to merit their displeasure," it "results in a continuous and pervasive restraint on all freedom of discussion that might reasonably be regarded as within its purview."[9] The laws invoked against me had provided precisely such a tool for abuse. Nowhere did they address the difference between the crime of impersonation and satire or humor. They contained no guidance whatsoever that would enable anyone to distinguish between parody, hoaxes, criticism, mimicry, and damage to reputation. As a result, there was a "pervasive threat" that prosecutors would apply these statutes abusively.

Implicitly, Kuby's argument to the federal district court also raised another question: If prosecutors were allowed to criminalize various forms of anonymous, offensive, and/or embarrassing speech that they disliked with all sorts of tools, then why draw the line there? The same kind of prosecutorial attitude could open the door to criminalizing a broad spectrum of forms of intellectual dishonesty, including what was commonly known as research fraud. After all, nobody had ventured to suggest that plagiarism enjoyed First Amendment protection. As a hypothetical example of where this might lead, an author who adopted ideas from another scholar without giving him appropriate credit could, in theory, be convicted of "intellectual property theft" on the grounds that he plagiarized with the intent to wrongfully obtain a benefit for himself and thereby lessen his colleague's reputation.

But to stretch our criminal laws to cover research fraud would clearly violate our tradition of intellectual freedom and institutional independence. Numerous works examine the history of plagiarism and other forms of academic fraud, but not one of them reports a single case treated as a criminal matter. All such cases, ranging from the "Piltdown man" claim to the most egregious recent falsifications of historical and scientific data, have regularly been handled on the academic, institutional level, or at the most as civil disputes.¹⁰ One would be hard pressed to find American legal decisions criminalizing academicians for offenses taking place in the *intellectual* realm; the criminal justice system has understandably focused its resources on the *tangible* harms and threats of a financial, bodily, or intolerably invasive nature that penal laws are meant to punish and deter.¹¹

> A similar underlying distinction can be seen, for example, in trademark litigation, where no violation occurs when one person uses another's trademark for purposes of commentary or criticism rather than to identify goods or services for sale.

What was true for plagiarism and other forms of serious research fraud was also true for online impersonation. American civil courts had handled dozens of lawsuits involving online impersonation, but apart from my case, there had been virtually no significant criminal prosecutions. Apparently, the only exceptions were several indictments brought in Texas under that state's online impersonation statute, one of them against a man who opened a Facebook profile in his former wife's name. Each of the trial courts confronted by those indictments declared the Texas provision criminalizing impersonation unconstitutional because it failed to define the word "harm" with sufficient clarity—precisely the problem that the New York courts handling my case had ignored in their decisions. Intermediate appellate courts had then reinstated two of the Texas indictments, holding that the undefined "harm" *was* sufficiently clear, but there was as yet no ruling from the Texas high court. Otherwise all such controversies throughout the United States had been consistently handled as civil disputes, with parody being judicially recognized as a constitutional defense in defamation lawsuits.¹²

One notable exception was a criminal case that had been filed not in the United States but in England; it was cited in our legal briefs because of the legal traditions the two countries share. This was the case of Howard Fredrics, the professor of music (and my fellow Oberlin alumnus) teaching at the time at Kingston

University in London. Fredrics had opened a satirical website under the name "Sir Peter Scott," which was also the name of a knighted British academic serving then as the university's vice-chancellor. Kingston University was a center, seemingly, of educational mayhem and extreme corruption, its nature detailed on the "Sir Peter Scott" website. Initially, Sir Peter had filed a complaint with the World Intellectual Property Organization, in relation to the domain name registered by Fredrics, sirpeterscott.com. WIPO determined that the vice-chancellor held no "trademark" rights to the name and dismissed the complaint. Then Sir Peter took the same action as Dr. Lawrence Schiffman: he complained to the police, and a British court convicted Fredrics in absentia of "harassment." The conviction, however, was eventually overturned on appeal, on the grounds that Britain's antiharassment laws were not intended to protect an individual's reputation, and that the website, containing as it did information of public interest, belonged to the highest category of protected speech.[13]

The British court's decision offered a sharp contrast to the stance taken by prosecutors and judges in Manhattan, for whom the issue of Schiffman's alleged plagiarism, far from being a question of public interest, was not only a "false accusation" but also irrelevant. What is more, during the sentencing hearing following my trial, Judge Berkman had suggested—in yet another ad hoc rationale having nothing to do with the laws actually invoked against me—that exposing academic misconduct through an act of impersonation would amount to an *invasion of privacy*. The Supreme Court had consistently ruled that the free flow of information outweighs privacy interests, but the court's entire First Amendment doctrine had been set aside and even turned on its head in the legal Wonderland of the Manhattan criminal court.[14]

"Where Was the Judge He Had Never Seen?"—Kafka

In the summer of 2015, I learned that John Bandler had resigned from his post at the DA's office and opened up a private legal and consulting practice "to help corporations and individuals in areas such as cybercrime investigations, cybersecurity, data privacy, and anti-money laundering." I had mixed feelings upon hearing the news. On the one hand, Bandler would now have fewer opportunities to harm people. On the other hand, he had gotten away with an assault on my rights, and the idea that he would now be regarded as a respected member of the legal community and an expert on "cybercrime" had something unpleasant about it.

But far more worrisome events were soon to unfold. The first stage of the federal proceedings took place in the New York Southern District court of Judge Katherine Polk Failla. Somehow, I had allowed Failla's past history as a prosecutor to lead me to fantasize that she would both rebuke Cyrus Vance Jr. and call out Vincent Rivellese's arguments for what they were. In a petition for habeas corpus—a procedure allowing relief when state courts fail to respect the federal constitutional rights of criminal defendants—Kuby confronted Failla squarely with both my demand for a new trial and the issues of criminal libel and satire. The answer, when it came, raised even more questions about the treatment intellectual controversies can expect to receive in the US court system.

In the opinion she issued on January 21, 2016, Failla ruled that the criminal libel argument was "defaulted" because it had not been raised as a separate issue at the New York Court of Appeals. The entire topic was brushed aside on a technicality: we were, in effect, supposed to see through the fog of Carol Berkman's wildly overbroad trial rulings and specifically focus on the "libel" issue in the state court proceedings, even though the court of appeals had not yet created the "damage to reputation" standard.[15]

In a particularly intriguing section of her decision, Failla went on to rule that the trial court's application of an erroneously broad standard was "harmless." Since I had testified that plagiarism is an extremely "serious" matter, no reasonable jury could, according to Failla, have found that I did not intend to damage a reputation by sending the "Larry Schiffman" emails.[16] And since the "Jonathan Seidel" email to the Royal Ontario Museum in Toronto inquired whether the museum planned to include Norman Golb in their list of speakers, that email might have been sent with the intent to secure "employment."[17] Failla did find that my "perplexing" emails disparaging the "filth from Chicago" had been wrongly criminalized, because a "properly instructed" jury might conclude that I had sent them to obtain only a "slight" amount of "personal satisfaction."[18] She did not mention, however, the fact that these emails directly mimicked Magen Broshi's description of Norman Golb as "filth." Throughout her opinion, she also failed to address the blatantly satirical content of my blogs, as well as the message they conveyed on their clear-cut surface—to wit, that an entire group of important researchers who had shed new light on the origins of the Dead Sea Scrolls were being silenced, smeared, and blackballed in museum exhibits. For Failla, as for Berkman and Abdus-Salaam before her, that substantive matter appeared to be simply irrelevant.

To support her rejection of my claim that the statutes, as interpreted by the New York Court of Appeals, would allow prosecutors to criminalize any parody they deemed inappropriate, Failla ruled that "a parody can only achieve its comedic or critical goals if the audience *knows* that the work is a parody."[19] This ruling constituted a draconian precept: it implies that satire and parody enjoy constitutional protection only if there is an *expectation* or *declaration* of satire, or if the parody is so *obvious* that no one could be fooled by it. Failla failed to provide any precedent for this principle and for good reason: it was arguably lacking in any legal or factual foundation.[20] Deadpan written satire and parody often confuse and fool people, but this does not normally affect their status as protected speech. The district court's theory of "known" satire misrepresented cultural history and social reality; it cast aspersion on a pervasive form of polemical discourse stretching back into antiquity. While policemen had routinely hunted down satirists in other countries and other times, in the United States, there was a Bill of Rights and a principle of the "free interchange of ideas."

> *"A parody can only achieve its comedic or critical goals if the audience* knows *that the work is a parody."*

With all due respect, Failla's understanding of how parodies achieve their goals was highly questionable; her ruling struck me as expressing an age-old philosophical disdain for the quality of *confusion* that characterizes so much satirical discourse. Perhaps unmindful of the Supreme Court's statement that the First Amendment "does not leave us at the mercy of *noblesse oblige*" and that an unconstitutional statute will not be upheld simply because officials have "promised to use it responsibly,"[21] she indicated that she was not convinced prosecutors would have any difficulty telling the difference between legitimate parodies and ones whose satirical nature is not clear. Welcome to the new American system of ordered liberty, where the nation's Bandlers get to decide whether a parody is confusing enough to merit arrest, prosecution, and incarceration on the grounds that it constitutes an act of criminal "deceit."

My argument that I should have been allowed to plead truth was, Failla concluded, "curious," because "at the very least, the statements were plainly not made by those to whom they were attributed."[22] But, as we saw earlier, one traditional form of satire involves "attributing statements" to individuals who did not make them, precisely to bring out the truth about something. In implying that if they wished to avoid the danger of prosecution, email satirists were now expected to limit themselves to *appropriate forms* of mimicry, Failla perpetuated a confusion—one very effectively used as a tool by the prosecutor at my trial—between the falsity in the "packaging" of such written messages and the truths they are intended to convey. It bears repeating that I would not have been arrested and prosecuted if I had merely sent out an email in Schiffman's name politely thanking recipients for attending a seminar.

That the myth of *reverential* parody, in the framework of my case, had now been declared something akin to a presumption of criminal law governing satire became very clear during a hearing on the case held at the Second Circuit Court of Appeals on June 23, 2017, when a panel of three appellate judges more or less spelled out that they had, on the one hand, little interest in any First Amendment issues that might be involved and, on the other hand, a highly particular view of the actual facts of the case. Judge Pierre Leval asserted (on what grounds is not clear) that the criminalized emails sparked an "investigation" at NYU, and analogized them to an act of violence.[23] As he put it, "If I shoot a gun out there, like this, in that direction, just because my purpose is—just because I want to enjoy the pleasure of shooting the gun, I still have to contemplate that it's going to cause the harm." The harm "contemplated" by the emails was harm to Lawrence Schiffman's "reputation" and "career." I wondered, as I listened, whether Leval's "pleasure of shooting the gun" analogy was in any way informed by his own academic experience, for he himself had served as an adjunct professor at NYU.

The panel did not address the reality of the truly devastating harm potentially inflicted on another scholar's academic reputation by the uncredited use of his ideas, nor the reputational harm inflicted, for example, by an article containing a crushing critique of another scholar's work; and it did not address the conflict between its own findings and nearly a century of Supreme Court jurisprudence. It also eschewed the topic of parody, or the problems involved in establishing a "line" between "deceit" and deadpan mockery. Judge Dennis Jacobs, known as an avid proponent of the First Amendment, remained silent on these issues throughout the hearing, just as Sheila Abdus-Salaam had remained silent through most of the hearing at Albany three years earlier.

In the context of *civil* litigation and trademark lawsuits, American courts have held that there must be some sort of clue that a text is a parody.[24] But even in the framework offered by civil trials, such clues are often notoriously difficult to detect. In a criminal trial, it would appear nearly impossible for a jury to determine *beyond a reasonable doubt* whether one or another deadpan parody contains enough clues to its parody status to be considered satirical. In issuing her unprecedented "recognizability" requirement, federal district court judge Failla had failed to discuss this difficulty, in the process offering prosecutors a green light to criminalize and punish protected speech. When Judge Jacobs wrote the federal Second Circuit appellate panel's decision, he relied on precisely that requirement, along with the new "damage to reputation" standard created by Albany, which Jacobs and the panel would now endorse as a matter of federal law.

Jacobs, described in The New York Times as a "funny, irreverent person with a love of history,"[25] began by summarizing his assessment of the Dead Sea Scrolls and the controversy surrounding them. The scrolls, he declared, "were ancient documents discovered ... in a group of caves near Jerusalem [sic]. Most academics [sic] think [sic] that they were written by a Jewish sect called the Essenes who reportedly [sic] lived nearby."[26] Next, he briefly and flatly ruled, following seven years of appellate litigation, that all the charges pertaining to "Frank Cross" and "Jonathan Seidel" were unconstitutional because there was no proof that the emails in the "names" of those two individuals were sent with the intent to damage their reputations; the "Frank Cross" ones were too "puerile," and the "Seidel" ones could have been intended to convey an "idea." Then, however, taking a firmer tone and, it needs to be noted, arguably substituting his own assessment for that of a jury that had made no such finding, Jacobs ruled that the "Larry Schiffman" emails had manifestly been sent not, apparently, to convey an "idea" but precisely with the intent to damage a reputation. As he put it, no reasonable jury could have found otherwise.

Perhaps concerned that this declaration might run into the objection not only that an allegation of plagiarism *is* an idea but that a *vast amount of satirical speech* is aimed precisely at damaging reputations, Jacobs then addressed my claim that my actual intent was to engage in satire and parody. He explained that I "misunderstand the genre" of parody, for "while it is true that a parody enjoys First Amendment protection notwithstanding that not everybody will get the joke, it is also true that parody depends on *somebody* getting the joke; parody succeeds only by its recognition as parody."[27] Really? Did my parody need to succeed *at all* to qualify as protected speech? A lawyer at the New York public defender's office who blogs under the name "Appellate Squawk" was quick to comment, "Holy cow! You mean the difference between crime and parody is whether the joke falls flat?" Apparently unable to resist the temptation to send an arrow of her own biting sarcasm in the direction of the court, the lawyer prefaced her comments with a figurative mirror in which, perhaps, the judges were meant to look at themselves: a partial photographic reproduction of Grant Wood's painting *American Gothic*. Quoting the "filth from Chicago" language used in my "Jonathan Seidel" emails, she pointedly signaled in conclusion, "*We* got the joke."[28]

> "Parody succeeds only by its recognition as parody."

So much for the conceit that seemed to have informed the entire judicial review of my case over seven years—namely, that each and every one of my words, at least in the "Larry Schiffman" emails, needed to be taken at face value, with utter seriousness, and without any room permitted for sharp, provocative, tongue-in-cheek irony or irreverence.

The implication of Jacobs's ruling seemed to be that I had engaged in satire at my own risk; since my parody, according to the panel, did not "succeed," having failed to garner "recognition," a crime was committed and punishment by incarceration at Rikers Island was in order; had it succeeded, it would have been no crime and I would not merit incarceration. As it happens, Jacobs's rationale was buttressed by his selective use of the evidence, for he omitted any mention of what was arguably the most overtly parodic of the emails, the one stating that Larry Schiffman would have been "banned from conferences around the world" if he had "given credit to this man"—as it happens, a descent into the patently ridiculous in an email that would be referred to by Fordham University's Arthur Hayes in a *Forward* op-ed piece as "an act of satire."[29] Ron Kuby had foregrounded this email in one of his briefs; Jacobs chose not to discuss it in his published opinion. Why cherry-pick the most deadpan quotes available and leave this message aside? If Jacobs believed that it failed to convey an "idea," or that no reasonable academic recipient would have understood it as a satire, or that it revealed nothing of my frame of mind and broader intent, why not say so?

Regardless of any protests or expressions of dismay from the likes of the New York public defender and Hayes, the introduction of a special "one person must get the joke" rationale into the law was the final, culminating legal result of my case. The development at work here was so important in the context of constitutional law that its meaning, too, bears repetition. The Second Circuit's new standard, erected as a principle of federal law in the context of a First Amendment challenge to a criminal prosecution, effectively required that satirical impersonations be obvious, rather than confusingly deadpan, in order to avoid prosecution, conviction of crimes, and jail.

The danger posed to satirical authors by the unprecedented standard of "known" or "recognized" satire could be seen from the fact that my emails *did* contain clues that should have alerted—and indeed did alert—readers that they were nothing but an accusatory send-up. No distinguished professor would describe plagiarism as a "minor failing" or attempt to suppress criticism of it on the grounds that "this is just the politics of Dead Sea Scrolls studies," crudely explaining that "if I had given credit to this man, I would have been banned from conferences around the world." The notion that a New York University department chairman would express fear of being internationally silenced if he appropriately credited a reputable source was in fact so obvious an instance of academic satire that no trained academic could take it seriously. The failure of two highly experienced NYU deans to openly acknowledge this fact, and its systematic bypassing not only by the prosecutor and judge at my trial but by an entire series of appellate judges, could only cast doubt on whether the collective effort to confront what I had done had in any way led to a more accurate understanding of the boundaries of satire. Had the quest for such an understanding been hindered, on some basic level, by the prosecution's repeated smears?

As if to emphasize that any empirical evidence of my actual intent was to be regarded as irrelevant, the various courts involved had focused exclusively, in the same cherry-picking fashion employed by the prosecutors, on those of my emails that conveyed mockery in a less overt, more deadpan manner. But even these had contained irony for those with an ear for it ("someone is intent on exposing me"), hyperbole ("my career is at stake"), understatement ("a minor failing"), belittlement, and personification—precisely the hallmarks of a lampoon. Indeed, to reiterate a point I've made above, *no professor would ever casually admit to plagiarism*. The preposterous nature of a declaration often suffices to indicate its satirical nature. Which must have *something* to do with why Dean Stimpson immediately knew that Schiffman could not have written the emails. The issue here was plain for all to see. As Judge Leval of the Second Circuit panel had himself stated in a decision he had written when he was still a lower federal court judge, "First Amendment protections do not apply only to those who speak clearly, whose jokes are funny, and whose parodies succeed."[30] Apparently, either the intervening years or the facts of my case had led him to modify his perspective; speaking with insufficient clarity was now like "shooting a gun out there," and a parody "succeeds only by its recognition as parody."

> *"First Amendment protections do not apply only to those ... whose jokes are funny, and whose parodies succeed."*

* * *

One additional aspect of the federal court decisions also deserves emphasis. Even assuming that my personification of Schiffman was so lacking in humor—so *accurate*, as it were—that it somehow required the neglect, or even reversal, of established legal principles, the reality was that my internet campaign as a whole had plenty of other satirical moments, as when I lauded the scroll exhibitors for preventing public confusion, or railed against the "filth from Chicago" that needed to be silenced. This contextualizing fact was also not mentioned by either the district court or the Second Circuit panel—just as they failed to mention Avi Katzman's original allegations of plagiarism, or my private emails to family members, where I had explained, long before my arrest, that my aim was to "inform people of the truth," and where I had asserted that the "plagiarism of Lawrence Schiffman" had been "exposed." If so much evidence was considered unworthy of mention in these crucial decisions upholding at least some of the verdicts in my case, then the possibility that prosecutors would continue to track down and arrest anonymous parodists who embarrassed people with clout and connections emerged as more than a disquieting phantasm. That possibility would increase if prosecutors, along with other members of the legal community, failed to fully appreciate, or to convey in their analyses (as would eventually be the case, for example, in a law review article published by a Mississippi judicial clerk), the intricacies, subtleties, and hazy distinctions of the Second Circuit's decision.[31]

A basic tool for exposing corruption and abuse of power seemed at risk of being suppressed. On February 16, 2018, the United States Supreme Court declined to hear an appeal of *People v. Golb*.

"Wise Men Say Nothing in Dangerous Times"—John Selden, *Table Talk*

During the next two months, I start getting nervous. The court date—Monday, April 16, 2018—at which my expected surrender will be arranged is approaching. All recourses have been exhausted. In view of the judges' interpretation of the facts, I'll be heading back to Rikers. The unconstitutional harassment statute was just a minor detail; clearly such behavior must not be tolerated.

Rikers Island: the world's largest penal colony;[32] one of the worst of the many festering, shameful sores in our society; the repugnant place where I had been held incognito, where a hateful guard had screamed at me, his face purple with rage, "Get that smile off your fucking face!" The law is the law. I tell my mom it's only a couple of months. The guards will make sure nothing happens to me. Deep down, what I'm most keenly aware of is the violence that's about to be done to the truth—the self-satisfied statement from the DA, the vicious smears that will be unleashed again in the press.

The night before April 16, I can't sleep. All the years since my arrest, the distortions, the oxymoronic arguments from the prosecutors, the lack of regard for the "truth is not a defense" unfairness of the trial on the part of the reviewing judges—all of it keeps swirling around in my head. I fall into a daze for a couple of hours and drag myself out of bed on time. I make it down to the criminal court. As I enter the room, I'm still thinking of how Kuby should answer if the prosecutor says this or that.

We wait around for half an hour, and then I'm called up to the defendant's table. Suddenly my heart starts pounding and I tell myself it's just a physical reaction.[33] For the next ten minutes, as the proceedings unfold, the pounding continues and I can barely focus on what's happening. I sit hunched over in the chair, hearing the pounding and increasingly certain that I'm going to collapse. No one seems to notice what's going on; I barely make out Elizabeth Roper, deputy chief of the Cybercrime and Identity Theft Bureau—and whose résumé includes working in the "official corruption unit of the Manhattan DA's office"[34]—arguing to Judge Laura Ward that the two-month jail sentence she had imposed in 2014 is still "appropriate" and that I should be incarcerated at Rikers. "The defendant," she suggests, "perpetrated a ... campaign to boost his father's reputation in the academic community."

As for the twenty-one convictions pertaining to Cargill, Goranson, Seidel, and Cross, all patently unconstitutional, all laboriously vacated after seven years of appellate litigation, they are simply irrelevant to my guilt; after all, Roper insists, it is the charges pertaining to the "Larry Schiffman" emails that were always the "core" of the case. In response, Kuby argues that according to the Second Circuit, an entire series of appellate judges were unable to figure out which forms of speech were criminal and which ones were constitutionally protected, and that it would serve no discernible purpose to jail me after the passage of so many years.

After Kuby is finished, Laura Ward gruffly asks me if I have something to say. At first I don't hear the question because my heart is still pounding; then I shake my head. She turns back to the prosecutor. "I couldn't sleep last night," I blurt out, as if trying to explain my physical reaction to the proceedings. Instantly I realize that I've just made a serious mistake.

Ward glances back at me and, as she turns again to Roper, "Well, yes," she says. Suddenly—against all my expectations—she addresses the prosecutor: "I agree that Mr. Golb has been punished enough. *Coming here so many times over all these years.* I'm going to let him go."

As simple as that. The pounding suddenly stops. Roper looks dumbfounded. Then she gets her nerve back and preserves her dignity: she demands an "order of protection" for Schiffman. Ward grants it, and explains that my final sentence is the time I've already served—the nights in the Tombs and at Rikers, and the probation where I was told that I had committed "fraud" and would be "finished" if I tried it again. Turning to me, Ward gives me a slightly humorous smile as she sums up her decision with one short sentence: "Mr. Golb, I hope I never see you here again." Is there a faint hint of an apology in her smile? As I leave the courtroom, Roper is still sitting there. She looks down at her papers, avoiding any eye contact.

In the midst of all the commotion, Robert Cargill is in Iowa, sending out a final tweet that appears to be aimed at me. For whatever reason, Robert has ceased blogging about my case during the federal appeal process; but he is clearly aware of my hearing, and perhaps even expects me to be sent to jail on this very day. His tweet reads simply "2 Samuel 12:12."[35] This passage from the Hebrew Bible, in which God (via Nathan) announces that David is going to be punished for plotting to kill Uriah and for stealing Uriah's wife, has already been cited by Cargill numerous times in his comments on my trial, including in his blog entry of September 20, 2010, announcing the "guilty" verdict. Here is the passage from the book of Samuel, together with the preceding verse:

> 11. Thus sayeth the Lord: Behold, I will raise up evil against thee out of thine own house, and I will take thy

wives before thine eyes, and give them unto thy neighbor, and he shall lie with thy wives in the sight of this sun.
12. For thou didst it secretly: but I will do this thing before all Israel, and before the sun.

Cargill's "creepy" tweet is reported to me by two female friends of mine who have accompanied me to the hearing. As I understand it, the meaning of 2 Samuel 12, as employed in this particular context, is that I "secretly" sinned by availing myself of anonymity, and that Cargill "raised up evil" against me by gathering information about my campaign and handing it over to New York's cutting-edge prosecutors. But I am still a bit puzzled by the analogy. For one thing, while Cargill did openly avow his efforts on behalf of the prosecution after March 5, 2009, his prior communications with Schiffman, and apparently with Bandler himself, that led to my arrest did not exactly take place in the open light of day. Nor was his collusion, evidenced in the margin of his *Virtual Qumran* film script, in an agreement "never to write down" Norman Golb's name exactly an open matter at the time it took place.

Ward's decision—dropping the sentence she herself had imposed four years previously—terminates, and leaves unfulfilled, the process that began in August 2008 with the Manhattan district attorney's formation of a special unit charged with investigating the Dead Sea Scrolls controversy. That process was marked by *close cooperation between a particular academic network and a massive overburdened and underfunded municipal prosecution system*. Designed to enforce draconian antidrug laws and to deal with both white-collar and violent crimes, the system depends on a smoothly running plea bargain process. The aim is to avoid trial and to move as many accused persons as possible—the majority of whom are without means and competent legal counsel—into prison as quickly as possible, saving large amounts of time and money and keeping the system going.

Unfortunately, the system had to deal with me, a recalcitrant defendant who pleaded not guilty and insisted on taking his case to trial. While I was recuperating from my physical and mental exhaustion during the days after Ward's stunning declaration, I couldn't help recalling a conversation I had had with a learned and experienced French academician in 1991, during my years in Paris. A meeting billed as a major international conference had been announced, dealing with the medieval Jewish history of France: an area in which, like that of the Dead Sea Scrolls, my father's work was both well known and the subject of intense intellectual and institutional controversy. Excited to see a program of the conference posted in a hallway of the university where I was residing, I quickly realized that my father was not included in the sea of announced attendees. That evening, I phoned him to verify that he had not been invited. He laughed mildly and explained that no one had informed him that the conference would be taking place—which, as he put it, was just "business as usual" in that field of studies.

A few days later, I happened to be near the office of a colleague and friend of my father's, a wiry gray-haired man who had for many years served as the editor of a journal dealing with religious and historical topics. I stopped in to pay him a visit, and during the course of our conversation, I mentioned the conference. Seeing that he, too, was aghast at the "politics" of the organizers, I told him that I planned to go to one of the sessions and to stand up and ask, during the question-and-answer session, "Why has Norman Golb not been invited to attend this conference?" "Ne le fais pas," he immediately said. "Don't do it. People will only use it to malign your father—they'll cluck their tongues and say, 'Look, Golb sent his son,' and so on and so forth. It's better just to ignore what they're doing, however outrageous and upsetting it is." I did go to the lectures, where I heard various attendees murmuring in the audience that "Golb wasn't invited," and another, from Tel Aviv, angrily protest on the stage that "Golb is not here." But I followed the

> The topic of the conference was "The Jews of Northern France in the Middle Ages." My father's books on the Jews of Rouen (the capital of medieval Normandy) had infuriated a number of French scholars who had always believed that there had never been a Jewish community of any importance in Rouen.

professor's advice, stayed silent, and watched the events unfold from a distance.

This book, in a sense, has been about my participation in a different conference—one in which, this time around, I've decided to speak up about a process of exclusion and blackballing unfolding over half a century in a major historical field.

The same professor in Paris, incidentally, also once taught me a trick: how to drop proof of academic malfeasance in an envelope and send it to two separate editors who had unwittingly allowed their journals to serve as the platform for the malfeasance, without comment and without affixing my name to the envelope. "When they see this," he noted, "they will be furious. A response will be solicited from the scholar who has been victimized, and the individual who did this will never be allowed to contribute to these journals again." Perhaps this is why I remembered my conversation with him about the 1991 conference so well. (To protect him, hopefully, from retaliation, I have refrained here from mentioning his name or the name of the journal he edited.)

When they charged me with fifty-two crimes, prosecutors expected I would act in a rational manner and accept a deal. But they had failed to grasp the full implications of my sense of commitment to the truth, of my strong solidarity with my father in the face of the abuse he was suffering at the hands of a network of academics whose works were characterized by various forms of charlatanry. The prosecutors expected that my legal training would lead me to do the "right" thing and plead guilty. But, defying all the odds, I refused to cooperate. The system was then faced with a mess that could have been the subject of a Kafka novel, and that would last nearly a decade, with one court after another creating a variety of legal rationales that took the case outside the "strict scrutiny" strictures imposed by a century of constitutional interpretation.

My trial would take place, pursuant to the prosecutor's

> The prosecutors didn't count on the fact that—certainly partly from my father—I had a long-hardened faith in critical inquiry and, doubtless more naively, in the rational course of justice.

specific request, before a unique and well-known criminal court judge. That judge, in turn, would make her opinion of satire and parody clear in the selective choice of definitions that she read to the jury. The subsequent litigation would reveal striking parallels to the process allowing "Qumran-Essene" pseudoscience to perpetuate itself despite the absence of any cogent evidence for its purported findings: the prosecution would present each of the courts with various modalities of distorted reasoning, fake allegations, and personal assaults on my character.

Clearly, the prosecutors in New York saw my resistance as a threat to the power and authority of the system in which they played such an important role. This factor removed *People v. Golb* from the realm of reasoned debate into one of ideological warfare. An academic dispute that in normal circumstances would have been looked into, at most, by an appropriate faculty committee became nothing less than a massively publicized struggle. Most oddly, the Manhattan DA's use of irrational arguments would conjure up the scroll monopoly network's own quasi-theological efforts to defend ideas that were unfounded and ideological in nature. The sectarian belief and the draconian enshrinement of the reputations of the group defending it would become two sides of the same coin. As in a self-realizing myth, baseless historical claims would be treated with the utmost respect, while an "any harms and benefits" principle would be invented and then modified, revised, and heightened into a remarkable doctrine that was arguably without any basis in American constitutional law.

This parallel neglect of scientific rationality and First Amendment precedent reflected a confluence of interests between the scrolls network and the Manhattan DA's office—a fact directly confirmed by the prosecutors taking sides in the scrolls debate itself.[36] According to the prosecutors, the research conclusions of Norman Golb were "unpopular" views, and whether history had been distorted by religiously motivated academics whose work lacked scientific merit was simply irrelevant. In the end, the scroll network's effort to maintain influence and authority would produce nothing less than a new legal principle: regardless of the First Amendment, regardless even of the truth, reputations impugned by parody that isn't "clear" enough can now be defended through criminal prosecution.

"The Greatest Enemy Is Despair"—Abraham Heschel

Even many months later—long after Laura Ward's decision, just one out of the dozens she rendered that week, had raised a few reporters' eyebrows and been ignored by the legal and academic communities—it was impossible to brush aside the impact the past nine years had had on me. My memories remained clear, as if everything had happened yesterday. But the impact was deeper than that. As a result of the legal process I had closely observed unfolding during and after my trial, my mind had grown accustomed to forcing itself into new ways of thinking. These were in line with the strategy developed by the prosecution in my case, but contrasted sharply with the ethical rules given, for example, in the American Bar Association's *Model Rules of Professional Conduct*, which strictly forbid lawyers and prosecutors from making misleading statements. As we have seen, the aim of the prosecutors' systematic distortions and omissions was to mislead the jury and the judges alike regarding my intent. The effects of the Manhattan DA's strategy were visible at every stage of the proceedings, including in opinions issued by the state and federal appellate courts.

> Rule 7.1 of the American Bar Association's *Model Rules of Professional Conduct* forbids lawyers and prosecutors from omitting "facts necessary to make [a] statement considered as a whole not materially misleading." But my entire case was built on doing precisely that: on carefully omitting any relevant background about the documented silencing and propaganda efforts of the Dead Sea Scrolls monopoly group and its associates and heirs.

Looking back, it's clear to me that the time it took for the process to play out made it more difficult for me to adjust to the fact that the actual workings of the criminal justice system didn't align with what I had once been taught at NYU's school of law. From one month to the next over nine years, I had been asked to accept the idea that twisting the truth was normal conduct on the part of highly trained prosecutors. Instead of accepting it, my resistance grew. Gradually, though, I reconciled myself to the system—at least to the extent that I grew convinced that no one can realistically hope to have any impact on it from the outside.

One spring morning in 2019, I sat wrestling with the mind-boggling Multistate Professional Responsibility Examination, a required first step for readmission to the New York State Bar. The questions on the exam presented long and elaborate ethical problems. Among the rules referred to was the one forbidding materially misleading statements (like "the accusations of plagiarism are false"), as well as the precept that "a prosecutor has the responsibility of a minister of justice and not simply that of an advocate," so that his duty is to seek "justice," not "convictions"; accordingly, for example, he must "make *timely disclosure* to counsel for the defendant of evidence or information that tends to ... mitigate the degree of the offense."[37]

Judges, of course, are also required to be "faithful to the law." In fact, they must avoid even an "appearance of impropriety," and they are not to be "swayed by partisan interests, public clamor or fear of criticism."[38] I had no reason to believe that any of the judges involved in overseeing and reviewing my case had fallen short of these fundamental ethical precepts. Rather, their decisions had been based on particular interpretations of the law, ones that struck me as plainly wrong and even dangerous in their implications for freedom of speech in this country and indeed everywhere in the world. Which, in a sense, was far worse than any ethical shortcoming would have been.

Despite my strong belief that there are right and wrong decisions, at one point as I rapidly penciled in my answers, the anxiety-sparking thought came over me that just as the various rules could be interpreted in different ways by real-life prosecutors and judges, each elaborate situation featured in the exam questions could actually be answered in more than one way, depending on how one wanted to see it. I realized that each of my instinctive solutions might have been slightly off base, for I had acquired a habit of seeing things through the eyes of experienced legal practitioners who seemed to be making choices that might in an exam room raise eyebrows but that were considered correct in view of the circumstances.

In the end, my disbarment would be summarily vacated by an order of New York's First Department on October 29, 2021. My motion for reinstatement, made on the grounds that the appellate courts had vacated the two wrongful felony convictions pursuant to which my license to practice law had been taken away from me, had gone unopposed—a tacit admission, as it were, that I had been wrongly disbarred to begin with. In addition to the exam results, the dossier I had submitted together with the motion included an affidavit recommending me, signed by a retired federal judge in Washington who had been following the Dead Sea Scrolls controversy for many years. The dossier also included another affidavit signed by a forensic psychiatrist, explaining that I suffered from no mental illness and that my decision to "impersonate" Schiffman had resulted simply from stress.

Meanwhile, controversy over satire had continued to galvanize public interest. One among many examples: California representative Devin Nunes had been subjected to persistent online mockery taking multiple forms that included hundreds of tweets parodying him. The tweets often presented themselves as statements made by his mother, and attacked him in ways that, according to Nunes, "no human being should ever have to bear and suffer in their whole life." Apparently seeking to make a point about the evils of online freedom, Nunes filed a lawsuit to try to suppress the "harassment." The move was met with an outburst of popular derision and indignation; Nora Benavidez, PEN America's director of US Free Expression Programs, called the lawsuit "a ridiculous attempt to use the court system to hold social media platforms accountable for what is ultimately constitutionally-protected satirical speech."[39] A judge ultimately threw the lawsuit out, ruling that Twitter cannot be sued for allowing people to post such material.[40]

While met with ridicule, the Nunes lawsuit once again pointed to a dangerous resurgent impulse to suppress forms of speech that are "unwanted." But the lawsuit, like nearly all contemporary efforts to suppress satire, was a civil matter. Nunes chose to litigate his grievance himself; he had no Morgenthau, Vance, or Bandler to come to his aid. Defending a *criminal* case in which First Amendment values are at stake is a dangerous—in many regards hallucinatory—experience. My conflict with one of New York City's most powerful academic-political establishments could easily have landed me on a prison-island where I could have been destroyed. The result: twenty-one convictions were eventually vacated; ten were kept intact. As all prosecutors know well, throw a lot of mud, some is bound to stick.

At bottom, the moral brigade's case lay in shambles. Large sums of taxpayer dollars had been squandered on a costly investigation of an academic controversy Bandler and his colleagues knew nothing about, and on a fruitless, nearly decade-long effort to have me incarcerated. Berkman's decisions had been gutted during the appellate process, and a trail of strange legal arguments had been left behind in the appellate courts. In a terrible humiliation that would continue to echo through the New York criminal justice system for years, one of the prosecutors' most precious debate-stifling tools, the aggravated harassment statute, had been declared unconstitutional on its face. They had, in a technical sense, won their impersonation battle and produced a deeply troubling exception to the First Amendment—a victory achieved at the cost of allowing a spotlight to be shed on the conduct of the academic on whose behalf they had brought the case to begin with. It was hard to imagine them deriving much satisfaction from the result.

Nevertheless, surviving in a power-based system from which any sort of meaningful conversation was excluded was, to put it mildly, daunting. I had lived on the knife's edge of ruin for nearly a decade. I took solace from friends, from books, and, at one point, from the documentary film *Man on Wire*, about Philippe Petit, the funambulist who in 1974 walked a tightrope between the twin towers of the World Trade Center. Somewhere in the film, Petit speaks of living "on the edge of life," of remaining true to his inner sense of what really matters. In my own way, I, too, felt suspended on a high wire where every step was risky, but I kept my balance by holding on to what really matters—a belief in the truth, a refusal to accept the falsehoods of others, no matter what the consequences. I continued to know, somewhere deep down inside, that the truth was a value worth defending especially when it was most fiercely under attack. For a decade, that knowledge had kept me steady on the rope. If my fight for justice was about anything, it was about protecting the truth when it comes under assault—whether that applies to the Dead Sea Scrolls, freedom of speech, or our criminal justice system. Too much is at stake for us not to risk everything to keep that value safe.

Epilogue

Eight years after my trial, the special building project for the Ingeborg and Ira Rennert World Center for the Dead Sea Scrolls—the massive Jerusalem complex destined to house the scrolls—was $17 million short, and the situation appeared to be the same at the time of writing.[1] Very likely, a dramatic removal of twenty-five thousand manuscript fragments from East Jerusalem, a move bound to cause serious tension with Jordan, no longer seemed urgent in view of the changed American and international political situation; or else funding for the planned World Center had become one more pawn in the game of internal Israeli politics. An eventual move, however, still seemed very much in the cards, especially in view of the role it would play in strengthening the Holy City's powerful draw for evangelical tourists.

Following my trial, in fact, the continuing religion-based scrolls enterprise was clearly a major success for the Israel Antiquities Authority—a factor undoubtedly feeding into its decision to develop a lucrative business arrangement with the venture in vulgarity known as the Museum of the Bible (or MOTB), an institution located near the National Mall in Washington and described by art historian Noah Charney as an "oversize piece of evangelical claptrap."[2] The arrangement apparently consisted in the receipt of money, along with a permanent exhibition space at the museum, in exchange for certain selections from the scrolls, to be loaned to the museum along with "cuneiform tablets from Abraham's time, materials from the First and Second Temples, and various other antiquities that go back to the Canaanite period."

> Charney indicates that when MOTB opened, some critics "expressed concern" that its "vast collection of more than 40,000 artifacts would be used as evangelical propaganda."

The developing picture soon took on a new dimension. In addition to texts loaned by the IAA, the DC museum put a variety of "Dead Sea Scroll" fragments on display that formed part of the massive antiquities collection amassed over the years by David Green, the billionaire founder of Hobby Lobby. There was only one problem with these fragments: like many of the other artifacts in Green's collection, no one had ever been able to figure out exactly where they came from and how they had entered the antiquities market. Doubts about their provenance, and indeed about their authenticity, quickly surfaced. After seeing them, Michael Langlois, a specialist in epigraphy and ancient history at the University of Strasbourg, asserted that "it's almost as though I could recognize the hand of the forger."[3] Toward the same time, a detailed study by Årstein Justnes of the University of Agder in Norway made it clear that certain scholars associated with the Dead Sea Scrolls monopoly team had been involved in what amounted to an elaborate effort to pass these forgeries off as authentic texts and integrate them into the "sect of Qumran" corpus.[4]

For his part, scrolls monopoly chief Emanuel Tov was "not convinced the fragments are fake."[5] Why would Tov—praised by some as

> When asked, several years after his retirement, if he knew that Dead Sea Scroll fragments were being exhibited at the Museum of the Bible, my father immediately replied that they were forgeries.

"perhaps the most important textual critic of the Hebrew Bible alive today,"[6] and who had, in 2017, been rewarded for his efforts on behalf of the monopoly with a position as Foreign Honorary Member in the American Academy of Arts and Sciences—need special proof to be convinced that dubious Hebrew manuscript fragments are fake, when the normal scientific expectation is that *authenticity* needs proving? In this regard, it is notable that even before lending his support to the Museum of the Bible, Tov had agreed to serve in a "senior" capacity with the Green Scholars Initiative (GSI), an organization that recruits poorly qualified academics whose activities, paid for by Hobby Lobby, then consist in legitimatizing, as it were, the Green family's collection by examining unprovenanced texts and declaring them to be the oldest known copies of one or another biblical passage.[7]

In practice, after they are examined, the texts rapidly disappear back into the collection, where they are unavailable for study by scholars at large.[8] The unique system at work here has grave implications: purchase of these texts and other unprovenanced artifacts encourages an illicit trade in antiquities benefiting terrorists, among others.[9] In their book *Bible Nation*, which exposes the largely fraudulent nature of the Hobby Lobby's educational enterprises, Candida Moss and Joel Baden describe Tov's willingness to participate in the unsavory "initiative" as being somehow ironical, because it was he, according to them, who "spearheaded ... the eventual opening of the Dead Sea Scrolls to the entire scholarly community."[10] Notably, the academics who join the GSI—most of them having no training in work with manuscripts, and most affiliated with evangelical educational institutions—are allowed to participate only if they sign rigid confidentiality agreements evidently meant to thwart not only accountability but almost any critical scrutiny of their work and of the Hobby Lobby collection itself. One "uninitiated" papyrus scholar told Moss and Baden how he had been denied access to the collection, but he offered the information under the condition that he "not ... be named for fear of professional retribution."[11]

A year after the publication of *Bible Nation*, on October 23, 2018, the Museum of the Bible announced that tests performed on five of the "Dead Sea Scrolls" fragments in Germany had revealed them to be forgeries, and that they would no longer be displayed. But other fragments (billed as some of the "most valuable artifacts") would continue to be displayed pending further testing; David Green himself "declined to comment."[12] Two months before the announcement, the museum had "quietly hired" Rena Opert, previously an employee of the US Holocaust Memorial Museum, to serve as "Jewish exhibits director."[13] Yonat Shimron of Religion News noted that Opert was "neither a curator nor a Judaica expert" but would "work on strategic planning."[14] Shimron pointed out that Moss, Baden, and others had accused the museum of treating "Judaism as a steppingstone for Christianity rather than a religion in its own right."[15] The same critics, she indicated, attributed a "fundamentally anti-intellectual orientation" to those behind the museum—an orientation rooted in the "evangelical understanding that the Bible is true and without error." Eventually, a further ramification would be added to this developing scandal when sociologist and investigative journalist Hella Winston would demonstrate that the museum's entire collection of Torah scrolls was in fact one of the main ingredients in a tax evasion scheme.[16]

Meanwhile, a press release from the Museum of the Bible had indicated that Lawrence Schiffman had "contributed to the museum's History floor and Narrative floor."[17] As criticism of the museum's biased orientation began to spread, Religion News informed its readers that "along with six other paid Jewish scholars," Schiffman had "signed agreements not to publicly criticize the museum," and that he did not agree with critics who had suggested that the museum's exhibits were oriented toward the "traditional Christian belief that Christianity is the fulfillment of biblical Judaism."[18] One apparent result of Schiffman's collaboration with the museum was visible in a dimly lit section (on the fourth floor of the colossal building) devoted to the Dead Sea Scrolls.

Here, visitors were informed that a "community" living at Qumran is "believed to have collected and written" the scrolls and, a bit later, more categorically but again without any supporting evidence, that the Essenes were the "Jewish religious group that collected the scrolls." One panel informed visitors that differences between the Masoretic text and the biblical Dead Sea Scrolls were trivial, so that "the Bible" had remained unchanged through history—evangelical propaganda that had no basis in reality.[19] No hint of any disagreement among historians about these claims was offered, but a special wall panel devoted to the Copper Scroll asserted that whether the treasures dryly listed in that major historical document ever "existed" is a "debated question." The question why such an artifact would have been "collected" and hidden in the caves along with the other scrolls by the wealth-eschewing Essenes was not addressed.

The "valuable artifacts" consisting of fake biblical scroll fragments would continue to be displayed until the spring of 2020, when the museum would be forced to admit that they were all forgeries. *National Geographic* would quote the museum's CEO,

Harry Hargrave, as stating that "The Museum of the Bible is trying to be as transparent as possible … We're victims—we're victims of misrepresentation, we're victims of fraud."[20] Lawrence Schiffman would be quoted in the same article as asserting that the importation of the fake scrolls was properly documented and that "the victims—despite the fact that it's embarrassing to admit that you were duped—have to go and explore all criminal and civil remedies with U.S., Israeli, and international authorities."

In the fall of 2018, I navigated the hallways of this old warehouse transformed into a symbol of evangelical power. During my little tour of the fraudulent scrolls exhibit, I felt like a visitor to another planet, where special rules existed for what could or could not be said and special punishments were prescribed for deviations from those rules. The museum's treatment of the scrolls was in tune with the exhibition policy that had taken shape before my trial: thanks to the "vigilance" of the exhibitors, as Robert Cargill had put it, those opposing the Qumranologists would "experience increasing difficulty in getting out their message." In implementing this policy, the exhibitors had, already a decade before any public controversy emerged around the Museum of the Bible, learned that they could benefit from the assistance of various prominent Qumranologists, including NYU's highly popular Jewish studies department chairman.

By now I was well aware, as Timothy Garton Ash observes, that while "free speech, like law, should be a bulwark for the weak against the strong," the "rich and powerful always try to bend it to their own purposes."[21] I was a bit troubled by the idea that I might bump into Schiffman in the room devoted to the scrolls—perhaps leading a tour and explaining that "scholars agree" about the scrolls and that they are "working together" to improve the museum's collection. What would happen if security became aware of my presence and informed me that I had been asked to leave? I had purchased my ticket with my debit card, and somehow this had led to my name—my real name—being printed on it. I fumbled for the ticket in my jacket pocket. Certainly, if an attempt were made to usher me to the exit, I would resist, and an argument would ensue. At the very least, I would demand some sort of an explanation, and then anything could happen. It would probably be best to quickly leave of my own accord, before someone spotted me. I located an escalator and made it down from the fourth floor and out to the street without prompting any incident. Walking across the National Mall in a chilly autumn breeze, I noticed that the grass was worn down. I headed to Union Station and got the first train back to New York.

I was glad to get out of there. I had done my job by witnessing the exhibit firsthand. As the train headed out of DC, it occurred to me that in some ways, the current phase of the scrolls saga was a bit like the crisis the entire country was going through—also with its roiling epicenter in Washington. I was in a reasonably good mood, but a tinge of indignation—of resentment!—lingered over the lies I had just seen on display, and over the fact that I had knowingly contributed to the museum's efforts by paying an entry fee.

I took out my pen and notepad and organized some of my thoughts. I wondered how archaeologist Yitzhak Magen would react if he saw the display I had just toured. A few days after my arrest, he had asserted that "not even a quarter of an Essene was at Qumran," that "the scrolls were the outcome of flight from Jerusalem and other areas that were densely settled with Jews," that the Qumranologists are just "a guild with money and conferences," that "it's beginning to change," and that the new theory "will finally win out."[22] He had reasserted these views in the final *Back to Qumran* report, which had been published by the Israel Antiquities Authority several months before Laura Ward dropped my jail sentence.

"A guild with money and conferences..."

At the time, I had no way of knowing that over the next few years, Magen's compelling contribution would be met not with reasoned debate but with an outpouring of renewed propaganda for the Essene theory. One press release emanating from an academic department would explain, for example, that a scholar had determined that Qumran was a gathering spot for Essene "pilgrimages"; as the *Times of Israel* explained (referring readers to the *Damascus Covenant* on which my father had done his PhD work at Johns Hopkins), researchers "believe [a] 1,000-year-old document from [the] Cairo Geniza shows [Qumran] hosted an annual event where [the] Essene sect gathered, bringing religious scriptures they left behind."[23] Archaeological findings that reinforced the Jerusalem theory of scroll origins would, on the other hand, be announced in a manner visibly designed to limit their significance. Such would be the case with a merchant's ledger dug up in the city's ruins, "inscribed with seven rows of mundane text" and dating from Second Temple times: a discovery making it all the more clear that there was "widespread literacy" at the time.[24] The reality of such literacy is precisely one of the basic facts that defenders of the Qumran-sectarian hypothesis had always sought to belittle; the legacy of that effort would be discernible in the declaration by one of investigators involved that the finding was "not the most important thing in the world."[25]

Some of the propaganda would take a slightly more sinister form, as when Jodi Magness of the University of North Carolina (and, following in the footsteps of Emanuel Tov, a 2019 inductee into the American Academy of Arts and Sciences) lashed out in a statement added on the second page of the new edition of her award-winning popular book on Qumran, inaccurately informing her thousands of readers that I had "spent two months in jail" and that "in the end" I had also been disbarred. With equal inaccuracy, she asserted in the same statement that my father, "a professor who studies medieval Jewish manuscripts," had argued not that the scrolls were the remains of libraries of the Jews of Jerusalem but that they had "originated in the Jerusalem Temple."[26] Several months after the publication of this offensive material, Magness would give a special presentation in which she would assert that the scroll caves "surrounded" Qumran; that a sect living there *must* have gathered the scrolls, even though, as she admitted in the same presentation, the vast majority of the scrolls had nothing sectarian about them; that the many water cisterns excavated at Qumran had served as ritual baths; and that the animal bones buried at the site were the remains of ritual sacrifices. In passing, she would refer to, and object to the title of, a "sensationalistic book, written during the 1980s, called *Who Wrote the Dead Sea Scrolls?*"[27]

What Magness would fail to tell her audience was that her claims and arguments had been rejected, and indeed refuted at length, by the Magen-Peleg team in their 450-page report.[28] According to the professional assessment of that team, only a single one of the cisterns, for example, had the archaeological characteristics of a ritual bath, the others all being used for the manufacture of pottery; and the "sacrificial" animal bones were *cooked*, not *burned* as is the case with the remains of sacrifices known from other archaeological digs—the simple, prosaic explanation for the burial of bones at Qumran being that the people who ate the cooked animals had figured out that burying their remains was the best way to keep scavengers away.[29]

> Per Magness's request, her presentation was not recorded by the hosting institution. Each member of her audience paid approximately sixty dollars to sign on to the Zoom presentation.

I knew nothing of the future exploits of the "new Essene sect" as I mulled over my visit to the massive Bible museum during my return trip to New York. Nor did I know that in the years to come, after the death of my father, a *National Geographic* issue devoted to the scrolls would eschew the misrepresentations of Schiffman, Magness, and others and give the Jerusalem-libraries theory the accurate treatment that it deserved.[30] What I did know was that in *Back to Qumran*, Yitzhak Magen had meted out his own brand of pointed ridicule to scholars who, according to him, were defending baseless, erroneous, and unscientific ideas. As the train slowly headed north through the slums of Philadelphia, I figured that Magen—a towering figure in the world of Israeli archaeology who would not be caught dead collaborating in any form with a phony institution like the one I had just visited—might be right about things beginning to change. Rationality and courage could still eventually prevail; new voices would certainly emerge; and the need for honesty, progress, and critical thinking would likely lead to renewed demands for an unbiased reassessment of the evidence. And, even if the ongoing Dead Sea Scrolls pseudoscience somehow remained "official" doctrine for years to come, more and more people would see the signs that the sectarian emperor had no clothes.

But that day was far in the future. In the here and now, I knew I had to write this book. Too much was at stake—the issues raised were too important to acquiesce in the distortions dished out in the court decisions, or in the silence of the academic community. What are the limits of protest when battling against injustices created by people in power? Should one merely offer a bit of polite criticism, so easily disregarded, when monopolists refuse to relinquish control, and seek to justify their continuing authority in defiance of critical, logical analysis of their position?

> According to the *National Geographic* 2022 special scrolls issue, "many scholars contest the identification of the Qumran community as Essene" and believe that the scrolls were only "transported to Qumran for safekeeping when Roman forces prepared to lay a siege around Jerusalem in 70 CE." Focusing on Norman Golb's multiple-Jerusalem-libraries theory, the author indicates that "support for this theory has been found in the difference in writing styles, as well as the great diversity of thought that the scrolls express."

As the train picked up speed, I thought of the trial of the Chicago Seven, where a federal judge had one of the defendants, Bobby Seale, bound and gagged. Were the judges in my case right to suggest that injustices in the academic milieu need to be tolerated because "careers" depend on them? At some point, when confronting systemic madness, one has to act in ways far outside the restraints of a "civility" code. In the end, I remained convinced that I had been right to feel that the choice was between doing whatever had to be done to expose the truth and lying down and letting those in power simply roll over their opponents. I had acted to bring a morally indefensible situation and a direct misuse of scholarship to the light of day—a misuse that had ended up obscuring the history of the Jews and of their contribution to the origins and ethos of

Western civilization. In acting as I had done, I had not only strayed outside the bounds of conventional normality but jeopardized my own livelihood. But the cause remained a legitimate, even necessary one: to bring some light where there had been too much darkness, and to end a scandalous abuse of authority motivated by ideologically driven hubris, greed, and a lust for accolade, all propped up on premises unsupported by a single shred of bona fide empirical proof.

I was still reviewing my notes when the train rolled into New York, Penn Station. I breathed a sigh of relief. It was only a short subway ride to Greenwich Village and my apartment. I had my work cut out for me. Putting everything together would not be easy, but I knew the fight would go on.

APPENDIX

Comparative Table of Selected Statements in Writings of
Norman Golb and Lawrence Schiffman

N. Golb	L. Schiffman
1. "The majority of the non-Biblical texts appear to be akin to, and at times identical with, well-known books of the apocryphal literature, which no writer could ever show, on the basis of internal evidence, to have been written by members of a single group or sect within ancient, pre-Tannaitic Judaism" (*PAPS*, 1980).	1. "The apocryphal compositions ... were composed outside the sectarian center and brought there"; "many compositions found at Qumran ... were widespread among various elements of the Jewish population" (*Reclaiming the Dead Sea Scrolls*, 33, 181).
2. It is "difficult to believe ... that the people living at Qumran practiced the laws and believed in the doctrines of only some of the scrolls," or "that it was there that the Essenes guarded and were able to preserve, more than any other group in ancient Judaism, the various works of Jewish literature comprising the apocryphal and apocalyptic writings, including works of these	2. The scrolls "provide the key to understanding what the sectarian library can tell us about other groups of Jews ... in that period"; "the texts in the Qumran corpus reveal many types of interpretation ... practiced by the Qumran sect as well as by other contemporary Jewish groups" (*Reclaiming the Dead Sea Scrolls*, xxvi, 211).

genres previously unknown" (*PAPS*, 1980).	
3. The popularity of apocalyptic ideas found in various scrolls and their influence on the mentalities of Jewish groups prior to 70 CE were "factors which may … help to explain the zeal which led to the Jewish War" (*PAPS*, 1980).	3. The influence of apocalyptic texts on the Jews of that time can be observed "in the messianic pressures for Jewish resistance against Roman rule that were factors in fueling the two Jewish revolts … both of which had messianic overtones" (*Bible Review*, October 1990).
4. The texts are "more than sufficient to show the mentality and religious outlook of various groups within Palestinian Judaism" before 70 CE. They "cast important new light on aspects of that period's history, particularly on the question of the influence of the beliefs and practices then current in Palestine on both the nascent rabbinic Judaism and the earliest forms of Palestinian Christianity" (*Biblical Archaeologist* 48 [June 1985]: 81–82).	4. "These documents are providing a critical background for the study of the later emergence both of rabbinic Judaism and of the early Christian church" (*Bible Review*, October 1990).
5. "The cogent inference to be drawn from the presence of Hebrew manuscripts at Masada is that Jewish sicarii inhabiting the site	5. "Very recently several fragmentary texts were published from Masada … occupied by the rebels during the Revolt against

possessed scrolls which they had brought there after taking the fortress ... while other Jews, of Jerusalem, took scrolls with them in addition to basic possessions needed for survival, in withdrawing to that site" (*PAPS*, 1980). In this, as well as his later articles, Golb specifically discusses the Sabbath Songs text.	Rome. In addition, a manuscript of the Sabbath Songs ... known in several manuscripts from Qumran, was found at Masada. Thus, the Jewish defenders of Masada possessed books of the same kind as those in the Qumran collection, but that were not directly associated with the sect itself. In other words, many of the works found at Qumran were the common heritage of Second Temple Judaism and did not originate in, and were not confined to, Qumran sectarian circles" (*Bible Review*, October 1990).
6. The manuscripts stemmed from first-century Palestinian Jews and were remnants of a literature showing "a wide variety of practices, beliefs, and opinions"; elucidation of the ideas and practices described in the scrolls might be best achieved "not by pressing them into the single sectarian bed of Essenism, but by separating them out from one another, through internal analysis, into various	6. "It is now becoming increasingly clear that the scrolls are the primary source for the study of Judaism in all its varieties in the last centuries before the Common Era. In short, this corpus does not simply give us an entry into the sect that inhabited the nearby settlement, but also has an enormous amount to tell us about the widely varying Judaisms of the Hasmonaean and

spiritual currents which appear to have characterized Palestinian Judaism of the intertestamental period" (*PAPS*, 1980).	Herodian periods" (*Bible Review*, October 1990). Responding to his own question whether his 1994 book was "revolutionary," Schiffman stated, "It is revolutionary to suggest that we should determine the scrolls' origins not through external evaluation and theoretical criteria, but rather through examination of the specific contents of the manuscripts" (*Reclaiming the Dead Sea Scrolls*, xxiv).
7. Golb discusses a biblical passage in the scroll known as the *Manual of Discipline*, which Qumranologists had long interpreted as implying that the members of the brotherhood group described in that manuscript should actually go live in the wilderness. Golb argues that the passage symbolically refers to study of the Torah (*PAPS*, 1980).	7. Discussing the same passage, Schiffman states that it has to be interpreted symbolically. "To prepare the way in the desert," he wrote, "means to interpret the Torah, specifically to explain it according to sectarian interpretations" (*Reclaiming the Dead Sea Scrolls* [1994], 95).
8. David Rothstein, UCLA dissertation on the Qumran phylacteries (University Microfilms, 1993): the circles responsible for	8. The Qumran phylacteries "bear witness to variations of custom, especially as regards the order and content of the biblical

these variegated religious amulets "constituted a broad spectrum of Palestinian (and diaspora) Jewry." Golb (*Who Wrote the Dead Sea Scrolls?* [1995], 103) appropriately cites Rothstein.	passages included in them" (*Qumran and Jerusalem* [2010]). Schiffman fails to cite Rothstein or Golb; he cites only authors who think members of a sect living at Qumran wore these phylacteries.
9. "We may note the lyrical richness of ancient Hebrew up to the very destruction of the Second Temple … and we observe that virtually all of this poetry, as well as over three quarters of the prose texts, was composed in Hebrew, disproving the view that Aramaic had overtaken Hebrew as the main language of the Jews of Palestine in the first century" (*Who Wrote the Dead Sea Scrolls?* [1995], 361). "There is little chance that we will ever be able to grasp the full magnitude of the creative power of this people in the days of the Hasmonaeans and their successors" (*Who Wrote the Dead Sea Scrolls?* [1995], 383).	9. The discovery of the scrolls "has reclaimed for us a new layer in the history of Hebrew language and literature. Like those before and after, this layer testifies eloquently to the linguistic and literary creativity of the Jewish people in their native language throughout their history" (*Qumran and Jerusalem* [2010], 62).
10. "[The scrolls] are the heritage of the Palestinian	10. "The challenge of Hellenism brought about the

Jews of that time as a whole, according to various parties, sects, and divisions that served as the creative source ... of a multitude of spiritual and social ideas" (*Who Wrote the Dead Sea Scrolls?* [1995], 383).	splitting of the Jewish community into various groups, each seeking to dominate the religious scene. The writings of some of these groups and information about others ... are preserved in the Dead Sea Scrolls ... We seek not only to describe the language and literature of the Qumran sect, but also to use their writings and the writings they collected as a means of uncovering information about a variety of Jewish groups of this period" (*Qumran and Jerusalem* [2010], 35, 37, 48).

NOTES

Notes to Chapter 1

[1] Eventually handed over by prosecutors along with other incriminating evidence, these items are in the author's files.

[2] The facts informing the thought processes outlined in this and the following paragraph, as well as those supporting the allegations made in the sidebar, will be documented throughout this book.

[3] I use the spellings "antisemitism," "antisemitic," and the like, rather than "anti-Semitism," for the reasons set forth by the International Holocaust Remembrance Alliance in a memorandum dated April 2015. See https://holocaustremembrance.com/resources/spelling-antisemitism ("the term antisemitism is today used to describe and analyze past and present forms of opposition or hatred towards Jews … The unhyphenated spelling is favored by many scholars and institutions in order to dispel the idea that there is an entity 'Semitism' which 'anti-Semitism' opposes. Antisemitism should be read as a unified term so that the meaning of the generic term for modern Jew-hatred is clear. At a time of increased violence and rhetoric aimed towards Jews, it is urgent that there is clarity and no room for confusion or obfuscation when dealing with antisemitism"); see also https://www.timesofisrael.com/whats-in-a-hyphen-why-writing-anti-semitism-with-a-dash-distorts-its-meaning/ and https://forward.com/culture/166092/should-anti-semitism-be-hyphenated/.

[4] See, for example, Arieh Shalev (NYU Langone Center), "Acute Stress Reactions in Adults," *Biological Psychiatry* 51, no. 7 (2002): 532–43.

[5] For the quotations in this and the following paragraphs, see People v. Golb, exhibit 46-A, a transcript of which is in the author's possession.

[6] For this expression, see Judaean hills tour guide and radio host Eve Harow's interview with Schiffman at https://soundcloud.com/thelandofisrael/rejuvenation-living-the-dead-sea-scrolls, and see https://jewishottawa.com/community-calendar/eve-harow--from-beverly-hills-to-the-judean-hills-1456242624 and https://www.wgbh.org/people/eve-harow. For a partial list of televised programs in which Schiffman has appeared, see https://www.imdb.com/filmosearch?role=nm2659013&job_type=self. Schiffman's performances are also documented in many YouTube videos: see, for example, https://www.youtube.com/watch?v=92hyhBXLaWE and https://youtu.be/dG8DnPy4R_U.

[7] While this term was used with a pejorative nuance for several decades to refer to a current-day revival of exaggerated puritanical propriety, its meaning is now often flipped by various commentators who proclaim the

need for a "new seriousness" in America. For the standard pejorative nuance, see, for example, Joe Kennedy, *Authentocrats: Culture, Politics and the New Seriousness* (Penguin, 2018). Kennedy is a professor of cultural studies at the University of Sussex.

[8] Although it was later removed from the district attorney's website, this release can still be read at https://web.archive.org/web/20090310010813/https://www.manhattanda.org/whatsnew/press/2009-03-05.shtml. Maxey Greene's professional LinkedIn page explains that she has left the DA's office and is a consultant whose skills include "marketing materials," "generating national and local media coverage," and "building press and business contacts."

[9] See, for example, https://gothamist.com/news/the-tombs-private-club-for-some-orthodox-jewish-jailbirds and https://nypost.com/2011/04/17/jailhoue-mitzvah-chutzpah/.

Notes to Chapter 2

[1] See Ron Robin, *Scandals and Scoundrels: Seven Cases That Shook the Academy* (Berkeley, 2004), 26, 82–83, 160–61, 214.

[2] Ibid., 207–8 (discussing a hoax perpetrated against the editors of the postmodernist journal *Social Text* by physics professor Alan Sokal). Robin's argument relies implicitly on a theory of democracy as *resistance to power*. It is worth noting that like many other ideas, this concept has emerged historically in various ways. To take but one example, the philosopher Emile Chartier (1868–1951), who wrote under the pen name "Alain" and was the revered high school teacher of Simone Weil, Raymond Aron, and others, defended a version of it in his political writings; according to him, power, by its very nature, corrupts those who hold on to it and leads to the tyrannical suppression of criticism; accordingly, "resistance" to power is one of the key "virtues of the citizen." See Alain, *Propos sur les pouvoirs* (Gallimard, 1985); these ideas are reiterated throughout the section of the book entitled "Les citoyens contre les pouvoirs." Unfortunately, Alain's personal form of resistance included privately expressing antisemitic views and sympathizing with the "sincerity" of Hitler.

[3] See Avi Katzman, "Anshe Hamearot," *Haaretz, Musaf*, 50, January 29, 1993.

[4] See Elisheva Carlebach, "Securing the Future of the Center for Jewish History: Independence Is Invaluable," *Forward*, November 28, 2007, available at https://forward.com/opinion/12132/securing-the-future-of-the-center-for-jewish-histo-00871/, and Lawrence Schiffman, ibid., at https://forward.com/opinion/12133/securing-the-future-of-the-center-for-jewish-histo-00872/. See also http://failedmessiah.typepad.com/failed_messiahcom/2007/12/the-future-of-t.html (commenting that "Lawrence Schiffman sticks to generalities

and avoids the details of his own plan, in effect arguing his case deceitfully").
5 For the IJCIC, see http://ijcic.net. For Schiffman's IJCIC role (including his service there as chairman of the board of governors) and other aspects of his career cited in this paragraph, see https://nyu.academia.edu/LawrenceSchiffman/CurriculumVitae.
6 See Schiffman's lengthy interview with Eve Harow at https://www.israelnationalnews.com/Radio/Author.aspx/1229; https://jewishottawa.com/community-calendar/eve-harow--from-beverly-hills-to-the-judean-hills-1456242624.
7 See, for example, Eric Herschthal, "Jewish Studies sans Religion?" (November 18, 2009), available at https://www.jta.org/2009/11/18/ny/jewish-studies-sans-religion. Schiffman is quoted as asserting that teaching secular Jewish culture is "an incorrect way to categorize Jewish phenomenon [*sic*]," a position, the article explains, that informs his opposition to the acceptance by NYU of grant money from the secularly oriented Posen Foundation. Secular Judaism emphasizes Jewish cultural and historical as opposed to religious identity. Throughout this book, I will use "secularism" and related terms to refer to an insistence on rationalist, critical, and empirical scholarly values.
8 See David Gibson in the *New York Times*, April 9, 2006, available at http://www.nytimes.com/2006/04/09/weekinreview/the-world-antisemitisms-muse-without-judas-history-might-have.html. Online references to Schiffman as a rabbi—all of them, according to his own criminal court testimony, false—include the following: https://nyulocal.com/the-ultimate-guide-to-the-city-part-5-nightlife-734aa2a31af2 ("NYU's own Rabbi Lawrence Schiffman"); https://www.thejc.com/comment/comment/stars-and-stripes-of-david-at-odds-1.57101 ("Rabbi Lawrence Schiffman, an Orthodox rabbi and world-renowned expert on the Dead Sea Scrolls at Yeshiva University"); https://www.torahanytime.com/#/speaker?l=792 (online lecture on "Seeing the Truth of Tanach through the World of Archaeology" delivered by "Rabbi Lawrence Schiffman"); https://www.youtube.com/watch?v=HvOVZmHwy4Q ("The Temple Mount with Rabbi Lawrence Schiffman—Jewish Spotlight Show"); https://www.ratemyprofessors.com/professor/2478157 ("Rabbi Schiffman is really great"); http://gatherthesparks.blogspot.com/2012/12/rabbi-lawrence-schiffman-on-gospels.html ("Rabbi Lawrence Schiffman on the Gospels"); and https://www.chabad.org/news/article_cdo/aid/2955336/jewish/Sinai-Scholarship-Top-Students-Academics-Explore-Torahs-Depths-at-National-Forum.htm (quoting "Rabbi Dr. Lawrence H. Schiffman, professor of Hebrew and Judaic studies at New York University and a world-renowned biblical scholar").

9 Students of rhetoric may wish to compare the "Larry Schiffman" emails with the old (and still commonly used) ironical technique known as apophasis. A classic example: "I say nothing of your Roguery, your Vices and your Ill Manners; but if I should, they are known to the whole World." See Anne Toner, "Apophatic Austen: Speaking about Silence in Austen's Fiction," in *XVII-XVIII, Revue de la Société d'études anglo-américaines des XVIIe et XVIIIe siècles* 73 (2016) (quoting Charles Bland's *The Art of Rhetoric* [London, 1706]); available at https://journals.openedition.org/1718/739. In apophatic discourse, the speaker generally calls attention to something by asserting that he will not mention it. In the emails, "Larry" calls attention to something by ordering others not to mention it, while in the same breath providing a link precisely to the material that must not be mentioned.

10 See https://web.archive.org/web/20100917105833/https://www.amny.com/urbanite-1.812039/rift-over-ancient-texts-leads-to-cyber-crimes-says-da-1.1137453.

11 Letter from interim associate dean Alicia Estes, dated February 5, 2018 (author's files).

12 The "Larry Schiffman" emails are gathered in People v. Golb, trial exhibit 16. For the reply to Peacock, compare Mervyn Peake's novel *Gormenghast*, chapter 39 ("Steerpike ... snatched up the candlestick ... In a moment, the [professor's] beard had shone out in sizzling fire"); and note the similarity between the names Peacock and Peake.

13 After receiving his degree, Peacock will become director of operations for the Sonoran Theological Group, an institution that provides "practical preparation for ministry." Peacock's online profile states that he "has served the church in a variety of capacities," that his "recent work looks at the necessity of humility in biblical studies," and that "he utilizes a theology of play both personally and professionally creating community in its wake." See http://www.sonorantheological.org/faculty-facilitators/ and http://www.sonorantheological.org/about/.

14 See People v. Golb, trial transcript, 188. In an article dated September 29, 2010, the *Huffington Post* would describe Catherine Begley as a "former special agent in the New York office of the FBI." The article would quote Begley as explaining that the "best way to insure [*sic*] that a counterfeit artwork doesn't resurface in the art world is to destroy or deface it. Shred it, incinerate it, stamp it so that no one will be fooled again." See Daniel Grant, "What Happens to Confiscated Art 'Fakes'?," available at http://www.huffingtonpost.com/daniel-grant/what-happens-to-confiscat_b_742118.html. After apparently moving from the bureau's art fraud unit to its health-care fraud task force, Begley would later be listed as regional security director at Merck & Co., specializing in "effective anti-counterfeiting strategy."

15 See John Leland, "Online Battle over Sacred Scrolls, Real-World Consequences," *New York Times*, February 16, 2013, available at

http://www.nytimes.com/2013/02/17/nyregion/online-battle-over-ancient-scrolls-spawns-real-world-consequences.html.

[16] See Stanley Cavell, *Must We Mean What We Say?* (Cambridge, 1958).

[17] See People v. Golb, trial exhibit C (included as appendix 2 in *The Qumran Con*) and trial transcript, 193–94.

[18] All the emails quoted in this and the next paragraph are gathered in People v. Golb, people's exhibit 15.

[19] This email is found among the documents gathered in People v. Golb, people's exhibit 16.

[20] See the online version of the article at http://web.archive.org/web/20080822092153/http://www.nowpublic.com/world/plagiarism-and-dead-sea-scrolls-did-nyu-department-chairman-pilfer-chicago-historian-s-work.

[21] See, for example, https://bobcargill.wordpress.com/2010/01/28/bombshell-ny-das-response-to-raphael-golbs-motion-to-dismiss-charges-and-suppress-evidence-reveals-norman-golbs-knowledge-of-the-campaign/. Cargill probably was unaware that the prosecution had distorted the excerpts' meaning by removing them from their context. For example: In the summer of 2008, my parents spent several weeks in Jerusalem. When they first arrived, my father could not access his emails on his laptop. My mother then instructed me to contact them via her Gmail account on the desktop computer lent by a colleague. The prosecution made this sound like my mother had been trying to protect my father from receiving evidence of nefarious activity on my part. Similar anodyne explanations exist for each of the excerpts in the chain of "evidence of intent" strung together by the prosecution.

[22] This followed my criticism of scroll exhibitions originally posted on the Spinoza's Lens website (and still available at http://web.archive.org/web/20111004040010/http://robertdworkin.wordpress.com/), which caught the eye of a reporter reviewing an exhibit in Raleigh, North Carolina. See the comments posted at http://web.archive.org/web/20100816144047/https://www.indyweek.com/indyweek/unraveling-the-continuing-mystique-of-the-dead-sea-scrolls/Content?oid=1210028 and http://web.archive.org/web/20110305011034/http://www.indyweek.com/indyweek/unraveling-the-continuing-mystique-of-the-dead-sea-scrolls/Content?oid=1210028.

[23] Dozens, possibly even hundreds, of media outlets carried articles based on Associated Press releases. For a small selection, see, for example, https://www.haaretz.com/world-news/u-s-lawyer-gets-jail-for-using-online-aliases-to-harass-people-in-dead-sea-scrolls-debate-1.325426; https://www.newsday.com/news/nation/ny-case-spotlights-dead-sea-scrolls-fake-emails-1.1572287; https://www.dailyherald.com/article/20101001/news/310019863/; https://www.chronicle.com/article/Cyberbully-Is-Found-Guilty-

on/124762; and https://wtop.com/news/2014/05/ny-court-upholds-online-impersonator-charges/.

[24] See, for example, John Eligon, "Identity-Theft Arrest in Dispute over Dead Sea Scrolls," *New York Times*, March 5, 2009, available at http://www.nytimes.com/2009/03/06/nyregion/06scrolls.html. Eligon quotes the district attorney's narrative without questioning its premises: "'This exemplifies a growing trend in the area of identity theft,' Antonia Merzon, an assistant district attorney, said during the news conference. 'It's very easy to open an account using any name you want on the Internet. There's nothing necessarily wrong with that. But when you start using another person's true identity for *some purpose*, you're crossing the line into a possible identity theft crime or impersonation crime'" (italics added).

[25] See, for example, John Eligon, "Dispute over Dead Sea Scrolls Leads to a Jail Sentence," *New York Times*, November 18, 2010, available at https://cityroom.blogs.nytimes.com/2010/11/18/dispute-over-dead-sea-scrolls-leads-to-a-jail-sentence/. The article fails to mention any controversy over the exhibitions. With respect to the plagiarism charges, it merely states the following: "Mr. Golb testified that the emails were merely parodies, but he maintained that he did believe Professor Schiffman had plagiarized from his father. Professor Schiffman denied those accusations."

[26] See Batya Ungar-Sargon, "Dead Sea Scrolls Go to Court," *Tablet*, January 14, 2013, at https://www.tabletmag.com/sections/arts-letters/articles/dead-sea-scrolls-go-to-court; cf. James McKinley, "Son of Dead Sea Scrolls Scholar Is Sentenced to Two Months in Jail," *New York Times*, July 14, 2014, available at https://www.nytimes.com/2014/07/15/nyregion/son-of-dead-sea-scrolls-scholar-is-sentenced-to-two-months-in-jail.html.

[27] My own claim of parody was, to be sure, mentioned in coverage of my trial testimony. See, for example, http://www.sandiegouniontribune.com/sdut-son-in-ny-dead-sea-scrolls-case-theres-no-crime-2010sep27-story.html.

[28] See https://nypost.com/2009/03/08/parting-dead-sea/.

[29] See http://www.nytimes.com/2012/09/26/nyregion/sock-puppetry-time-honored-tradition-thrives-online.html.

[30] See http://www.nytimes.com/2013/02/17/nyregion/online-battle-over-ancient-scrolls-spawns-real-world-consequences.html. On Schiffman's status as an "authority," compare Carl Sagan's "baloney detection kit," in *The Demon-haunted World: Science as a Candle in the Dark* (Random House, 1995), 212.

[31] See People v. Golb, 102 A.D.3d 601, 960 N.Y.S.2d 66 (1st Dept. 2013).

[32] See Golb v. Attorney General of the State of New York, No. 15-cv-1709, 2016 WL 297726 (S.D.N.Y. Jan. 21, 2016).

[33] See Goodacre's blog item of March 13, 2009, on the "ethics and practicalities of blogging in the wake of the Raphael Golb affair,"

available at https://ntweblog.blogspot.com/2009/03/ethics-and-practicalities-of-blogging.html. In casting doubt on the "academic" nature of the pseudonymous (and satirical) discourse used in my campaign, Goodacre fails to confront the fact that I am not affiliated with a university, and that my intent, far from being to abide by the polite customs of interdepartmental "civility," was to call attention to a scandal in the academy—one whose existence he apparently does not wish to recognize.

[34] See https://jonathanturley.org/2009/03/09/who-wrote-the-dead-sea-scrolls-emails-lawyer-charged-with-impersonating-nyu-professor/.

[35] The *New York Daily News* item used by Turley as the source for information on the contents of one of my emails will later be removed from that publication's website; it is available at https://web.archive.org/web/20101006101424/https://www.nydailynews.com/news/ny_crime/2009/03/05/2009-03-05_dead_sea_scrolls_stir_cyberhoax_west_vil-1.html.

[36] See https://www.washingtonpost.com/politics/2022/01/27/biden-scotus-pick-conservative-criticism/.

[37] See https://jonathanturley.org/about/.

[38] The second entry can still be read online at https://web.archive.org/web/20100808072831/http://tzvee.blogspot.com/. The first is in the author's files.

[39] Italics added. See https://steveawiggins.com/2010/10/01/crimeless-victim/ and https://steveawiggins.com/2014/07/22/dead-see-scrolls/.

[40] See http://blog.simplejustice.us/2010/07/20/a-prosecution-2000-years-in-the-making/.

[41] Supina's comment was copied and reposted on the site of British blogger Geoff Hudson. See https://www.blogger.com/comment.g?blogID=14512636&postID=8772262647332441374&bpli=1&pli=1.

[42] See https://latin4everyone.wordpress.com/2013/02/ (commenting that if "even scholars of classical antiquity" "fall victims to such abuse, then wider academia is surely far more vulnerable"). Hinke was the last American arrested for evading the Vietnam War draft (he and others were pardoned by Jimmy Carter); his writings include *Free Radicals: War Resisters in Prison* (TrineDay, 2017).

[43] See comment 43 at https://web.archive.org/web/20130527155344/http://newsdesk.tjctv.com/2013/04/investigation-reveals-additional-questionable-identity-with-connections-to-broydes-scholarship/.

[44] Arthur Hayes, "Censorship Redux: The 21st Century Attack on the First Amendment Right of Public Criticism by the Use of Cyberharassment, Cyberstalking and Online Impersonation Laws," in *Sympathy for the Cyberbully: How the Crusade to Censor Hostile and Offensive Online Speech Abuses Freedom of Expression* (New York, 2017), 175.

[45] Kembrew McLeod, *Pranksters: Making Mischief in the Modern World*

(New York University Press, 2014), 53, 67 (quoting cultural historian Lori Landay, *Madcaps, Screwballs, and Con Women: The Female Trickster in American Culture* [Philadelphia, 1998], 2).

[46] See Michael Bugeja, "Satire Explores Unspoken Truths but Is Often Misunderstood," in Iowa Capital Dispatch, June 25, 2021. Available at https://iowacapitaldispatch.com/2021/06/25/satire-explores-unspoken-truths-but-is-often-misunderstood/.

[47] See Seymour-Smith's introduction to Joseph Conrad's *The Secret Agent* (Penguin, 1990), 14.

[48] See Rivlin's introduction to Eliahu Schwarz, *To Jerusalem With Love: 142 Sketches of Life in the Holy City* (Jerusalem, 1971), 147. Rivlin was best known for his Hebrew translations of the Koran (published in 1936) and of the *Arabian Nights* (published in thirty-two volumes between 1947 and 1971).

[49] See Erasmus, *Adages, I i 1 to I v 100* (Collected Works: Volume 31), translated by Margaret Mann Phillips (Toronto, 1982), 449.

[50] An English translation of the *Epistolae* would be reprinted in 1964 and 1972, with commentary treating them as a "basic text of European humanism." See F. G. Stokes (tr.), *On the Eve of the Reformation: "Letters of Obscure Men"* (New York, 1964) [1515–17]. This notwithstanding, the text is no longer included in humanities course syllabi. For the reception of the letters in Europe when they were first passed around, see the far more detailed introduction to Stokes's original translation of 1909, at liii.

[51] See the discussion of apophasis, above, note 9.

[52] Stokes (tr.), *On the Eve of the Reformation*, introduction to 1909 edition, liii.

[53] George A. Test, *Satire: Spirit and Art* (Tampa: University of South Florida Press, 1991), 10.

[54] See the anonymous article "Pasquin and Pasquinades," published in the October 1860 edition of the *Atlantic Monthly*, available at https://www.theatlantic.com/magazine/archive/1860/10/pasquin-and-pasquinades/627768/. Despite the obvious importance of the pasquinades to anyone interested in the history of censorship and freedom of speech, they are today apparently the object of widespread ignorance among American academics. In February 2012, conservative First Amendment specialist Eugene Volokh of UCLA would assert on his blog that he had "just learned" the meaning of the "term," referring readers to a brief series of definitions that include, for example, "an abusive lampoon or satire, esp one posted in a public place." See https://volokh.com/2012/02/24/pasquinade/.

[55] *Atlantic Monthly*, ibid.

[56] For details, see the anonymous 1860 *Atlantic Monthly* article cited in the previous note.

[57] See the *Stanford Encyclopedia of Philosophy*, at https://plato.stanford.edu/entries/pascal/.

⁵⁸ See Blaise Pascal (préf. Louis Cognet), *Les Provinciales* (Paris: Bordas, 1992), i–lxxxv.

⁵⁹ For more on the satirical nature of the first great modern novel, see Nathalie Grande, "Conscience, volonté et distance critique dans *La Princesse de Clèves*," in *MaLiCe* (Aix-Marseille, 2021), available at https://cielam.univ-amu.fr/malice/articles/conscience-volonte-distance-critique-dans-princesse-cleves.

⁶⁰ John Bunyan, *The Pilgrim's Progress from This World, to That Which Is to Come* (New York: Fleming H. Revell, 1903) [1678], 223. Discussions of Bunyan's use of satire include Brean S. Hammond, "*The Pilgrim's Progress*: Satire and Social Comment," in Vincent Newey, ed., *The Pilgrim's Progress: Critical and Historical Views* (Totowa, NJ, 1980), 118–31, and Brainerd Stranahan, "Bunyan's Satire and Its Biblical Source," in Robert Collmer, ed., *Bunyan in Our Time* (London, 1989), 50–51.

⁶¹ See the doctoral dissertation of Erin Ashworth-King, *The Ethics of Satire in Early Modern English Literature* (2009), 1–6, available at https://core.ac.uk/download/pdf/210598372.pdf. The scope of the decree may actually have been broader: it ordered the burning of certain volumes of verse satire by various authors and then declared that "no satires or epigrams be printed hereafter."

⁶² See https://johnmarston.leeds.ac.uk/the-works/marstons-poems/ (Leeds University page on the poems of John Marston). The works burned pursuant to the 1599 decree included Marston's "Metamorphosis of Pygmalion's Image," a work filled with angry satire that the poet had published under the pseudonym "W. Kinsayder."

⁶³ See *Universal Jewish Encyclopedia*, vol. 9 (1943), 21; T. J. Cardy, *A Dictionary of Literary Pseudonyms in the English Language* (Mansell, 1999). See also Saul Chajes, *Pseudonymen-Lexikon der hebraischen und jiddischen Literatur* (Bamberger, 1933). The widespread use of literary pseudonyms was by no means limited to the nineteenth century. "George Orwell," for example, is a pseudonym. The *Encyclopedia Britannica* entry on Orwell explains that "few people but relatives knew his real name was [Eric] Blair. The change in name corresponded to a profound shift in Orwell's lifestyle, in which he changed from a pillar of the British imperial establishment into a literary and political rebel." By the same token, current-day objections to pseudonymous commentary are far from a recent development.

⁶⁴ See, for example, Michael Hanrahan, "Defamation as Political Contest during the Reign of Richard II," *Medium Aevum* 72, no. 2 (2003): 272n1 ("In 1379 and again in 1389 Richard II re-enacted the hundred-year-old scandalum magnatum statute, which Edward I had originally instituted in 1275 to prevent social discord by suppressing slanderous reports about the great men of the realm"), and Michael Kahn, "The Origination and Early Development of Free Speech in the United States: A Brief Overview," *Florida Bar Journal* 76 (October 2002): 71 ("The seeds of seditious libel

originated in a collection of laws known as Scandalum Magnatum, which was passed in 1275 and outlawed any speech that contributed to discord between the king and his people. Sir Edward Coke, as attorney general, reported to the infamous Star Chamber in a case in 1606 that libel of a government official is a greater offense than a private libel and even a true libel may be punished").

[65] T. J. Carty, *A Dictionary of Literary Pseudonyms in the English Language* (Mansell: London, 1995), lists forty-one pseudonyms used by Swift. See, for example, Judith Mueller, "*A Tale of a Tub* and Early Prose," in Christopher Fox, ed., *The Cambridge Companion to Jonathan Swift* (2003), 208 (observing that "parody is intrinsically unstable and subversive" and that "in imitating the sort of writing Swift finds objectionable, *A Tale of a Tub* risked being objectionable itself, as its initial reaction showed").

[66] See, for example, https://www.bachelorandmaster.com/essay/a-modest-proposal-critical-commentary.html (describing the work as a "very cruel and dangerous satire on the politics of Great Britain") and https://littlevillagemag.com/prairie-pop-a-guide-to-the-satirical-hits-inspired-by-a-modest-proposal/ (mass walkout of dignitaries provoked by Peter O'Toole's reading of the work at a theater opening in 1984).

[67] See Chiara Frenquellucci, "Forged Letters and Literary Hoaxes: Satire and the Epistolary Novel in Girolamo Gigli's 'Il gazzettino' and 'Il collegio petroniano delle balie latine,'" in *Italica* 88, no. 2 (Summer 2011): 163–77, 163–64, 166, 169–70.

[68] See *The Spirit of Laws* (1748), book 12, ch. 12–13 (tr. Thomas Nugent, 1750). Available at https://press-pubs.uchicago.edu/founders/documents/amendI_speechs3.html.

[69] For details, see Robert Darnton, *The Devil in the Holy Water, or the Art of Slander from Louis XIV to Napoleon* (Philadelphia, 2011).

[70] See, for example, Gregory Dowd, *Groundless: Rumors, Legends, and Hoaxes on the Early American Frontier* (Johns Hopkins Press, 2016), 187–204; see also C. Mulford, "Benjamin Franklin's Savage Eloquence: Hoaxes from the Press at Passy, 1782," *Proceedings of the American Philosophical Society* 152, no. 4 (2008): 490–530.

[71] See *On Parody*, by Arthur Shadwell Martin (New York, 1896), 18.

[72] See ibid. and, for a thorough account, Ben Wilson, *The Laughter of Triumph: William Hone and the Fight for the Free Press* (London, 2005).

[73] See Charles Knight, *The Popular History of England*, vol. 8 (London, 1862), 87.

[74] For details, see, for example, https://www.mtsu.edu/first-amendment/article/1017/seditious-libel and https://firstamendmentwatch.org/history-speaks-the-end-of-seditious-libel-1964/.

[75] For Buratti, see https://www.treccani.it/enciclopedia/pietro-buratti_(Enciclopedia-Italiana)/. As for Courier, he published many antimonarchical pamphlets under the name "Paul-Louis, Winemaker."

Today, however, he is mostly remembered for his discovery of a missing section from Longus's *Daphnis and Chloe* in a Florentine manuscript. In a public letter of 1810, he mocked several personages in Florence for their response to a stain of ink he had accidentally left on the manuscript in question—a response motivated, according to Courier, by their shame at not having spotted the missing passage themselves, and by their hatred of foreigners; in a later preface, he clarified that the attacks orchestrated against him at the time were due to his refusal to dedicate his edition of Longus to Élisa Bonaparte, the emperor's sister. See Paul-Louis Courier, tr., *Les Pastorales de Longus* (Merlin, 1825), 271–333. Imprisoned for two months in 1821 after criticizing the Count of Chambord in one of his biting pamphlets, Courier was assassinated in 1825 at the age of fifty-three, a crime that was long suspected to be connected with his writings, although it was apparently committed by disgruntled employees.

[76] *Journal des Freres Goncourt*, December 9, 1885 (my translation). For the novel, see Desprez-Fèvres, *Autour d'un cloche* (1884).

[77] See Herman Melville, *The Confidence Man* (Grove Press, 1961 [1857]), 164. In the same passage the confidence man goes so far as to suggest that irony is "satanic."

[78] See Mark Sussman, "The 'Miscegenation' Troll," *JSTOR Daily*, February 20, 2019, available at https://daily.jstor.org/the-miscegenation-troll/.

[79] See H. Silverstein and C. Arnold, *Hoaxes That Made Headlines* (New York, 1986), 82.

[80] See R. Kent Rasmussen, *Critical Companion to Mark Twain: A Literary Reference to His Life and Work* (Facts on File, Inc., 2014), 332–33 and 658.

[81] See http://www.twainquotes.com/Galaxy/187006a.html.

[82] See the text of Twain's speech at https://www.laphamsquarterly.org/scandal/opinion-page.

[83] For readers' confusion of two Poe satires with reality, see McLeod, *Pranksters*, 81–81 (noting that one of them was "written in the style of a medical report. ... Poe declined to comment on its fictional status").

[84] Italics added. I have also added proper capitalization to Cargill's lowercase text both here and elsewhere. See https://bobcargill.wordpress.com/2009/11/08/on-recent-news-about-the-cloak-and-browser-case-against-raphael-golb/.

[85] See Doe v. 2TheMart.com Inc., 140 F. Supp. 2d 1088, 1092 (W.D. Wash. 2001), and Columbia Insurance Co. v. Seescandy.com, 185 F.R.D. 573, 578–80 (N.D. Cal. 1999). The Supreme Court has recognized these rights in many cases. See, for example, Watchtower Bible and Tract Society of New York, Inc. v. Village of Stratton, 536 U.S. 150 (2002); Buckley v. American Constitutional Law Foundation, 525 U.S. 182, 197–99 (1999); McIntyre v. Ohio Elections Comm., 514 U.S. 334, 341–42 (1995) (using pseudonyms to illustrate anonymity); and NAACP v. Alabama, 357 U.S. 449, 461 (1958). In Reno v. American Civil Liberties Union, 521 U.S. 844 (1997), the Supreme Court stated that the internet is a public forum of

preeminent importance, and held that First Amendment rights are fully applicable to communications over the internet.

[86] For Rousseau's abandonment of his five children, see Matthew Mendham, "Rousseau's Discarded Children: The Panoply of Excuses and the Question of Hypocrisy," *History of European Ideas* 41, no. 1 (2015): 131–52. The anonymous pamphlet, entitled *Sentiment des citoyens* (1864), was in fact written by Voltaire; Rousseau was confused, frustrated, and deeply angered by the anonymous nature of the text, wrongly guessing its author to be someone else (for Voltaire generally used pseudonyms). For Rousseau's attacks on anonymity and pseudonymity, see Jean Dagen, "Secrets de Polichinelle?," *Revue Voltaire*, no. 8 (PUPS, 2008): 15–28.

Notes to Chapter 3

[1] See Jacobson's September 17, 2004 interview with Elizabeth Manus in *Something Jewish* at https://web.archive.org/web/20040917170926/http://www.somethingjewish.co.uk/articles/1185_howard_jacobson.htm ("I don't know what kind of trouble this gets somebody into, a disputatious mind … That's what shapes the Jewish sense of humor, that's what shaped Jewish pugnacity or tenaciousness"). Jacobson, whose novel *The Finkler Question* won the Booker Prize in 2010, is occasionally described as a British version of Philip Roth.
[2] See New York Stock Exchange, Inc. v. Gahary and Zito, 196 F. Supp. 2d 401 (S.D.N.Y. 2001).
[3] See http://www.nytimes.com/2002/04/23/business/big-board-drops-trademark-suit.html.
[4] See http://www.aaup.org/AAUP/pubsres/policydocs/contents/electcomm-stmt.htm; and http://web.archive.org/web/20041206234022/http://www.aaup.org/statements/REPORTS/04AFelec.htm.
[5] See Hustler Magazine, Inc. v. Falwell, 485 U.S. 46 (1988).
[6] See Phil Tinline, *Ghosts of Iron Mountain* (Scribner, 2025); see also "Hoax of Horror? A Book That Shook White House," U.S. News & World Report, November 20, 1967. Lewin's avowal is today treated as a lie and his satire taken at face value and presented as evidence of a "deep-state conspiracy" by radical right-wing radio, YouTube and cable TV presenters with audiences of millions; the antisemitic *Protocols of the Elders of Zion* are occasionally presented as corroborating proof.
[7] See the discussion of the Yes Men in McLeod, *Pranksters*, 268–71.
[8] See http://theyesmen.org/.
[9] Lani Boyd, "The Yes Men and Activism in the Information Age" (MA diss., Louisiana State University, 2002), iv. Available at http://etd.lsu.edu/docs/available/etd-04142005-174336/unrestricted/Boyd_thesis.pdf.
[10] See https://www.theguardian.com/media/2004/dec/04/india.broadcasting.

[11] See Peter Lewis, "Computer Jokes and Threats Ignite Debate on Anonymity," *New York Times*, December 31, 1994, available at http://www.nytimes.com/1994/12/31/us/computer-jokes-and-threats-ignite-debate-on-anonymity.html.

[12] See Steven Weinberg, "Sokal's Hoax," *New York Review of Books*, August 8, 1996, 11–15. The text of this article is available at https://physics.nyu.edu/sokal/weinberg.html.

[13] See https://en.wikipedia.org/wiki/Sokal_affair.

[14] See, for example, Jennifer Schuessler, "Hoaxers Slip Breastaurants and Dog-Park Sex into Journals," *New York Times*, October 4, 2018, available at https://www.nytimes.com/2018/10/04/arts/academic-journals-hoax.html. At present, anyone who wishes to contribute to such efforts can automatically create a new jargon-filled hoax article by using the sophisticated computer program known as the "Postmodernism Generator." See http://www.elsewhere.org/pomo/.

[15] See Terry Neal, "Satirical Website Poses Political Test," *Washington Post*, November 29, 1999, available at http://www.washingtonpost.com/wp-srv/WPcap/1999-11/29/002r-112999-idx.html.

[16] See Massie Ritsch, "Parody Web Sites Skewer Campaigns," *Los Angeles Times*, available at http://articles.latimes.com/2000/apr/23/news/mn-22599.

[17] See Henry David Thoreau, *Walden* (New York, 1910), 7.

[18] See Rall v. Hellman, 284 A.D.2d 113 (2001); https://www.villagevoice.com/1999/11/23/drawn-to-battle/; and http://observer.com/1999/09/red-herring-editor-does-double-duty-as-bush-fundraiser/.

[19] McLeod, *Pranksters*, 127, 175.

[20] See Ryan Mac, Benjamin Mullin, Kate Conger, and Mike Isaac, "A Verifiable Mess: Twitter Users Create Havoc by Impersonating Brands," *New York Times*, November 11, 2022, available at https://www.nytimes.com/2022/11/11/technology/twitter-blue-fake-accounts.html.

[21] See Jess Rauchberg, "Impersonation and Parody: Shitposters Satirically Mock Elon Musk's Chaotic Twitter Takeover," Conversation, November 15, 2022, available at https://theconversation.com/impersonation-and-parody-shitposters-satirically-mock-elon-musks-chaotic-twitter-takeover-194503.

[22] See, for example, Nathan Allebach, "A Brief History of Internet Culture and How Everything Became Absurd," March 19, 2019, available at https://medium.com/swlh/a-brief-history-of-internet-culture-and-how-everything-became-absurd-6af862e71c94.

[23] See, for example, https://theoutline.com/post/2558/death-of-the-internet-net-neutrality-donald-trump-alt-right-gamergate-facebook-twitter.

[24] People v. Golb, trial transcript, 1246.

[25] See, for example, People v. Golb, trial transcript, 1240 ("This was for maliciousness, not for parody"), as well as the district attorney's First

Department response brief of August 2012, 43 ("defendant's intent to defraud went way beyond an innocuous attempt to convince the email recipients that he was Schiffman simply for the fun of it"), available at https://raphaelgolbtrial.files.wordpress.com/2011/11/district-attorneys-response-brief-in-the-raphael-golb-case.pdf.

[26] Libel means "damage to reputation." In the common-law tradition, the attribution of reputation-damaging statements to another person was a recognized form of libel. As one court declared in New York in 1929, "To publish in the name of a well-known author any literary work, the authorship of which would tend to injure an author holding his position in the world of letters, has been held to be a libel." And already during the nineteenth century, it was understood that "if A. writes a libelous letter in B.'s name to C., *the libel is upon B.* as well as upon C., if it contains language which would subject B., *had he written it*, to public hatred and contempt." See Ben-Oliel v. Press Publishing Co., 251 N.Y. 250, 167 N.E. 432 (1929), and State v. Hollon, 80 Tenn. (12 Lea), 482.

[27] See A. Jay Wagner and Anthony L. Fargo, *Criminal Libel in the Land of the First Amendment* (International Press Institute, special report issued in October 2012, revised and reissued in September 2015), 38n83 (citing 1965 N.Y. Laws 1030 [eff. Sept. 1, 1967]), available at http://legaldb.freemedia.at/wp-content/uploads/2015/05/IPI-CriminalLibel-UnitedStates.pdf.

[28] See Norman Golb, *Who Wrote the Dead Sea Scrolls?* (Scribner, 1995), 215.

[29] People v. Golb, trial transcript, 1228–29.

[30] See Rule 200.11(c) of New York's Uniform Rules.

[31] Transcript of the September 23, 2009, hearing (author's files), at 2, 4. Berkman made no mention of Rule 200.11(c) and provided no further explanation of the grounds for the administrative judge's decision.

[32] See Association of the Bar of the City of New York, *Joint Report of the Committee on Criminal Advocacy and the Committee on the Criminal Courts on the Assignment of Judges in the Criminal Term of Supreme Court in New York County*, available at https://www2.nycbar.org/Publications/reports/show_html_new.php?rid=50 ("The Appellate Division, 1st Department, has ruled that assignment of judges is an administrative matter and litigants have no judicially enforceable right to the random assignment of judges").

[33] See https://abovethelaw.com/2007/03/judge-of-the-day-carol-berkman/.

[34] Berkman's order of February 11, 2010, is in the author's files and can be read online at https://dssruling.files.wordpress.com/2010/04/raphael_golb_ruling.pdf.

[35] See ibid., 2n1.

[36] See College Republicans at San Francisco State University v. Reed, 523 F. Supp. 2d 1005, 1018 (N.D. Cal. 2007) (noting that such "civility" requirements "might well require students to forsake the means of communication that are most likely to be effective"). See also Marshall v.

Amuso (E.D. Pa. Nov. 17, 2021) (blocking enforcement of school board "civility policy") and Speech First, Inc. v. Fenves, 979 F.3d 319, 338–39 (5th Circuit 2020) (reinstating an action to block the University of Texas at Austin from enforcing campus regulations forbidding "incivility" along with "harassment," defined by the university as including any form of "hostile or offensive speech, oral, written, or symbolic"; the court signaled "the consistent line of cases that have uniformly found campus speech codes unconstitutionally overbroad or vague"), and see IOTA XI Chapter of Sigma Chi Fraternity v. George Mason Univ., 993 F.2d 386 (4th Cir. 1993) (blocking George Mason University from disciplining students who engaged in an "ugly woman" contest, which, however "crude," "sexist," and "racist" it might be, was protected speech because it was "inherently expressive" and conveyed a "message of satire and humor").

[37] See https://www.nyu.edu/about/policies-guidelines-compliance/policies-and-guidelines/guidelines-speech-speakers-dissent.html.

[38] See, for example, Steve Kolowich, "The Fall of an Academic Cyberbully," March 20, 2009, available at https://www.chronicle.com/article/The-Fall-of-an-Academic/30977.

[39] On the sordid history of the plea bargain system, see William J. Stuntz, *The Collapse of American Criminal Justice* (2011). For the suggestion that criminal defendants could "crash the system if they demanded their constitutional rights and refused to plea to crimes they did not commit," see, for example, Michelle Alexander, "Go to Trial: Crash the Justice System," *New York Times*, March 10, 2012, available at http://www.nytimes.com/2012/03/11/opinion/sunday/go-to-trial-crash-the-justice-system.html. See also Emily Yoffe, "Innocence Is Irrelevant," *Atlantic*, September 2017, available at https://www.theatlantic.com/magazine/archive/2017/09/innocence-is-irrelevant/534171/.

[40] See Michael Shnayerson, "Sand Simeon," *Vanity Fair*, August 1998, available at https://www.vanityfair.com/magazine/1998/08/sandsimeon199808; see also Aaron Elstein, "Inside Ira Rennert's Dirtiest Businesses: Epic Pollution at His La Oroya Refinery in Peru Has Put the Reclusive Billionaire and His Business Practices in the Spotlight," *Crain's New York Business*, November 27, 2011, available at http://www.crainsnewyork.com/article/20111127/FINANCE/311279990/inside-ira-rennerts-dirtiest-businesses. Rennert's mining business is allegedly responsible for the poisoning and maiming of hundreds of Peruvian children; he has attempted to have an ongoing civil lawsuit seeking damages dismissed on a variety of technicalities. See https://news.bloomberglaw.com/litigation/renco-cant-upend-order-barring-contact-in-peruvian-smelter-case. He was also found liable for inappropriately siphoning off funds from the business for the construction of a massive luxury mansion in the Hamptons. See https://www.reuters.com/article/rennert-malpractice/billionaire-rennert-

files-malpractice-lawsuit-over-213-million-judgment-idINKBN1EY20J. For his "wall of honor" status as a donor to the Museum of Jewish Heritage, see https://mjhnyc.org/supporters/.

41 See the list of contributors at http://www.elections.ny.gov:8080/plsql_browser/CONTRIBUTORA_CO UNTY?ID_in=C36419&date_From=01/01/2008&date_to=10/16/2017&A MOUNT_From=5000&AMOUNT_to=1000000&ZIP1=&ZIP2=&ORDE RBY_IN=A&CATEGORY_IN=ALL. Under New York law, the maximum amount that can be contributed to a district attorney in an election cycle is $57,000. See https://www.nytimes.com/2017/11/15/nyregion/defense-lawyers-donations-district-attorney.html.

42 See http://www.wlrk.com/aoemmerich/, https://www.scribd.com/document/8682354/Vance-Invite, http://www.archaeology.org.il/contact.html, and http://www.wlrk.com/ContactUs/.

43 See Greg Donahue, "Crime of the Centuries," *New York Magazine*, February 15, 2023, available at https://nymag.com/intelligencer/article/michael-steinhardt-antiquities-stolen-artifacts.html.

Notes to Chapter 4

1 See, for example, Edward Rothstein, "Peering into the Mystery of Those Enigmatic Fragments," *New York Times,* October 6, 2008, available at http://www.nytimes.com/2008/10/07/arts/design/07scrol.html.

2 Rothstein, ibid. One member of the group, David Noel Freedman, was the son of a Jewish immigrant from Romania who wrote gags for Eddie Cantor, but he had converted to Christianity and been ordained as a Presbyterian minister in 1944, eight years after the death of his father. For de Vaux's antisemitic policies and Action Française membership, see also Michael Baigent and Richard Leigh, *The Dead Sea Scrolls Deception* (London, 1991), 26–27.

3 Caution, as it were, was thrown to the desert wind. For Roland de Vaux's original, more sober assessment quoted in the sidebar, see James Vanderkam and Peter Flint, *The Meaning of the Dead Sea Scrolls* (HarperOne, 2013), 13.

4 Kathleen Howard and Curators of the Israel Museum, eds., *Treasures of the Holy Land: Ancient Art from the Israel Museum* (New York, 1986), 269. The "list of contributors" indicates that the section of the catalog on the Dead Sea Scrolls was written by Magen Broshi, the then curator of the Shrine of the Book wing of the Israel Museum in Jerusalem. Ibid., 23.

5 See Malka Rabinowitz, "Dead Sea Scrolls come from Jerusalem, U.S. professor says," *Jerusalem Post*, June 9, 1970, 4.

6 "The Problem of Origin and Identification of the Dead Sea Scrolls," *Proceedings of the American Philosophical Society* (1980), 1-24; and see

also the other articles listed in Golb, *Who Wrote the Dead Sea Scrolls?*, bibliography, 423-431.

[7] On the known tunnels leading out from Jerusalem, which may have been used by escaping refugees who brought scrolls with them, see N. Golb, "Newly Discovered Tunnel May Once Have Carried Dead Sea Scrolls," The Forward, Oct. 24, 2007, available at: https://forward.com/opinion/11873/newly-discovered-tunnel-may-once-have-carried-dead-00675/.

[8] See "The Problem of Origen," 11.

[9] Ibid. Even the most adamant Qumran-Essene ideologues have been forced to recognize the "extraordinarily varied" contents of the scrolls, as well as the fact, signaled in the sidebar, that the manuscripts retrieved from the caves are only a portion of the ones originally hidden. See, for example, Sidnie White Crawford, *Scribes and Scrolls at Qumran* (Eerdmans, 2019), 146 and 238.

[10] Letter of June 15, 1980.

[11] Joel L. Kraemer, Michael G. Wechsler, Fred Donner, Joshua Holo, and Dennis Pardee, eds., *Pesher Nahum: Texts and Studies in Jewish History and Literature from Antiquity through the Middle Ages Presented to Norman (Nahum) Golb* (Studies in Ancient Oriental Civilization: Oriental Institute, 2012), 4, 7.

[12] Ibid., 4.

[13] For this and the following quotes, see Rothstein, "Peering into the Mystery of Those Enigmatic Fragments," *New York Times, Oct*ober 6, 2008. See also Baigent and Leigh, *The Dead Sea Scrolls Deception*, 26–27. The authors indicate that de Vaux had a "flair for public relations," but that "behind his personable facade, [he] was ruthless, narrow-minded, bigoted and fiercely vindictive."

[14] See Tony Long, "Aug. 7, 1991: Ladies and Gentlemen, the World Wide Web," *Wired*, August 7, 2007, available at https://www.wired.com/2007/08/dayintech-0807-2/.

[15] See https://vnnforum.com/showpost.php?p=929170&postcount=88.

[16] John Noble Wilford, "John Strugnell, Scholar Undone by His Slur, Dies at 77," *New York Times, Dec*ember 9, 2007, available at http://www.nytimes.com/2007/12/09/us/09strugnell.html.

[17] See http://www.nytimes.com/2013/05/17/world/europe/geza-vermes-dead-sea-scrolls-scholar-dies-at-88.html.

[18] See People v. Golb, trial transcript, 174–75.

[19] See "Unscrolling Judeo-Christian Tradition: The New York Newsday Interview with Lawrence Schiffman," *New York Newsday*, May 27, 1992, at 73–76. See also John Noble Wilford, "Monopoly over Dead Sea Scrolls Is Ended," *New York Times, Sept*ember 22, 1991, and Schiffman's letter to the *Chicago Sentinel*, December 5, 1991, in which he expressed his concern that with their liberation, the scrolls would henceforth be "subject to interpretation without the benefit of the painstaking scholarship required for preparation of a text edition."

[20] "Grad Students Study Legendary Dead Sea Scrolls," *Washington Square News*, March 5, 1992.
[21] See https://www.jta.org/1990/12/13/archive/editor-of-dead-sea-scrolls-fired-after-attacking-judaism-and-israel.
[22] For the events summarized in the following paragraphs, see Golb, *Who Wrote the Dead Sea Scrolls?*, chapter 8, 217–47.
[23] See Golb, *Who Wrote the Dead Sea Scrolls?*, 222, and Sara S. Hodson, "Freeing the Dead Sea Scrolls: A Question of Access," *American Archivist* 56 (Fall 1993): 690–703, here 693, available at http://americanarchivist.org/doi/pdf/10.17723/aarc.56.4.w213201818211541?code=same-site.
[24] See Hodson, "Freeing the Dead Sea Scrolls," 695.
[25] See John Noble Wilford, "Monopoly over Dead Sea Scrolls Is Ended," September 22, 1991, available at http://www.nytimes.com/1991/09/22/us/monopoly-over-dead-sea-scrolls-is-ended.html, and Clyde Haberman, "Israel to Revise Rules on Scrolls," October 28, 1991, available at http://www.nytimes.com/1991/10/28/world/israel-to-revise-rules-on-scrolls.html.
[26] Ron Grossman in *Chicago Tribune*, August 2, 1993, available at http://articles.chicagotribune.com/1993-08-02/news/9308020063_1_ben-zion-wacholder-martin-abegg-dead-sea-scrolls.
[27] Ibid.
[28] See, for example, David Nimmer, "Copyright in the Dead Sea Scrolls: Authorship and Originality," *Houston Law Review* 38, no. 1 (2001): 159, and Neil Wilkof, "Copyright, Moral Rights and the Choice of Law: Where Did the Dead Sea Scrolls Court Go Wrong?," ibid., 463.
[29] See Donceel and Donceel-Voûte, "The Archaeology of Khirbet Qumran"; idem, "Les ruines de Qumran réinterprétées," *Archeologia* 298 (1994) 24-35; idem, "'Coenaculum': La salle à l'étage du locus 30 à Khirbet Qumrân sur la Mer Morte," in Rika Gyselen, Marthe Bernus-Taylor et al. (eds.), *Banquets d'Orient* (Leuven: Peeters, 1992), 61-84. Writing in the *Oxford Handbook of the Dead Sea Scrolls* (2010), Eric Meyers refers to the Donceels' "sudden departure from the project," misleadingly suggesting that they just decided to quit, without explaining the circumstances that led to their "departure." Meyers also states that this departure "did not help promote their ideas," without mentioning their continued research outside of any "project" defined and controlled by Father de Vaux's successors. Ibid., 26-27.
[30] See Yitzhak Magen, Yuval Peleg, et al., *Back to Qumran (Jerusalem, Israel Antiquities Authority, 2018), 140-42*.
[31] The caption of the key Figure 117 on page 114 of the team's final report will certainly rile those who continue to seek to belittle my father's impact on this field of studies.
[32] The "Back to Qumran" excavations revealed that the site was rich in the natural resources needed for pottery manufacture. According to my father,

Qumran's original strategic status as a fortress is not necessarily contradictory to its exploitation for agricultural and commercial purposes. Josephus, in his descriptions of Herod's forty-year rule, makes clear that the king tried to develop his lands to their fullest through many building works, commercial enterprises, and agricultural projects.

[33] Magen and Peleg, *Back to Qumran,* 142.

[34] *Back to Qumran,* 105, 127. Since, as Magen points out in the preface to the report (ibid., xi), Qumranology is characterized by a web of "articles and theories...all of which [have] to be read, and every opinion quoted," I will note here in passing that J. Magness (*The Archaeology of Qumran,* 103-104), while dogmatically referring throughout to Qumran as "the sectarian settlement," strenuously objects to the Magen-Peleg team's conclusion that the site served for a time as a pottery production center. The report has thus been "answered," and can now safely be ignored in Qumranological circles. But, while Magness has updated her book with a variety of references to Magen and Peleg, and while she quarrels here and there with one or another of their conclusions, she fails to provide her readers with a full and adequate explanation of the reasons why the Israeli team, after a decade reexamining the site and reevaluating all the evidence, felt compelled to reject virtually every aspect of the interpretation of Qumran that she has inherited from Father de Vaux.

[35] Ibid., xii.

[36] See Yizhar Hirschfeld, *Qumran in Context* (Peabody, MA., 2004); Janine Zacharia, "Evidence of Dead Sea sect found after 2000 years," Reuters, January 8, 1998; available at: http://tcoto.klaxo.net/rel/essenes.htm. Hirschfeld's identification is disputed by Magen and Peleg (*Back to Qumran,* 141); they see the Ein Gedi finds as also reflecting the flight of refugees from Jerusalem during the Great Revolt.

[37] See, for example, Jürgen Zangenberg, "Zwischen Zufall und Eigenartigkeit," in Jörg Frey, Carsten Claußen, and Nadine Kessler, eds., *Qumran und die Archäologie* (Tübingen, 2011), 121–46.

[38] Ibid, 142.

[39] See the obituary by Elizabeth Simson, available at https://www.academia.edu/92244402/Oscar_White_Muscarella_1931_2022_Obituary_, and the one by Neil Genzlinger of the *New York Times,* available at https://www.nytimes.com/2022/12/22/arts/oscar-white-muscarella-dead.html.

[40] In an article published in 1990 and entitled "The Significance of the Scrolls," Lawrence Schiffman stated that "beginning in 1985 with a conference held at New York University, and continuing to the present, contradictions of the 'official' Essene hypothesis were voiced as the field of learning advanced. Gradually a new non-consensus began to emerge." In fact, Norman Golb's publicly known opposition to the Essene theory began in 1970, and his first published work opposing that theory appeared in 1980. In an apparent reflection of the policies of exclusion discussed earlier in this chapter, Schiffman simply did not invite Golb to attend the

1985 NYU conference. (The conference proceedings would be titled *Archaeology and History in the Dead Sea Scrolls: The New York University Conference in Memory of Yigael Yadin*—yet, despite this foregrounding of archaeology and Yadin in the title, not a single article in the volume dealt with archaeology. The question, broached by Golb in his 1980 article, of whether any archaeological evidence pointed to inhabitation of Qumran by a sect was thus left entirely unaddressed.) The proceedings of Schiffman's 1985 NYU conference also appeared in 1990. See Lawrence Schiffman, "The Significance of the Dead Sea Scrolls," 23; ibid., ed., *Archaeology and History in the Dead Sea Scrolls: The New York University Conference in Memory of Yigael Yadin*, JSOT/ASOR Monograph Series, no. 2 (Sheffield 1990). For similar exclusion tactics also apparently practiced by Schiffman at another NYU conference, see http://failedmessiah.typepad.com/failed_messiahcom/2007/05/nyu_academic_is.html (asserting that Schiffman was "responsible for the NYU 'scholarly' conference on the late [Lubavitcher] Rebbe [Menachem Mendel Schneerson]" and "barred anyone with largely negative views of Schneerson from participating").

[41] For David Sarna's postings, see page 178.

[42] See https://bobcargill.wordpress.com/2009/11/08/on-recent-news-about-the-cloak-and-browser-case-against-raphael-golb/.

[43] See the compendious analysis in the late Gordon Moran's *Silencing Scientists and Scholars in Other Fields: Power, Paradigm Controls, Peer Review, and Scholarly Communication* (London, 1998).

[44] "The Problem of Origin and Identification of the Dead Sea Scrolls," 24.

[45] See N. Golb, *Who Wrote the Dead Sea Scrolls?*, 211-215, 310-318, 423-24.

[46] L. Schiffman, "The Significance of the Dead Sea Scrolls," *Bible Review*, VI, no. 5, Oct. 1990, p. 24.

[47] See ibid., *Reclaiming the Dead Sea Scrolls* (Doubleday, 1994), xxi and 413.

[48] For details, see *The Qumran Con*. In addition to the other figures listed, it should be noted that precisely the same misrepresentation is found in a paper authored by an undergraduate student in 2010 and submitted to Alex Jassen in "partial fulfillment" of Jassen's course on the scrolls at the University of Minnesota. See: https://www.academia.edu/1446275/Resurrecting_the_Dead_Sea_Scrolls_Communities_An_Alternative_Vew_of_Qumran_and_the_Scrolls. Jassen received his Ph.D. under Schiffman's guidance and initially taught courses on the scrolls at Minnesota, before himself receiving a position at New York University. It is unclear what exactly gave rise to the student's error, but it appears to have gone uncorrected.

[49] See Charlotte Hempel, "Qumran Community," in Lawrence Schiffman and James VanderKam, eds., *Encyclopedia of the Dead Sea Scrolls* (Oxford, 2000), 750; available at

https://www.oxfordreference.com/view/10.1093/acref/9780195084504.001.0001/acref-9780195084504-e-435.

[50] Golb, in his 1995 book, had asserted that under the dire circumstances they were facing, "the more thoughtful inhabitants of Jerusalem would have behaved no differently than other people facing a siege. They had little choice but to hide away their wealth, their books, even the phylacteries that eventually turned up in such relative abundance in the Qumran caves." See *Who Wrote the Dead Sea Scrolls?*, 145. That *some* of the scrolls may have come from the Temple was, he acknowledged, a reasonable conclusion, particularly in view of the fact that some of the artifacts listed in the Copper Scroll seem to be identical with ones described as having belonged to the Temple in rabbinical texts. But this acknowledgment that Rengstorf may not have been *entirely* off the mark with his theory of Temple priests using Qumran as a summer resort and keeping a library there, was a different cup of tea from Hempel's description, which reversed the terms of the discussion, magnified this one aspect of Golb's theory, and suggested that he had boldly argued, *following* Rengstorf, that the scrolls "belonged" to the Temple, and had tacked onto it the claim that they also included texts hidden by "individual wealthy citizens." Importantly, this latter claim was itself misleading. While many of the scrolls presumably did come from collections owned by well-to-do individuals, others, including the *Manual of Discipline*, contained passages reflecting the idea that contact with money was defiling. Golb had never suggested that only wealthy people were "thoughtful" enough to hide their scrolls; nor had he denied that the scrolls included writings of wealth-eschewing groups. Hempel's summary was thus misleading in more ways than one.

[51] See https://library.biblicalarchaeology.org/department/reviews-72/.

[52] For the Stanford policy statement quoted in the sidebar, see https://plato.stanford.edu/guidelines.html. Schiffman and VanderKam were apparently aware of these norms. Their aim, they asserted in their introduction (p. x), was "to encompass *all scholarship* on the scrolls to date, making use of the research of many scholars of international reputation." (Italics added.)

[53] Abuses of this sort are of course widespread in academic culture. See G. Moran, *Silencing Scientists and Scholars in Other Fields*.

[54] In an article on "policy makers and propaganda in epistemic networks," James Weatherall, Cailin O'Connor, and Justin Bruner focus on a pair of manipulative techniques they call "biased production" and "selective sharing." They explain that "the propagandist endeavors to bias the total body of evidence" available to others, and they point out that to counter this effort, "particularly when evidence is relatively difficult to get or equivocal, it is essential that policy makers (and the public) have access to a complete, unbiased sampling of studies." When production is biased, "epistemically poor results" may follow—results that can also be produced by bias or selective sharing in the media. While "journalists

often select scientific studies to feature in articles," few of them are "experts in the relevant literatures, and in any case, the goal is rarely to give a uniform and even-handed characterization of all available evidence. To the contrary, journalistic practices often encourage, or even require, journalists to share ... only the most striking, surprising, or novel studies." See Weatherall, O'Connor, and Bruner, "How to Beat Science and Influence People: Policy Makers and Propaganda in Epistemic Networks," January 8, 2018, 14–15, draft article available at https://arxiv.org/pdf/1801.01239.pdf.

[55] For quotes in this paragraph and other pertinent passages, see Thomas Kuhn, *The Structure of Scientific Revolutions* (University of Chicago Press, 1962), 93, 136–37, 148–49, 151, 158. Kuhn suggests that these facts distinguish "scientific work ... from every other creative pursuit except perhaps theology." The classic examples of the use of force to suppress new scientific ideas are, of course, the trials of Galileo and Giordano Bruno.

[56] For earlier statements, by J.T. Milik, J.A. Fitzmyer, and J. Greenfield, of the distinction that had occasionally been proposed, between "sectarian" scrolls purportedly written at Qumran, and others which must have come from "elsewhere," see N. Golb, "The Problem of Origin," *PAPS* (1980), 15 n. 25.

[57] See *Who Wrote the Dead Sea Scrolls?*, 303.

[58] Ibid., 215 and 423n75.

[59] Thomas Mallon, *Stolen Words: Forays into the Origins and Ravages of Plagiarism* (New York, 1989), 176.

[60] Ibid., 152, 156.

[61] See letter of May 1980 to Norman Golb from Jonas Greenfield in Jerusalem, describing a letter received from Sarna. Norman Golb Papers, Special Collections Research Center, University of Chicago, box 15 ("Sarna Letter to Greenfield, 1980").

[62] "The Significance of the Dead Sea Scrolls," 24. In his letter of August 29, 2008, to administrators at NYU, Schiffman would speak of "multiple Judaisms." See Norman Golb's discussion at https://isac.uchicago.edu/sites/default/files/uploads/shared/docs/schiffman_response_2010nov30.pdf, 9.

[63] Philip Davies, "Sadducees in the Dead Sea Scrolls?," in Zdzislaw Kapera, ed., *Qumran Cave 4—Special Report* (Cracow, 1991), 89, 94 (italics in original). Quoted at greater length in Golb, *Who Wrote the Dead Sea Scrolls?*, 212n.

[64] Norman Golb would make precisely this point in his response (reprinted in *The Qumran Con* as appendix 3, pages 381–413) to the "Confidential Letter" that Schiffman composed and distributed to certain NYU faculty members and to Manhattan prosecutors. The idea that the presence of works by *various* groups in a body of texts must be explained by a hypothesized group's need to read the writings of *other* groups (to engage in "polemics with its neighbors," as Schiffman puts it in *Reclaiming*, xxvi)

puts the cart before the horse and is inherently arbitrary, because, in the absence of external proof, there is no way of knowing *which* of the various groups felt it needed to read *whose* writings. Furthermore, since the manuscripts hidden in several caves have almost entirely disintegrated, it is difficult to know what sort of significance to attribute to the discovery, by chance, of several relatively intact copies of a particular text in other caves where conditions were not as bad.

[65] Schiffman's failure to examine, in his polemics on the scrolls, the history of certain key ideas that he was presenting must be seen in tandem with his apparent reluctance to discuss, in a meaningful way, opposing interpretations. One reviewer, for example, found reading Schiffman's book *Reclaiming the Dead Sea Scrolls* to be "like hearing one conclusory position in a scholarly debate, without hearing the responses from the other scholars." See https://www.librarything.com/work/576353/reviews/66472487. By contrast, my father's research on the scrolls proceeded through a critical examination (1) of the empirical evidence and (2) of the claims made by previous scholars.

[66] See Norman Golb's analysis of the Qumran-Essene "paradigm" of previous scholarship in "The Problem of Origin and Identification of the Dead Sea Scrolls," 1980. For my own use of the same method, see my article "Rumor, Knowledge and Politics in Verga's *I Malavoglia*, in *Italian Quarterly*, vol. 42, nos. 163-64 (2005), 33-53.

[67] This email was passed along to Norman Golb, and the author has a copy of it in his files.

[68] "The Significance of the Dead Sea Scrolls," 24. It should be noted that in listing several articles by Golb in the bibliography of *Reclaiming* (see above, note 47) and in adducing them as purported evidence for his "Temple" misrepresentation of Golb's theory, Schiffman omitted Golb's key 1980 and 1985 articles. This omission could only leave readers with the impression that Golb's work in the field dated not from *well before* but from *around the same time* as Schiffman began publishing his own "widely varying Judaisms" claims on the scrolls.

[69] Email of May 31, 2004. Norman Golb Papers, Special Collections Research Center, University of Chicago, box 59 ("Jacob Neusner, 2004").

[70] For a full discussion of the apparent relationship between Schiffman's views and Norman Golb's, see *The Qumran Con*, chapter 5, and in particular the side-by-side table of statements by Schiffman and earlier ones by Golb on pp. 108-112.

[71] *New York University Faculty Handbook*, 76, 92, available at http://www.nyu.edu/osp/pdf/FacHbk200S.pdf.

[72] American Historical Association, www.historians.org/pubs/Free/ProfessionalStandards.cfm#Plagiarism, last visited December 1, 2009 (italics added).

[73] *New York University Faculty Handbook*, 101.

[74] Mallon, *Stolen Words, 35 and* passim.

[75] People v. Golb, 253 (Catharine Stimpson) and 307 (Richard Foley).
[76] Available at https://www.historians.org/jobs-and-professional-development/statements-standards-and-guidelines-of-the-discipline/statement-on-standards-of-professional-conduct.
[77] See, for example, Mallon, *Stolen Words, 101*: "*If the material that you present can* be assigned to a source, it probably *ought* to be assigned to a source" (italics in original).
[78] See "Academic Integrity: Acknowledging Your Sources," Princeton University, available at https://www.princeton.edu/pr/pub/integrity/pages/sources/.
[79] See Jon Wiener, *Historians in Trouble: Plagiarism, Fraud and Power in the Ivory Tower* (The New Press, 2004).
[80] For the Jewish concept of intellectual theft (Heb. *genevat da'at*) as outlined in the sidebar, see the article by Erica Brown of Yeshiva University, "The Plagiarist's Dilemma—Stealing, Lying, and Impersonation," at https://www.myjewishlearning.com/article/plagiarism/.
[81] In view of perpetual conflicts over what can and cannot remain online (including with regard to the Dead Sea Scrolls), it is worth emphasizing the description of the internet by its inventor, Tim Berners-Lee, as "a method of *storing knowledge* using hypertext documents" (italics added). See https://www.wired.com/2007/08/dayintech-0807-2/.
[82] See Jacoby, *The Last Intellectuals*, and works cited there. That a major critique originally made by liberals and social democrats such as Jacoby and his predecessors would eventually be in large measure co-opted—together with basic First Amendment issues—by social and cultural conservatives, and indeed by right-wing zealots, is an irony of American social and institutional history.
[83] For quotes in this paragraph and other pertinent remarks, see Jacoby, *The Last Intellectuals*, 121, 127, 135, 138, 143–45, 152, 154–56, 200, 235.
[84] To get a sense of this tendency's deleterious impact, one need only peruse syllabuses for academic courses on the scrolls, which for the most part omit any mention of opponents of the sectarian hypothesis, including in lengthy bibliographies. Three examples among many: "The Dead Sea Scrolls and the Biblical World" (Azusa Pacific University course taught by Michael DeVries), available at https://www.academia.edu/30708506/UBBL_420_The_Dead_Sea_Scrolls_and_the_Biblical_World; "Dead Sea Scrolls" (University of Texas course taught by Jonathan Kaplan), available at file:///C:/Users/Laptop/Downloads/Dead%20Sea%20Scrolls%20Syllabus%202013.pdf; "Dead Sea Scrolls Syllabus" (Duke University course taught by Anathea Portier-Young), available at https://www.academia.edu/15230391/Dead_Sea_Scrolls_Syllabus. So much for allowing students to make up their own minds about major historical controversies!
[85] The most frequent object of such personal innuendos is, of course, my father. Already in the above-cited *American Scholar* exchange, John

Trever (who had photographed the first seven Dead Sea Scrolls in 1948) had expressed the hope that Norman Golb would "not ... harass ... the world of biblical scholarship" with his criticism. See also the statement by John Collins (of the Yale Divinity School), in *Journal of Religion* 81, no. 2 (April 2001): 324, that Golb's contribution on the scrolls to the third volume of *The Cambridge History of Judaism* consisted of "idiosyncratic polemics." On Magen Broshi's remarkably crude variation on this trope, see page 94.

[86] See Thorstein Veblen, *The Theory of the Leisure Class* (New York, 1994) [1899], 232-33 (asserting also that "the men who have occupied themselves with…efforts to widen the scope of human knowledge have not commonly been well received by their learned contemporaries"); Henry Adams, *The Education of Henry Adams*, 377, 450. For Adams's "conspiracy of silence" claim as applied to the Dead Sea Scrolls, see again numerous academic course syllabi.

[87] See Gwynned de Looijer, *The Qumran Paradigm* (Durham University Ph.D. dissertation, 2013), 244-46. Available at http://etheses.dur.ac.uk/7727/1/TheQumranParadigmGdL2013.pdf?DDD32+.

[88] See the many scroll-related entries on the blog of Jim Davila at https://paleojudaica.blogspot.com/. Following my father's death, Davila would reiterate that the Jerusalem theory of scroll origins is "probably ultimately wrong," without pointing his readers to any of the publications of Magen, Peleg, and others confirming that theory. See https://paleojudaica.blogspot.com/2020/12/norman-golb-1928-2020.html.

[89] Magen, Peleg, et al., *Back to Qumran* (Jerusalem, Israel Antiquities Authority, 2018), xi.

[90] Ibid., xvi, 138, 140.

[91] See N. Golb, *Who Wrote the Dead Sea Scrolls?*, 230.

[92] See Kraemer, Wechsler, et al., *Pesher Nahum*, 4.

[93] See the 1997 exchanges between Goranson and Lemche, the late Frederick Cryer, and several other scholars on the "Orion" forum at http://orion.mscc.huji.ac.il/orion/archives/1997b/threads.html#00388, including in particular http://orion.mscc.huji.ac.il/orion/archives/1997b/msg00391.html ("Really, Steven ... there's no need for innuendo about a fine scholar like Golb, even if you happen not to agree with him. Golb is staying in Jerusalem at the flat of the late—and much lamented—Jonas Greenfield"); http://orion.mscc.huji.ac.il/orion/archives/1997b/msg00796.html (apparently referring to Goranson as a "bully" and an "obscurantist"); and http://orion.mscc.huji.ac.il/orion/archives/1997b/msg00398.html ("The moderator should be very diligent in filtering away any mail with indications of political agendas open or hidden. The usual hint of anti-semitism should never be allowed to pass without being openly stated, so that we know what we are up against"). See also Goranson's exchange with Cryer at http://www.mail-

archive.com/orion@panda.mscc.huji.ac.il/msg00791.html.

[94] John Noble Wilford, "Debate Erupts over Authors of the Dead Sea Scrolls," *New York Times, Dec*ember 24, 2002.

[95] Author's files; Norman Golb Papers, Special Collections Research Center, University of Chicago, box 25 ("Jacob Neusner, 2002–2012").

[96] News items reflecting a new "consensus" that there were not one but *two* principal theories of scroll origins included the following: *USA Today*, January 2, 2007 ("The nature of the settlement at Qumran is the subject of a lively academic debate. The traditional view ... is [etc.]. The second school says," etc.); *Wall Street Journal*, September 26, 2008 ("There are two competing theories about the scrolls," etc.); *Jewish Week*, October 20, 2008 (The Jewish Museum's current scrolls exhibit "highlights a roiling scholarly debate that continues to hound the scrolls," etc.); the Jewish Museum in New York's press release of September 12, 2008 ("Scholars have two basic theories about who used the scrolls," etc.); *Le Monde*, November 5, 2008 (article by Alain Beuve-Méry, the grandson of *Le Monde*'s founder Hubert Beuve-Méry), available at http://www.lemonde.fr/culture/article/2008/11/05/les-manuscrits-de-la-mer-morte-viennent-detre-traduits-en-francais_1115194_3246.html ("The ties between the Essenes ... and Qumran have now been reduced to nothing, just as the major American historian and paleographer Norman Golb had already written"). Mr. Beuve-Méry indicates that the new French translation of the scrolls, in nine volumes prepared by researchers of the younger generation, has been organized not according to "cave," as in translations prepared by members of the Dead Sea Scrolls monopoly group, but in accordance with the inductive approach that Golb has been recommending for years.

[97] See https://web.archive.org/web/20051221115756/ and http://web.israelinsider.com/bin/en.jsp?enPage=ArticlePage&enDisplay=view&enDispWhat=object&enDispWho=Article%5El3983&enZone=Culture&enVersion=0&.

[98] See Magen, Peleg, et al., *Back to Qumran* (2018), xii. For insights on the history and political consequences of Christian archaeological efforts in Palestine beginning in the nineteenth century, see Andrew Lawler, *Under Jerusalem: The Buried History of the World's Most Contested City* (Doubleday, 2021).

[99] See https://en.parks.org.il/ParksAndReserves/qumran/Pages/default.aspx.

[100] Compare the methods used by evangelical scholars to defend their claims, discussed in Mark Elliott, Kenneth Atkinson, and Robert Rezetko, eds., *Misusing Scripture: What Are Evangelicals Doing with the Bible?* (Routledge, 2023), 32-33 ("citing critical scholarship dubiously"), 37-38 ("orienting their academic discourse toward other evangelicals"), and 104-05 ("referencing other authorities, mainly other evangelicals"). Different versions of ancient biblical texts contain a plurality of often contradictory readings. Evangelicals attempt to explain away these contradictions, because otherwise they could not answer the question, *which* of the

versions is inerrant? For the meaning of the term "evangelical" and a discussion of evangelical beliefs regarding the Bible, along with the implausibility of those beliefs and their incompatibility with basic scholarly values, see, in the same work, Kenneth Atkinson, "The Error of Biblical Inerrancy: The Bible Does Not Exist," 79-92, as well as the introduction, 10-38, and Robert Rezetko's contribution, again in the same work, "Building a House on Sand: What Do Evangelicals Do When They Do Textual Criticism of the Old Testament?," 95-117. See also *Who Wrote the Dead Sea Scrolls?*, 338 ("the Jews of the first and second centuries B.C. would not even have known what the word 'Bible' or its Hebrew equivalents meant. The 'Bible' as such did not yet exist then, but was only in the [long] process of coming to be formed").

[101] See http://www.jpost.com/Business/Business-Features/Evangelical-tourism-could-bring-10-million-visitors-a-year, http://mfa.gov.il/MFA/PressRoom/2014/Pages/Christian-tourism-to-Israel-2013.aspx, and https://www.bloomberg.com/news/articles/2017-09-19/zionist-evangelicals-trail-trump-to-holy-land-with-cash-in-hand.

[102] See http://mfa.gov.il/MFA/AboutIsrael/Spotlight/Pages/Christian-tourism-to-Israel.aspx. Approximately 209,000 American Christian tourists to Israel in 2011–12 self-identified as pilgrims. See Hillary Kaell, *Walking Where Jesus Walked: American Christians and Holy Land Pilgrimage* (New York University Press, 2014), 209n2.

[103] See http://diplomacy.co.il/diplomatic-magazine/economy/3673-summary-of-2016-a-turning-point-for-tourism-to-israel-increase-of-about-4-in-incoming-tourism-to-israel-in-2016-over-the-previous-year-all-time-record-for-incoming-tourism-in-last-four-months-of-the-year-september-december.

[104] See http://www.archaeology.org.il/conservation.html.

[105] See https://www.haaretz.com/settlementdollars/.premium-1.707158, https://www.vanityfair.com/magazine/1998/08/sandsimeon199808, and http://www.motherjones.com/politics/2012/07/hamptons-ira-rennert-mansion-helicopter/#. The obscenity arguably involved in naming a building housing the oldest existing copies of the Hebrew Bible after a magnesium magnate would be disregarded as the plans moved ahead.

[106] See Ira Rabin and Oliver Hahn, "Dead Sea Scrolls Exhibitions around the World: Reasons for Concern," *Restaurator. International Journal for the Preservation of Library and Archival Material* (May 17, 2012): 101–21; Sarah Everts, "Dead Sea Scrolls–Scientists in Berlin Criticize Israeli Cultural Authorities for Treatment of Sacred Documents," *C&EN Artful Science* (blog), June 22, 2012, available at http://cenblog.org/artful-science/2012/06/22/dead-sea-scrolls-scientists-in-berlin-criticize-israeli-cultural-authorities-for-treatment-of-sacred-documents/.

[107] See the IAA loan agreement at http://www.antiquities.org.il/images/forms/loan_agreement.pdf. It is not clear if the sum of $250,000 is per scroll fragment, or in exchange for as many fragments as a museum requests—which would mean that a

museum could request a hundred fragments rather than the usual dozen or so and still pay the same sum. Notably, the contract specifies that any exhibit contents added by the borrowing institution "must be approved" by the IAA.

[108] See the articles gathered at https://isac.uchicago.edu/research/individual-scholarship/individual-scholarship-norman-golb.

[109] See chapter 9 of the Museums Association code of ethics, available at http://www.museumsassociation.org/publications/10963.

[110] American Alliance of Museums code: http://www.aam-us.org/resources/ethics-standards-and-best-practices/code-of-ethics. See also the code of the Association of Art Museum Directors at: https://aamd.org/about/code-of-ethics (stating that museum directors will uphold the "public trust" and "perform their professional duties with honesty, integrity, and transparency").

[111] Being associated with a Christian educational institution did not in itself, of course, prove bias. In reviewing the 1996 edition of the *Oxford Classical Dictionary*, Jeffrey Peterson of the Austin Graduate School of Theology in Texas (formerly known as the Institute for Christian Studies) had gone out of his way to note that the entry on the Dead Sea Scrolls in the dictionary, by Martin Goodman, "mentions the hypothesis that these texts constitute the remains of private libraries rescued from the Roman siege and destruction of Jerusalem ... rather than the documents composed or collected by a sect resident in the Judaean desert ... but there is no mention of relevant bibliography or even the name of the University of Chicago professor who developed this hypothesis." See *Libraries and Culture* 33, no. 4 (1998): 455–56. Peterson suggested that such efforts to suppress information useful to readers interested in learning more about an important opposing view were well known among Biblicists. As he put it, "This is characteristic of the mode of response of many scrolls scholars to the 'Jerusalem library hypothesis' but is no less regrettable for that." (Compare Peterson's accurate description of the Jerusalem-libraries theory of scroll origins with the misrepresentations disseminated by Schiffman and others.)

[112] Sandi Dolbee, "S.D. Gets Rare Chance to Ponder Biblical Mystery: Dead Sea Scrolls Exhibit Coming in '07," May 16, 2005, available at http://legacy.sandiegouniontribune.com/news/communities/churches/2005 0516-9999-1n16scroll.html.

[113] See Donald Harrison, "Exciting Plans Disclosed for San Diego's Exhibition of the Dead Sea Scrolls in 2007," jewishsightseeing.com, January 26, 2006, available at http://www.jewishsightseeing.com/dhh_weblog/2006-blog/2006-01/2006-01-26-dead_sea_scrolls.htm.

[114] Kelly Bennett, "Overseeing the Scrolls: Questions for Risa Levitt Kohn," June 2, 2007, available at http://www.voiceofsandiego.org/topics/news/overseeing-the-scrolls-questions-for-risa-levitt-kohn/.

115 See Stan Wilson, "Visiting Qumran, Home of the Dead Sea Scrolls," special to ASSIST press, November 6, 2007, available at http://www.swkfaithandfamily.org/articles/Qumran.htm.

116 Mike Boehm, "A Lively Debate over the Dead Sea Scrolls," June 26, 2007, available at http://articles.latimes.com/2007/jun/26/entertainment/et-scrolls26.

117 Barbarella Fokos, "Fragments of the Past: Dead Sea Scrolls Controversies," *San Diego Reader*, July 5, 2007, available at https://www.sandiegoreader.com/news/2007/jul/05/fragments-past/#.

118 See Bennett, "Overseeing the Scrolls."

119 See https://isac.uchicago.edu/sites/default/files/uploads/shared/docs/dss_review_sandiego_catalogue_2007.pdf.

120 NowPublic was a "citizen journalism" website, meaning that reporting on the site took the form of ordinary people disseminating news, information, and commentary. (Some of the other terms commonly used to express the same concept are "street journalism" and "guerrilla journalism.") The site was purchased by the Anschutz oil and gas company in 2009 and was closed down in 2013. Courts have frowned on claims that citizen journalists have fewer First Amendment rights than "members of the news media." See, for example, Pulliam v. Fort Bend County, Texas et al. (S.D. Tex. June 20, 2023), available at https://ij.org/wp-content/uploads/2022/12/ECF-48-Order-Granting-Defendants-Motion-to-Dismiss-in-Part-and-Denying-in-Part.pdf ("independent" journalist who uploaded films he made of the police to his own website entitled to just as much constitutional protection as professionally employed media journalists).

121 See Charles Gadda, "Did Christian Agenda Lead to Biased Dead Sea Scrolls Exhibit in San Diego?," available at http://web.archive.org/web/20080430220643/www.nowpublic.com/culture/did-christian-agenda-lead-biased-dead-sea-scrolls-exhibit-san-diego, and see the exchange with Pam Fox Kuhlken in the comments at http://web.archive.org/web/20080417212226/http://www.nowpublic.com:80/culture/christian-fundamentalism-and-dead-sea-scrolls-san-diego. See also https://museumethics.wordpress.com/author-responds-to-dead-sea-scrolls-criticism/. In his trial testimony, Robert Cargill would deny having any knowledge of the identity of "B. Ralph," but would then admit to having used multiple pseudonyms to let me "know that he knew who I was." In this regard, Cargill's gathering of information on the identity of "Charles Gadda" deserves special mention. See the results of his effort at http://archive.li/AyKSH#selection-6725.65-6741.123.

122 See, for example, http://www.sandiegouniontribune.com/sdut-dead-sea-scrolls-exhibit-lives-on-2007oct19-story.html, https://www.sandiegohistory.org/journal/v53-3/pdf/SDNHM.pdf, https://www.jweekly.com/2007/06/29/dead-sea-scrolls-exhibit-comes-to-san-diego/, and http://www.sdnews.com/view/full_story/302594/article--%CB%9CDead-Sea-scrolls--exhibit-poised-to-tantalize.

¹²³ Although it has since been deleted, the widely read blog of Pastor Jim West (ThD from Andersonville Theological Seminary in Georgia; at the time ministering in Kansas City) offered a good example. For other Christian blogs organically advertising the San Diego exhibit, see, for example, http://evidenceforchristianity.org/review-of-the-dead-sea-scrolls-exhibit-at-san-diegos-museum-of-natural-history/.

¹²⁴ Meg Sullivan, "Virtual Qumran Sheds New Light on Dead Sea Scrolls Discovery Site," UCLA Newsroom, June 18, 2007, available at http://newsroom.ucla.edu/releases/Virtual-Qumran-Sheds-New-Light-7935. (Meg Sullivan is senior public information officer at UCLA.)

¹²⁵ Pepperdine defines itself as a "Christian university ... rooted in the Church of Christ heritage." See https://www.pepperdine.edu/spiritual-life/christian-university/. The Churches of Christ, sometimes also called the "Restoration Movement," share a "commitment to evangelism and mission" and a "New Testament emphasis." See http://cofcaustralia.org/about/.

¹²⁶ Tom Tugend, "Armchair Archeologists [sic] Can Explore Qumran Virtually," available at https://web.archive.org/web/20070910205934/http://jewishjournal.com/home/preview.php?id=17788.

¹²⁷ See, for example, "Dead Sea Scrolls Site Once a Fortress?" at http://www.nbcnews.com/id/19749433/#.WciB6rYrInc; see also "Warriors May Have Occupied Dead Sea Scrolls Site" at http://www.foxnews.com/story/2007/07/13/warriors-may-have-occupied-dead-sea-scrolls-site.html and "Warriors Once Occupied Dead Sea Scrolls Site" at https://www.livescience.com/1682-warriors-occupied-dead-sea-scrolls-site.html.

¹²⁸ See, for example, https://charlesgadda.wordpress.com/warriors-occupied-qumran-scrolls-battle-continues-july-17-2007/ and https://charlesgadda.wordpress.com/dead-sea-scrolls-qumran-fortress-team-responds-to-criticism-july-19th-2007/.

¹²⁹ I was not alone in signaling this problem, for Pastor Jim West also initially expressed doubts about the originality of the claims conveyed in the film. West, however, then went to considerable lengths to promote the film, even using images from it (including the imaginary reconstruction of a scriptorium at Qumran, which an entire series of archaeologists claim never existed) for his blog header. Early in 2010, West would delete his then-existing blog in its entirety, thereby effacing any digital trace of his online support for the San Diego exhibit. Cf. https://charlesgadda.wordpress.com/dead-sea-scrolls-qumran-fortress-team-responds-to-criticism-july-19th-2007/ and https://drjimwest.wordpress.com/2007/07/13/qumran-warrior-central/. Only faint hints are still available on the Wayback Machine; see, for example, http://web.archive.org/web/20071001212606/http://drjimwest.wordpress.com/. West would begin posting the current version of his blog,

https://zwingliusredivivus.wordpress.com/2010/01/, on January 29, 2010.

[130] For the citations from Tigchelaar's article in the sidebar, see *Review of Biblical Literature*, August 2010, available at https://lirias.kuleuven.be/bitstream/123456789/270251/3/7241_7884.pdf. Notably, Tigchelaar's critique was similar to the one leveled by Norman Golb in 1995 at the earlier, comparable speculative effort—leading Magen to *abandon* the original "Operation Scroll" proposal.

[131] With respect to the peer review process, my father once said that "when dealing with the Dead Sea Scrolls, one must always ask: Who are the peers doing the reviewing?" Golb's scholarly writings on the Dead Sea Scroll exhibitions and various other topics were always subject to professional review at the Oriental Institute before appearing online.

[132] National Geographic, "Writing the Dead Sea Scrolls," available at https://www.youtube.com/watch?v=4rN79yvpi1k&feature=youtu.be. The statements quoted are made toward the end of the program, starting at 38:00. See also https://isac.uchicago.edu/sites/default/files/uploads/shared/docs/the_mystery_of_national_geographic_solved.pdf.

[133] See, for example, https://robertcargill.com/2009/04/04/full-text-of-dr-cargills-remarks-at-the-pepperdine-gsep-panel-discussion-on-racism-and-homophobia/ and https://www.change.org/p/pepperdine-overturn-your-decision-to-deny-recognition-to-lgbt-students/c/1805970.

[134] See https://web.archive.org/web/20100415115309/ and http://www.bobcargill.com:80/Docs/ROBERT_CARGILL_RESUME_WEB.pdf. References to Christianity.com would no longer appear in Cargill's résumé following 2010.

[135] Italics added. See https://www.femalefirst.co.uk/celebrity/Nicole+Kidman-3525.html. See also https://www.nydailynews.com/archives/gossip/nicole-calls-scripture-doctor-article-1.610796 ("The face of Chanel has been studying with Dr. Robert Cargill, an adjunct professor of religion at Pepperdine University who has supervised archeological digs in Israel").

[136] See http://www.nytimes.com/2013/02/17/nyregion/online-battle-over-ancient-scrolls-spawns-real-world-consequences.html. In a 2015 biographical statement, Cargill would confirm that he "was raised as a Christian (Churches of Christ)" but had since become an agnostic, also asserting on the same page his belief that "Christian insistence upon ... a literal interpretation of the biblical text is greatly harming modern Christianity." See https://web.archive.org/web/20150708142137/http://www.bobcargill.com:80/about.htm.

[137] See Brian Howe, "Unraveling the Continuing Mystique of the Dead Sea Scrolls," Indy Week, August 6, 2008, available at https://www.indyweek.com/indyweek/unraveling-the-continuing-mystique-of-the-dead-sea-scrolls/Content?oid=1210028, archived at http://web.archive.org/web/20100816144047/https://www.indyweek.com/indyweek/unraveling-the-continuing-mystique-of-the-dead-sea-

scrolls/Content?oid=1210028.

[138] See Margaret Rose, *Parody: Ancient, Modern, and Post-modern* (Cambridge University Press, 1993), 26–28.

[139] For a sampling, see, for example, http://scrolls-in-san-diego.blogspot.com/, http://www.voiceofsandiego.org/letters/other-side-of-the-scrolls/, http://www.freerepublic.com/focus/religion/1860981/posts, http://www.bloggernews.net/13551, http://discardedlies.com/entry/?33674_, http://sdnews.com/view/full_story/302772/article-Letters-to-the-editor, https://timothyfishbane.wordpress.com/2008/07/09/scandal-criticism-follows-scrolls-exhibit-to-raleigh-info-and-links/, https://robertdworkin.wordpress.com/, https://biblicalraleigh.wordpress.com/2008/07/17/unc-professor-admits-hes-not-a-scrolls-expert-defends-biased-museum-exhibit/, and https://biblicalnewyork.wordpress.com/2008/07/28/new-yorks-jewish-museum-announces-dead-sea-scrolls-exhibit-recognizes-lack-of-consensus-on-scrolls-origins/.

[140] See, for example, http://web.archive.org/web/20071030172823/www.nowpublic.com/culture/dead-sea-scrolls-exhibit-misleads-public.

[141] See, for example, the comments posted under the articles appearing at http://web.archive.org/web/20080417212226/http://www.nowpublic.com:80/culture/christian-fundamentalism-and-dead-sea-scrolls-san-diego, http://web.archive.org/web/20080430220643/www.nowpublic.com/culture/did-christian-agenda-lead-biased-dead-sea-scrolls-exhibit-san-diego, and http://web.archive.org/web/20080523144157/http://www.nowpublic.com/culture/charity-fund-involved-dead-sea-scrolls-conflict. Many similar discussions about the scroll exhibits took place on the Internet Infidels web forum, but that site was later removed from the internet. See also the results of the investigative efforts of Robert Cargill, at http://archive.li/AyKSH#selection-6725.65-6741.123.

[142] See the remarks by Steve Mason of York University at http://web.archive.org/web/20080523144157/http://www.nowpublic.com/culture/charity-fund-involved-dead-sea-scrolls-conflict. Mason, of course, did not entirely agree with my treatment of the group meeting at SBL where he had been faced with the "impossible task" of answering four papers delivered mostly by Qumran-Essene traditionalists. See *The Qumran Con*, chapter 8, p. 189 and note 35.

[143] See, for example, the comments posted under the articles appearing at http://web.archive.org/web/20080417212226/http://www.nowpublic.com:80/culture/christian-fundamentalism-and-dead-sea-scrolls-san-diego, http://web.archive.org/web/20080430220643/www.nowpublic.com/culture/did-christian-agenda-lead-biased-dead-sea-scrolls-exhibit-san-diego, and http://web.archive.org/web/20080523144157/http://www.nowpublic.com/culture/charity-fund-involved-dead-sea-scrolls-conflict. Many similar

discussions about the scroll exhibits took place on the Internet Infidels web forum, but that site was later removed from the internet.

[144] In addition to the items listed in the notes above, see, for example, *People v. Golb*, trial exhibits 12, 14A, 17–19, 30, 40A, 40B, and 40C, and http://archive.li/AyKSH#selection-6725.65-6741.123 ("a number of typed letters were sent to each of the museums that hosted the Dead Sea Scrolls exhibitions … Each of the letters were mass mailed to each of the members of the museum board of directors and administrators").

[145] Levitt Kohn's regrets were expressed in an interview with the *National Post* dated March 7, 2009.

[146] The words running from "it may be many years" to "our lives today" were eventually omitted. See http://web.archive.org/web/20080810021032/ and http://www.nowpublic.com:80/culture/dead-sea-scrolls-coming-new-york, and compare http://web.archive.org/web/20110514205831/ and http://www.thejewishmuseum.org:80/site/pages/onlinex.php?id=196&live_stat=DeadSeascrolls.

[147] See http://web.archive.org/web/20110716163428/ and http://www.thejewishmuseum.org/site/pages/press.php?id=140.

[148] For the following quotations, see https://timothyfishbane.wordpress.com/.

[149] Only a few electronic traces remain of this comical blog, posted by Geoff Hudson, online. See, for example, https://web.archive.org/web/*/http://aliasesofjeffreygibson.blogspot.com/*. Hudson's many postings were in part the inspiration for my own pseudonymous campaign. After I began posting, Hudson even suggested that my own blogs were written by Gibson!

[150] Gibson in fact went further: he specifically doxed me as the author of the Charles Gadda blogs, and accused Norman Golb of criminal conduct, the alleged crime consisting in the quotation, for purposes of academic criticism, of Robert Cargill's marginal comments in his film script.

[151] See above, page 94.

Notes to Chapter 5

[1] People v. Golb, trial transcript, 426. (The transcript states "disinfected." Here and elsewhere I have corrected obvious typographical errors.)

[2] Pretrial order of February 11, 2010, 2n1. Available at https://dssruling.files.wordpress.com/2010/04/raphael_golb_ruling.pdf.

[3] See https://abovethelaw.com/2007/03/judge-of-the-day-carol-berkman/.

[4] See http://www.nytimes.com/2001/03/30/nyregion/judge-clearly-not-amused-sentences-a-subway-impostor.html and https://longreads.com/2015/05/05/the-boy-who-loved-transit/.

[5] See https://nypost.com/2012/04/25/judge-a-deal-buster/.

[6] See https://longreads.com/2015/05/05/the-boy-who-loved-transit/.

[7] People v. Golb, voir dire transcript, 64.

[8] Ibid., 74.

[9] Ibid., 79.

[10] Ibid., 80.
[11] Ibid., 205–7.
[12] Ibid., 208, 210.
[13] Ibid., 24–25.
[14] Ibid., 41.
[15] See ibid., 124.
[16] Ibid., 140.
[17] People v. Golb, pretrial order of February 11, 2010; trial transcript, 5–6.
[18] See the Committee on Public Safety report at http://info.sen.ca.gov/pub/09-10/bill/sen/sb_1401-1450/sb_1411_cfa_20100412_141750_sen_comm.html.
[19] People v. Golb, trial transcript, 23–25.
[20] Ibid., 25–26.
[21] For all these terms, see, for example, Brief for Respondent-Appellee [Cyrus Vance Jr.], United States Court of Appeals for the Second Circuit, January 26, 2017. See also People v. Golb, trial transcript, 1246.
[22] People v. Golb, trial transcript, 19.
[23] Ibid., 35.
[24] See Diane Barth, "Why We Love to Hate Whistleblowers," *Psychology Today*, August 17, 2018, available at https://www.psychologytoday.com/us/blog/the-couch/201808/why-we-love-hate-whistleblowers.
[25] Breitbart, of course, had popular whistleblowers like Daniel Ellsberg and Frank Serpico in mind. It is worth noting that various parties acting on behalf of the American right wing have recently presented themselves as whistleblowers, claiming that their message is being suppressed and that they are victims of the "cancel culture." While such claims are central to the mass appeal of neofascist movements, they flaunt the standards normally used to judge truth and accuracy.
[26] People v. Golb, trial transcript, 149, 157–58; see also 250, 295, 300–302, 322, 1218–19, 1222–23, 1249, 1255, 1260, 1265.
[27] Ibid., 144.
[28] Ibid., 151.
[29] Ibid., 190.
[30] See, for example, People v. Golb, trial transcript, 179 (court doesn't see "relevance" of questions about Schiffman's role in the monopoly); 187 (court doesn't see relevance of "inquiry" into Schiffman's continued misrepresentations of Norman Golb's theory); 205 (court does not "care" whether or not People investigated truth of allegation of plagiarism); 216 (court objects to relevancy of Katzman's article accusing Schiffman of plagiarism).
[31] Ibid., 220.
[32] See, for example, Robert Cargill's entry at https://bobcargill.wordpress.com/2009/11/08/on-recent-news-about-the-cloak-and-browser-case-against-raphael-golb/ (asserting that "Golb was actively attempting to disguise his identity while making false …

accusations," claiming that I "spewed ... libel and defamation ... online," and warning that this claim "will be taken up in civil court after the conclusion of the criminal trial"; this warning, it should be noted in passing, never became a reality). See also the same author's later entry at https://bobcargill.wordpress.com/2010/01/25/now-where-have-i-seen-this-before-using-aliases-to-support-or-attack-an-idea/ (suggesting, among other things, that I wrote an article that was "false" because it "accused [Schiffman] of plagiarizing," and that the alleged "falsity" of this "accusation" is part of what renders my impersonation of Schiffman "illegal"; note that this entry of Cargill's was posted two weeks after Carol Berkman ruled that the truth or falsity of my accusations was "irrelevant" to whether or not I committed a crime, since, by her own admission, "libel is no longer a crime in New York").

[33] See People v. Golb, trial transcript, 174–75.

[34] Ibid., 217.

[35] Ibid., 217.

[36] Ibid., 185–86.

[37] See *Firing Line Debate*: "That Freedom of Thought Is in Danger on American Campuses," available at https://www.youtube.com/watch?v=oTA_juB-VSE.

[38] See https://www.chronicle.com/article/On-Becoming-a-Phoenix-/134658.

[39] The letter was leaked by Brian Leiter of the University of Chicago Law School. See http://leiterreports.typepad.com/blog/2018/06/blaming-the-victim-is-apparently-ok-when-the-accused-is-a-feminist-literary-theorist.html.

[40] In a controversy-sparking article of 1999, Nussbaum charged Butler with arguing that "we are all, more or less, prisoners of the structures of power," and that there is nothing anyone can do about the structures except "to parody them, to poke fun at them, to transgress them in speech." Nussbaum condemned this view as a form of moral abdication. "Parodic performance," she suggested, "is not so bad when you are a powerful tenured academic in a liberal university. But ... when [Butler] tells women in desperate conditions that life offers them only bondage, she purveys a cruel lie, and a lie that flatters evil by giving it much more power than it actually has." See Martha Nussbaum, "The Professor of Parody," *New Republic*, February 22, 1999, available at http://faculty.georgetown.edu/irvinem/theory/Nussbaum-Butler-Critique-NR-2-99.pdf. For the "visceral response within the academy and beyond" sparked by Nussbaum's article, see https://www.nytimes.com/1999/11/21/magazine/who-needs-philosophy.html.

[41] See, for instance, confidential letter signer John Hamilton's assertion that he "can imagine" Ronell "crossing lines in a campy way; usually it was nothing more than fun," and that, while she "certainly does write over-the-top emails," if the graduate student involved had been "upset" by the emails, "he could have chosen to work with someone else." Available at

http://blog.lareviewofbooks.org/essays/avital-nimrod-sexual-harassment-campy-communications-nyu/.

[42] See Jay's review of Ronell's *Fighting Theory* in *Artforum*, May 2011, available at https://www.artforum.com/print/201105/avital-ronell-s-fighting-theory-28050. Jay points to various statements of this sort by Ronell, such as her complaint that "as soon as someone has a little magnetism with students, as soon as the 'children' start to listen, one sets out on the road to crucifixion." See also Bernd Hüppauf, "A Witch Hunt or a Quest for Justice: An Insider's Perspective on Disgraced Academic Avital Ronell," *Salon*, September 8, 2018, available at https://www.salon.com/2018/09/08/a-witch-hunt-or-a-quest-for-justice-an-insiders-perspective-on-disgraced-academic-avital-ronell/. Hüppauf, who originally hired Ronell when he was chairman of NYU's German department, indicates that Ronell transformed the department into "a hand-selected group of disciples" where "dissent was heresy, and heretics would be reprimanded or excommunicated."

[43] People v. Golb, 676 (suggesting to the prosecutor that "perhaps you want to think about whether or not you want to confuse the jurors as totally as you've confused the Judge").

[44] Ibid., 665–76, 1250.

[45] Ibid., 277–79, 281, 285, 287–88.

[46] Ibid., 276–86.

[47] Ibid., 275, 283–85.

[48] Ibid., 288.

[49] Ibid., 307.

[50] Ibid., 265, 311.

[51] See People v. Golb, trial transcript, 251, 253–54, 263, 307, 322.

Notes to Chapter 6

[1] People v. Golb, trial transcript, 409–69.

[2] See https://www.flynnfh.com/obituary/patrick-phillip-mckenna/.

[3] It is worth noting, with respect to both Lawrence Schiffman and Jonathan Seidel, that Orthodox Jewish law forbids what is known as *mesirah*, or the act of turning over a fellow Jew to gentile legal authorities, particularly if they might be corrupt, or if doing so could lead to incarceration. The law's modern applicability is a subject of some debate among rabbinical authorities, but it has been invoked even to prevent observant Jews in Brooklyn from informing on or testifying against child molesters. For rabbinical sources, see https://www.sefaria.org/sheets/350168.8?lang=bi&with=all&lang2=en.

[4] People v. Golb, trial transcript, 27.

[5] Ibid., 613–15, 618.

[6] These counts, like most of the miscellaneous charges, will be vacated by the New York Court of Appeals, on First Amendment grounds and for lack of any sort of criminal conduct.

[7] Ibid., 631–35. Goranson would continue to defend his Qumranological claims long after my trial. In fact, he would reiterate them in a July 1, 2024, review posted on Amazon, on the Early Writings website, and in at least one other online forum. My aim, he there suggests, has been to "promote" the views of Norman Golb, rather than to criticize misrepresentations and blackballing. Needless to say, he does not mention his own role in the effort to criminalize my campaign of criticism and satire.

[8] Ibid., 639.

[9] See Cargill's résumé at https://clas.uiowa.edu/classics/sites/clas.uiowa.edu.classics/files/field/cv/Cargill%20Resume%202018.pdf.

[10] See the evidence gathered by Cargill at http://archive.li/AyKSH#selection-6725.65-6741.123.

[11] People v. Golb, trial transcript, 723.

[12] Ibid., 770.

[13] See Dan Milmo, "Elon Musk Threatens to Sue Anti-Defamation League over Lost X Revenue," *Guardian*, September 5, 2023, available at https://www.theguardian.com/technology/2023/sep/05/elon-musk-sue-adl-x-twitter.

[14] For all quotes from Cargill's "exclusive," see People v. Golb, defendant's trial exhibit H-1, available at https://raphaelgolbtrialtranscripts.files.wordpress.com/2011/03/cargillarticle.pdf.

[15] See People v. Golb, defendant's exhibit H-1.

[16] This is a slight inaccuracy on Cargill's part. Mr. Broshi did not "write" the comment; he uttered it in a moment of anger, in response to a question put to him by Avi Katzman in an interview published in *Haaretz* on October 4, 1991.

[17] Mr. Broshi, curator of the Shrine of the Book from its inception in 1964 until 1994, had an MA in archaeology from the Hebrew University, but not a PhD.

[18] See People v. Golb, trial transcript, 763–68.

[19] People v. Golb, trial exhibit, 3.

[20] People v. Golb, trial transcript, 788.

[21] Ibid., 805–6.

[22] See Robert Cargill, "The State of the Archaeological Debate at Qumran," *Currents in Biblical Research* 10, no. 1 (October 2011): 112–14, and see the list of his writings since then in his curriculum vitae at https://clas.uiowa.edu/religion/sites/clas.uiowa.edu.religion/files/field/cv/Cargill%20CV%202015.pdf.

[23] See Shanks's announcement at https://www.biblicalarchaeology.org/daily/archaeology-today/archaeologists-biblical-scholars-works/hershel-shanks-my-final-first-person/; for Cargill's later departure from this position, see https://www.biblicalarchaeology.org/first-person-bob-cargill/and-now-for-

something-completely-different/.

24 See https://clas.uiowa.edu/religion/people/robert-r-cargill. In his announcement of his departure from BAR (see previous note), Cargill will state that he plans to continue his "teaching and research as a tenured professor ... at the University of Iowa."

25 People v. Golb, trial transcript, 26.

26 See https://biblicalraleigh.wordpress.com/. The admission came in private email correspondence between Ehrman and "Jerome Cooper," a pseudonym I used to contact him with an inquiry as to how he had come to be invited to lecture at the Raleigh exhibit. In the course of this exchange, Ehrman explained his scholarly position by stating, "I am not an archaeologist or scrolls expert myself, but ... everyone whom I know who is personally committed to doing research on the scrolls thinks that the Essenes probably wrote them." He added that in his opinion, it was legitimate for the museum "to present the *opinio communis* of scholarship, and let the experts wrangle over it." For Ehrman's views on religion, humanism, and the importance of skepticism, see https://ffrf.org/outreach/awards/emperor-has-no-clothes-award/item/21383-ffrf-s-emperor-honor-to-truth-telling-bible-scholar.

27 People v. Golb, trial transcript, 812–17.

28 See S. W. Crawford, "The Identification and History of the Qumran Community in North American Scholarship," in D. Dimant, ed., *The Dead Sea Scrolls in Scholarly Perspective: A History of Research* (Brill, 2012), 14. In support of this assertion, Crawford referred her readers to a few pages rehashing the usual arguments in a book by doctrinaire Qumranologist James VanderKam that appeared before my father's 1995 book was published, as well as to a chapter of the 2002 edition of Jodi Magness's book on Qumran, in which Magness briefly objects to the interpretation of Qumran as a "fort." These were perhaps not strong sources on which to base such a categorical conclusion, particularly in view of Crawford's failure to inform her readers that virtually all of Magness's claims had been rejected by the Magen-Peleg archaeological team.

29 See Crawford's article, "The Qumran Collection as a Scribal Library," in S. W. Crawford and Cecilia Wassen, ed., *The Dead Sea Scrolls at Qumran and the Concept of a Library* (Brill, 2016), 120. In her book *Scribes and Scrolls at Qumran*, published three years later, Crawford will more accurately assert that according to Golb, "the scrolls were part of *library holdings* from Jerusalem." Later in the same work, however, she will again object to the view that the "collection" consisted of "scrolls brought down from *several* libraries in Jerusalem at the time of the First Jewish Revolt, *or deposited in the caves by the temple authorities*" (italics added). See pages 169 and 239 of that book. Nowhere will Crawford directly address Norman Golb's argument that the scrolls are only part of a *wider* phenomenon of scroll hiding in response to the siege of Jerusalem. Crawford's case largely rests on interpreting the scrolls as a

single coherent "collection" rather than as the partial remains of thousands of manuscripts that were hidden in *various* locations. Her insistence on this view spills over into further inaccuracies when she states, "This *collection* was not a frozen relic of *a collection* brought from elsewhere to be hidden in the caves, as several have suggested" (italics added). Crawford, in a footnote, here signals Golb along with Magen and Peleg. But, unlike Crawford, neither my father nor Magen and Peleg have ever suggested that the scrolls were the remains of a single "collection." Ibid., 146.

[30] Crawford's own attempt to define a unifying "sectarianism" in the scrolls is similar to previous efforts of Devorah Dimant and Florentino García Martínez. Those efforts have been severely criticized by other scholars: a fact that Crawford does not divulge to her readers. See, for example, Zangenberg, "Zwischen Zufall und Eigenartigkeit," 129, and de Looijer, *The Qumran Paradigm*, 34–87. For Crawford's parallel effort to demonstrate a connection between the scrolls and Qumran based, for example, on a few scroll fragments containing what appear to be writing exercises and lists of false prophets and the like, see my analysis in *The Qumran Chronicle* (Vol. 31: December, 2023), pp. 49-50. It should also be observed that my father, in view of the known existence of tunnels leading out from Jerusalem, concluded that the scrolls, either in part or in whole, may have been hidden *during* the siege, and not merely before it, as twice stated by Crawford. See above, chapter 4, note 7.

Notes to Chapter 7

[1] Richard Posner, *The Little Book of Plagiarism* (New York, 2007), 78.
[2] People v. Golb, trial transcript, 1083. For Bandler's question on whether I think I'm smarter than the jurors, see ibid., 1102.
[3] Ibid., 1106–7. For Breitbart's question as to whether he has "disaffected" Berkman in view of the "faces" she is making, see ibid., 426.
[4] Ibid., 1114–15.
[5] People v. Golb, people's exhibit 15.
[6] See http://www.nytimes.com/2010/09/28/nyregion/28scrolls.html.
[7] Ibid., 1134.
[8] The reactions of arrestees, and the ease with which they are mentally manipulated by those in whose custody they find themselves, are the subject of a wide body of research. One study concludes that police interrogation "can best be understood as a confidence game based on the manipulation and betrayal of trust." See Richard Leo, "Miranda's Revenge: Police Interrogation as a Confidence Game," in *Law and Society Review* 30, no. 2 (1996): 259–88. The susceptibility to manipulation is no minor matter: it has resulted in the well-documented phenomenon of false confessions and wrongful convictions based on them throughout the United States. See, for example, Saul Kassin, "False Confessions: Causes, Consequences, and Implications for Reform," *Current Directions in*

Psychological Science 17, no. 4 (2008): 249 (indicating that "despite the commonsense belief that people do not confess to crimes they did not commit, 20 to 25% of all DNA exonerations involve innocent prisoners who confessed," and that "recent analyses reveal ... that these discovered instances represent the tip of an iceberg").

[9] The author's files contain a copy of Martin Garbus's statement. For the difference between civil lawsuits and criminal prosecutions, and the decriminalization of libel in New York in 1965, see above, chapter 3, pages 56-58.

[10] The 170 instances are scattered through the People v. Golb trial transcript, on these pages: 25–26, 30, 64, 66–67, 73, 78, 89–91, 110, 112, 137, 139, 141, 147–49, 154, 156–58, 226, 240, 242, 244–45, 247–50, 252–55, 258, 260, 295–96, 300–304, 318–24, 461–62, 466, 623, 628–29, 646, 656, 712, 714–15, 717–20, 722, 727, 729, 734–36, 740, 742–44, 1080–81, 1104–5, 1129–30, 1218–21, 1228–30, 1239–41, 1247–49, 1254–55, and 1260.

[11] Ibid., 1218–20, 1228–29, 1230, 1240–41, 1246, 1255.

[12] Ibid., 1244.

[13] Ibid., 1244.

[14] Ibid., 25; see also 1244.

[15] See Bernard Harcourt, *Critique and Praxis* (Columbia University Press, 2020), 385, 387 (quoting in part from Candice Delmas, *A Duty to Resist* [Oxford University Press, 2018], 21).

[16] For Pessoa, see People v. Golb, trial transcript, 1025.

[17] For the sidebar quote, see Philip Margulies and Maxine Rosaler, *The Devil on Trial: Witches, Anarchists, Atheists, Communists, and Terrorists in America's Courtrooms* (New York, 2008), 1.

[18] People v. Golb, trial transcript, 1240. For my ability to "stir up controversy," see ibid., 1246.

[19] See People v. Golb, trial transcript, 1018–20.

[20] See Fyodor Dostoevsky, *Crime and Punishment*, tr. Richard Pevear and Larissa Volokhonsky (Vintage Classics, 1993), I.6, 70.

[21] People v. Golb, trial transcript, 1269.

[22] Ibid., 1280.

[23] Italics added. See the definitions gathered at https://www.thefreedictionary.com/parody; see also the American Heritage Dictionary definition of *impersonate*, which includes "To imitate the appearance, voice, or manner of; mimic."

[24] Simon Dentith, *Parody* (Routledge: New York, 2000), 20. Dentith further indicates (ibid., 189) that "most forms" of parody are "shot through with more or less mocking or derisive imitations or anticipations of the other's word." See also Webster's Ninth, second definition ("a feeble or ridiculous imitation"), and the *Princeton Encyclopedia of Poetry and Poetics* (Princeton University Press, 2012), 1255ff. (the satirist "serves as self-appointed prosecutor, judge, and jury, exposing and condemning the worst excesses of human behavior, sometimes with the object of provoking the wicked to guilt, shame, rage, and tears").

[25] People v. Golb, trial transcript, 1281.
[26] Many articles describe the widespread, and palpably racist, use of rap song lyrics to secure criminal convictions. See, for example, Sam Levin, "When Rap Lyrics Are Used against You in Court: 'They Silenced Me for 21 Years,'" *Guardian*, September 3, 2022, available at https://www.theguardian.com/us-news/2022/sep/03/california-mckinley-mac-phipps-rap-music-black-rappers.
[27] People v. Golb, trial transcript, 1281.
[28] Ibid., 1287.
[29] Ibid., 1281.
[30] Section 33.07(b) of the Texas Penal Code provides a useful contrast: it forbids sending a communication "with the intent to cause a recipient of the communication to *reasonably* believe that the other person authorized or transmitted the communication."
[31] For the circumstances of the case that prompted the *Onion*'s brief, see https://www.nytimes.com/2022/10/04/us/the-onion-supreme-court.html. The brief is available at https://www.supremecourt.gov/DocketPDF/22/22-293/242292/20221003125252896_35295545_1-22.10.03%20-%20Novak-Parma%20-%20Onion%20Amicus%20Brief.pdf.
[32] People v. Golb, trial transcript, 651, 1127.
[33] See https://jonathanturley.org/2010/10/01/new-york-lawyer-convicted-of-impersonating-nyu-professor/.
[34] See Jonathan Turley, "Harm and Hegemony: The Decline of Free Speech in the United States," *Harvard Journal of Law and Public Policy* 45 (2022): 571–701, available at https://www.harvard-jlpp.com/wp-content/uploads/sites/21/2022/07/TURLEY_VOL45_ISS2.pdf. Turley's "cancel culture" argument rests largely on eliding the difference between governmental suppression of constitutionally protected speech (a wrong that, he accurately point out, has been common in American history) and decisions by privately owned entities like Twitter as to how they want their platforms to be used. Since those decisions are themselves protected by the First Amendment, Turley's effort is arguably an attack on free speech values rather than the defense of them that it presents itself as being. For Turley's views on Twitter (and his apparent approval of Elon Musk's proposal to charge users eight dollars for "verified" accounts), see also the commentary at https://abovethelaw.com/2022/11/jonathan-turley-elon-musk-twitter-verified/.
[35] See https://googlegazer-blog-blog.tumblr.com/post/5867455275/guilty-as-charged-the-trial-of-raphael-golb and https://web.archive.org/web/20100918091948/http://greedwatcher.com/.
[36] David Sarna and Laurence E. Schiffman, *A Computer-Aided Critical Edition of the Tosefta Sotah* (Waltham, MA, Jewish Theological Seminary of America, 1970).
[37] People v. Golb, sentencing transcript, 24, 30.
[38] Ibid., 25.

[39] Ibid., 22.
[40] The reality of suicides at Rikers Island has, in recent years, become a matter of increasing notoriety, despite the efforts of authorities to have such matters treated with discretion. See, for example, Erum Salam, "'Abject Neglect': Critics Report Chaotic and Deadly Conditions on Rikers Island," *Guardian*, October 19, 2021, available at https://www.theguardian.com/us-news/2021/oct/19/rikers-island-abject-neglect-chaotic-conditions-deaths. More generally, Rikers has become "notorious for its culture of brutality." See Jennifer Gonnerman, "Do Jails Kill People?," *New Yorker*, February 20, 2019, available at https://www.newyorker.com/books/under-review/do-jails-kill-people. Investigations of deaths at the complex are "buried … behind bureaucratic walls." See Graham Rayman, "Investigations of Inmate Deaths on Rikers Island Can Take Years as Frustrated Families Feel Stonewalled," *New York Daily News*, April 24, 2022, available at https://www.nydailynews.com/new-york/nyc-crime/ny-rikers-death-investigations-delayed-families-stonewalled-20220425-i4c4iyatkvf43p3je7ryljyada-story.html.
[41] See Matt Katz, "NYC Must Pay as Much as $300 Million after People Posted Bail and Weren't Released," Gothamist, November 30, 2022, available at https://gothamist.com/news/nyc-must-pay-as-much-as-300-million-after-people-posted-bail-and-werent-released.
[42] See Ashley Southall and Jan Ransom, "Once as Pro-prosecution as Any Red State, New York Makes a Big Shift on Trials," *New York Times*, May 2, 2019 (noting that until the law was overhauled in 2019, New York had "one of the most restrictive rules in the country regarding turning over the government's evidence"). Available at https://www.nytimes.com/2019/05/02/nyregion/prosecutors-evidence-turned-over.html.
[43] People v. Golb, trial exhibit C, 2, 10; trial transcript, 308. The text, reprinted as appendix 2 in *The Qumran Con*, is available online at http://www.sirpeterscott.com/images/schiffmancorrespondence.pdf.
[44] Norman Golb, "The Confidential Letter Composed by Prof. Lawrence Schiffman of New York University," 1, 3–5, 9. Available at https://isac.uchicago.edu/sites/default/files/uploads/shared/docs/schiffman_response_2010nov30.pdf. Reprinted as appendix 3 of *The Qumran Con*, pages 397–413.
[45] Ibid., 10, 12.
[46] See comment 43 by Lawrence Kaplan (in relation to Prof. Michael Broyde's use of pseudonyms) at http://newsdesk.tjctv.com/2013/04/investigation-reveals-additional-questionable-identity-with-connections-to-broydes-scholarship/.
[47] Email of December 9, 2010, from Joel Kraemer to Norman Golb, a copy of which is in the author's files.
[48] The Yeshiva University press release has since been deleted. See https://roshyeshiva.wordpress.com/ and

https://web.archive.org/web/20110115045650/http://blogs.yu.edu/news/2011/01/12/president-joel-appoints-vice-provost/. The text read, in pertinent part: "Professor Schiffman will lead the effort to 're-imagine' undergraduate education at Yeshiva University," said President [Richard] Joel. "This undertaking will involve restructuring the undergraduate colleges. ... The vice provost will work ... to strengthen and foster a student experience of excellence and success and provide the optimum environment for faculty scholarship and teaching. ... Professor Schiffman's reputation as a scholar, his academic vision and his commitment to Torah u'Maddah [law and learning] exemplify our mission," said President Joel. "His boundless energy, his strong leadership skills and his collegial sensibilities make him the ideal person to further that mission in our undergraduate schools."

[49] See Luke Tress, "NY Officials: Yeshiva U Must Explain Public Funds as It Won't Recognize LGBTQ Group," *Times of Israel*, January 12, 2023, available at https://www.timesofisrael.com/ny-officials-yeshiva-u-must-explain-public-funds-as-it-wont-recognize-lgbtq-group/.

[50] "Living the Dead Sea Scrolls," audio interview with Eve Harow.

[51] See https://web.archive.org/web/20210516100815/https://bobcargill.wordpress.com/2010/09/30/dr-golb-found-guilty/.

[52] See https://web.archive.org/web/20200922212622/https://robertcargill.com/2011/01/12/quote-of-the-day-on-dead-sea-scrolls-scholarship/.

[53] See https://web.archive.org/web/20200809055332/http://targuman.org/2011/01/12/i-worry-for-my-friend-dr-robert-cargill/.

[54] See http://www.twincities.com/2010/03/12/dead-sea-scrolls-exhibit-goes-on-display-in-minn/. It is to be hoped that Alex Jassen's participation in this joint project allowed him to correct the misapprehension about the nature of Norman Golb's theory that he had apparently obtained from Schiffman. See above, chapter 4, note 48.

[55] See Norman Golb's review of the Milwaukee exhibit at https://isac.uchicago.edu/sites/default/files/uploads/shared/docs/milwaukee_dss_exhibit_2010.pdf.

[56] On the Discovery Center exhibit, see http://www.nytimes.com/2011/10/29/arts/design/the-dead-sea-scrolls-at-discovery-times-square-review.html and https://tomverenna.wordpress.com/2012/01/08/review-of-the-dead-sea-scrolls-exhibit-at-the-discovery-center/.

[57] See Lauren Green, "Dead Sea Scrolls in a Command Performance on Broadway," Fox News, November 10, 2011, available at http://www.foxnews.com/us/2011/11/10/dead-sea-scrolls-command-performance-on-broadway/.

[58] "The Dead Sea Scrolls Exhibit: An Unsolicited Opinion," December 15, 2011, available at http://mlsatlow.com/2011/12/15/the-dead-sea-scrolls-

exhibit-an-unsolicited-opinion/ (accessed April 7, 2015).

59 "Thou Shalt Suspend Disbelief: Dead Sea Scrolls Come to Times Square Tourist Land," February 2, 2012, available at http://forward.com/articles/150628/thou-shalt-suspend-disbelief/ (accessed April 7, 2015).

60 "Review: Dead Sea Scrolls Come to Times Square … and the Ten Commandments Too," December 25, 2011, available at http://tzvee.blogspot.com/2011_12_01_archive.html (accessed April 7, 2015).

61 This and the following quotes are from the author's transcription made during a visit to the exhibit. The same statement will be repeated in the Cincinnati exhibit and elsewhere. See 5–6 of Norman Golb's review at https://isac.uchicago.edu/sites/default/files/uploads/shared/docs/golb_excerpts_2012_dss_cincinnati_exhibit.pdf.

62 For further information on inaccurate statements in the Dead Sea Scroll exhibits, see Norman Golb's discussion at https://isac.uchicago.edu/sites/default/files/uploads/shared/docs/decline_of_qumranology.pdf.

Notes to Chapter 8

1 This release was later removed from the district attorney's website. It is available at https://web.archive.org/web/20101007085419/http://www.manhattanda.org/whatsnew/press/2010-09-30c.shtml.

2 See http://blog.simplejustice.us/2010/10/01/golb-convicted-making-sockpuppets-criminals/.

3 See, for example, https://www.nytimes.com/2019/07/09/nyregion/cyrus-vance-epstein.html and https://www.cnn.com/2018/03/19/entertainment/times-up-cyrus-vance/index.html.

4 See http://manhattanda.org/appeals.

5 See People v. Golb, trial transcript, 238, 254, 263, 316.

6 See ibid., 195–96; http://www.tabletmag.com/jewish-arts-and-culture/books/121361/dead-sea-scrolls-go-to-court (indicating that "in a recent telephone interview, Schiffman himself insisted that he suffered no harm" from being portrayed as admitting to plagiarism).

7 For the emails cited in this paragraph, see People v. Golb, people's exhibit 15.

8 See Mr. Rivellese's response brief in the federal court, 8–10, 22, available at https://raphaelgolbtrial.files.wordpress.com/2011/11/raphael-golb-v-new-york-appellants-reply.pdf.

9 See "A Trial on Identity Theft, with Scholarly Discourse," *New York Times*, September 27, 2010, A25, at http://www.nytimes.com/2010/09/28/nyregion/28scrolls.html ("'I used … satire, irony, parody and any other form of verbal rhetoric …' he said,

likening himself to Voltaire"). For the prosecution's rhetoric quoted in this paragraph, see the federal court of appeals response cited in the previous note, 10–12, 15, 24.

[10] See, for example, Skilling v. United States, 561 U.S. 358 (2010) (narrowing the scope of the "honest services fraud" statute, 18 U.S.C. § 1346).

[11] Author's files.

[12] See Golb v. Attorney General of the State of New York, No. 15-cv-1709, 2016 WL 297726 (S.D.N.Y. Jan. 21, 2016), 52.

[13] The text of the district attorney's response brief, written by Vincent Rivellese, is available at https://raphaelgolbtrial.files.wordpress.com/2011/11/district-attorneys-response-brief-in-the-raphael-golb-case.pdf.

[14] See "The Phenomenon of Internet Impersonation," available at https://raphaelgolbtrial.wordpress.com/the-phenomenon-of-internet-impersonation/.

[15] On the history of alt-right websites, see Maura Conway, Logan Macnair, and Ryan Scrivens, "Right-Wing Extremists' Persistent Online Presence: History and Contemporary Trends," International Centre for Counter-Terrorism policy brief, October 2019, available at https://icct.nl/app/uploads/2019/11/RWEXOnline-1.pdf.

[16] See http://sirpeterscott.com/images/23.10.09comet.jpg, http://sirpeterscott.com/images/30.7.10comet.jpg, http://sirpeterscott.com/images/150509comet.jpg, http://riveronline.co.uk/the-uni-spent-half-a-million-of-public-money-to-keep-me-silent/, and https://www.timeshighereducation.com/news/disgruntled-ex-lecturer-and-his-muse-show-stomach-for-a-fight/419827.article. See also the lively debate in the House of Commons on efforts (ultimately rejected by the British courts) to criminalize the online activities of Fredrics and of Ian Puddick, available at https://www.youtube.com/watch?v=0vJ3c8px4Vo.

[17] See http://www.usatoday.com/news/education/2011-04-18-college-presidents-impersonated-twitter.htm.

[18] See http://chronicle.com/article/When-a-Twittering-College-P/47269/.

[19] See Jim Dwyer, "2,000-Year-Old Scrolls, Internet-Era Crime," *New York Times*, November 6, 2009, available at http://www.nytimes.com/2009/11/08/nyregion/08about.html.

[20] See https://web.archive.org/web/20071218112815/https://long18th.wordpress.com/2007/12/11/satire-and-the-fake-first-person-voice/.

[21] See https://www.theatlantic.com/technology/archive/2012/02/learning-cormac-mccarthy-twitter-hoax/332358/.

[22] See https://www.theguardian.com/technology/2011/sep/29/sock-puppets-twitterjacking-digital-fakery.

[23] See the *Atlantic* article cited in note 21.

[24] See, for example,

https://www.theguardian.com/commentisfree/2013/sep/03/snowden-manning-assange-new-heroes.

25. See https://www.theguardian.com/commentisfree/2015/feb/07/aaron-swartz-suicide-internets-own-boy. Swartz was charged with crimes worth a seven-year prison sentence, including wire fraud, computer fraud, and theft of information from a computer.

26. See https://www.wired.com/2015/01/barrett-brown-sentenced-5-years-prison-connection-stratfor-hack/.

27. See http://www.nytimes.com/2013/12/14/world/asia/a-karzai-impersonator-finds-fame-and-misfortune.html and http://www.mcclatchydc.com/news/nation-world/world/article24568384.html.

28. See http://www.nytimes.com/2011/02/14/business/media/14link.html. See also Koch Industries v. Does (Youth for Climate Truth), 2011 WL 1775765 (D. Utah): Koch filed a trademark suit; lawyers for the authors of the release argued that it was parody and that "lifting anonymity must be the purpose of the lawsuit"; the district court dismissed the suit.

29. See "Spoof Twitter Account Ignites First Amendment Lawsuit," *New York Post*, June 13, 2014, available at https://nypost.com/2014/06/13/spoof-twitter-account-ignites-first-amendment-lawsuit/, and "Police Raid over Tweets Leads to Lawsuit against Peoria Mayor," *Chicago Tribune*, June 13, 2014, available at http://www.chicagotribune.com/news/local/breaking/chi-peoria-mayor-twitter-20140612-story.html.

30. Author's files. The Berkman Center at Harvard University has since been renamed the Berkman Klein Center for Internet and Society.

31. In a footnote to the proposed research project, I suggest that "an example would be the online publication, by a journalist named Bill Wyman, of a 'confessional' history of the Rolling Stones, purportedly written by Mick Jagger and intended for 'archives' kept by the group's former bassist, also fortuitously named Bill Wyman. Many readers were initially fooled." See http://www.slate.com/articles/news_and_politics/low_concept/2010/11/please_allow_me_to_correct_a_few_things.html.

32. I here referred the Berkman Center directors to Evgeny Morozov, *The Net Delusion: The Dark Side of Internet Freedom* (New York, 2011).

33. See the second letter of "Brutus," in the *Anti-Federalist Papers*, November 1, 1787, available at http://www.constitution.org/afp/brutus02.htm.

34. Thomas v. Collins, 323 U.S. 516, 530 (1945).

35. For Nazi parades, see National Socialist Party of America v. Village of Skokie, 432 U.S. 43 (1977). For offensive slogans at a gay funeral, see Snyder v. Phelps, 562 U.S. 443 (2011). For political speech as the First Amendment's "core," see, for example, Meyer v. Grant, 486 U.S. 414 (1988), and Buckley v. Valeo, 424 U.S. 1 (1976).

36. United States v. Eichman, 496 U.S. 310 (1990); Virginia v. Black, 538 U.S. 343 (2003). See also Dandridge v. Williams, 397 U.S. 471, 484

(1970), and Thornhill v. Alabama, 310 U.S. 88, 97 (1940).

[37] McIntyre v. Ohio Elections Comm'n, 514 U.S. 334, 346 (1995).

[38] See Garrison v. Louisiana, 379 U.S. 64 (1964), and Ashton v. Kentucky, 384 U.S. 195, 199–200 (1966). Various state high courts around the country have since held many criminal libel statutes to be unconstitutionally vague and overbroad.

[39] Hustler Magazine, Inc. v. Falwell, 485 U.S. 46 (1988); see also R.A.V. v. City of St. Paul, Minn., 505 U.S. 377, 414 (1992) ("the mere fact that expressive activity causes hurt feelings, offense, or resentment does not render the expression unprotected").

[40] The nine traditional categories of speech that are *not* protected by the First Amendment are (1) advocacy intended, and likely, to incite imminent lawless action; (2) obscenity; (3) speech integral to criminal conduct; (4) so-called "fighting words"; (5) child pornography; (6) false and malicious defamation, subject to the requirement that truth and good faith be allowed as affirmative defenses (but bear in mind that the Supreme Court famously held a criminal libel statute unconstitutional in 1966, and that libel has since been decriminalized in most American states, including New York); (7) certain additional forms of false speech, including perjury, impersonation of a *public official*, and fraud, defined by the Supreme Court as "a misrepresentation that is material, upon which the victim relied, and which caused actual injury"; (8) so-called "true" threats; and (9) speech presenting some grave and imminent threat that the government has the power to prevent, "although," says the Supreme Court, "a restriction under the last category is most difficult to sustain." See Brandenburg v. Ohio, 395 U.S. 444 (1969); Miller v. California, 413 U.S. 15 (1973); Giboney v. Empire Storage & Ice Co., 336 U.S. 490 (1949); Chaplinsky v. New Hampshire, 315 U.S. 568 (1942); New York v. Ferber, 458 U.S. 747 (1982); New York Times Co. v. Sullivan, 376 U.S. 254 (1964); Gertz v. Robert Welch, Inc., 418 U.S. 323 (1974); Virginia Bd. of Pharmacy v. Virginia Citizens Consumer Council, Inc., 425 U.S. 748, 771 (1976); Virginia v. Black, 538 U.S. 343, 344 (2003); Near v. Minnesota ex rel. Olson, 283 U.S. 697, 716 (1931); and United States v. Alvarez, 567 U.S. 709 (2012).

[41] See, for example, Brown v. Entertainment Merchants Ass'n., 564 U.S. 786 (2011); see also Sorrell v. IMS Health, 564 U.S. 552 (2011), and R.A.V. v. City of St. Paul, 505 U.S. 377, 382 (1992).

[42] See, for example, Brown v. Entertainment Merchants Ass'n, 131 S.Ct. 2729, 2738 (2011), and United States v. Playboy Group, 529 U.S. 813.

[43] See, for example, Ashcroft v. ACLU, 542 U.S. 656, 660 (2004).

[44] See, for example, People v. Golb, sentencing hearing, 30–31 (admonishing the defendant that "you seem to believe that you were carrying a banner for the First Amendment and what you were doing is a form of yelling fire in that crowded theatre").

[45] See, for example, Illinois ex rel. Madigan v. Telemarketing Associates, Inc. 538 U.S. 600, 620 (2003).

[46] See Michel de Montaigne, "Apologie de Raimond Sebond," in *Essais*, vol. 2 (Garnier-Flammarion, Paris, 1979), 232; cf. ibid., "De la colere," 376.
[47] See People v. Golb, trial transcript, 1247.
[48] Turner Broadcasting Sys., Inc. v. FCC, 512 U.S. 622, 643 (1994); City of Cincinnati v. Discovery Network, Inc., 507 U.S. 410, 428–29 (1993).
[49] See Reed v. Town of Gilbert, 135 S.Ct. 2218, 2227 (2015).
[50] See Honeyfund.Com Inc v. Governor, State of Florida, No. 22-13135 (11th Cir. 2024), available at https://media.ca11.uscourts.gov/opinions/pub/files/202213135.pdf. For the quotation in the sidebar, see page 13 of the court's opinion.
[51] See State v. Bishop, 787 S.E.2d 814, 818–21 (N.C. 2016).
[52] See https://blog.simplejustice.us/2014/05/14/golb-decided-and-the-sockpuppet-dies/.
[53] On the puzzling later effort of Christopher Dunn of the New York Civil Liberties Union, see below.
[54] See People v. Golb, 960 N.Y.S.2d 66 (1st Dept. 2013) (Jan. 29, 2013), at 1, available at https://law.justia.com/cases/new-york/appellate-division-first-department/2013/9101-2721-09.html.
[55] Ibid., at 1. I have deleted the court's internal brackets. The trademark case cited by the panel is Cliffs Notes, Inc. v Bantam Doubleday Dell Pub. Group, Inc., 886 F.2d 490, 494 (2d Cir. 1989).
[56] Ibid., at 3.
[57] United States v. Alvarez, 567 U.S. 709, 132 S.Ct. 2537, 2548 (2012).
[58] For the details in this and following paragraphs, see http://volokh.com/2013/03/13/prof-lawrence-schiffmans-lawyer-demands-removal-of-post-containing-the-text-of-a-court-opinion/, http://blog.simplejustice.us/2013/03/13/schiffman-meet-streisand-update-x4/, and https://www.techdirt.com/articles/20130314/17275122332/internet-is-baseless-legal-threats-popehat-greenfield-volokh-triple-streisand-edition.shtml.
[59] See http://blog.simplejustice.us/2013/03/13/schiffman-meet-streisand-update-x4/. The comments Schiffman and Rieders were apparently attempting to have removed include, for example, one posted on Greenfield's blog in 2010: "One possibility that doesn't seem to be addressed in this interesting and quite troubling piece is that Professor Schiffman was simply afraid of being exposed for real and serious past plagiarism, and had a feeling Professor Golb's son couldn't be stopped otherwise." See https://blog.simplejustice.us/2010/07/20/a-prosecution-2000-years-in-the-making/.
[60] See https://votelawrenceschiffman.wordpress.com/.
[61] See https://www.theguardian.com/higher-education-network/blog/2012/jun/07/academic-debate-online-aliases-sock-puppets.
[62] See https://raphaelgolbtrial.files.wordpress.com/2011/11/raphael-golb-amicus-brief.pdf.

63 See the transcript of the hearing, 16–19, available at http://www.nycourts.gov/ctapps/arguments/2014/Mar14/Transcripts/032514-72-Oral-Argument-Transcript.pdf, and see the video webcast at http://www.nycourts.gov/ctapps/arguments/2014/Mar14/032514-72-Oral-Argument-Webcast.asx.

64 See https://www.nyclu.org/en/publications/column-parody-jerry-falwell-and-dead-sea-scrolls-debate-new-york-law-journal. In both this article and the one that he posted after Albany's decision, Dunn presented the prosecution's inaccurate narrative of the case as fact, asserting, for example, that Norman Golb's views "have not been accepted by the academic community." This misleading statement was made in apparent ignorance of widely available reporting, including in the *New York Times*, on developments in the scrolls controversy over the years. No comment or response was solicited from me before or after either of Dunn's two articles appeared.

65 The New York Court of Appeals' May 13, 2014, decision is available at http://www.nycourts.gov/ctapps/Decisions/2014/May14/72opn14-Decision.pdf.

66 Personal correspondence, author's files.

67 See http://www.nydailynews.com/new-york/dead-sea-scrolls-case-harassment-law-tweaked-article-1.1791551.

68 See, for example, John Leland, "Top Court Champions Freedom to Annoy," *New York Times*, May 13, 2014, available at https://www.nytimes.com/2014/05/14/nyregion/top-court-champions-freedom-to-annoy.html, and Adrianne Jeffries, "New York Court Upholds the Right to Be Annoying," Verge, May 14, 2014, available at https://www.theverge.com/2014/5/14/5716814/new-york-court-upholds-the-right-to-be-annoying. Jeffries seems to have had some difficulty understanding what I was alleged to have done, for she inaccurately asserted that I had "called" academic media departments and had "sent an email ... linking to an article written under another false identity and suggesting Schiffman plagiarized it." She did, however, append a statement about my campaign that I gladly submitted to the Verge in lieu of a comment on her article.

69 See Christopher Dunn, "The Annoying First Amendment Thicket of Aggravated Harassment," June 5, 2014, available at https://www.nyclu.org/en/publications/column-annoying-first-amendment-thicket-aggravated-harassment-new-york-law-journal.

70 See http://blog.simplejustice.us/2014/05/14/golb-decided-and-the-sockpuppet-dies. See also the discussion by Jacob Sullum at http://reason.com/blog/2014/05/14/new-yorks-highest-court-upholds-the-righ.

71 People v. Golb, 23 N.Y.3d 455, 466 (2014).

72 A. C. Bradley, *Shakespearean Tragedy: Lectures on Hamlet, Othello, King Lear, Macbeth* (London, 1905), 207.

73 See D. E. Fehrenbacher and V. Fehrenbacher, eds., *Recollected Words of Abraham Lincoln* (Stanford University Press, 1996), 43, and Anthony Gross, *Lincoln's Own Stories* (New York, 1912), 109.

74 See Ashton v. Kentucky, 384 U.S. 195, 200–201 (1966).

75 People v. Golb, 23 N.Y.3d 455, 471 (2014).

76 See https://www.washingtonpost.com/news/volokh-conspiracy/wp/2014/05/13/impersonating-someone-online-with-intent-to-injure-his-reputation-is-a-crime-in-new-york/. For Volokh's curiously *separate* discussion of Albany's aggravated harassment ruling (hence giving readers the mistaken impression that what took place at the trial was more neat and comprehensible than it actually was), see https://www.washingtonpost.com/news/volokh-conspiracy/wp/2014/05/13/new-yorks-aggravated-harassment-statute-is-unconstitutionally-overbroad-and-vague/. Volokh had learned the meaning of the term "pasquinade" two years earlier: see https://volokh.com/2012/02/24/pasquinade/.

77 Volokh's silencing of Lippman's dissent appeared to be the same "out of cite, out of mind" treatment that the Qumranologists had long given the research findings of Norman Golb. See Gordon Moran, *Silencing Scientists and Scholars in Other Fields*, 137, 141. The fact that Jonathan Lippman was a judge, rather than a scholar, hardly lessened Professor Volokh's scholarly duty to address a dissenting opinion that, on First Amendment grounds, directly confuted the rationale of a decision that he, himself a First Amendment scholar, had chosen to support.

78 See especially his amicus brief in *United States v. Alvarez*, arguing in favor of the constitutionality of the Stolen Valor Act, which made it a crime to falsely boast that one had been awarded a military medal. Volokh's brief has been removed from the American Bar Association website but may still be read at https://web.archive.org/web/20120309094647/https://www.americanbar.org/content/dam/aba/publications/supreme_court_preview/briefs/11-210_petitioneramcu2profs.authcheckdam.pdf. The Supreme Court rejected Volokh's reasoning. See above, note 57.

79 In his article "The First Amendment and Criminal Libel Law," Volokh recognizes that "one can certainly be worried about the … potential chilling effect" of criminal libel laws, and suggests that "this may help explain why they have largely fallen out of favor." Nonetheless, he concludes that such laws "are constitutional." Available at https://reason.com/2019/04/10/the-first-amendment-and-criminal-libel-l/. But see, for example, Article 19 Global Campaign for Free Expression, "Briefing Note on International and Comparative Defamation Standards" (London, 2004), 2–6 ("There is a strong and growing body of law in support of the principle that criminal defamation is itself a breach of the right to freedom of expression … The clear view of … the international bodies that have considered the matter is that the imposition of custodial sanctions through criminal defamation laws is disproportionate and

unnecessary to protect individual reputations, particularly when alternative measures—including apologies, corrections and the use of the right of reply—can effectively address any harm to reputation without exerting a chilling effect on freedom of expression"). Available at https://www.article19.org/data/files/pdfs/analysis/defamation-standards.pdf. Without recourse to a highly particular—and indeed atavistic—doctrine of constitutionality, it is difficult to reconcile the "principle that criminal defamation is itself a breach of the right to freedom of expression" with the claim that criminal libel laws are "constitutional."

[80] Em dashes added. See http://blog.simplejustice.us/2014/05/14/golb-decided-and-the-sockpuppet-dies/.

[81] See https://bobcargill.wordpress.com/2014/05/13/ny-court-of-appeals-upholds-19-convictions-against-raphael-golb-in-dss-case/.

[82] See https://bobcargill.wordpress.com/2014/07/14/raphael-golb-re-sentenced-to-2-months-in-prison-3-years-probation/ and https://bobcargill.wordpress.com/2015/03/05/appeal-denied-dr-golb-to-serve-2-month-prison-sentence/.

[83] See Robert Cargill, *The Cities That Built the Bible* (HarperCollins, 2017), 206–8.

[84] See https://www.nysenate.gov/legislation/bills/2013/S7869.

[85] Hayes, *Sympathy for the Cyberbully*, 149–61, 160.

[86] See https://www.saratogacountycriminaldefenselawyerblog.com/2015/02/harassment.html.

[87] See https://blog.ericgoldman.org/archives/2014/05/dead-sea-scrolls-impersonation-case-convictions-partially-affirmed.htm.

[88] See https://h2o.law.harvard.edu/text_blocks/30600.

[89] See Ralph Waldo Emerson, "New England Reformers," *Essays*, 2nd ser. (1883), 269, and "Intellect," *Essays*, 1st ser. (1903), 341.

[90] See, for example, Shuttlesworth v. City of Birmingham, 382 U.S. 87 (1965).

[91] *National Law Journal*, April 13, 2017. Available at http://www.nationallawjournal.com/id=1202783688030/NY-Judges-Suspected-Suicide-Shines-Light-on-Silent-Struggle?slreturn=20170318004757.

Notes to Chapter 9

[1] See http://www.htronline.org/about-us/ and http://www.nytimes.com/2003/08/06/nyregion/robert-j-ward-77-a-senior-federal-judge.html.

[2] See Adonis v. Philippines (UNHRC, 2011) 1815/2008, paragraphs 8.7–10, available at http://www.bayefsky.com/pdf/philippines_t5_ccpr_1815_2008_scan.pdf; http://www.pen-international.org/newsitems/african-court-imprisonment-

for-defamation-violates-freedom-of-expression/; Cumpănă and Mazăre v. Romania, No. 33348/96 (ECHR 2004); Affaire Belpietro c. Italie, No. 43612/10 (ECHR 2013); Affaire Mika c. Grèce, No. 10347/10 (ECHR 2013); Mariapori v. Finland, No. 37751/07 (ECHR 2013); https://www.thebureauinvestigates.com/blog/2012-02-07/prison-time-for-libel-infringes-human-rights-unhrc-decides; and https://www.theguardian.com/uk/2009/oct/25/house-of-lords-libel-laws.

[3] See, for example, David Pritchard, "Rethinking Criminal Libel: An Empirical Study," *Communication Law and Policy* 14, no. 3 (2009): 303–39 (finding sixty-one criminal libel prosecutions initiated in Wisconsin in a sixteen-year period).

[4] Article 49.3 of the Charter of Fundamental Rights of the European Union states, "The severity of penalties must not be disproportionate to the criminal offense." While United States Supreme Court case law forbids "grossly" disproportionate sentences, American criminal sentencing codes have no equivalent to article 49.3.

[5] See T.V. ex rel. B.V. v. Smith-Green Cmty. Sch. Corp., 807 F. Supp. 2d 767, 789 (N.D. Ind. 2011). Available at https://casetext.com/case/tv-v-smith-green-community-school-corporation.

[6] See, for example, https://www.article19.org/data/files/pdfs/conferences/criminal-def-eu-ngo-paper.pdf.

[7] See http://business.time.com/2013/01/22/can-you-go-to-jail-for-impersonating-someone-online/.

[8] Thornhill v. Alabama, 310 U.S. 88, 97 (1940).

[9] Ibid., 97–98.

[10] See, for example, the various cases discussed in Wiener, *Historians in Trouble*, and Mallon, *Stolen Words*.

[11] See, for example, https://www.law.cornell.edu/wex/criminal_law (noting that the common law recognized nine felonies—murder, robbery, manslaughter, rape, sodomy, larceny, arson, mayhem, and burglary—along with a variety of misdemeanors, including assault, battery, false imprisonment, perjury, and intimidation of jurors). For trademark law, see Rubin v. Coors Brewing Co., 514 U.S. 476, 496 (1995) (Stevens, J., concurring) (trademark restrictions apply only to "transaction-driven speech," which "usually does not touch on a subject of public debate"). See also Taubman v. Webfeats, 319 F.3d 770, 775 (6th Cir. 2003) (use of the domain name "shopsatwillowbend.com" to comment on a shopping mall called "Shops at Willow Bend" was protected speech because the use was not "in connection with the sale ... or advertising of any goods or services"); Bosley Medical Institute, Inc. v. Kremer, 403 F.3d 672 (9th Cir. 2005) (use of the domain name "bosleymedical.com" to criticize Bosley Medical Institute, Inc. was protected speech because the defendant did not offer a competing service); and Lucasfilm Ltd. v. High Frontier, 622 F. Supp. 931, 934 (D.D.C. 1985) (because the defendants were "selling [only] ideas," there could be no trademark infringement).

¹² For civil cases see, for example, Hustler Magazine, Inc. v. Falwell, 485 U.S. 46 (1988); Campbell v. Acuff-Rose Music, Inc., 510 U.S. 569, 582 (1994); Draker v. Schreiber, 271 S.W.3d 318 (Tex. Ct. App. 2008); Fisher v. Dees, 794 F.2d 432, 437–38 (9th Cir. 1986); New Times, Inc. v. Isaacks, 146 S.W.3d 144, 147 (Tex. 2004); and T.V. v. Smith Green Community School (Northern District of Indiana 2011 U.S. Dist. LEXIS 88403). — As for the Texas criminal court cases, none of them were prosecuted under the clause of that state's impersonation statute that criminalizes electronic communications sent with the intent that the recipient "reasonably believe" they were written by an impersonated party (a requirement, of course, utterly lacking in the New York statute used to prosecute me). See, for example, https://search.txcourts.gov/SearchMedia.aspx?MediaVersionID=0775e54f-9043-43ff-aa78-1a853493ef7a&coa=coa01&DT=Opinion&MediaID=a1bb6733-54e6-4cee-9a16-b97a83e33dd5 and https://search.txcourts.gov/SearchMedia.aspx?MediaVersionID=97c0a393-19f4-445d-831e-4c42eda8acdc&coa=coa07&DT=Opinion&MediaID=23c99c1f-d306-407e-942c-6b36ab2af9e3.

¹³ See http://sirpeterscott.com/images/150509comet.jpg and http://sirpeterscott.com/images/30.7.10comet.jpg and note 8 to this chapter.

¹⁴ See Cohen v. California, 403 U.S. 15, 21 (1971), and Organization for a Better Austin v. Keefe, 402 U.S. 415, 420 (1971).

¹⁵ See Golb v. Attorney General of the State of New York, No. 1:2015cv01709 (S.D.N.Y. 2016), 47, available at https://law.justia.com/cases/federal/district-courts/new-york/nysdce/1:2015cv01709/439393/25/.

¹⁶ Ibid., at 31.

¹⁷ Ibid., at 33–44.

¹⁸ Ibid., at 29.

¹⁹ Ibid., at 45.

²⁰ An example of a court adhering to an appropriate standard can be found in Campbell v. Acuff-Rose Music, Inc., 510 U.S. 569, 583 (1994), where the Supreme Court explained that "parody serves its goals *whether labeled or not*, and there is no reason to require parody to state the obvious (*or even the reasonably perceived*)" (italics added). See also, for example, San Francisco Bay Guardian v. Superior Court, 17 Cal. App. 4th 655, 660 (1993) ("The fact that … a few people … stated that they did not recognize the letter as a joke does not raise a question of fact … [T]he *very nature of parody … is to catch the reader off guard at first glance*, after which the 'victim' recognizes that the joke is on him to the extent that it caught him unaware" [italics added]).

²¹ United States v. Stevens, 559 U.S. 460, 480 (2010).

22. See Golb v. Attorney General of the State of New York, No. 1:2015cv01709 (S.D.N.Y. 2016), 48.
23. An audio of the hearing is available at https://www.courtlistener.com/audio/30877/golb-v-attorney-general-of-th/?type=oa.
24. See, for example, Laura Little, "Just a Joke: Defamatory Humor and Incongruity's Promise," *Southern California Interdisciplinary Law Journal* 21 (2011): 35–36, 39. For the jury's capacity to evaluate claims of damage to reputation in the context of *civil* statutes, see, for example, Carter v. Helmsley-Spear, Inc., 861 F. Supp. 303, 327n14 (S.D.N.Y. 1994) (vacated in part on other grounds, 71 F.3d 77 [2d Cir. 1995]), and Wojnarowicz v. American Family Association, 745 F. Supp. 130, 140 (S.D.N.Y. 1990).
25. See Benjamin Weiser, "Hang Him Up? The Bad Judge and His Image," *New York Times*, January 27, 2009 (applying these terms to the late Judge Charles L. Brieant, Jr. and asserting that they are a "fair description of Judge Jacobs as well"), available at https://www.nytimes.com/2009/01/28/nyregion/28portrait.html.
26. Golb v. Attorney General of the State of New York, 870 F.3d 89, 92 (2017).
27. Ibid., 102.
28. See "When Is Parody a Crime? When Nobody Gets It," available at https://appellatesquawk.wordpress.com/2017/09/08/when-is-parody-a-crime-when-nobody-gets-it/.
29. Arthur Hayes, "Raphael Golb Is Facing Jail Time—for Parodying a Dead Sea Scrolls Scholar," *Forward*, October 12, 2017, available at http://forward.com/opinion/385050/raphael-golb-is-facing-jail-time-for-parodying-a-dead-sea-scrolls-scholar/.
30. See Leval's opinion in Yankee Publishing Inc. v. News America Publishing, Inc., 809 F. Supp. 267, 280 (SDNY 1992). Other decisions that are hard to reconcile with Jacobs's opinion include those mentioned above in note 17. See also New Times, Inc. v. *Isaacks*, 146 S.W.3d 144, 147 (Tex. 2004) ("The satiric effect emerges only as the reader concludes by the very *outrageousness* of the words that the whole thing is a put-on"), and Fisher v. Dees, 794 F.2d 432, 437–38 (9th Cir. 1986) ("*Destructive* parodies play an important role in social and literary criticism and thus merit protection").
31. See Yitzchak Besser, "Web of Lies: Hate Speech, Pseudonyms, the Internet, Impersonator Trolls, and Fake Jews in the Era of Fake News," *Ohio State Technology Law Journal* 17, no. 2 (2021): 233–75, at 255–58. The author, who presents *People v. Golb* as "one of the most famous impersonator-troll cases," summarizes the Second Circuit's decision by broadly stating that the panel "upheld the constitutionality of the criminal impersonation statute." This statement, read in the context of the article, creates the misleading impression that the panel affirmed not merely the "Larry Schiffman" convictions but all the convictions under review,

including those pertaining to "Seidel" and "Cross." The words "satire" and "parody" appear nowhere in Besser's discussion—exactly the approach one can expect future prosecutors to take.

[32] So it was described by Jennifer Wynn of John Jay College in her revealing book entitled *Inside Rikers* (New York, 2001); I am unaware of any diminution since then in the size of this "carceral archipelago" (again Wynn's term, borrowed from Foucault), although plans have vaguely been aired to shut the place down permanently.

[33] "Trust your body," Rupi Kaur had written, "it reacts to right and wrong / better than your mind does." *The Sun and Her Flowers* (Toronto, 2017), 212.

[34] See https://www.nytimes.com/2011/09/18/fashion/weddings/elizabeth-roper-david-shanies-weddings.html.

[35] See https://twitter.com/xkv8r/status/985912123250356226?s=03.

[36] See Norman Golb, "Aspects of the Roles of Truth and Fiction in the Current Struggle over the Meaning of the Dead Sea Scrolls," available at https://isac.uchicago.edu/sites/default/files/uploads/shared/docs/the_role_of_truth.pdf.

[37] See Rule 3.8 of the New York Rules of Professional Conduct, available at https://www.nycourts.gov/ad3/AGC/Forms/Rules/Rules%20of%20Professional%20Conduct%2022NYCRR%20Part%201200.pdf.

[38] See the New York Code of Judicial Conduct, available at https://ww2.nycourts.gov/rules/chiefadmin/100.shtml#01.

[39] See https://pen.org/press-release/devin-nunes-twitter-defamation-lawsuit/. But see also McClatchy California Opinion Editors, "Devin Nunes Wants to Intimidate the Press with Lawsuits—and He's Not Alone," April 12, 2019, available at https://www.sanluisobispo.com/opinion/article229138344.html (suggesting that the lawsuit should be seen as part of a "disturbing trend of high profile lawsuits against media organizations" and was designed to "scare critics who can't afford legal costs").

[40] See Brian Pietsch, "Devin Nunes Can't Sue Twitter over Cow and Mom Parodies, Judge Says," *New York Times*, June 25, 2020, available at https://www.nytimes.com/2020/06/25/us/politics/devin-nunes-cow-tweets.html.

Notes to Epilogue

[1] The $17 million figure is stated by Lawrence Schiffman in "Living the Dead Sea Scrolls," audio interview with Eve Harow, available at http://thelandofisrael.com/living-the-dead-sea-scrolls/ and https://soundcloud.com/thelandofisrael/rejuvenation-living-the-dead-sea-scrolls.

[2] See Eric Cortellessa, "As Priceless Israeli Artifacts Head to a Controversial DC Bible Museum, Some Wonder Why," *Times of Israel*, May 1, 2016, available at https://www.timesofisrael.com/as-priceless-

israeli-artifacts-head-to-a-controversial-dc-bible-museum-some-wonder-why/. When the museum opened in the fall of 2017, art and architecture critic Philip Kennicott observed that "small claims based on material or scientific evidence are juxtaposed with larger claims about the truth of biblical narratives in a way that confuses fact and speculation." See "The New Bible Museum Tells a Clear, Powerful Story. And It Could Change the Museum Business," *Washington Post*, November 15, 2017, available at https://www.washingtonpost.com/entertainment/museums/the-new-bible-museum-tells-a-clear-powerful-story-and-it-could-change-the-museum-business/2017/11/15/6fc76f40-c98e-11e7-8321-481fd63f174d_story.html. Katherine Stewart would later report that the museum's "task is to embed a certain set of assumptions in the landscape of the capital." See "The Museum of the Bible Is a Safe Space for Christian Nationalists," *New York Times*, January 6, 2018, available at https://www.nytimes.com/2018/01/06/opinion/sunday/the-museum-of-the-bible-is-a-safe-space-for-christian-nationalists.html.

[3] See Megan Gannon, "Are the Museum of the Bible's Dead Sea Scrolls Fakes?," available at https://www.livescience.com/60985-dead-sea-scroll-forgeries.html, and Candida Moss and Joel Baden, *Bible Nation: The United States of Hobby Lobby* (Princeton, 2017), 34–35.

[4] See Årstein Justnes, "Fake Fragments, Flexible Provenances: Eight Aramaic 'Dead Sea Scrolls' from the 21st Century," in Mette Bundvad and Kasper Siegismund, eds., *Vision, Narrative, and Wisdom in the Aramaic Texts from Qumran: Essays from the Copenhagen Symposium, 14–15 August, 2017* (Leiden: Brill, 2019). See also, by the same author, "The Provenance of the Dead Sea Scrolls: Five Examples," in Neil Brodie, Morag M. Kersel, and Josephine Munch Rasmussen, eds., *Variant Scholarship: Ancient Texts in Modern Contexts* (Sidestone Press, 2023), a work that raises the issue of whether "the academy should engage with ancient texts and text-bearing objects of uncertain provenance."

[5] See Daniel Burke, "Mystery at the New Bible Museum: Are Its Dead Sea Scrolls Fake?," available at https://www.cnn.com/2017/11/17/us/bible-museum-fakes/index.html. The article states that Emanuel Tov "is perhaps the world's leading expert on the Dead Sea Scrolls." For the rather stunning ethical implications of Tov's reluctance to admit the texts are forgeries, see *Variant Scholarship* (previous note).

[6] Moss and Baden, *Bible Nation*, 71. The authors interviewed Tov during the preparation of their book and thank him in their preface.

[7] See ibid., 63–98.

[8] Ibid.

[9] Ibid.

[10] *Bible Nation*, 81–82. The authors say nothing about Tov's efforts to protect the monopoly, including his documented threats of legal action against those who defied it. While focusing on the unprovenanced nature of the Green collection's scroll fragments, they take the sectarian origin of the scrolls for granted, citing only John Collins of the Yale Divinity

School as an authority in this regard. And despite the fact that "on its fifth floor, the Museum of the Bible will lend space to exhibits drawn from and curated by the Israel Antiquities Authority and the Vatican Museum" (ibid., 156), they make no mention of the various IAA-loaned, evangelically oriented scroll exhibits discussed in this chapter.

[11] Ibid., 70.

[12] See Daniel Burke, "Bible Museum Says Five of Its Dead Sea Scrolls Are Fake," available at https://www.cnn.com/2018/10/22/us/bible-museum-fake-scrolls/index.html. In the wake of the forgery scandal, several Christian educational institutions, including the Southwestern Baptist Theological Seminary in Fort Worth, Texas, and the School of Theology at Azusa Pacific University in California, began to suspect that they, too, had been fooled into purchasing forged scroll fragments. See D. Burke, "After Bible Museum Scandal, More American Christians Suspect They Bought Fake Dead Sea Scrolls," available at https://www.cnn.com/2018/10/26/us/evangelicals-dead-sea-scrolls/index.html.

[13] See Yonat Shimron, "DC's Bible Museum Hires a Jewish Exhibits Director as It Overhauls Staff," available at https://religionnews.com/2018/10/10/dcs-bible-museum-just-hired-a-jewish-exhibits-director-as-it-overhauls-its-staff/.

[14] Ibid.

[15] On the museum's evangelical agenda and its historical roots, see Jill Hicks-Keeton and Cavan Concannon, *Does Scripture Speak for Itself? The Museum of the Bible and the Politics of Interpretation* (Cambridge University Press, 2022).

[16] See Hella Winston, "How Much Is an Unkosher Torah Worth?," *Jewish Week*, April 13, 2020, available at https://jewishweek.timesofisrael.com/how-much-is-an-unkosher-torah-worth/.

[17] See https://www.museumofthebible.org/press/press-releases/new-bible-museum-to-unveil-its-approach-to-creating-exhibit-content-and-tackling-provenance (release date October 4, 2017).

[18] See Yonat Shimron, "DC's Bible Museum Hires a Jewish Exhibits Director as It Overhauls Staff," available at https://web.archive.org/web/20181011014104/https://religionnews.com/2018/10/10/dcs-bible-museum-just-hired-a-jewish-exhibits-director-as-it-overhauls-its-staff/. The original version of this article was later deleted from the Religion News website, and a new version was posted in which the quoted language ("who along with six other paid Jewish scholars signed agreements not to publicly criticize the museum") was replaced with the words "Schiffman, who, like the rest of the advisory board, is paid." It is unknown how or why this editorial modification came about. Candida Moss and Joel Baden refer to scholars they interviewed who unsuccessfully tried to steer the museum away from its evangelical perspective, and who "cannot be named because of the terms of the

nondisclosure agreement they signed." *Bible Nation*, 172. For commentary on the museum's obvious Christian bias, see, for example, Jill Hicks-Keeton, "The Museum of Whose Bible? On the Perils of Turning Theology into History," January 24, 2018, available at http://www.ancientjewreview.com/articles/2018/1/24/the-museum-of-whose-bible-on-the-perils-of-turning-theology-into-history, and Melissa Bailey Kutner, "Hobby Lobby's Museum of the Bible Steals; Does It Also Lie?," May 3, 2018, available at https://eidolon.pub/hobby-lobbys-museum-of-the-bible-steals-does-it-also-lie-ee09a3335e3f.

[19] See the discussion in *Misusing Scripture*, above, chapter 4, note 100.

[20] See Michael Greshko, "'Dead Sea Scrolls' at the Museum of the Bible Are All Forgeries," *National Geographic*, March 13, 2020, available at https://www.nationalgeographic.com/history/2020/03/museum-of-the-bible-dead-sea-scrolls-forgeries/.

[21] See Timothy Gordon Ash, *Free Speech: Ten Principles for a Connected World* (Yale University Press, 2016), 292.

[22] See https://www.haaretz.com/1.5086601, archived at http://web.archive.org/web/20190412082605/https://www.haaretz.com/1.5086601.

[23] "Ancient Text Said to Solve Mystery of Why Dead Sea Scrolls Were Placed in Qumran," *Times of Israel*, September 28, 2010, available at https://www.timesofisrael.com/1000-year-old-document-may-reveal-why-dead-sea-scrolls-were-stashed-in-qumran/. See also Nir Hasson, "New Study Solves the Mystery of Dead Sea Scrolls Site," *Haaretz*, August 29, 2021, available at https://www.haaretz.com/archaeology/.premium.HIGHLIGHT-dead-sea-scrolls-site-mystery-solved-qumran-jerusalem-1.10155326. Many other reports on the same theme can be found online.

[24] See Amanda Borschel-Dan, "2,000-Year-Old Ledger Found in City of David Points to Widespread 2nd Temple Literacy," *Times of Israel*, May 17, 2023, available at https://www.timesofisrael.com/2000-year-old-ledger-found-in-city-of-david-points-to-widespread-2nd-temple-literacy/.

[25] Ibid. (quoting Esther Eshel of Bar Ilan University).

[26] See J. Magness, *The Archeology of Qumran and the Dead Sea Scrolls*, 2nd ed. (Eerdmans, 2021), 2. As indicated earlier, Magness had already misrepresented my father's views in 1994, claiming that he had argued that Qumran was a "Roman fort": see pages 1–2 of my father's article at https://isac.uchicago.edu/sites/default/files/uploads/shared/docs/schiffman_response_2010nov30.pdf. The misrepresentation in her 2021 book was arguably worse, because it allowed her to suggest to her readers that my father's conclusions, and also those of the Magen-Peleg team, were quirky, isolated manifestations, rather than closely related perspectives growing out of a series of pathbreaking historical and archaeological investigations. Magness would not be the last to distort and belittle the nature of my father's contribution. The July 1, 2024 Amazon review of the present book by Stephen Goranson would assert that Karl Rengstorf had

proposed that the scrolls came from "one" library; Golb, that they came from "several" libraries. By avoiding any mention of the Temple in summarizing Rengstorf's idea, the two theories are again made to seem far more closely related than they really are.

[27] These and many similar assertions were made in a two-part "continuing education class" given, via Zoom, on October 19 and 21, 2021, to an audience of 92nd Street Y subscribers. An audio recording of the presentation is in the author's possession.

[28] The gist of Magness's only comment on *Back to Qumran*, made at the very end in response to a question from a member of the audience as to whether any recent research had led her to change her views on anything, was that the excavations of the Magen-Peleg team had dealt "mainly with garbage dumps outside the site." So much for the standards of truth and rational inquiry on the Dead Sea Scrolls lecture circuit!

[29] Since, as Yitzhak Magen points out in the preface to the final *Back to Qumran* report (page xi), Qumranology is characterized by a preposterous mass of "articles and theories … all of which [have] to be read, and every opinion quoted," I must note that J. Magness (*The Archaeology of Qumran* [2021], 103–4), while continuing to refer throughout to Qumran as "the sectarian settlement," strenuously objects to the Magen-Peleg team's conclusion that the site served for a time as a pottery production center. The official IAA-sanctioned report has thus been *answered* and can now safely be ignored in Qumranological circles where Magness is regarded as an authority. Magness, to be sure, has updated her book (originally published in 2002) with a variety of references to the Magen-Peleg report, but while she quarrels here and there with one or another of their conclusions, she arguably fails to provide her readers with a full and adequate explanation of the reasons why the Israeli team, after a decade spent reexamining the site, felt compelled to reject virtually every aspect of the interpretation of Qumran that she has inherited from Father de Vaux.

[30] See Jean-Pierre Isbouts, *The Dead Sea Scrolls: 75 Years since Their Historic Discovery* (National Geographic, 2022), 36–37.

INDEX

Abdus-Salaam, Sheila (judge), 231, 234, 238, 239, 240, 241, 251
Abram Curry (falsely named as source by Mark Twain), 48
Academic lampoon. *See* Parody, Satire
Acts of Torah, 126
Adler, Simon (pen-name), 171
African Court of Human Rights, 243
Aliases. *See* Pseudonyms
Alt-right websites, 208, 210
American Academy of Arts and Sciences, 269, 274
American Association of Criminal Defense Lawyers, 222
American Association of University Professors, 51
American Civil Liberties Union, 155, 222
American Friends of the Israel Antiquities Authority, 66
American Gothic, 253
American Humanist Association, 155
American Schools of Oriental Research, 155
Annoying speech, criminalized, 63, 204, 214, 219, 231
Anonymity, 27, 40, 45, 149, 205, 228, 244, 297, 330
  perennial use by satirists, 39–47
Antisemitism, 4, 149, 208, 285
  mocked in *Letters of Obscure Men*, 39
Archeology (magazine), 150, 152
Ardis, Jim (mayor of Peoria), 212
Arrest at gunpoint, 1
Ash, Timothy Garton, 272
Ashton v. Kentucky (1966), 233, 242, 243
Assange, Julian, 211
Atlantic, 210, 299
Austin Graduate School of Theology, 312
Back to Qumran (Magen-Peleg report on excavations), 273
Baden, Joel, 270
Balasubramani, Venkat, 239
Bandler, John (prosecutor), 5, 6, 7, 8, 9, 10, 14, 23, 24, 51, 54, 57, 117, 119, 121, 122, 124, 125, 126, 131, 132, 133, 134, 136, 137, 138, 139, 140, 141, 142, 143, 144, 148, 154, 155, 156, 159, 160, 161, 162,

163, 164, 165, 166, 167, 168, 169, 170, 171, 172, 175, 177, 191, 192, 204, 205, 219, 238, 247, 248, 266
- argues to the jury that 'this was not for parody, this was for maliciousness', 169
- asserts the defendant is a 'menace,' because he 'knows how to twist words and stir up controversy', 57, 169, 170
- claims that the defendant intended to gain a thousand dollars through his 'fraudulent scheme', 27, 31, 131, 132, 205, 225
- informs the defendant that 'when there's someone like Dr. Schiffman,' mimicry is not 'allowed', 7

Barth, Diane, 123
Begley, Catherine (Special Agent at FBI), 22
Benavidez, Nora, 265
Berkman Center for Internet and Society, 212, 213
Berkman, Carol (criminal trial judge), 23, 24, 60, 61, 62, 63, 64, 65, 113, 115, 117, 118, 119, 120, 121, 124, 126, 127, 133, 138, 139, 140, 141, 142, 143, 144, 145, 148, 154, 157, 159, 160, 161, 162, 163, 164, 165, 166, 173, 174, 175, 177, 178, 191, 206, 213, 218, 240, 242, 244, 247, 248, 330
- admonishes the defendant that 'your criminal intent brought you a parody over the line', *177*
- agrees to preside over trial at prosecutor's request despite rule requiring random selection of judge, 60
- explains that six months at Rikers Island will teach the defendant not to 'imitate someone in that manner', 179
- instructs jurors not to examine 'legal issues of free speech', 174
- instructs jurors that satire and parody are light forms of comedy, 173
- prevents the defendant from testifying that his intent was to engage in satire, 164
- rules that "neither good faith nor truth is a defense", 63

Berners-Lee, Tim
Bible Nation (Baden and

Moss), 270
Biblical Archaeology Review, 155
Bill of Rights (United States Constitution), 214
Blake, Aaron, 33
Bloody Massacre Near Carson (Mark Twain), 47
Boehm, Mike
Book of Samuel, 258
Boyd, Lani, 53
Bradley, Andrew, 233
Brady, Christian, 197
Brandeis University, 85, 177
Braunstein, Susan, 133, 134
Breitbart, David, 14, 60, 61, 62, 65, 116, 117, 118, 123, 125, 126, 127, 128, 135, 138, 139, 140, 141, 142, 143, 144, 145, 147, 148, 159, 160, 161, 162, 164, 165, 166
Bridges, Jeff, 117
Broshi, Magen, 151, 152, 153, 249, 321
Brown University, 198, 209
Brown, Barrett, 211
Bugeja, Michael, 38
Bunyan, John, 41, 42, 293
Buratti, Pietro, 46
Bush, George W., 53
Butler, Judith, 130
Cahn, Edmond, 2
California State University, 26
California State University at Chico (academic integrity policy), 26
Cambridge History of Judaism
Campbell, Naomi, 14
Campus 'civility' codes, 63, 231
Cargill, Robert, 28, 29, 81, 125, 146, 149, 150, 151, 152, 153, 154, 155, 197, 237, 238, 257, 258, 259, 272, 289, 295, 318, 319, 321, 322, 335
  effort to suppress N. Golb's critique and citation of his film script
  his views on the expectation of satire and parody, 48
  his work on the Virtual Qumran film shown to the public at the 2007 San Diego scrolls exhibit
  reaction to online criticism of his film, 150–52
  trial testimony of, 149–55
Caricature, 212
Catholic University of Leuven
Charney, Noah, 268
Chicago Maroon, 36
Chicago Seven, trial of the, 276
Child pornography, 216
Christianity, 35, 198, 199, 270, 271

Chronicle of Higher Education, 130
Civil cases, distinguished from criminal, 56, 58
Clemens, Samuel. *See* Twain, Mark
Code of Ethics of the Museums Association (London), 159
Collins, John, 340
Columbia College in Chicago, 28
Columbia University, 209, 240
Compelling state interest doctrine, 216, 217, 221
Confessions of Jean-Jacques Rousseau, 49
Confessions of St. Augustine, 179, 183, 185, 189
Copper Scroll, 271
Courier, Paul-Louis, 46
Crawford, Sidnie White, 155, 156, 157, 158
Crime and Punishment (Dostoevsky), 172
Criminal libel, 43, 165, 206, 233, 234, 242, 243, 248
scandalum magnatum, 43
Cross, Frank Moore, 27, 146, 155, 156, 164, 257
Cross-burning. *See* Expressive conduct
Cryer, Frederick
Cyber-bullying statute, held unconstitutional in North Carolina, 221
David, Larry ("Curb Your Enthusiasm"), 2
Davies, Philip
Dead Sea Scroll exhibitions "politics" of exhibitors, 58
Dead Sea Scrolls, 1, 3, 4, 10, 15, 24, 26, 27, 29, 31, 32, 34, 58, 65, 67, 124, 138, 139, 140, 141, 142, 146, 148, 151, 153, 163, 171, 189, 192, 193, 197, 198, 199, 203, 218, 229, 249, 252, 254, 259, 260, 265, 267, 270, 271, 275, 276, 290, 312, 327, 328, 338, 339, 340, 341, 342, 343
as remains of Jerusalem-area libraries, 199
U.S. exhibitions, 3, 10, 58
Defamation, 233, 242, 246, 331, 334, 335, 336, 339, *See also* Libel, Criminal libel
Defoe, Daniel, 43
Dentith, Simon, 173
Desprez, Louis, 46
Dickens, Charles, 46
Discovery Times Square (exhibition space in New York), 198, 199, 200
Dostoevsky, 172
Dow Chemical (Bhopal gas tragedy), 53
Duke University, 28, 146, 147, 156
Dunn, Christopher, 230, 231,

232, 235
Dwyer, Jim, 31, 329
Early Case Assessment Bureau, 5, 10
Edelstein, Sam (pen-name), 171
Edict of the King of Prussia (Ben Franklin), 45
Ehrman, Bart, 156
Electronic Frontier Foundation, 244
Eligon, John, 34, 205, 290
Emerson, Ralph Waldo, 240
Emmerlich, Adam, 66
Epstein, Jeffrey, 202
Erasmus, 40
Essenes, 252, 271, 322
European Court of Human Rights, 243
Evangelical tourism to Israel, 204
Expressive conduct, 215
Failla, Katherine Polk (judge), 248, 249, 250, 251
   rules that parody is only entitled to First Amendment protection 'if the audience knows that the work is a parody', 249
Fake news. *See* Alt-right websites
False speech, harmful forms of, 57
Fernich, Marc, 222, 232
Fèvre, Henry, 46

Fey, Tina, 173
Fields, Weston, 275
First Amendment, 8, 15, 16, 27, 52, 55, 57, 61, 62, 63, 120, 165, 168, 171, 173, 214, 215, 216, 217, 218, 220, 221, 223, 226, 231, 234, 236, 238, 241, 244, 245, 247, 250, 251, 252, 254, 255, 262, 266, 291, 320, 330, 331, 334
   dissemination of information, ideas and opinions as essence of free speech, 15
   use of verbal provocation to make a point, 16
First Appellate Division, 191, 223, 225, 226, 229
Flag desecration. *See* Expressive conduct
Foley, Richard, 134, 135, 137
Fordham University, 38, 238, 253
Fox News, 198
Franklin, Benjamin, 45, 171, 294
Franks, Lucinda, 67
Fredrics, Howard, 208, 246, 247, 329
Freedman, David Noel
Friedenberg, Daniel, 134
Friedman, Jesse (pen-name), 171
Galileo, 129
Garbus, Martin, 165, 166,

324
Gazzetino (Gigli), 44
George Washington University, 33, 176, 198, 235
Georgetown University, 209
Gibson, Jeffrey, 28, 146, 175, 176, 287
Gigli, Girolamo, 44
Global news services, 15
   use as propaganda tool by D.A., 15, 30
Golb, Norman, 2, 19, 20, 24, 26, 27, 29, 32, 35, 36, 62, 64, 66, 127, 128, 132, 133, 134, 136, 143, 146, 147, 148, 151, 152, 153, 154, 155, 163, 171, 175, 205, 228, 248, 249, 260, 262, 318, 326, 328, 339
   claimed 'unpopularity' of his research conclusions adduced as evidence of criminality, 27, 39, 64, 66, 122, 175, 207, 262
   confirmation of his conclusions by Israeli and European archaeologists, 273
   response to 'confidential' attack of L. Schiffman, 194
Goldman, Eric, 239
Goodman, Martin, 312
Goranson, Stephen, 28, 146, 147, 148, 149, 257
Gore, Al, 55

Green Scholars Initiative, 269
Green, David, 269, 270
Greene, Maxey, 25, 27
Greenfield, Jonas
Greenfield, Rebecca, 210
Greenfield, Scott, 35, 201, 222, 227, 232, 236
Guardian, The, 228
Guilty plea bargains, 65, 259, 261
   at core of U.S. criminal justice system, 65
   deal refused, 65
Haaretz, 19, 26, 152, 153, 286, 321, 342
Haley, Alex, 242
Harassment, 9, 11, 15, 16, 23, 28, 54, 57, 63, 65, 121, 129, 146, 171, 172, 214, 219, 223, 224, 225, 229, 231, 232, 238, 247, 256, 265, 299, 320, 333, 335
   'aggravated harassment' statute declared unconstitutional, 231
Harcourt, Bernard, 168
Hargrave, Harry, 272
Harow, Eve, 196, 197, 285, 287, 327, 339
Harper's, 115
Harvard Divinity School, 28
Harvard University, 2, 16, 28, 146, 156, 212, 213, 240, 330
Hayes, Arthur, 38, 238, 239, 253, 254, 291, 335, 338

Hebrew Bible, 35, 200, 269
Hebrew University, 321
Hellman, Danny, 55
Heschel, Abraham, 263
Hirschfeld, Yizhar, 29
Hoaxes, 39, 45, 48, 53, 54, 55, 56, 208, 245, *See also* Satire
   more effective than "conventional" forms of criticism, 18
Hobby Lobby, 269, 270, 340, 342
Hone, William, 45, 46
Hudson, Geoff, 291
Hustler v. Falwell (1988), 216
Hyperbole, 212
Iago (Shakespeare character), 232–35, 240
Impersonation, 11, 15, 23, 31, 53, 56, 63, 65, 120, 121, 136, 146, 171, 172, 208, 210, 211, 216, 223, 232, 235, 243, 244, 245, 246, 247, 290, 331, 337, *See also* Parody; Satire
   of Catholic authorities in *Letters of Obscure Men*, 39
   of University of Chicago dean, 30
Incriminating evidence, 25–26
Influencing a debate (as criminal motive), 10, 25, 28, 62, 123, 146

Inside Higher Education, 209
Internet
   moral ambiguity of, 57
Interrogation, 4–10
Intertestamental Judaism, 199
Irony, 35, 173, 212, 244, 253, 255, 328
Israel Antiquities Authority, 268, 273, 341
Israel Museum, 153, 193
Jacobs, Dennis (judge), 251, 252, 253
   rules that parody will only benefit from First Amendment protection if it is 'recognized' as parody, 252
Jacobson, Howard, 51
Jacoby, Russell
Jerusalem, 25, 122, 153, 155, 193, 199, 252, 268, 273, 274, 275, 312
Jewish Forward, 198
Jewish Museum in New York, The, 25, 31, 63, 123, 132, 133, 155, 156, 160, 161, 162, 163, 167, 197, 204
Jobs, Steve, 209
John Paul Jones (impersonated by Ben Franklin), 45
Johns Hopkins University, 274
Joselit, Jenna Weissman,

198
Justnes, Årstein, 269
Kafka, Franz, 27, 247, 261
Kansas State University, 209
Kapera, Z. J.
Kaplan, Lawrence, 37, 194
Karzai, Hamid, 211
Katzman, Avi, 19, 26, 31, 58, 125, 127, 128, 129, 135, 136, 167, 193, 205, 223, 255, 286, 318, 321
  interview with Schiffman, 19
Kaufman, Peter (pen-name), 20, 171
Kingston University, 208, 247
Koch Industries, 212
Kraemer, Joel, 194, 195
Kuby, Ronald, 61, 62, 116, 117, 118, 131, 133, 134, 138, 150, 151, 152, 153, 154, 155, 160, 180, 181, 188, 191, 206, 207, 220, 230, 243, 245, 253, 257
Kuhlken, Pam Fox
Kuhn, Thomas
Kunstler, William, 117
La Fayette, Madame de, 41
La Princesse de Clèves (Madame de La Fayette), 41, 293
Langlois, Michael, 269
'Larry Schiffman' Gmail 'confessions', 9, 18, 20, 21, 27, 63, 121, 129, 136, 160, 167, 170, 197, 203, 219, 248, 252, 257, 288
Legal Aid Society, 61, 114
Lehman family, 67
Leland, John, 31, 288
Letters of Obscure Men, 38, 39, 47, 292
Leval, Pierre (judge), 250, 251, 255
  abandons his own view that 'First Amendment protections do not apply only to those whose jokes are funny and whose parodies succeed', 255
Levitt Kohn, Risa, 151, 198
Lewin, Leonard, 52
Libel, 43, 57, 58, 121, 172, 215, 232, 236, 239, 242, 243, 244, 248, 293, 294, 298, 331, 334, 335, 336, *See also* Criminal Libel, Defamation
Lieberman, Abraham, 196
Lincoln, Abraham, 47, 233
Lingua Franca, 54
Lippman, Jonathan (judge), 229, 234
Little Book of Plagiarism (R. Posner), 159
Louis XV, 45
Madame de Pompadour, 45
Madame du Barry, 45
Magen, Yitzhak, 29, 133, 273, 275
Magness, Jodi, 274, 275, 343
Mallon, Thomas, 336

Man on Wire (film), 266
Manhattan District Attorney. *See* Morgenthau, Robert; Vance, Cyrus; *see also* Bandler, John; Rivellese, Vincent; Roper, Elizabeth
Manning, Chelsea, 211
Massachusetts Institute of Technology, 211
Mayer-Schönberger, Viktor, 210
Mazella, David, 209
McCain, John, 209
McCarthy, Joseph, 169
McClatchy Washington Bureau, 212
McGill University, 37, 194
McKenna, Patrick (police officer), 1, 2, 5, 11, 23, 25, 138, 139, 140, 141, 142, 145
  declares under oath that "the allegations of plagiarism are false", 23
McLeod, Kembrew, 38, 53, 56, 291, 295, 296, 297
Melville, Herman, 47
Meyers, Eric, 148
Milwaukee Public Museum, 198
Miranda rights, 5
Miscegenation, 47
Model Rules of Professional Responsibility, 263
Modest Proposal (Swift), 44
Molinos, Miguel de, 40
Montaigne, Michel de, 219, 332
Montesquieu, 44
Morgenthau, Robert (Manhattan D.A.), 24, 25, 66, 192, 238, 266
  press release issued by, 14
  role as chairman of Museum of Jewish Heritage, 66
Moss, Candida, 270
Multi-State Professional Responsibility, 264
Muscarella, Oscar White
Museum of Jewish Heritage, 66
Museum of the Bible, 268, 269, 270, 271, 272, 340, 341, 342
Musk, Elon, 56
Narrative, established by prosecutor, 30
National Association of Criminal Defense Lawyers, 229
National Geographic, 146, 155, 271, 275, 342, 343
National Law Journal, 241
Nazi slogans, 215
Neusner, Jacob
New Jersey Star-Ledger, 35
New Testament
New York Court of Appeals, 214, 229, 233, 242, 243, 248, 249, 320, 333
New York Newsday
New York Post, 14, 31, 113, 115, 330

New York Stock Exchange, 51
New York Times, x, 14, 22, 31, *32*, 34, 67, 125, 130, 163, 205, 211, 212, 228, 287, 288, 290, 297, 299, 326, 328, 329, 331, 339, 340
New York University, 2, 4, 5, 7, 8, 13, 15, 16, 18, 19, 21, 22, 23, 24, 26, 28, 31, 54, 63, 65, 121, 128, 129, 131, 132, 134, 135, 170, 192, 193, 194, 196, 198, 203, 205, 209, 220, 225, 231, 251, 254, 263, 272, 285, 287, 292, 320, 326
  "Public Safety" (security forces), 21
  Elmer Bobst library, 18, 28, 63
  Elmer Bobst Library, 231
  faculty code of conduct, 26, 128, 135
  failure to investigate allegations of misconduct, 26
New York World, 47
Newgate Prison, 43
North Carolina Museum of Natural Sciences (Raleigh), 156
North Carolina Supreme Court, 221
North Caroline Supreme Court, 221
NowPublic, 20, 26, 27, 135, 136, 150
Nude demonstrations. *See* Expressive conduct
Nunes, Devin, 265, 266, 339
Nussbaum, Martha, 130
NYU emails, 7
Obama, Barak, 200
Obus, Michael (judge), 60
Oceania's Ministry of Truth. *See* Orwell, George
On Liberty (J.S. Mill), 215
Opert, Rena, 270
Oriental Institute, 151, 154, 193
Orion Center (Hebrew University), 148
Orwell, George, 226
Othello (Shakespeare), 232, 240, 333
Oxford Classical Dictionary, 312
Palin, Sarah, 173
parody, 236
Parody, 5, 24, 31, 34, 38, 39, 51, 53, 55, 57, 59, 62, 64, 117, 130, 144, 164, 168, 169, 173, 176, 177, 210, 212, 223, 230, 245, 246, 249, 250, 251, 252, 253, 255, 262, 263, 290, 294, 297, 319, 324, 328, 330, 337, 338, *See also* Satire
Pascal, Blaise, 41, 293
Pasquinades, 40
Pasquinades (anonymous satires affixed to statute of Pasquino in Rome), 40

Peacock, Cory, 21, 22, 288
Peer review process
  as an argument for silencing critics of Qumranology, 151
  mocked by academic hoaxes, 54
Peleg, Yuval, 29, 275, 343
Peltz, Jennifer, 35
PEN America, 222, 265
Pepperdine University
Perjury, 216
Personification, 212
Pessoa, Fernando, 168
Peterson, Jeffrey, 312
Petit, Philippe, 266
Pfann, Stephen, 155
Piltdown man, 245
Plagiarism, 3, 7, 14, 18, 22, 23, 26, 29, 31, 32, 35, 63, 64, 65, 122, 123, 126, 127, 128, 129, 134, 135, 136, 137, 143, 144, 151, 159, 165, 166, 170, 174, 192, 193, 203, 204, 205, 209, 218, 222, 242, 245, 246, 247, 248, 254, 255, 256, 264, 289, 290, 318, 328
Poe, Edgar Allen, 48, 295
Pope, Alexander, 50
Posner, Richard, 159
Postmodernist academic culture (mocked by Sokal), 54
Postmodernist literary theory about the "death of the author"
  adhered to by NYU dean Catharine Stimpson, 129
Praise of Folly (Erasmus), 40
Pretending to be someone else, 7, 8, 121, 212, *See also* Parody; Satire
Probation, Department of, 178, 201
Provincial Letters (Pascal), 41
Pseudonyms, 2, 3, 15, 41, 147, 154, 155, 160, 205, 207, 294, 326
  prevalence of their use in literary history, 42
  used by Jonathan Swift, 44
Psychological abuse of inmates, 187
Qumran, x, 127, 151, 155, 193, 197, 199, 203, 262, 271, 273, 274, 275, 321, 340, 342, 343
  cisterns, 274, 275
  military fort, 150
  pottery at, 275
  room designated as
Qumranology, 122, 152, 155, 194, 272, 273
  characterized by effort to suppress bibliographical information on Jerusalem libraries theory, 312
Rall, Ted, 55

Random selection of judges in criminal cases, 60
Raskolnikov. *See Crime and Punishment* (Dostoevsky)
Reclaiming the Dead Sea Scrolls (L. Schiffman)
Refusal to cooperate, 2
Religion News, 270, 271, 341
Rennert, Ira, 66, 201, 203, 268, 299
Report from Iron Mountain, 52
Reznick, Joshua (pen-name), 171
Richter, Rosalyn (Judge), 191
Rieders, Clifford A., 226, 227
Rikers Island, 181–91, 242, 256, 258
　intake process, 184
　orientation film, 186
　removal from system, 191
　sanitary conditions, 182, 183, 185
　TB test at 3 a.m., 184
Rivellese, Vincent (prosecutor), 229, 248
Robin, Ron, 18, 244
Ronell, Avital, 129, 130, 319, 320
Roper, Elizabeth (prosecutor), 257, 258
Rothstein, Edward
Rousseau, Jean-Jacques, 49
Royal Ontario Museum, 248

Rush Limbaugh, 54
Sadducees
Samuel Gerrish (impersonated by Ben Franklin), 45
San Diego Natural History Museum, 26
Santa Clara University School of Law, 239
Sarna, David, 81, 177
Sarna, Nahum, 81, 85, 177
Satire, 3, 16, 31, 38, 39, 40, 43, 44, 45, 47, 48, 51, 52, 53, 54, 55, 57, 64, 117, 127, 168, 173, 175, 205, 208, 209, 210, 212, 213, 216, 223, 245, 248, 249, 250, 252, 253, 254, 262, 265, 266, 294, 299, 328, *See also* Parody
　banned in 1599, 42
Satlow, Michael, 198
Saturday Night Live, 212
Scandals and Scoundrels (Robin, Ron), 18
Schiffman, Lawrence, 7, 8, 9, 13, 14, 16, 18, 19, 20, 21, 22, 23, 24, 25, 26, 27, 30, 31, 34, 58, 63, 64, 65, 117, 121, 122, 123, 124, 125, 126, 127, 128, 129, 130, 131, 132, 133, 134, 135, 136, 137, 139, 141, 142, 143, 144, 146, 150, 151, 155, 159, 160, 161, 162, 163, 164, 166, 167, 168, 170, 171, 172, 178,

192, 193, 194, 196, 197, 198, 203, 204, 207, 209, 219, 220, 221, 222, 225, 226, 227, 228, 229, 230, 235, 247, 248, 250, 251, 252, 253, 255, 256, 257, 258, 265, 271, 272, 275, *See also* 'Larry Schiffman'
Gmail 'confessions'
   argues that the Dead Sea scrolls contain 'widely varying Judaisms'
   asserts that "nobody reads" NYU's faculty code of conduct, 128
   asserts that 'nobody believed' the 'Larry Schiffman' Gmails, 21
   'confidential' attack on N. Golb, 24, 129, 137, 150, 193, 319
   interprets and denies Avi Katzman's allegations, 128
   special treatment by FBI, 22
   trial testimony, 124–28
Schmidt, Stephen, x
Science Museum of Minnesota, 197
Scott, Sir Peter, 208, 247
Scott-Heron, Gil, 114
Seale, Bobby, 276
Search warrant, 1, 23, 60, 138, 139, 142, 145
Second Circuit Court of Appeals, 241, 250

Seidel, Frederick (poet), 171
Seidel, Jonathan (rabbi in Oregon), 27, 146, 171, 248, 252, 253, 257, 320
Selden, John, 256
Shakespeare, 232, 233, 234
Shanks, Hershel, 155, 321
Shimron, Yonat, 270
Shortest-Way with the Dissenters (Defoe), 43
Shrine of the Book, 151, 153, 193, 321
Smith, Mark, 21
Smith, Robert S. (judge), 229
Snowden, Edward, 211
Social Text, 54
Social value of hoaxes, satire, etc., 56–57
Society of Biblical Literature, 154, 155
Sokal, Alan, 54, 286, 297
Spirit of the Laws, The (Montesquieu), 44
Steinbeck, John, 202
Stern, Tuvia, 16
Stimpson, Catharine, 128, 129, 130, 133, 135, 255
Stolen Valor Act, 225
Stolen Words (Th. Mallon), 336
Strauss-Kahn, Dominique, 202
Strict scrutiny. *See* Compelling state interest doctrine
Supina, Greg, 35–37

Independent Chronicle (Boston newspaper, 45
Supreme Court, 52, 206, 214, 215, 216, 217, 218, 220, 223, 225, 233, 240, 242, 243, 245, 247, 250, 251, 256, 298, 331, 334, 336, 337
Swartz, Aaron, 211
Swift, Jonathan, 43–44
Syntactical disturbance, as taught at NYU, 130
Tablet Magazine, 31
Tanner, Simon, 226, 228
Test, George, 40
The Cities that Built the Bible (R. Cargill), 238
The Pilgrim's Progress (John Bunyan), 41
The Rape of the Lock, 50
Theological Faculty of Cologne, 39
Tietz, Jeff, 115
Times of Israel, 274
Tombs (jail complex in lower Manhattan), 2, 11
   fight between detainees, 13
   fingerprinting, 11
   racial profiling in, 12
   detention conditions at, 12
Toole, John Kennedy, 2
Tov, Emanuel, 269, 270, 274, 340
Trigger warnings, 49
Trump, Donald, 210
Turley, Jonathan, 33, 176, 235, 238, 291, 325
Twain, Mark, 47, 48, 295
Twitter, 56, 208, 265, 297, 325, 330, 339
U.S. Free Expression Programs. *See* Pen America
U.S. Holocaust Memorial Museum, 270
Understatement, 212
United Nations Human Rights Commission, 243
United States v. Alvarez (2012), 225
Universal Jewish Encyclopedia, 42
University of Agder, 269
University of California in Los Angeles, 25, 28, 149, 170, 204, 226, 235
University of Chicago, 2, 30, 130, 154, 193, 312, 319
University of Iowa, 38, 155, 322
University of Kentucky, 197
University of Nebraska, 155
University of North Carolina at Chapel Hill, 156, 274
University of Strasbourg, 269
University of Texas at Austin, 209
Vance, Cyrus, Jr. (Manhattan D.A.), 66, 131, 201, 202, 203, 248, 266, 300, 318
   accepts $34,500 from

founder of World Center for the Dead Sea Scrolls, shortly after my indictment, 66
Vance, Cyrus, Jr. (Manhattan D.A.), 238
Vassar College, 209
Vatican, 341
Vaux, Roland de
Virtual Qumran (film), 150
Volokh, Eugene, 226, 227, 229, 235, 236, 334
Voltaire, 205
Wachtell, Lipton, Rosen & Katz, 66
Waffenschmidt, Thomas, 227
Ward, Laura (judge), 242, 257, 258, 259, 260, 263, 273
Ward, Robert J. (judge), 242
Washington Post, The, 33
Washington Square News
Weinstein, Harvey, 202
Wesch, Michael L., 209
Wesleyan University, 209
Whistleblowing, popular enmity towards, 123
White, Albert (pen-name), 171
Who Wrote the Dead Sea Scrolls?, 2, 26, 36, 134
Wiggins, Steve, 35
Wikipedia, 142
Wilford, John Noble, 32
Williams, Terry (police officer), 5
Winston, Hella, 271
Wire, 210
Wood, Grant ("American Gothic"), 253
World Center for the Dead Sea Scrolls, 66, 201, 203, 268
World Intellectual Property Organization, 247
World Trade Center, 266
World Trade Organization, 53
Wu, Timothy, 240
Yadin, Yigael
Yes Men, 53, 121, 209, 296
Yeshiva University, 196, 227, 228
Zahavy, Tzvee, 33, 34, 51, 198
Zimmerman, Matt, 244
Žižek, Slavoj, 210

www.ingramcontent.com/pod-product-compliance
Lightning Source LLC
LaVergne TN
LVHW051822080426
835512LV00018B/2681